AGRICULTURAL SOCIOLOGY

HARPER'S SOCIAL SCIENCE SERIES

UNDER THE EDITORSHIP OF F. STUART CHAPIN

AGRICULTURAL SOCIOLOGY

A Study of Sociological Aspects
of American Farm Life

WALTER L. SLOCUM

PROFESSOR OF RURAL SOCIOLOGY

WASHINGTON STATE UNIVERSITY

HARPER & BROTHERS PUBLISHERS, NEW YORK

AGRICULTURAL SOCIOLOGY: A Study of Sociological Aspects of American Farm Life

Copyright © 1962 by Walter L. Slocum

Printed in the United States of America

Library of Congress catalog card number: 62-8879

Contents

IV. SOCIAL SYSTEMS: NETWORKS OF RELATIONSHIP — 271

V. COMMUNITY DEVELOPMENT — 505

Editor's Introduction

Despite the fact that in 1960 only 9 percent of the population of the United States lived on farms, agriculture is still an industry and an occupation of great importance in the national economy. It is not always realized that matters of verbal definition influence the understanding of recent changes in agriculture, and this complicates any effort to generalize about the characteristics of farming people. The author considers these problems of scientific description against the background of his first hand knowledge of agriculture in Pakistan and among Oriental peoples. His approach is, however, modern rather than historical, as will be seen in his use of some contemporary concepts and principles derived from recent research in such areas as communication, decision-making processes, reference group principles, role behavior, social action patterns, social systems, and voluntary associations. In several of his chapters the titles indicate his approach, as for example, Chapters 8 through 13, 17, and 25. All in all the author's treatment is refreshing and well oriented to the needs of students in courses in rural sociology.

F. STUART CHAPIN

Asheville, N. C.
October, 1961

Preface

The decision to write this book was made following my return to academic life in August of 1951 after an absence of nine years, during which I served in the U.S. Navy's military government program and in two departments of the federal government. The rural sociology textbooks then available were not fully satisfactory to me as material for use in presenting the results of studies dealing with various aspects of the sociology of agriculture. At one time or another I have used most of these books as texts or reference works in my teaching at Washington State University.

This book is an attempt to organize and interpret the relevant results of a half-century of research by rural sociologists and other social scientists on the sociological aspects of agriculture and farm life. The data are presented within an explicit sociological frame of reference similar to that used by many contemporary American sociologists, but sociological concepts are regarded as means of achieving understanding rather than as ends. The reader who has had a recent introductory course in sociology will be familiar with most of the concepts.

The focus of the book is upon American agriculture as an occupation and a way of life. It emphasizes not only recent and emergent changes in agriculture and farm life but also the social and cultural backgrounds against which such changes must be evaluated.

Intimate familiarity with American agriculture and farm life on the part of the reader has not been assumed. This seems justifiable for several reasons. Probably no single person is highly conversant with all aspects of American agriculture. The ever-increasing specialization in occupational roles within agriculture means that there is increasing need for specific information about the characteristics of the social system and culture patterns associated with diverse types of agriculture. At the same time it is essential to recognize that the interdependence of the farm and nonfarm segments of our society has been accentuated rather than diminished by the growth of specialization.

The continuing decline in the farm population means that there is an increasing need to provide nonfarm people with current, systematic information about how farm people live and work. This was perhaps less necessary some generations ago when most Americans were either farm residents or farm reared, because then the rural heritage was a part of their own personal experience. Urban dwellers, who now comprise the majority of the American population, may be assumed to have relatively little accurate knowledge of the subject.

People in foreign countries have many misconceptions about farm life in America, some of which may be based on the tendency of social scientists to study and report on problem situations rather than basic uniformities.

Although I am greatly indebted to many people, I have not asked any of them to share the responsibility for what I have said in this book. Specifically, I wish to acknowledge my debt to Paul H. Landis and George W. Hill for arousing my interest in rural sociology and to the former for encouraging me to return to the field. J. H. Kolb, retired Chairman of the Department of Rural Sociology at the University of Wisconsin, contributed much to my approach to the study of farm life. I am also indebted to many rural sociologists who have contributed to the growing fund of sociological information about agriculture and farm life through research papers, bulletins, books, and other publications, and to my students at Washington State University and at the University of the Panjab, Lahore, West Pakistan. I wish also to acknowledge the secretarial assistance of my wife, Esther L. Slocum, in preparing the book.

It is my hope that this work will be of assistance to three principal categories of users: first, college and university students who intend to enter some agricultural field; second, other college and university students who are concerned about agricultural work and life in their prospective future roles as citizens; and third, all adults who have some interest in or responsibility for agriculture.

WALTER L. SLOCUM

AGRICULTURAL SOCIOLOGY

1

Introduction

This book is a sociological analysis of the social and cultural factors that influence the lives of those who depend in full or in part on the occupation of agriculture. It is concerned with the dynamic processes of life—cooperation, competition, decision-making—and with the systems of interpersonal and group relationships directly involved in agriculture. It is also concerned with the participation of the farmer and his family in the broader systems of social relationships, among them the church, community, state, and nation. The forces that influence farmers' decisions and actions and their means and aims are also of concern. This interest leads to the field of culture, including cultural change, and in turn makes it necessary to pay some attention to agricultural history because of the time dimension inherent in culture. Some traditions and customs have long roots.

The focus of the study is agricultural, but some comparisons will be made with nonfarm life to help us better understand the unique characteristics of American farm life as well as the features it shares with urban and rural nonfarm ways.

If we knew enough, our story might begin with the dawn of agriculture in prehistoric times when men first began to live sedentary lives. However, we know little about the circumstances of early tillers of the soil, although we may suppose from the findings of archaeologists and anthropologists that their lot was hard. We may be sure that life was short. We may assume too that early agriculturists had a narrow outlook and lived in a small social world. Certainly this was true of the serfs in medieval Europe who were bound to the soil and lived in squalor; it is true today of the poverty-stricken agricultural villagers of India, Pakistan and the Middle East.

We shall not attempt to trace in detail the gradual improvement over the centuries of the technology, economic circumstances, and living conditions of farmers in the western world. It is well to remember, nonetheless, that agriculture has developed from modest beginnings. Agricultural surpluses are a relatively new phenomenon, even now confined to a few advanced countries.

Great changes have occurred in American agriculture since colonial times. Yet we should not overlook the fact that in comparison to primitive cultivators, the colonists were equipped with a fairly advanced technology. They had domesticated animals; they had plows and some other farm implements; they practiced crop rotation, used animal manure as fertilizer, and cultivated their growing crops to control weeds and conserve moisture. There was, of course, a great deal of hard, monotonous hand labor, and hours were long and comforts few by contemporary standards.

The changes which have altered farm life in America have complex roots. Basically, however, they stem from the forces unleashed by the industrial revolution which began shortly before the Revolutionary War.

URBAN INFLUENCES

Many scholars have called attention to the polar differences between life in a metropolis and life in a little isolated community of farm people. In America, these differences seem to be disappearing under the dominant and pervasive influence of urban centers. By 1960, only 9 percent of the nation's population lived on farms. This is a great contrast to 1790, when only six communities in America had as many as 8000 people.

Specialization is an outstanding characteristic of the metropolis, perhaps the distinguishing characteristic; only in great centers of population can a large enough clientele be found to warrant it. This is a fact of the greatest importance for cultural change, for it is chiefly through extreme specialization that technology is advanced. There are very few generalists in the city. Almost all workers are specialists in one way or another, even those who fill relatively routine occupational roles. Integration of specialized work is accomplished through business firms, governmental agencies, medical clinics, and other forms of social organization. Not only does specialization exist in every city, but there is specialization among cities. Washington, D.C., for example, provides principally governmental administrative services, New York is the great center of finance, Hollywood is the entertainment capital of the nation, and Rochester, Minnesota, is an outstanding medical center.

An important aspect of metropolitan living for great numbers of the employed urban population is the daily journey to and from work. Those who live on farms or rural acreages are enabled to hold city jobs by rapid horizontal transportation in subways, street railways, commuters' trains, and, of course, automobiles, and vertical movement in elevators. Many consequences flow from this pattern of life which may take from a few minutes to two hours or even more daily, and which for five days a week largely removes the adult urban male from contact with his family for most of each working day.

Great contrasts of wealth and poverty are to be found in cities. In some there are demarcations by ethnic or racial concentration, as in Chinatown, Little Italy, Ghetto, or Black Belt. There are also distinctive areas based on economic status, known by such names as the Gold Coast, the Slums, Skid Row.

Life in great cities is characterized by a large number of transitory and other superficial contacts, and the social structure by a plethora of interest groups and formal organizations rather than by informal assembly. Urban people generally know each other only segmentally, in specific roles, rather than as whole personalities as in the little rural communities or neighborhoods of the past. Primary group contacts do, of course, exist in the family, in kinship, friendship, and fraternal groups, and to some extent within various occupational associations.

Family life in the metropolis tends to be democratic, with emphasis on individualism rather than group values. The typical urban family has been classified by some students as a matriarchy because of the absence of the husband-father at work and because of the tendency for women to do most of the purchasing.

Changes in business, industry, and politics affect the agricultural operations of the modern farmer. He knows it. The changes in his farming methods due to the application of science are profound. Urban values and patterns of life greatly influence contemporary farm life. A farmer's world still involves primary relationships with family members, kinfolk, neighbors, and friends, but in advanced countries he also has many contacts with others. He may do his shopping in the city. If he is an American, he probably is a member of at least one farm cooperative; he is likely to be a church member; and he may belong to the Rotary Club or a similar service organization.

RECENT CHANGES IN AMERICAN AGRICULTURE

An important change which has recently occurred in America is the rise of part-time farming. Many farmers have taken part- or full-time work off their farms. They continue to live on their farms and to conduct some agricultural operations, but they have income from nonfarm sources. At the same time, some urban workers have moved to a farm residence from which they commute to urban jobs, a development of major importance, as we said. In some American states, more than half of those who operate farms also work elsewhere over 100 days a year.

A successful commercial farmer is not to be likened to an old-world peasant. He is an intelligent, literate businessman. If he is sometimes perplexed and hard put to solve his problems it is because he is confronted with situations that cannot be handled by individual action in traditional ways. But many farmers are highly resourceful in solving problems on their own farms. The record of fabulous expansion in farm production in the second quarter of the twentieth century shows that American farmers have learned to put the findings of agricultural scientists to work. The successful farmer has his eye trained on the agricultural experiment stations of the land-grant colleges.

Commercial farms have grown larger and farming operations more complex. Consequently, capital requirements have increased. The modern farmer no longer depends on human or animal power. He may still work long hours, but his work is that of managing his business and operating his machines. This is a far cry from the sheer physical drudgery of his grandfather's day.

With the passing of the land frontier, the prospect of moving up the agricultural ladder from hired hand to full owner, once the traditional goal of the American farm boy, has lost importance. Ownership is now generally attained in other ways. However, it still seems to be true the world over that most farmers were reared on farms.

But in America most farm boys do not become farmers; our cities are peopled with rural migrants and their descendents, some in high places and others working as factory operatives, clerks, or service workers.

The typical operator of a modern American commercial farm is well educated. Some are college graduates. There is now time for reading, watching television, and many other activities that were unknown a generation ago.

Of course, not all American farmers are successful. Some are poorly educated and poorly housed, and produce barely enough to keep body and soul together. Furthermore, the image of the American farmer as a self-reliant individualist who neither asks nor needs help from others has faded. Nearly all are now members of co-operatives. In the last 25 years American agriculture has benefited greatly from research conducted by scientists supported largely by public funds. The increased productivity thus achieved has been so tremendous that the federal government has enacted crop control and price support legislation which greatly affects the freedom of farmers. The problem of disposing of surplus agricultural products is still far from solution, and average farm incomes are still far below the average nonfarm level.

Contrasted with this picture, there are still many millions of agricultural people in underdeveloped areas of the world who produce little if anything for the market. These people cultivate small plots with primitive technology. Illiterate and poverty-stricken, their lot is constant toil, disease, and in many cases hunger and early death. Most live in agricultural villages. In spite of their poor situation or perhaps because of it, they do not accept change readily.

In some Communist countries, farmers live and work on collective farms. Compared to American farmers, their lot is evidently hard and their productivity low. In other modern capitalistic countries like England, France, and Germany, farmers are apparently efficient and thrifty but more like the traditional European peasant than the American farmer in their attitudes. We shall find that the range of variation in agricultural operations and in the outlook and daily lives of the people who till the soil is very great. Insofar as possible, we shall take a dynamic rather than a static point of view, recognizing that we are living in a transitional period in human history.

THEORETICAL PREMISES

Of central importance in understanding the nature of human relationships in agriculture is an appreciation of the fundamental teachings of three closely related disciplines: cultural anthropology, sociology, and social psychology.

This is not a book on social theory. Nevertheless, it seems essential at the outset to present some of the basic theoretical premises
which underlie the discussion. These ideas will be developed in
greater detail as the book progresses.

1. There is now general agreement among social scientists that differences in social training or *socialization* are of greater importance
   than biological or hereditary differences in explaining human attitudes and behavior.
2. *Socialization* is a process of personality development which continues throughout the whole lifetime of the person, although special significance is attached to the training received in the early
   years.
3. The *culture* of the society, including folkways, mores, laws, and
   values, is basically a product of social interaction between people.
   Those whose interactions give rise to modifications in culture are,
   of course, conditioned and influenced by their own cultural
   heritage.
4. *Culture* influences conduct through its impact on the social training of the individual.
5. All distinctively human behavior involves direct or indirect interaction with other persons. Indirect interaction is defined as contact through mass media like the radio, television, newspapers,
   magazines, and books.
6. Interpersonal relationships occur within and with reference to
   social systems and create patterns which, in turn, may be regarded
   as social systems. In one sense, these are part of the culture; in
   another sense, they are regulated by it.

THE NATURE OF CULTURE

We will examine selected aspects of the cultural heritage which
are of major importance to agriculture. But first it seems worth

while to familiarize ourselves with some of the general features of culture.

For sociological purposes culture may be defined as the values, customs, language, institutions, technologies, laws, and other norms which are shared by members of a social system. Culture is handed down from the past both recent and remote. Linton has called it the social heritage.[1]

Perhaps the most significant aspect of culture is the fact that only human beings have it. Lower forms of life are equipped in varying degrees to cope with the complexities of existence, but they are unable to communicate behavior patterns except through imitation or instinct. The vertebrates have an adaptive capacity based on the ability to imitate other individuals of the same species to some extent. Insects are evidently equipped with elaborate biologically transmitted complexes of instinctive behavior; thus a wasp can reproduce all the essential aspects of wasplike behavior even though it never sees its parents.

It was once thought that this was true of humans, but it is now generally conceded that human beings are equipped with relatively few if any instinctive patterns of behavior. All common attitudes, values, and patterns of participation in the affairs of men are learned and all unique habits derive their significance from the general or customary patterns which exist in a particular society or system of social relationships.

All human societies have culture. The content differs but all have customs, all have language, all have the same major institutions, all have some type of technology, norms, and enacted laws which are shared by the members of the society.

Although culture is found wherever there are human societies, culture is not the same as society. Certain insects like ants and termites have societies but no culture. Only man has both. As Kroeber has pointed out, human society and culture always co-occur; thus any phenomenon involving relationships between people necessarily has both a cultural and social aspect.[2]

The most important medium for the communication of culture is

[1] Ralph Linton, *The Study of Man*, Appleton-Century, 1936, p. 80.
[2] A. L. Kroeber, *The Nature of Culture*, University of Chicago Press, 1953, p. 7.

language, both written and oral, which is as well an integral part
of culture. Socialization is the basic process of learning; culture
is learned in connection with social roles.[3] It is possible for people
to communicate to others through language reasonably clear
definitions of situations which may be encountered and to give instructions with respect to the behavior considered appropriate to
such situations in terms of the culture. Of course, for communication
of culture there must be receptiveness and learning ability as well as
the ability to communicate instructions.

Most sociologists and many anthropologists agree that culture
consists of nonmaterial phenomena, ideas, techniques, values, and
the like rather than of objects. Sutherland, Woodward, and Maxwell have suggested the term *culture object* for the material objects associated with particular parts of the culture.[4] Familiar culture objects associated with agriculture include farm machines,
domesticated animals, and plants which produce food and fiber.

CUSTOMS

A *custom* is a habit which is learned, performed, and transmitted
socially. However, not all habits are customs; those that are peculiar
to individuals are obviously not customs. When thinking about
the significance of various customs to the members of a social system,
it is useful to classify them as *folkways* and *mores*, terms suggested a half-century ago by William Graham Sumner. In Sumner's
usage, a *folkway* is a custom which has grown out of experience and
is handed down within a social system without rational reflection.
The folkways are the "right" ways of doing various things. As he
puts it, "There is a right way to catch game, to win a wife, to make
oneself appear . . . and so on in all the cases which can arise."[5]

Although the folkways are the right ways to do things because
they are the expected ways, they do not have moral sanctions associated with them. One who violates the folkways does not
threaten the values of the group, and consequently he is not usually

[3] The process of socialization is discussed in Chapter 11.
[4] R. L. Sutherland, J. L. Woodward, and M. A. Maxwell, *Introductory Sociology*, 4th ed., Lippincott, 1952, p. 21.
[5] William G. Sumner, *Folkways*, Ginn, 1906, p. 2.

punished, although he may be regarded as eccentric, ignorant, or uncouth.

The *mores,* on the other hand, are customs which are regarded by members of the social system as vital and essential to the maintenance or welfare of the group or other social system; they involve moral issues. Violation of the mores generally involves severe penalties, including ostracism or even death.

COMMUNITY VERSUS SOCIETAL NORMS

It is easy to overemphasize the significance of any factor which is singled out for study. This is true of community subculture also. When we recognize differences between communities we should not blind ourselves to their similarities not only in outward form but also in culture. In contemporary America and other modern nations, there are a large number of societal influences. The modern communication media of television, radio, daily newspapers, and magazines subject citizens everywhere to many of the same stimuli. These have an impact upon the socialization of the individual and obviously contribute to the development of similar patterns of value and attitudes.

CULTURE TRAITS, PATTERNS, AND AREAS

One way of looking at culture is to analyze it from the standpoint of its component parts. Anthropologists have identified the culture trait as the simplest aspect. Kroeber says, however, that the most profitable aspects to study seem to be culture patterns or configurations.[6] It is clear that most culture traits do occur in patterns or configurations and that some evaluation is placed upon such configurations by the members of a social system. On a higher level of abstraction, it is possible to think of certain broad patterns of culture including many configurations as culture types. These constructs are sufficiently distinctive to create images of major types of agriculturalists of different nations. Thus we may speak of American farmers, Chinese coolies, Indian villagers, and Italian peasants. We can easily supply adjectives characterizing each type; we may say, for instance, that the Indian villager is disease-ridden,

[6] Kroeber, *op. cit.,* p. 5.

poorly housed, poorly clad, poorly fed, and dominated by values which apparently make him content with his lot. A description like this one will be a caricature to some extent but will contain much truth.

Anthropologists have also identified culture areas. These are generally broad geographic areas within which certain types and patterns of culture are fairly typical. The entire United States, because of its common customs and traditions and language, might be regarded as a culture area—in fact, the area probably should be extended to include the English-speaking part of Canada which, though its governmental forms and political traditions differ, shares with the U.S. a common language and many customs. Even within such an area as the United States it may be possible to distinguish cultural subareas characterized by distinctive traditions and values. Certainly with respect to the prevalent attitudes toward integration of the races the South is a different culture area from the North. Taylor and Loomis and Beegle have taken the position that type of farming may distinguish a culture area.[7] We will discuss this and related matters in more detail later.

At this point it may be worth while to note that the basic idea of the culture area has been generalized from the relationship of certain culture patterns to geographic areas observed by anthropologists in their studies of preliterate people. But more than geography is involved. The immensely productive techniques of the American Corn Belt farmer are not used in all areas where they seem appropriate, apparently because of the relationship between social systems and culture. Not all social systems are able to utilize the same culture patterns. Modifications in economic and social organization seem to be required for the successful application of science to agriculture.

UNIVERSALS, ALTERNATIVES AND SPECIALTIES

Linton has taken a position which seems sound—that the content of the culture of any major society is so incredibly rich that no single individual can comprehend the whole of it. It follows that

[7] See Carl C. Taylor, *et al.*, *Rural Life in the United States*, Knopf, 1949, chap. 19; C. P. Loomis and J. A. Beegle, *Rural Social Systems*, Prentice-Hall, 1950, chap. 8.

the members of any social system participate to varying degrees in the total culture associated with the system. Linton suggests a three-fold classification of culture in terms of the extent to which members of a social system participate in it.

1. *Universal aspects of culture.* These are the ideas, customs, and other aspects of culture which all normal adult members of the social system participate in. They may be thought of as the core of the culture.

2. *Specialties.* These are elements of culture which only some members of the social system participate in. An example is the division of labor into men's work and women's work where men may have only a vague general knowledge of things that women do or vice versa. In addition there are a great many aspects of technology which are known only to specialists; thus we have doctors, electronics experts, automobile and tractor mechanics, and agricultural specialists like entomologists and plant pathologists.

3. *Alternatives.* These include methods of effectuating aspects of the culture which are shared by certain individuals but are not common to all the members of a social system. These include the particular value systems and customs of a given family or other reference group relating to the use of alternative culture objects for common purposes, as for instance the use of animals, automobiles, airplanes, or other modes of conveyance for transportation.[8]

VALUES

The scientific study of values as an aspect of culture has not progressed very far. This is especially true of values associated with different types of agriculture in contemporary societies. In spite of this, a great deal has been written on the subject of rural values.[9]

There is no doubt that some of the reasons for specific attitudes toward agriculture are to be sought in traditional values. In the United States, W. A. Anderson has made a number of statistical

[8] Linton, *op. cit.*, p. 382.

[9] See P. A. Sorokin, C. C. Zimmerman, and C. J. Galpin, *A Systematic Source Book in Rural Sociology*, University of Minnesota Press, 1930, vol. I, chaps. I, II; Paul H. Landis, *Rural Life in Process*, 2nd ed., McGraw-Hill, 1948, chap. 9; Murray A. Straus, *A Technique for the Measurement of Values in Rural Life*, Washington AES Technical Bulletin 29, August, 1959.

studies of selected aspects of rural values.[10] Straus has also done some work on the subject.[11] Iwanska has investigated some of the values of part-time farmers, using anthropological techniques.[12]

CULTURE CHANGE

The tempo of culture change in both the rural and urban contemporary world is very high. As far as America is concerned, the diverse cultural backgrounds of European immigrants who settled on American farms have now largely disappeared so that the ethnic differences from one locality to another are much smaller than was the case a generation or so ago. In the process of assimilation, the culture of the earlier English-speaking settlers was, of course, greatly modified, although it continued dominant.

The great changes taking place in agriculture at the present time have their origin in the general stream of culture. These will be discussed in some detail later.

Considered abstractly, culture change is attributable basically to two interrelated processes: innovation and borrowing. Innovation is the phenomenon through which new ideas appear and new technology is invented. Borrowing is the process by which these creations are diffused from the innovator to the rest of the population. Material artifacts, while not considered for present purposes to be part of the culture, are nevertheless associated with the spread of culture; hence the techniques of utilizing the new developments and equipment are diffused at the same time as the material artifacts themselves or shortly thereafter.

Culture change is not necessarily the same as social change, although broadly conceived social change may be classified as a form of culture change. The term *social change* is reserved for changes in social organization. Sometimes social change must precede and prepare the way for other culture changes. For example, rural electrification in the U.S. made little progress until the establishment of the Rural Electrification Administration.

[10] W. A. Anderson, *A Study of the Values in Rural Living*, Cornell University AES Memoir 277, 1947.

[11] Straus, *op. cit.*

[12] Alicja, Iwanska, *Good Fortune: Second Chance Community*, Washington AES Bulletin 589, June, 1958.

SOCIOLOGICAL ASPECTS OF A SOCIAL SYSTEM

Social systems are relatively permanent operating networks or patterns of interpersonal relationships among people. The concept as used in this book includes both informal groups and formal organizations. Even such abstract collectivities as social classes, castes, and other forms of stratification may, under certain circumstances, be regarded as social systems.

The term social system has a dynamic rather than a static connotation. Any given social system develops through interaction, and its functioning may involve many different types of interaction including both cooperation and conflict. Transitory relationships should not be regarded as social systems—a casual contact between two strangers, a spectator crowd at a county fair, or a radio or television audience. The organizations promoting the fair and athletic contest and the radio and TV corporations, on the other hand, would properly be classified as social systems.

Parsons sometimes uses the term social system in such a way as to include an entire population having a common culture. Within this terminology one would then have to consider concrete forms of association as subsystems.[13] For present purposes it seems preferable to use the traditional word society for nations having a common culture, reserving the term social systems for the more or less distinctive parts of a society.

What are the essential sociological aspects of a social system? A full answer to this question can become very involved, as Loomis has demonstrated.[14] For present purposes attention may be focused on three aspects.

1. Insofar as the structure of the system is concerned, there are social statuses or positions and associated roles, each with rights, duties, and authority. These are sometimes called *status roles;*[15] in this discussion we will ordinarily use the term *role* to include both concepts.

Each social system is composed of a set of interdependent

[13] Talcott Parsons, *The Social System,* Free Press, 1951.
[14] See C. P. Loomis, *Social Systems,* Van Nostrand, 1960, Essay 1.
[15] *Ibid;* Ralph Linton, *The Study of Man,* Appleton-Century, 1936.

statuses and associated roles which must be performed in order for the system to function. The nature of this *role set* determines the structure of the system.

Each status has some social rank and carries with it certain rights and obligations that affect the performance of the role. Some statuses have less rank than others and hence may carry more obligations and duties than rights and authority, as, for example, the status of family servant. In any established social system these expectations are well known to all members. In some types of systems status roles change slowly, whereas in others they may change rapidly.

2. Every social system has some boundaries of physical location or territorial distribution. These may be local, as for a village, or nearly unlimited, as in the case of the United Nations. Frequently there are also other boundaries, such as those found between the Aberdeen Angus Association and the Hereford Association or between a high school and a college.

3. There is the associated culture, including values and standards, ends or objectives, norms governing behavior of participants, and related aspects of its culture. The culture associated with a particular social system consists of (a) general societal culture, which pertains to all members of the larger society, and (b) distinctive objectives, values and norms which pertain specifically to the system. The latter arise over time out of the problems and experiences of the members of the social system as they perform their roles. Values or norms of a specific system may represent only minor departures from societal values or norms, or as in the case of Dukhobors, there may be major differences. Some are closed systems which can be entered only by birth while others are open to all who may be interested.

It is obvious that some social systems have a more complicated form of organization or structure than others. The simplest, of course, are the intimate face-to-face relationships which may be characterized as primary groups. These include relationships of various kinds, such as the family, the clique, the play group, the gang, college fraternities, and certain types of communities.

Persons associated with any given social system usually share certain central values or objectives. For example, the members of a particular farm family will have a common set of values which may differ to some extent from the values held by members of other families in the same locality because they have a common background of tradition and experience which is not shared fully by other families. Depending upon the nature of the interaction within the system, they have to a greater or lesser degree a "we" feeling, a sense of belonging. This is not to deny that antagonistic feelings may arise between the members of various social systems as they play their diverse roles.

Any individual is influenced by the contacts that he has with people in various social systems. In the performance of his specific role within the system he will be influenced by the expectations which other members of the system have communicated to him concerning that role. Membership in important social systems, which we will call his reference groups,[16] may also affect behavior not directly related to the actual performance of his role within the system. He will also give consideration to the impact of other behavior on his status within the reference group.

Everyone belongs to a number of social systems. Systems are linked together in this way and many also have functional relationships to each other. However, the role expectations of various social systems do not always fit neatly with each other; a person may thus suffer from serious role conflicts at times because of the variations in the expectations of the different systems with which he is associated.

In a complex modern society like that of the United States, social systems tend to develop around specialized interests even in rural areas. Emphasis is usually upon attainment of specified objectives through rational action. Integration, insofar as it is achieved, occurs chiefly through conscious efforts of leaders to pool resources to solve common problems. In contrast, the social systems of primitive societies and of rural segments of underdeveloped countries tend to be oriented toward members considered as whole persons. Traditional procedures are often regarded as sacred. Lesser social systems found in the tradition-bound little community are likely to be well integrated in the sense that the norms are relatively

[16] See Chapter 11 for a discussion of reference groups.

stable, well known and mutually reinforcing, being based upon likenesses of members.[17]

QUESTIONS FOR FURTHER STUDY AND DISCUSSION

1. Make a list of customs followed by members of your own family. Classify these as folkways and mores.

2. Can you identify any norms which you think are more or less unique to your home community? How do these differ from the relevant societal norms?

3. Contrast the probable events of one day in your grandparents' family with one day in your own family. Do you think that it is likely that changes of similar magnitude will occur in the next thirty years?

4. Make a list of the social systems of which you are a member. What are the requirements for membership in each system listed?

SELECTED REFERENCES

Ralph Linton, *The Study of Man*, D. Appleton-Century, 1936.
Charles P. Loomis, *Social Systems*, Van Nostrand, 1960.

---

[17] Technical sociological terms used to refer to the polar types of social relationships in modern urbanized societies include: secular, *Gesellschaft*, contractual and rational. Those which refer to the opposite types found in less urbanized societies include: sacred, *Gemeinschaft*, familistic and traditional (see Loomis, *op. cit.*, essay 2; Earl H. Bell, *Social Foundations of Human Behavior*, Harper, 1961, chap. 15).

I

RURAL PEOPLE

Nobody knows how many rural people there are in the world today, but it is certain that the great majority of the population of the world is rural. Harris and Ackerman in 1946 estimated that more than two-thirds earn their livelihood through agricultural work.[1] It is a modern paradox that in the United States, which has great agricultural surpluses, a relatively small proportion of the population is engaged in agriculture, while India and Pakistan with their chronic food shortages have a very high proportion in farming.

Although there is a high correlation between rural residence and dependence upon agriculture, rural people are not necessarily farmers; neither do all farmers live on the land which they cultivate.

[1] Joseph Ackerman and Marshall Harris, eds., *Family Farm Policy,* University of Chicago Press, 1947, p. 39.

2

Rural Population Characteristics
and Trends

Information concerning the number of rural farm and rural non-farm people at selected periods together with information concerning selected population characteristics such as age, sex, race, residential stability, marital status, and occupation is collected by most national governments through taking the census from time to time. Although much of the data is not specifically designed to serve their purposes, sociologists have found that analyzing these demographic characteristics enables them to infer many relationships and general situations which assist materially in understanding culture patterns and the functioning of social systems. This chapter presents an analysis of some of the significant characteristics and trends in the farm population.

The characteristics of the people who make up the population—farm, rural, nonfarm, and urban—frequently change materially from one census date to another. These changes are normal. They result from modifications of social and economic conditions which are in turn expressions of human interrelationships. The U.S. Bureau of the Census has adopted the wise policy of using sample surveys between decennial census dates, which enables us to keep abreast of many important changes.

Information concerning the characteristics of specific categories of the farm and rural nonfarm population would be extremely useful if available. Unfortunately, the definitions used by data-collecting organizations are not uniform from one country to another or from one census date to another. There are even difficulties involved in comparing data from the U.S. *Census of Agriculture* and the U.S. *Census of Population and Housing* for a particular date.

For example, the farm population of the United States as defined in the 1950 *Census of Population and Housing* included all persons living on places which the person who was interviewed by the census taker considered to be a farm or ranch. This procedure did not correspond with the definition used in the *Census of Agriculture*, which deals with farms, farm production, and farm operators. To be classified as a farm in the 1950 *Census of Agriculture*, a place must have had at least 3 acres which produced agricultural products valued at $150 or more in 1949, or, if under 3 acres in size, it must have had sales of agricultural products of $150 or more. The definition of a farm was changed materially for the 1959 *Census of Agriculture*: at that date sales of agricultural products of $250 were required for places of less than 10 acres and sales of $50 for places of 10 acres or over. The same definition was also employed in the 1960 *Census of Population.*

This change in definition contributed materially to the sharp decline in the farm population, which was reported to be only 15,669,000 in April 1960 according to the new definition in comparison to 19,839,000 on the basis of the old. The reclassification involved greater shifts than these figures suggest. A total of 5,355,000 people were moved out of the farm category while 1,185,000 were shifted from the nonfarm to the farm classification. Many of the latter were operators of horticultural enterprises which they did not regard as farms or part-time farmers whose key occupational roles were not agricultural.

Those who were shifted out of the farm group by the new definition were essentially nonagricultural as far as their occupational affiliations were concerned. There are more than 5,000,000 rural people, then, who consider that they live on farms but will no longer be included in the farm population because they receive little economic support from agriculture.

The demographic characteristics of the farm populations will, of course, be altered to some extent by the changed definition. Information from the April 1960 *Current Population Survey* shows that the change in definition had much less effect in the North Central region than in other census regions. The percentage decreases due to definition were: North Central, 9.0; Northeast, 28.4; South, 24.2; and West, 24.0. The median age of the farm population is 26.4 under the new definition compared to 26.2 under the old. However, the new farm population does include relatively more children under 14 and more older persons 65 years of age and over. The median net money income of those families shifted out of the farm population in 1959 was $3621 compared to $2800 for the new farm population. The ratio of males to females in the group shifted to the nonfarm residential categories was 102.1 compared with 109.3 in the new farm population. The change in definition apparently did not alter the proportions of white and nonwhite people in the farm population.

There were two main reasons for the change in definition in 1960.[1] The first is the fact that evidence from a 1957 sample survey indicated a great increase in the number of people who claimed they lived on farms but who lived on places which did not meet the definition of a farm used by the agricultural census. The second reason was the desire by the Bureau of the Census and users of census data for a definition of farms for use in the agriculture census which would not allow places to be classified as farms on the value of production without sale of agriculture products. Without a corresponding change in the farm population definition there would have been greater disparity between the two censuses.

While the new definition should result in greater comparability between the agricultural and population censuses, it certainly creates major problems for comparing data collected in 1960 with farm population data from earlier censuses.

The fact that information about population characteristics is collected by the *Census of Population and Housing* rather than by the *Census of Agriculture* means that it has been impossible, except on a special study basis, to analyze population data according to type of farming, size of farm, or economic classification of the farm enterprise.[2] For example, one cannot make a detailed analysis of the characteristics of the 583,000 prosperous commercial farmers who in 1954 produced agricultural products valued at $10,000 or more. In 1954 the products sold by these farmers accounted for 58 percent

[1] Calvin L. Beale and Gladys K. Bowles, *The 1960 Definition of Farm Residence and Its Marked Effects on Farm Population Data*, U.S. Department of Agriculture, Agricultural Marketing Service, February, 1961.

[2] A special study made cooperatively by the U.S. Department of Agriculture and the U.S. Bureau of the Census does provide some information about the characteristics of the population on different types of farms in 1950 (see U.S. Bureau of the Census, *Farms and Farm People—Population, Income and Housing Characteristics by Economic Class of Farm*, 1952).

of all market sales. Information from a special study indicates that the people on prosperous farms may differ in important respects from other farmers.[3]

Students of rural life have long noted a tendency for certain farm population characteristics including family composition, sex ratio, fertility, and residential stability to be different from those found among urban or rural nonfarm segments of a population, and census data reveals that many differences still exist in the United States between the farm population considered as an aggregate and the urban population, though it is also clear that the differences are diminishing. The circumstances of life in agricultural areas in earlier generations in the U.S. and the conditions of cultivators today in underdeveloped parts of the world are materially different from those found among American farm people today. The modern American farm population resembles the urban population more than it does the farm population of 1900.

Some farm people, especially those who reside on prosperous commercial farms, not only have practically all of the amenities of life generally available to city dwellers but in some cases have a much higher standard of living than found in urban populations. Others are very poor. This observation is introduced here to caution the student against accepting sweeping generalizations about the characteristics of farm people. There is, at least in the U.S., so much variation in social, economic, and other characteristics within the farm population that averages may conceal meaningful differences. Population information needs to be analyzed and utilized with care. The user must take into account applicable definitions and methods of collection, and when data are obtained from samples the extent of sampling variability should be noted. Utilized by the perceptive student of social and economic relationships on a state or local level, population data can be extremely useful for social planners, organizations, and agencies.

RURAL POPULATION IN SELECTED COUNTRIES

It is not possible to make exact comparisons between countries because of differences in definitions used by census organizations. Perhaps the best available information is the percentage of econom-

[3] *Ibid.*

ically active males in agriculture. Even this figure, however, cannot be had for China, the USSR, and certain other countries with substantial populations. Furthermore, this percentage gives no direct information about farm populations, or rural people who depend on services to farmers for their livelihood.

The data of Table 1 shows a tremendous variation among the countries listed, ranging from 6 percent in the United Kingdom to 83 percent in Algeria. Since some of the data were collected more than 15 years ago, considerable changes may have occurred in some countries.

The paucity of comparable information for earlier dates in many countries makes it impossible to trace with any degree of precision

TABLE 1. Percent of Economically Active Males in Agriculture in Selected Countries

Continent and Country	Year	Percent	Continent and Country	Year	Percent
Africa			Pakistan	1951	76
Algeria	1948	83	Philippines	1948	63
Egypt	1947	52	Europe		
North America			Austria	1951	25
Canada	1951	23	Belgium	1947	13
USA	1950	15	Czechoslovakia	1947	29
USA[a]	1961	8.6	Denmark	1950	29
			France	1946	33
South America			East Germany	1946	23
Argentina	1947	30	West Germany	1950	17
Brazil	1950	56	Ireland	1949	46
Bolivia	1950	69	Italy	1951	43
Chile	1952	37	Norway	1947	35
Ecuador	1950	62	Sweden	1945	30
Paraguay	1950	63	United Kingdom	1951	6
Venezuela	1950	48			
			Oceania		
Asia			Australia	1947	19
Ceylon	1946	50	New Zealand	1951	22
India	1951	69			
Japan	1947	50			

SOURCE: *United Nations Demographic Yearbook,* 1956, Table 12.
[a] "Monthly Report on the Labor Force," *Employment and Earnings,* U.S. Bureau of Labor Statistics, January, 1961.

the growth in numbers of urban, rural, farm, and rural nonfarm populations. In the United States and Canada and in the countries of western Europe, industrial development has been accompanied by a substantial and still continuing increase in the urban population. This trend in the United States will be discussed in greater detail below. It is not certain whether the expansion of industry in India, China, and other previously nonindustrialized countries with large concentrations of population will generate this type of urban growth and a subsequent decline of the farm population. The culture of these countries is vastly different from that which western countries had prior to industrial development. Furthermore, advances in technology permit decentralization of some industries.

RURAL POPULATION TRENDS IN THE UNITED STATES

During colonial times the relatively sparse population was principally rural. In 1790 when the first census of the total population of the United States was made, there were 3,929,000 people of whom more than 96 percent lived outside the six cities with 8000 or more inhabitants. In 1850, 87.5 percent of the population was rural; only 12.5 percent lived in the 85 cities having 8000 or more people.

The rapid settlement of the United States after 1850 was accompanied by large numerical increases in both the urban and the rural population. The prospect of free agricultural land and the companion prospect of unparalleled social and economic opportunities attracted large numbers of European immigrants, many of whom settled on farms in the northern part of the country.

The farm population was counted as a separate segment of the rural population for the first time in 1920. At that time there were 31,393,000 farm people or 29.7 percent of the total population of the U.S. It has been estimated that the peak number of American farm dwellers was reached in 1910 when there were an estimated 31,855,000 people, comprising roughly 35 percent of the total population. Between 1920 and 1930 the farm population declined to 31,158,000. This trend was reversed in the 1930s due chiefly to adverse economic conditions in the cities, and a slight increase was registered in 1940. The labor needs of industry and the Armed Services during World War II stimulated a tremendous increase in farm-to-city migration with the result that there were 7,000,000 less people on farms in 1950 than in 1940. The downward trend of the farm population continued during the 1950s while the total population of the United States increased very rapidly; in April, 1960, there were 15,669,000 farm people comprising 8.7 percent of the civilian population of the U.S.[4] As noted earlier, the decline in the 1950s was due in part to a change in definition.

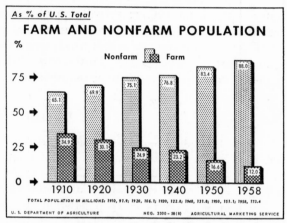

FIG. 1. Farm and Nonfarm Population, 1910-1958. The proportion of the population on farms has declined drastically.

The close relationship between the farm and the rural nonfarm population in many sections of the United States leads us to an examination of the trends in the latter.[5] Since 1910 when the rural farm and nonfarm segments of the rural population were estimated separately,[6] the rural nonfarm population has been increasing even as the farm population has decreased. This has occurred in spite of a reclassification in 1950 of approximately 8,000,000 people as urban residents who under previous definitions would have been counted as a part of the rural nonfarm population. Starting with 18,118,000 in 1910, the rural nonfarm figure increased to 27,029,000 in 1940 and to 54,295,000 or 30.2 percent of the national total in 1960 (Table 2).

[4] U.S. Bureau of the Census, *Estimates of the Rural Farm Population of the United States, April 1960,* Series Census-AMS (P-27), No. 29, April 18, 1961.

[5] Since 1900 the U.S. Census Bureau has used a population of 2500 as the point of separation between rural and urban.

[6] Estimated for 1910.

Table 2. Population Trends in the United States by Residence, 1790-1960

Year	Total	Urban Number	Urban Percent	All Rural Total	All Rural Percent	Rural Nonfarm Number	Rural Nonfarm Percent	Rural Farm Number	Rural Farm Percent
1790	3,929,214	201,655	5.1	3,727,559	94.9				
1850	23,191,876	3,543,716	15.3	19,648,160	84.7				
1870	38,558,371	9,902,361	25.7	28,656,010	74.3				
1900	75,994,575	30,159,921	39.7	45,834,654	60.3				
1910	91,972,266	41,998,932	45.7	49,973,334	54.3	18,118,341	19.7[a]	31,854,993	34.6[a]
1920	105,710,620	54,157,973	51.2	51,552,647	48.8	20,159,385	19.1	31,393,262	29.7
1930	122,775,046	68,054,823	56.2	53,820,223	43.8	23,662,710	19.3	30,157,513	24.5
1940	131,669,275	74,423,702	56.5	57,245,573	43.5	27,029,385	20.5	30,216,188	23.0
1950	150,687,361	96,457,686	64.0	54,229,675	36.0	31,181,325	20.7	23,048,350	15.3
1960	180,004,000[b]	110,040,000	61.1	69,964,000	38.9	50,125,000	27.9	19,839,000	11.0
1960	180,004,000[c]	110,040,000	61.1	69,964,000	38.9	54,295,000	30.2	15,669,000	8.7

[a] Estimated.
[b] Old definition of farm population.
[c] New definition of farm population.

Source: U.S. Bureau of the Census, *Estimates of the Rural Farm Population of the United States, April 1960*, Series Census-AMS (P-27), No. 29, April 18, 1961; and *Estimates of the Population of the United States, January 1, 1950, to March 1, 1961*, Series P-25, No. 226, April 17, 1961.

The increase in the rural nonfarm population is to be explained partly by the increase in services to farmers which has accompanied the application of scientific and technological developments to agriculture and partly by the location in rural areas of plants for processing agricultural products after they leave the farm and before they enter the grocery store. Perhaps even more important than either of these two developments, however, has been the tremendous increase in the number of people who live in the country but work in a city. It reflects a belief on the part of many Americans that rural living is more wholesome than urban living. Many parents feel that the country is a better place to raise a family than the city. It should be noted again that many of the people classified by the census as members of the farm population are part-time farmers who actually obtain more of their income from nonfarm than from farm sources. This point will be discussed in greater detail later.

DISTRIBUTION OF THE U.S. FARM POPULATION BY REGION

The farm population of the United States is not distributed evenly throughout the country. There are vast areas, including the arid and semiarid West and the mountains, which are submarginal for agriculture. Furthermore, the large-scale mechanized types of agriculture practiced in some fertile areas will support relatively small agricultural populations.

The percentage classified as rural farm varies from state to state. In 1950 only Mississippi, Arkansas, and North Dakota had as many as 40 percent of their people living on farms. The farm population comprised between 30 and 40 percent of the total in South Dakota, North Carolina, South Carolina, Kentucky, Tennessee, and Alabama. At the other extreme, in Massachusetts, Rhode Island, Connecticut, New Jersey, and New York less than 5 percent of the population was rural farm.

In 1959 only seven states had as many as 150,000 farms: Texas led with 227,000; North Carolina was in second place with 190,000; Iowa reported 174,000; Missouri had 163,000; Tennessee had 157,000; Illinois had 154,000; and Kentucky had 150,000. In terms of absolute numbers, the bulk of the farm population is located in the Cotton and Corn Belts.

Like the farm group, the rural nonfarm population is also distributed unevenly throughout the United States. In 1950, high proportions of the population were classified as rural nonfarm in the South Atlantic region and in the mountain states of the West. West Virginia reported 44.9 percent of its population as rural nonfarm in 1950. This high figure doubtless is due to the predominance of the coal mining industry in West Virginia. Vermont with 42.1 percent rural nonfarm people was not far behind. The following 13 states also reported that 30 percent or more of their people lived in rural nonfarm areas in 1950: Maine, New Hampshire, North Dakota, Virginia, North Carolina, South Carolina, Kentucky, Montana, Wyoming, New Mexico, Arizona, Nevada, and Oregon.

People who live in small towns and other rural nonfarm areas have not been studied as carefully as urban and farm populations. Nevertheless, the characteristics and problems of these people are of considerable concern to farmers and farm organizations and agencies, for many of the wage earners in the rural nonfarm population make their living by providing various services, agricultural and otherwise, to farmers. Most of them are in interaction with farmers informally, as members of formal voluntary organizations, and as joint participants in various services offered by community institutions and government agencies. Even in the urban fringe the encroachment of nonfarm people in previously agricultural areas creates major economic and social problems for farm people.

RURAL POPULATION CHARACTERISTICS

As indicated above, characteristics like family size, composition, age distribution, sex ratio, and marital status frequently differ in degree between the farm population of a country and the urban or rural nonfarm segments. Reporting on data collected by the U.S. Census Bureau in 1940, Hagood found sharp contrasts between the farm group and urban people with rural nonfarm people in an intermediate position as far as most population characteristics examined by the Census were concerned.[7]

Slocum and Stone examined systematically the extent to which the farm population of Washington conformed in 1950 to traditional

[7] Margaret J. Hagood, "Dynamics of Rural Population," in Carl C. Taylor et al., Rural Life in the United States, Knopf, 1949, p. 228.

ideas about rural-urban differences. On the basis of this analysis, they concluded that for the population of the state of Washington at that date "conformity did exist for most of the items on which comparisons were possible":

1. Farm families were somewhat larger.
2. Farm adults tended to be less well educated.
3. Aged parents were more often found in farm homes.
4. A higher proportion of farm women were married.
5. Farm income was generally lower although this was not true in eleven counties.
6. The farm population contained a higher proportion under fifteen and over sixty-four.

It should be added, however, that in most cases the differences were not great. . . .

Conformity with traditional expectations concerning rural-urban differences was not found for the following:

1. The rural birth rate has been ~~~ ~~ than the urban birth rate.
2. Farm girls did *not* marry at younger ages than nonfarm girls.
3. There were fewer males per 100 females in the farm population than in the rural nonfarm population. This may have been due principally to the influence of several large military establishments whose members were classified as rural nonfarm.[8]

The differences observed were not as great as those reported by Hagood for the population of the U.S. in 1940 and were probably less than those existing in the country as a whole in 1950, but there were many indications of continued rural-urban convergence during the decade of the 1950s. The decrease in differences between rural farm and urban populations in this country is due to the eager participation of farm people in social and cultural change. This, however, is clearly an exceptional situation as far as most of the rest of the world is concerned. The available information indicates that great differences between rural and urban populations still exist in most countries, especially in the parts of the world which have experienced little industrial development.

[8] Walter L. Slocum and Carol L. Stone, *The Farm People of Washington at Mid-Century,* Washington Agricultural Experiment Station Bulletin 557, February, 1955, p. 39. Throughout the present work, Agricultural Experiment Station will be abbreviated AES.

Let us now look in greater detail at the social implications of significant population characteristics for which information is available from census sources.

AGE DISTRIBUTION

The age distribution of any population has an important bearing upon many social phenomena. For one thing, the presence of excessively large numbers of people in the dependent age categories of childhood or old age may restrict the social activities and as well adversely affect the economic potential of a farm family. For another, as T. L. Smith has correctly observed, rural populations which ordinarily have a higher concentration of people of advanced age are likely to be more conservative, due to the fact that older people tend to accept new ideas less readily than younger people. There is also much truth in the further point made by Smith that in rural society control of property is likely to be retained by older people longer than in urban areas. He points out that this permits the older people to have a large voice in the control of the affairs of rural communities.[9] Along the same lines, Kolb and Brunner have called attention to the constructive contributions of young people in the settlement and subjugation of the frontier. These authors also suggest that the increase in the proportion of older people in the population has brought pressure for legislation to provide social security benefits for the aged.[10]

A special survey made by the U.S. Census Bureau in March, 1960, showed that 8.6 percent of the rural farm population was 65 or over compared to 7.7 percent of the rural nonfarm and 9.3 percent of the urban population.[11] This represents a reversal of the 1950 farm and nonfarm positions; at that time, 7.5 percent of the rural farm population was 65 or older compared to 8.3 percent of the rural nonfarm and 8.2 percent of the urban population. The change suggests that the long-time tendency for farmers to retire to nearby towns may have been arrested.

[9] T. Lynn Smith, *The Sociology of Rural Life,* 3rd ed., Harper, 1953, pp. 41, 76-80.
[10] John H. Kolb and Edmund deS. Brunner, *A Study of Rural Society,* 4th ed., Houghton Mifflin, 1952, p. 39.
[11] *Household and Family Characteristics, op. cit.*

The high incidence of children traditionally found among farm populations has been noted by many writers. The farm group has frequently been referred to as the "seedbed" of the nation's population. This aspect of population dynamics will be discussed in greater length in the section dealing with fertility.

The presence in the rural population of persons in the dependent ages may be expressed in terms of a dependency ratio derived by ascertaining the number of persons under 18 and over 65 per 1000 persons in the productive years 18-65. The ratios for March, 1960, computed by this method are rural farm 945, rural nonfarm 908, and urban 756. Price has suggested that the heavy dependency load carried by the rural population is an important factor in explaining differences between rural and urban levels of living.[12]

There is evidence that the dependency ratios are highest among the families that are the least prosperous.[13]

SEX COMPOSITION

The sex composition of a population has important implications for various aspects of social relationships including opportunities for marriage. Landis has drawn attention to the tendency in frontier areas, where there is a predominance of adult males, for a spirit of bravado to prevail with an abnormal number of gambling houses, brothels and violent deaths, and high drunkenness and suicide rates.[14] Landis also suggests that a large excess of females in a community may lead to higher divorce rates, greater aggressiveness on the part of women in their relationships with men, and perhaps the development of new patterns of family life.[15]

Traditionally men have outnumbered women among all segments of the population of the United States. Males outnumber females at birth by about 105.7 to 100.[16] In 1959, due to the cumulative effect of the longer life expectancy of women, there were more females than males in the general population (95.2 males per 100 females). As in

[12] Paul H. Price, "The Rural Population," in A. L. Bertrand, ed., *Rural Sociology*, McGraw-Hill, 1958, p. 57.
[13] *Farms and Farm People, op. cit.*, p. 51.
[14] P. H. Landis and P. K. Hatt, *Population Problems*, 2nd ed., American Book, 1950, pp. 78-80.
[15] *Ibid.*, pp. 80-82.
[16] *Ibid.*, pp. 59-60.

earlier periods, however, men outnumbered women among the farm people (105.7 males per 100 females). The 1959 sex ratio in the rural nonfarm segment of the population was 98.8 males per 100 females and in the urban population 91.6 males per 100 females.[17]

These residential differences in the sex ratio are not due to any inherent tendency on the part of farm mothers to bear significantly more male children than their urban sisters. The explanation is to be sought rather in the selective character of rural-urban migration. Movements from farms to urban areas have involved more women than men. In the early adult years, farm girls migrate to cities to enter occupations which are open to women only in such areas. Agriculture is primarily an occupation for males. There is also believed to be a tendency for widows to migrate to towns and cities rather than to assume the direction of farm operations.[18] Many of the women who migrate to towns and cities undoubtedly marry urban residents.

The great mobility of the American population, both farm and nonfarm, has doubtless encouraged the tendency for American men and women to select their mates on the basis of personal choice rather than considerations of socioeconomic class position, family lineage, or kinship as in many other countries.[19]

Marital Status

In 1950, a larger proportion of adult women were married among the rural farm population than the urban with the rural nonfarm population occupying an intermediate position. The situation was reversed for men. Data from a special analysis of the 1950 Census of Agriculture and Population show that at that time farm operators (90 percent) were much more likely to be married than all farm males aged 14 or over (64 percent), probably because they were older and in a more favorable economic position than the rest of the farm group.[20]

[17] U.S. Bureau of the Census, *Civilian Population of the United States, by Type of Residence, April 1959 and 1950,* Series P-20, No. 98, January 25, 1960.

[18] Smith, *op. cit.,* p. 81.

[19] See Landis and Hatt, *op. cit.,* p. 75; Slocum and Stone, *op. cit.,* p. 17.

[20] *Farms and Farm People, op. cit.,* p. 58.

There were more widowed women than widowered men in all residential categories in 1950. However, there were relatively fewer in the rural farm population. The percentages support the belief that many widows migrate from farms rather than assume the burden of farm operations.

Divorced persons were least frequently found in the farm population and most frequently found in the urban with the rural nonfarm population occupying an intermediate position. These data tend to confirm a widespread conviction that divorces are less prevalent among farm people. Kolb and Brunner offer the opinion that this difference is due to a more conservative attitude of rural families toward divorce and greater stability in family relationships.[21] The proportion of widowed and divorced males was highest in 1950 among residential farmers and operators of low-income farms, probably due chiefly to the higher proportion of aged in these categories.[22]

EDUCATIONAL ATTAINMENTS

Belief in education is one of the dominant values in contemporary American society. Formal education is widely regarded as the most desirable method of occupational preparation. The educational channel is also widely used as a means of attaining higher social status. With the advent of scientific methods of farming, education has also assumed a greater occupational significance to farm people than formerly; many farmers are now aware of the vocational value of education.

In spite of this, the farm population of the United States still lags far behind the rural nonfarm and urban segments. Among persons 25 years of age and over in 1957, educational attainments of both men and women were lowest for the rural farm population and highest for the urban population among both whites and nonwhites. The median number of years of school completed was 8.6 for the farm population compared to 10.6 for the total population 25 years old and over. Rural farm women tend to have more education than rural farm men.

The educational achievements of farm people differ to a considerable extent from one part of the United States to another. In the

[21] Kolb and Brunner, op. cit., p. 42.
[22] Farms and Farm People, op. cit., p. 58.

state of Washington, for example, one-third of the adults aged 25 or over in 1950 had completed high school as compared with only one-fifth of all farm adults in the United States as a whole.

The trend toward a high-school education among the farm people in the United States apparently started its rapid upward acceleration about 30 or 35 years ago. Census data indicate progressively higher percentages of high-school graduates with decreasing age. The rapid acceleration in the rate of increase started with those who would have been of high school age in the late 1920s.

The superior educational achievements of urban and rural non-farm adults reflected by the census data are due in part to selective migration in the past of better-educated farm people to urban and village areas. However, the differences may also be attributed to some extent to the fact that the tendency for young people from farms to go to high school and college is a culture pattern of relatively recent origin which has not yet spread to all parts of the United States.

Although the farm population contained relatively fewer college graduates than the urban or rural nonfarm population, nevertheless in March, 1957, there were more than 792,000 people over 25 on farms who had completed a year or more of college. Nearly 265,000 of these were college graduates.[23] These numbers are sufficiently great to provide a substantial supply of college-trained leadership in the farm population. As might be expected, these people tend to be concentrated in areas of highest farm incomes.

Why do marked differences in educational attainments exist among the states? A basic reason is, of course, the fact that in the U.S. responsibility for education is a state rather than a federal function. Furthermore, within most states there has been a great deal of local responsibility for elementary and secondary education. The state of Washington which, as noted previously, has a much higher level of educational achievement than the national average among farm adults may assign at least part of the credit to the fact that for a considerable number of years the state has had a system of consolidated schools. Free transportation has been provided for those living outside the incorporated limits of the place where the school is

[23] U.S.Bureau of the Census, *Educational Attainment: March 1957*, Series P-20, No. 77, December, 1957.

located. This, of course, makes it fairly easy for farm youth to attend high school if they wish to do so. An underlying factor of considerable importance is that together with other states along the Pacific Coast Washington was settled relatively late by people who were themselves descended from migrant stock. Most students of migration believe that there is a tendency for the most adventuresome to migrate, leaving the conservatives behind. If this is true, then the fact that the Pacific Coast generally was settled last is of profound significance in explaining the readiness which the people of this section of the United States have shown toward the acceptance of change. The foreign-born have never been of great significance in the population of this area, although the great bulk of adults ever since territorial days have come from outside the state.

It may be anticipated on the basis of economic and social changes occurring throughout the United States that the pattern of educational achievement found among the farm people in the Pacific states will become the expected nationwide pattern.

Kolb and Brunner[24] have noted that educational support tends to be lowest in the areas where the educational achievements and economic status of the farm people are the lowest. Thus there is a tendency for low educational attainments to be self-perpetuating. This is a matter of national interest. The history of rural-urban migration in America reveals that many of the citizens of prosperous urban centers come from poor farm areas. Proponents of federal support for education have called attention to the long-term interest of urban areas in the children of poor farm families.[25]

OCCUPATIONAL COMPOSITION

The farm labor force has been declining steadily for many years —there were 10,450,000 persons regularly employed in agriculture in 1929 compared to 5,723,000 in 1960.

There may have been a time in the history of the United States when almost every able-bodied adult male who lived on a farm was engaged in agricultural work on a full-time basis. This situation no longer exists. In 1959, 45 percent of all farm operators did some

[24] Kolb and Brunner, op. cit., p. 319.
[25] See Chapters 4 and 21.

off-farm work; 30 percent worked off their farms 100 days or more.[26] In addition, substantial numbers of farm wives worked on off-farm jobs. There is little doubt that the development of part-time farming and the corollary increase in the number of persons holding dual occupational roles one of which is agriculture has served to keep the farm population from declining even more drastically than it has since 1940.

Farmers and farm laborers had higher rates of multiple job holding in 1958 than any other major occupational category except protective service workers. Jobs of all types and status levels were

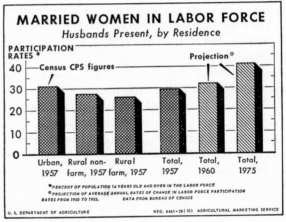

FIG. 2.   Farm Wives Employed in 1957.

held by farmers, but the major concentration was in "blue-collar" jobs as craftsmen, operatives, and laborers.[27]

Many married farm women work for pay; 26 percent of married farm women living with their husbands were employed outside the home in 1957[28] (Fig. 2). Most of them were employed in non-agricultural occupations.

A point that deserves special mention is the fact that the pro-ductive aspects of farming are predominantly regarded as men's

[26] U.S. Bureau of the Census, *1959 Census of Agriculture—Preliminary*, Series AC59-1, January, 1961.

[27] U.S. Bureau of the Census, *Multiple Jobholding: July 1958*, Series P-50, No. 88, April, 1959.

[28] U.S. Bureau of the Census, *Marital Status of Workers: March 1957*, Series P-50, No. 76, November, 1957.

work in the U.S. Farm women may help with field work to a limited extent during rush seasons and some perform farm chores, particularly with poultry, but the fact is that throughout much of the country the role of the farm wife is held to be that of a homemaker whose duties include care of the house, taking the primary responsibility for the children, and preparing meals.

Iwanska found that people tend to believe women should be glamorous.

A woman should be glamorous. Her place is at home and in the community. It is not in the barn, not even in the garden, because glamour is clearly uncompatible (sic) with such hard physical work.

"Women just aren't made for this sort of work," Good Fortune housewives say. "Their hands get rough and they age much earlier than they would otherwise; it isn't healthy for them."

There are still quite a few partner wives in Good Fortune. These not only keep gardens and chickens. They work side by side with their husbands in the barn and in the fields. Sometimes partner wives devote considerably more time to farming than their husbands who work outside. But as a rule the husbands of partner wives are bitterly criticized for letting their wives work so hard. Sometimes they are even suspected of forcing them to work so hard "so they can be lazy and have time for beer drinking."[29]

The fact that a large proportion of the farm population does not depend upon agricultural pursuits for a major part of its livelihood has great significance in terms of their personal experiences, interpersonal relationships, and attitudes about agricultural programs and problems. There can be little question that a person who occupies some nonfarm job as his principal occupational role has substantially different daily experiences and personal relationships than one who occupies a full-time job on a farm. These individual experiences and relationships obviously influence attitudes. It may be assumed that everyone who lives on a farm has some interest in agriculture. It is also fairly obvious that a person whose major occupational role is that of a full-time farmer has a much more vital interest in prices for agricultural products and other aspects of agricultural policy than one who earns most of his living from a nonfarm job.

The great decline in the number of people gainfully employed in agriculture has occurred primarily because of the development of

[29] Alicja Iwanska, *Good Fortune: Second Chance Community*, Washington AES Bulletin 589, June, 1958, p. 30.

farm technology, including the adoption of gasoline engines as sources of energy. As this has taken place, the occupation of agriculture itself has undergone additional specialization. It is still true that most farmers do their work in the open air in close association with the soil and living plants and animals, but the meaning of agriculture from an occupational point of view is no longer simple. The typical American commercial farmer is not a peasant chained to an unrelenting routine established by his animals or plants. He is a specialist. There are vast differences in the occupational roles of a cattle rancher, a wheat farmer, an orange grower, a corn-hog producer, a dairyman, or a fruit farmer, to mention a few of the principal fields of commodity specialization.[30] Similar changes have occurred within the ranks of farm labor. Many farm workers today are specialists who draw premium wages because of their skills. Furthermore, many of the operations previously performed by farm laborers—for instance, crop dusting, application of farm fertilizers, and orchard spraying—have now been taken over by firms of agricultural specialists who provide services to many different farmers on a contract basis.

A very important requirement for the modern farm operator in America is a knowledge of business principles. Successful operation of a commercial farm under present-day competitive market conditions demands a rather high degree of managerial skill. In addition, a farmer who is interested in keeping up with developments in farm technology must have a considerable amount of education. To stay abreast of developments in plant breeding, farm chemicals, and livestock nutrition, for example, requires the equivalent of a college course in agriculture which includes substantial work in chemistry, agronomy, and animal husbandry.

To get the most out of his land, the farmer needs to understand the importance of soil testing and crop rotation. On most farms operated on a family basis, the farm operator must have considerable mechanical skill in order to keep his machines in good repair.

This brief account of some of the ramifications of the occupational roles included under the heading of agriculture should be sufficient to make it clear that a commercial farm in the U.S. is no

[30] See Chapter 7 for a discussion of the regional distribution of various types of farming.

place for a person without ability and education.

From an occupational standpoint as well as in many other ways, the current position of people engaged in agriculture may be regarded as interdependent. The traditional self-sufficient farmer of colonial times produced little if anything for the market. He grew and processed his own food and erected his own shelter with his own hands, perhaps with some help from his neighbors. His wife turned homespun yarn into rough clothing. As we have noted above, commercial farmers today are often specialists. Many wheat farmers, for example, keep no dairy animals and obtain their milk, bread, and other groceries from the market just as if they were nonfarm people.

The sociological importance of occupation has been stated clearly by Dr. Alba Edwards, a former employee of the United States Bureau of the Census:

> The most nearly dominant single influence in a man's life is probably his occupation. More than anything else, perhaps, a man's occupation determines his course and his contribution in life. And when life's span is ended, quite likely there is no other single set of facts that will tell so well the kind of man he was and the part he played in life as will a detailed and chronological statement of the occupation, or occupations, he pursued. Indeed, there is no other single characteristic that tells so much about a man and his status—social, intellectual, and economic— as does his occupation. A man's occupation not only tells, for each workday, what he does during one-half of his waking hours, but it indicates, with some degree of accuracy, his manner of life during the other half— the kind of associates he will have. the kind of clothes he will wear, the kind of house he will live in and even, to some extent, the kind of food he will eat. And, usually, it indicates, in some degree, the cultural level of his family.[31]

FACTORS IN RURAL POPULATION GROWTH

The growth of rural population is determined by three factors known to students of population as the *vital processes*—births, deaths, and migration. Births and deaths will be discussed in this section, and migration subsequently.

[31] Alba M. Edwards, *Comparative Occupation Statistics for the United States, 1870 to 1940*, Special Report, U.S. Bureau of the Census, *116th Census of the U.S.: 1940*, 1943, p. xi.

REPRODUCTIVE PATTERNS

In the United States as well as in many other countries, rural birth rates have been higher than urban as a general rule. From an economic standpoint, farmers traditionaly viewed an additional male child as an asset since he joined the farm labor force at a fairly early age. Because food and shelter were largely provided by the farm, an additional mouth to feed would not fall with as great an impact on a farmer as upon a city dweller. Furthermore, most rural populations have placed a positive value upon the production of children. Apparently the mores banned family limitation in some cases. In *The Golden Bough,* Frazer suggests that preliterate rural folk practiced fertility rites on the assumption that high human fertility would encourage greater fertility in crops and animals.[32] In most western countries, on the other hand, relatively small families have come to be regarded as desirable by urban families.[33]

Information concerning births depends chiefly upon the establishment of accurate registration and recording procedures. In the United States valid information dates from 1920. Comparable data are still unavailable for many of the underdeveloped countries which have the greatest concentration of rural people. In India and Pakistan, for example, the record of births and deaths is kept by illiterate village officials in most cases. The "record" consists of a simple count of births by sex within specific periods. Information from studies in these countries indicates that the crude birth rate is approximately 50 per 1000 or about twice that in the U.S.[34]

Births are not normally recorded or tabulated according to the residential and occupational classification of parents. Consequently, it is necessary to rely upon census sources for data which reflect the reproductive behavior of rural farm people. These data show that traditional residential differences continue to persist. In 1957, the number of children ever born to women who had ever been

[32] Sir James Frazer, *The Golden Bough,* Macmillan, 1958.

[33] Landis and Hatt, *op. cit.,* p. 178.

[34] Kingsley Davis, *The Population of India and Pakistan,* Princeton University Press, 1951; W. L. Slocum, Jamila Akhtar, and Abrar Fatima Sahi, *Village Life in Lahore District,* Lahore, Social Sciences Research Center, Panjab University Press, October, 1959.

married was substantially greater for rural farm residents than for those who lived in rural nonfarm or urban areas. For women 15 to 44 years of age the number of children per 1000 women was: rural farm 3009, rural nonfarm 2356, and urban 2035.[35]

Another indicator of fertility is the total number of children born to women who have passed through the childbearing period. Information collected through a survey conducted by the U.S. Census Bureau shows the following number of children ever born per 1000 women ever married who were aged 45 or over in April, 1957: rural farm 3910, rural nonfarm 3069, and urban 2514.[36]

There are indications, however, that recent increases in birth rates have been smaller in rural farm areas. Between 1950 and 1957, "the average number of children ever born per 1000 women of all marital classes, standardized for age, increased about 26 per cent in urban areas . . . 12 per cent in rural-nonfarm areas . . . and 10 per cent in rural-farm areas."[37]

In the rural population, the highest fertility is to be found in relatively isolated sections like the Appalachian Mountain areas of Kentucky and Tennessee, western Virginia and North Carolina, southern West Virginia, and Alabama. It is also high in isolated sectors of Louisiana, in the Ozark Mountain area of Arkansas and Missouri, in the most inaccessible parts of Utah, Colorado, Arizona, and Nevada, and on the Indian reservations in the Dakotas. This pattern suggests that in locales where farming is relatively little commercialized traditional patterns of rural fertility still exist. Further confirmation of this view is the finding that 1950 fertility ratios when standardized for age and marital status were inversely related to economic classification of farms.[38]

Although the data presented above show that rural-urban differentials in reproductive behavior still exist in the United States, rural birth rates have declined materially from pioneer times. The fertility decline in the rural-farm population has not been as great as the decline in the nonfarm population.[39] However, the above informa-

[35] U.S. Bureau of the Census, *Fertility of the Population: March 1957*, Series P-20, No. 84, August, 1958.
[36] *Ibid.*
[37] *Ibid.*
[38] *Farms and Farm People, op. cit.*, p. 60.
[39] Taylor *et al., op. cit.*, p. 238.

tion indicates that the upsurge in the birth rate which occurred during the 1950s has not been so great in rural as in urban areas. Price has suggested that rural-urban fertility differentials will eventually disappear in the U.S.;[40] this may occur, but it is likely that differences will persist longer in some sections of the country than in others.

The prospect of the disappearance or even the reversal of traditional farm-nonfarm fertility differentials in this country is a reflection of social and cultural change. One change of great significance is the tendency for farm males to marry later than nonfarm males. In addition, the rising level of education and the greatly increased exposure of farm people to urban ideas has doubtless broken down much of the traditional rural resistance to birth control. Furthermore, the long-standing inverse correlation between income and number of children is no longer generally true for the U.S. Many married people have sufficient control over conception to make it possible for them to plan their families in terms of resources and personal desires.[41] Population control in this country is not a matter of great concern at present, although it cannot be said that this will be true indefinitely. So far as the world as a whole is concerned, the specter of overpopulation is a menace which threatens to wipe out the gains of technology and science. Since the great majority of the people of the world are agricultural, this matter is of concern to rural sociologists in many countries.

LONGEVITY AND MORTALITY

As we have already noted, the proportion of aged is increasing in all residential segments of the population. This is of course due to a reduction in mortality rates and consequent longer life.

Compared to countries like India and Pakistan or to earlier periods in the United States, the present American life expectancy is little short of amazing. In 1957, the expectation of life at birth was 67.1 years for a white male and 73.5 for a white female. For nonwhites the comparable expectancies were 60.3 and 65.2.[42] This represents a

---

[40] Paul H. Price, "The Rural Population," in Bertrand, ed., *op. cit.*, p. 66.

[41] Observation by Dr. Irene Taeuber at the Pakistan Population Seminar, Karachi, September 12, 1959.

[42] U.S. Bureau of the Census, *Statistical Abstract of the United States: 1960*, 1960, p. 59.

TABLE 3. Expectation of Life at Birth for Selected Dates and Countries

| | | Expectation of Life in Years | |
		Male	Female
U.S.A.	1956[a]		
	White	67.3	73.7
	Nonwhite	61.1	65.9
U.S.A.	1900-1902[a]		
	White	48.2	51.1
	Nonwhite	32.5	35.0
Japan[b]	1921-1950	42.1	43.2
	1957-1958	63.7	68.1
India	1930-1941[c]	32.0	31.4
Sweden[d]	1941-1945	67.1	69.7
Canada[d]	1947	65.2	69.0
France[d]	1946-1948	62.5	68.0

[a] U.S. Bureau of the Census, *Statistical Abstract of the U.S.*: 1959, pp. 60-61.

[b] Minoru Tachi and Toshio Kuroda, *Trends in Population Growth and Economic Development in Japan,* paper presented at the Pakistan Population Seminar, September, 1959.

[c] Kingsley Davis, *The Population of India and Pakistan,* Princeton University Press, 1951, p. 242.

[d] W. S. Thompson, *Population Problems,* McGraw-Hill, 1953, p. 233.

notable improvement during the 50 years since 1900, when lives were much shorter (Table 3). If the life span of man is 100 years, as Dublin has suggested, further increases in longevity may be anticipated.[43]

A feature of mortality rates which has attracted considerable attention in recent years is the fact that women have longer life expectancies than men in the United States and other western countries. This is not true of countries like India and Pakistan, where hazards of childbirth result in a high mortality rate for women in the childbearing period. On the average a white woman in the

[43] L. I. Dublin, in E. V. Cowdry, ed., *Problems of Ageing,* 2nd ed., Williams and Wilkins, 1942, p. 109.

U.S. may be expected to live 6.4 years longer than a man. Coupled with the fact that American men tend to marry women on the average two years younger than themselves, this means that most women, including those who live on farms, can expect several years of widowhood.

Prior to the development of modern sanitation methods and medical care, rural areas had an advantage over cities in respect to health. Sorokin, Zimmerman, and Galpin concluded that there was ample evidence to support the conclusion that in the past country people had lower mortality rates than city people.[44]

Information available for the United States[45] indicates a somewhat longer life expectancy for rural areas. Although the hazards of life in cities have been reduced by sanitary conditions and the availability of medical treatment, urban mortality rates continue to exceed those of rural populations. In 1958 there were 10.1 deaths per 1000 in the urban U.S. compared to 8.4 in rural areas.[46] According to Sorokin, Zimmerman, and Galpin, the following factors tend to give an advantage to rural populations:

> There are several factors that seem not only to be responsible for the relatively lower rural mortality but that also seem to be sufficient to counterbalance the effect of the environmental factors lowering urban death rates: lower density of population in the country; greater integrity of the rural family; greater maternal care of the child in the rural family; the outdoor character of agricultural work; better country air; more healthful nature of agricultural work; "the greater peace of mind" of the rural people. . . ; and finally, a generally better adaptation of human beings to the rural environment.[47]

Nonwhites have somewhat higher mortality rates than whites in the United States as a whole and in the farm population. This undoubtedly reflects the fact that in general the economic circumstances and levels of living of nonwhites are less favorable than those of the white population.

[44] P. A. Sorokin, C. C. Zimmerman, and C. J. Galpin, *A Systematic Source Book in Rural Sociology*, University of Minnesota Press, 1932, III, 121.

[45] Smith, *op. cit.*, p. 153.

[46] U.S. Department of Health, Education, and Welfare, *General Natality and Mortality by Counties, Urban and Rural Areas, and Specified Urban Places*, section 11 of *Vital Statistics of the United States, 1958*, 1960.

[47] Sorokin, Zimmerman, and Galpin, *op. cit.*, p. 135.

The spectacular increase in the number of people in the world during the last 50 to 100 years is not due to any increase in birth rates, for these have been falling except in backward areas where they have remained constant at a high level, but rather to very substantial decreases in death rates.

As Landis and Hatt have pointed out, the chief factors responsible for death are famine, malnutrition, war, accidents, and disease. There has never been a famine in the United States, although conditions existing in the Great Plains Area during the drought-depression years would have led to famine if it had not been for an abundance of food, adequate transportation, and the humanitarian aspects of American society. But it is certain that famine has taken a great toll of life in the old world. During the historic past millions of rural people have perished because of famine in India, China, Russia, and other parts of the globe.[48] Malnutrition occasioned by short food supplies and faulty food habits, while less spectacular than famine, has undoubtedly contributed materially to mortality among rural people. Traditional food habits are yielding slowly in advanced countries to scientific knowledge concerning human nutritional requirements, but even in the U.S. nutrition specialists have criticized the diet of rural families. Diseases specifically produced by malnutrition include pellagra, rickets, scurvy, and beriberi. In addition, malnourished persons doubtless fall prey to the ravages of other diseases, like tuberculosis. Perhaps the most spectacular advances of medical science have been in the control of epidemic diseases like smallpox, yellow fever, and malaria. Many of the diseases of childhood such as scarlet fever, measles, chicken pox, and mumps have also been controlled. The last great epidemic in the U.S. with high death rates was the influenza epidemic following World War I.

Farm accidents due to encounters with farm animals and machinery still constitute an important cause of death. Automobile accidents doubtless also take a substantial toll of farm people as well as others. Accident injury rates are somewhat higher among farm people than nonfarm people.[49] Prodipto Roy, in fact, has described farming as one of the world's most dangerous jobs. He

[48] Landis and Hatt, op. cit., pp. 137-138.
[49] See Statistical Abstract of the United States: 1960, op. cit., Table 75, p. 68.

found in a study in two Washington counties that one of every four farms had an accident in 1959.[50]

QUESTIONS FOR FURTHER STUDY AND DISCUSSION

1. Look up the trends in the rural farm population of your state in census reports. Discuss the implications of these data.
2. What are the principal factors in the continuing increase in the rural nonfarm population?
3. Why is the heaviest concentration of the U.S. farm population found in the South? Is this situation likely to change? Explain your answer.
4. What are the probable reasons for the disproportionate number of people over 65 years of age in the farm population?
5. Discuss the implications of falling rural farm birth rates in view of the past importance of farm families as a source of population growth.
6. Discuss the implications of recent increases in life expectancy in terms of opportunities for young people to get established in farming.

SELECTED REFERENCES

Bogue, Donald J., *The Population of the United States,* Free Press, 1959.
Landis, P. H., and P. K. Hatt, *Population Problems,* 2nd ed., American Book, 1950.
Slocum, Walter L., and Carol L. Stone, *The Farm People of Washington at Mid-Century,* Washington AES Bulletin 557, 1955.
Smith, T. Lynn, *The Sociology of Rural Life,* 3rd ed., Harper, 1953.
Taylor, Carl C., *et al., Rural Life in the United States,* Knopf, 1949.

[50] Prodipto Roy, *Accidents to Farm People,* Washington Agricultural Extension Service EM 2088, July, 1960. (Mimeo)

3

Physical and Mental
Characteristics and Health

The developmental potentiality of both rural and urban people
depends upon their biological heredity. Basic capacity of this kind,
as Gesell has said, is "a gift of nature."[1] Although it is likely that
few ever attain their full potential, nevertheless there are biological
limits to development. An ape cannot be trained to become a man,
nor can a moron be changed into a genius through education. Furthermore, with reference to the sociological implications of heredity,
there are certain inborn and unchangeable physical characteristics,
such as skin color, which have an important influence on the social
rank and the life chances of the human individual in a particular
society.

There is a fairly widespread belief, a sort of folk knowledge, that
has been handed down from the past which holds that farmers
and villagers in general have inferior physical and mental characteristics when compared to urban people. And those who hold this
view sometimes argue that the alleged gap is widening. This opinion
is based upon the fear that the migration of rural youth to cities
selects the best individuals and that this may have a serious effect
on the quality of the rural population. As E. A. Ross once said, "In
New England there are rural counties which have been losing their
best for three or four generations, leaving the coarse, dull, and hide-
bound. The number of loafers in some slack-water villages of the
middle states indicates that the natural pacemakers of the locality
have gone elsewhere to create prosperity. In parts of southern Michi-

[1] Arnold Gesell, "Growth Potentials of the Human Infant," in A. M. Lee,
ed., *Readings in Sociology*, Barnes & Noble, 1951, p. 65.

gan, Illinois, Wisconsin, and even as far west as Missouri, there are communities which remind one of fished out ponds populated chiefly by bullheads and suckers."[2] The evidence on selective migration will be examined later.[3]

Most American farm people would doubtless vehemently reject the allegation that they are physically or mentally inferior in any way. However, we should not dismiss the possibility that there are some rural-urban differences without examining the evidence.

DIFFERENCES IN PHYSICAL CHARACTERISTICS

Sorokin, Zimmerman, and Galpin examined the evidence available up to about 1930 concerning physical differences between rural and urban populations in various parts of the United States and Europe.[4] Very little additional evidence seems to have been accumulated since that time.[5]

STATURE, HEAD SHAPE, SIZE, AND PIGMENTATION

With respect to stature, the evidence revealed that in some localities the rural population was taller, whereas in other localities the reverse was true. The same sort of inconsistencies were evident in studies on the shape of the head, which is one of the criteria utilized in determining racial affiliation. Similar findings were reported with respect to other physical characteristics such as body weight and build and pigmentation (skin and hair color).[6]

These apparently inconsistent findings were reconciled by Sorokin, Zimmerman, and Galpin on the basis of a theory proposed by an Italian scholar, Rodolfo Livi. The two elements involved in Livi's theory are: (1) that human physical characteristics like those named above are determined to a considerable extent by biological heredity; and (2) that rural populations tend to be more homogeneous than urban because there traditionally has been less mobility

[2] E. A. Ross, *The Outlines of Sociology*, Century, 1923, p. 22.
[3] Chapter 4.
[4] P. A. Sorokin, C. C. Zimmerman, and C. J. Galpin, *A Systematic Source Book in Rural Sociology*, University of Minnesota Press, 1932, vol. III.
[5] T. Lynn Smith, *The Sociology of Rural Life*, 3rd ed., Harper, 1953.
[6] Sorokin, Zimmerman, and Galpin, *op. cit.*, chap. XVII.

among rural people. This means that the population of a city is more likely to be composed of migrants from different places and consequently to include different physical stocks. Thus stature or any other physical characteristic of a city population is likely to manifest greater variability than is found in the population of the nearby rural area. Consequently, in a city surrounded by a rural area where the native population is tall, for example, the population is likely to be shorter on the average because it includes not only tall rural migrants but also people from other places where the population is shorter. In such a case the immigration of short individuals obviously lowers the average stature.[7] Smith agrees that Livi's theory is adequate to explain the existing evidence, but he also acknowledges that in the case of stature there seemed to be no uniform differences between rural and urban populations.[8]

If it is true that differences in physical characteristics of this type which formerly existed are disappearing in countries like the United States, this may reasonably be attributed to the mobility of the rural population which has actually amalgamated or intermixed stocks as well as intermingled people with varying characteristics in both urban and rural areas.

RACE

Perhaps the most important single physical characteristic from the standpoint of influence on social relationships in the rural U.S. is race. Walter has defined race in the following words: "A race is a large division of human beings distinguished from others by relatively obvious physical characteristics presumed to be biologically inherited and remaining relatively constant through numerous generations."[9] He goes on to say that the characteristics most commonly used in racial classifications include color of skin, head form, stature, and facial features.[10]

This is not the place to enter into a discussion of the fine points of racial differences. For present purposes it will suffice to say that the farm population of the U.S. may be divided racially into whites,

[7] *Ibid.*, pp. 17-18.
[8] Smith, *op. cit.*, p. 87.
[9] P. A. F. Walter, Jr., *Race and Culture Relations*, McGraw-Hill, 1952, p. 5.
[10] *Ibid.*, p. 6.

Negroes, and other nonwhites including chiefly Indians, Japanese, and Filipinos. In 1950 there were only about 175,000 other nonwhites in the rural-farm population.

Perhaps because the Negroes were imported by southern planters principally for use as field hands, there is a widespread tendency to think of American Negroes as predominantly rural. This is no longer true, although there were proportionately more Negroes in the farm population (13.7 percent) than in the rural nonfarm (8.0 percent) or urban populations (9.7 percent) in 1950.

In 1950, 3,158,000 Negroes were classified as rural farm and an additional 2,491,000 as rural nonfarm. A much larger number, 9,-393,000, were urban residents. This represents a considerable change from earlier times. In 1940 more than half of the Negroes in this country were classified as rural and about half of these lived on farms. The change reflects a heavy migration of rural Negroes to the north and west and to southern cities.

Even so the population of the southeastern states continued to have a heavy concentration of Negroes in 1950; the states with the largest proportions of Negroes in 1950 were Mississippi (45.5 percent), South Carolina (38.9 percent), Louisiana (33.1 percent), Alabama (32.1 percent), and Georgia (30.9 percent). The 1960 census will probably reveal additional changes in the regional and rural-urban distributions of Negroes.

In the rural South, most Negroes have always had lower socio-economic status than most white people. Because race is established by birth and it is impossible for a Negro to become white, Negroes have been referred to by some writers as a caste. It is true that caste membership is fixed by birth, but caste as a form of social stratification prescribes for members specific caste-oriented values and behavior norms which apparently are not generally found among American Negroes.[11]

It is certainly true, however, that being a Negro has important social and economic consequences in the rural South. Negroes have had their own churches, interest groups, and neighborhoods. Until the 1954 desegregation decision of the U.S. Supreme Court, most southern states maintained separate elementary and secondary school systems for Negroes and whites. This was done on the assump-

[11] See Chapter 17 for a discussion of caste.

tion that this "separate but equal" treatment adequately met the requirements of the Constitution of the United States. The problems of integration have not been studied adequately from a sociological point of view. It is clear, however, from press reports that in some areas of the South the previous pattern of relationships between white people and Negroes has been disrupted.

With respect to population characteristics, Negroes exhibit somewhat different characteristics from whites. In the farm population, for example, the 1950 sex ratio for Negroes was 102.5 compared to 110.2 for whites. The median number of years of school completed by Negroes 25 years of age and over in the farm population was much lower than among whites (4.3 years for Negro males and 8.4 years for white males). More of the nonwhite females over 14 were single (25.8 percent for nonwhites and 19.7 percent for whites), and there was a higher incidence of widows in the nonwhite than in the white farm population (17.6 and 10.0 percent, respectively).

MENTAL CHARACTERISTICS

Mental characteristics are generally considered to be of greater importance than physical in relation to personal achievements and interpersonal relationships. Adequate data pertaining to intelligence, mental health, and personality traits are extremely difficult to obtain. In the following discussion we will attempt to evaluate some of the available evidence which seems to be relevant to the question.

RURAL-URBAN DIFFERENCES IN INTELLIGENCE

There are many definitions of intelligence. For present purposes the concept may be defined as the ability to understand information and to utilize it in the solution of problems.[12]

Many efforts have been made by American and foreign psychologists to develop measures for testing the intelligence of individuals, particularly school children. The operational definition of the intelligence quotient (IQ) for children is the mental age divided by the chronological age. The mental age in this operation is ascertained by comparing the score of a person on a pencil-and-

[12] See Smith, *op. cit.*, pp. 112, 113.

paper test of some length to the average for individuals of his own age. The content of most intelligence tests is drawn principally from urban rather than rural experience worlds.

Sorokin, Zimmerman, and Galpin summarized the findings of 65 studies which compared the intelligence quotients of rural and urban children in various parts of the United States and Europe up to about 1930.[13] With only a few exceptions, the urban children achieved higher scores. Similar studies since that time have yielded generally comparable results.[14] Since it is not possible by the use of any test yet devised to separate innate from acquired ability, these results are not surprising.

Intelligence tests applied by the U.S. Army in World War I indicated that recruits from agriculture rated much lower than those from most other occupational classes. In this connection, however, it must be borne in mind that many capable farm workers were exempted from military service because they were considered essential to agriculture.[15]

A study made by Shimberg in 1929 investigated the hypothesis that the lower scores of rural children on intelligence tests were due more to the nature of the tests than to innate intellectual differences. Two intelligence tests were constructed, one based upon rural experience and worded in agricultural terms and the other based on urban experience. On the rural-oriented test, the urban children were found to be a full year behind the rural. On the urban-oriented test, the opposite results were obtained.[16]

There is little question that in terms of the problems and experiences encountered in the urban setting, people with a farm background have been at a definite disadvantage, at least initially. At the same time, there is ample evidence that many people who have been reared on farms have successfully overcome the handicap of a rural background. There is some evidence that a substantial amount of formal education greatly assists in overcoming the intellectual

[13] Sorokin, Zimmerman, and Galpin, op. cit., pp. 266-281.

[14] Smith, op. cit., p. 113.

[15] See John H. Kolb and Edmund deS. Brunner, A Study of Rural Society, 4th ed., Houghton Mifflin, 1952, p. 51.

[16] Myra E. Shimberg, "An Investigation into the Validity of Norms with Special Reference to Urban and Rural Groups," Archives of Psychology, no. 104, 1929; summarized in Sorokin, Zimmerman, and Galpin, op. cit., pp. 282-286.

handicap of a farm background. Hatch and Landis studied 1091 persons who entered the State College of Washington without previous college experience and found that while students from farms tended to rank slightly lower during their first college term than those from urban and rural nonfarm areas, this was a temporary condition. The students from farms showed greater improvement in scholastic performance than others; furthermore, they were more persistent, as shown by the fact that fewer dropped out of college during the first year and a larger proportion graduated.[17] Landis concludes that the farm students had the ability to make scholastic adjustments as effectively as urban students in the college setting. It is his opinion that this type of achievement is more satisfactory than psychological tests as a basis for comparing rural-urban intelligence.

A probability sample of approximately one-fourth of all students who entered the State College of Washington as freshmen in 1951, 1952, and 1953 was studied to ascertain factors associated with withdrawal from college. It was found that residence in rural areas had no bearing on the chances of academic survival.[18]

Other efforts to assess or evaluate the intelligence of rural versus urban people have been made by noting the residential origin of people who have achieved positions of sufficient distinction to be listed in *Who's Who in America* and comparable records (for example, *RUS*, which lists living rural leaders). A study by Visher of *Who's Who in America* for 1922-1923 showed that 74.1 percent of those listed were born in cities and towns or villages, although in 1870, the census year nearest to the average date of birth of persons listed, 70 percent of the population lived on farms.[19] Kolb and Brunner have criticized this approach, pointing out that *Who's Who* selects people whose achievements are important to urban society rather than those who have made outstanding contributions to agriculture. A study by Sorokin and Zimmerman of farm leaders given 12 lines or more in the 1925 edition of *RUS* found that a greater

[17] Raymond W. Hatch and Paul H. Landis, "Social Heritage as a Factor in College Achievement," *Research Studies in the State College of Washington,* December, 1942, pp. 215-272.

[18] W. L. Slocum, "Social Factors in Academic Mortality," *College and University,* Fall, 1956, p. 58.

[19] Cited in Kolb and Brunner, *op. cit.,* p. 53.

share of agriculture leaders came from farms than from cities.[20] Similar results were found by Thaden in a study of the 1930 edition of *RUS*: 83.5 percent of Thaden's sample had some farm background, which he interpreted to mean that positions of leadership in agriculture are more likely to be attained by persons who have been reared on farms.[21]

The evidence certainly cannot be interpreted to mean that rural people as a category are more intelligent than urban people, and on the other hand, it seems reasonably clear that most of the established measurements of intelligence and achievements are biased in favor of urban experience worlds and values; consequently, it cannot be concluded that rural people as a category are inferior to urban. The fact seems to be, as Landis has pointed out, that the way the mind is developed is of fundamental importance in understanding the achievements which can be expected.[22] As we shall note in further detail in the discussion on socialization, the culture of one's reference groups is of fundamental importance in explaining conduct.[23]

Feeblemindedness

There is a class of mental defectives known as the feebleminded whose mental incapacity is due either to heredity or to arrested development. On December 31, 1957, there were 158,365 mental defectives and epileptics in public and private hospitals.[24] The residence of these patients was not reported.

Landis has noted that the rate of commitment to institutions of those officially defined as feebleminded has been only about half as high in rural areas as in urban populations. The rate of commitment prior to 1948 was about 40-45 per 100,000 for rural areas as compared to 80-85 per 100,000 for cities, although there are some

[20] P. A. Sorokin and C. C. Zimmerman, "Farmer Leaders in the United States," *Social Forces*, September, 1928, pp. 33-45.

[21] J. F. Thaden, "Characteristics of Persons Listed in RUS," *Rural Sociology*, December, 1937, pp. 429-443.

[22] Paul H. Landis, *Rural Life in Process*, 2nd ed., McGraw-Hill, 1948, p. 109.

[23] See Chapter 11.

[24] U.S. Bureau of the Census, *Statistical Abstract of the United States: 1959*, 1959.

variations in this rate from one section of the country to another.[25]

Commenting on the probable reasons for this difference, Landis suggests that urban families are more likely to send their feeble-minded members to institutions than are rural families. Thus, although there is no reason to believe that more feebleminded persons are produced in rural than in urban homes, it seems likely that a somewhat higher percentage of the mentally defective are at large and not confined to mental institutions in rural areas.[26]

PERSONALITY TRAITS

Rural sociologists and others have been intrigued by the possibility that some aspects of the rural farm environment may be responsible for distinctive personality traits. After a review of the relevant literature up to 1948, Landis offered the following list of personality traits said to be characteristic of farmers:

Farmers are supposed to be conservative, individualistic, superstitious, fatalistic, to possess stability, to lack cooperative qualities, to be of a magical turn of mind, mystical in outlook, to be religious, dogmatic, prejudiced, strait-laced in morals, stern and just, patient, stolid, introspective, versatile, impressionistic, suspicious, to possess much common sense, to be of sound and adequate judgment, to be independent in forming judgments, to possess deep convictions, to be meditative, to have fixed purposes, to have endurance, to be immune to radicalism, to have peace of mind, to practice simplicity, to feel aversion for fads and show, to practice thrift and frugality, to assume responsibility readily, to have initiative, to be resourceful, frank, hospitable, sympathetic, to lack socialization, to be characterized by hardiness, to be pessimistic, to brood over injuries. They are supposed to be emotionally intensive, highly suggestible, shy, sentimental, to lean toward the emotional in religious expression, to be conformists, to lack idealism, to love nature, to have a developed artistic sense, to like gossip, to be moody, to be given to resignation, to have a tendency to be discouraged, to be orthodox in religion, to be introverted, silent, to think and speak directly, to be democratic, to lean toward "fogyism," to be unprogressive, realistic, intolerant, naive, skeptical, serious, clannish, economical, complaining, honest, stubborn, easygoing, reticent, gullible, trustworthy, conventional,

[25] Landis, *op. cit.*, p. 111.
[26] *Ibid.*, pp. 111-112.

tenacious, nonmercenary, unselfish, neighborly, friendly, wholesome, and narrow-minded.[27]

As we shall see later in discussing the process of socialization, the formation of personality traits is principally determined by culture and other environmental influences. Consequently, as the conditions of life on farms are altered, so-called rural personality traits will also change. Empirical studies made in the state of Washington and other parts of the United States indicate that differences in the values of farm and urban people are diminishing. Since personality traits are to a very large extent reflections of fundamental values, traditional rural-urban differences in personality traits will also diminish and perhaps eventually disappear.

T. L. Smith, after his review of the literature on this subject, has concluded that rural sociologists in the U.S. agree to some extent that the farmer is

. . . (1) conservative and orthodox—that he tends to accept rural culture as it came to him and to preserve its values; this being the case, it is not surprising that at certain times and places traits such as the magical mind, suggestibility, "fogyism," etc., have been assigned to him; (2) thrifty and frugal, traits necessary to survival when dealing with nature, which may exhibit unfriendly aspects for years at a time; (3) fatalistic, in the sense that he has no mechanistic explanation of the universe, thinks the vagaries of the weather and the seasons cannot be accurately predicted, and resigns himself to make the best of what the future may bring; (4) possibly actuated by the tendency to be suspicious of strangers, who are not frequent enough so that he becomes accustomed to them; and (5) more outspoken and frank than city people, many of whom might lose their jobs, meet economic boycott or political reprisals if they spoke their minds too freely.[28]

The conclusion of the present writer is that such differences as may exist in personality traits between rural and urban people are due to differences in role expectations in their social systems. As far as so-called rural personality types are concerned, these are for the most part caricatures based on some aspects of occupational roles.

---

[27] *Ibid.*, p. 120.
[28] Smith, *op. cit.*, p. 125.

HEALTH

The sociological implications of ill health have not been explored for either farm or nonfarm segments of the population. There is no doubt, however, that performance of many roles is profoundly affected by physical and mental health. It is well recognized that physical disabilities may greatly impair the ability of a farmer to do manual labor. It is less well known that the way he fills the roles of husband and father also may be affected by how well he feels. The ill person frequently makes many demands upon those who are well.

PHYSICAL HEALTH

American farmers and their families have shared in the tremendous advances in sanitation, medicine, and medical care which have occurred in the last 50 years. As noted previously, these developments have resulted in a rise in longevity and a consequent increase in the number and proportion of the aged. It is well to remember, however, that many rural people in under-developed countries have not yet benefited fully from modern medical care and sanitation.

The fact that the fatal epidemic diseases have been conquered does not mean that illness has been banished; much illness still remains among all segments of the population. The question then arises, is there more or less ill health among farm people than among others?

This subject was investigated about 1930 by Sorokin, Zimmerman, and Galpin. They reviewed information from isolated studies in the United States and abroad as well as the results of many examinations of military recruits. Their general conclusion was that the available evidence indicated better health among the rural than the urban population, although there were a few diseases like pellagra which were more prevalent in rural areas. But they also observed that there was more difference between upper and lower classes of the urban population than between similar strata within the rural population.[29]

[29] Sorokin, Zimmerman, and Galpin, *op. cit.*, pp. 95-96.

The results of physical examinations given to a sample of men inducted into military service during World War II indicate that there was a lower rejection rate among white urban recruits than among whites from rural areas (24.7 percent of white urban draftees and 26.2 per cent of white rural farm draftees were rejected). Among Negroes the rejection rate for rural draftees was 38.0 percent and for urban draftees 32.6 percent.[30] These rates may suggest that the health of farm males of draft age was inferior to that of urban males. Mapheus Smith found that farm workers had higher disqualification rates than any other occupational categories,[31] but that a large proportion of rejected farm workers were disqualified for mental deficiency. The refined data revealed that agricultural workers actually had fewer physical defects than other workers. He concluded that ". . . the physical status of the agricultural population was superior to that of the rest of the population."[32]

The heavy economic impact of illness on the farm population of the U.S. is indicated by a nationwide sample survey of 4000 family units made in 1935 by the Department of Agriculture. Health care was found to rank fifth among family expenditures, with an average of $240 for this purpose in 1955. It was exceeded only by housing, food, clothing, and transportation. This study did not explore the economic or social consequences of inability to perform essential farm tasks because of illness.[33]

A statewide sample survey made in Michigan in 1948 provides the most comprehensive information yet available concerning the types of illness and health needs of rural people. The survey, which was supported financially by the Michigan State Medical Society, utilized a list of 27 "symptoms." The list was validated by having medical doctors examine a random sample of persons to whom the questionnaire had been given. Approximately 80 percent agreement was obtained. The authors reported:

[30] Mapheus Smith, *Selective Service Contributions to Knowledge of Rural-Urban Differences in Physical and Mental Status,* unpublished paper, U.S. Selective Service System, p. 4. (Based on a 10 percent sample of first examinations, November, 1940–September, 1941, and approximately 20 percent of examinations made during November and December, 1943.)

[31] *Ibid.,* p. 8.

[32] *Ibid.,* p. 11.

[33] A. L. Bertrand and D. G. Hay, *Farmers' Expenditures for Health Care in 1955,* U.S. Department of Agriculture, Agricultural Information Bulletin 191.

. . . the findings of the survey regarding unmet need for medical attention show that more medical care is needed throughout the population. The amount of unmet need, however, is greatest in the open country and in villages.

. . . Among the socio-economic factors associated with unmet needs, gross family income was an important one in all sample areas. Miles to the nearest town having a doctor, an ecological factor, was also associated with amount of unmet need. The unmet needs increased with distance. . . . There were no marked differences among the open country, village, metropolitan and urban families regarding the number of times a doctor was consulted. Likewise, care of the patient in his home by a doctor occurred in all areas with a high degree of uniformity. About 7 per cent of the population had received such care during the 6 months' period.[34]

Since 1948, the symptoms approach developed in Michigan has been used in some other states. The specific information concerning the types and incidence of illness would be expected to differ in other parts of the country, but unmet needs for medical care are prevalent.[35]

A study by McNamara in two areas of Missouri revealed that at least 5 percent of the people in his sample were unable to work on a given day because of disabling illness and that in addition illness of a nondisabling nature affected the working efficiency of 20 to 30 percent of the farm working force. Chronic or prolonged illness in his opinion is a serious problem among farm people. McNamara also came to the conclusion after reviewing field experiences that the actual extent of illness was underreported by his respondents.[36] The Michigan Health Survey reported that a significantly higher proportion of open-country respondents than of urban residents lost working time because of illness.[37]

The U.S. National Health Survey has provided current data on certain aspects of rural-urban differentials in health conditions. The information comes from interviews conducted during the period July, 1957-June, 1958, with a nationwide probability sample of

[34] C. R. Hoffer et al., *Health Needs and Health Care in Michigan*, Michigan AES Special Bulletin 365, June, 1950, pp. 32-34.

[35] A. L. Bertrand, ed., *Rural Sociology*, McGraw-Hill, 1958, p. 282.

[36] R. L. McNamara, *Illness in the Farm Population of Two Homogeneous Areas in Missouri*, Missouri AES Research Bulletin 504, July, 1952.

[37] Hoffer et al., op. cit., p. 18.

American households.[38] More than 168,000 persons were covered by the interviews, which means that the data can be trusted to reflect with reasonable accuracy health conditions as perceived by respondents.

The survey data shows a remarkably small amount of difference between residential segments of the population in terms of number of days of disability per person per year (Table 4). Rural farm

TABLE 4. Number of Days of Disability per Person per Year by Residence, United States, July, 1957–June, 1958

Residence	Restricted Activity Days	Bed Disability Days	Work- Loss Days[a]	School- Loss Days[b]
All areas	20.0	7.8	10.1	8.4
Urban	19.7	7.9	9.8	9.0
Rural nonfarm	20.0	7.5	9.9	7.8
Rural farm	21.5	7.6	12.2	7.3

[a] Computed for persons 17 years of age and over classified as "usually working," i.e., those who reported working as their major activity during the 12-month period preceding the week of interview.
[b] Computed for children 6-16 years of age.
SOURCE: U.S. National Health Survey, *Disability Days, United States, July 1957–June 1958*, U.S. Public Health Service Publication 584-B-10, May, 1959, Table 2, p. 16.

children of school age lost less school time than either rural or urban children. Rural farm adults, on the other hand, reported more days of restricted activity and lost more working days than urban adults; rural nonfarm adults occupied an intermediate position in both cases. Residential differences in the number of days sick in bed were slight but favored rural farm people.

Residential differences in the incidence of chronic health problems

[38] The U.S. National Health Survey is a continuing program under which the Public Health Service makes studies to determine the extent of illness and disability. It was authorized in July, 1956, by Public Law 652, 84th Congress. The sample for the national household survey was designed and selected by the Bureau of the Census which also conducted the interviews and processed the data for the Public Health Service. (See U.S. National Health Survey, *Concepts and Definitions in the Health Household-Interview Survey*, U.S. Public Health Service Publication 584-A3, September, 1958.)

TABLE 5. Percent Distribution of Persons by Limitation of Activity due to Chronic Conditions According to Sex and Residence, United States, July, 1957–June, 1958.

Sex and Residence	All Persons	Persons with No Chronic Condition	Persons with One or More Chronic Conditions			
			Total	With No Limitation of Activity	With Partial Limitation of Activity[a]	With Major Limitation of Activity[b]
Both Sexes						
All areas	100.0	58.6	41.4	31.3	8.0	2.1
Urban	100.0	58.4	41.6	31.7	7.6	2.2
Rural						
nonfarm	100.0	58.7	41.3	31.4	7.9	2.0
Rural farm	100.0	59.4	40.6	28.7	9.9	2.0
Male						
All areas	100.0	60.9	39.1	29.4	6.9	2.8
Urban	100.0	61.0	39.0	29.7	6.4	2.8
Rural						
nonfarm	100.0	60.7	39.3	29.6	6.9	2.9
Rural farm	100.0	60.3	39.7	28.0	9.2	2.5
Female						
All areas	100.0	56.5	43.5	33.0	9.0	1.5
Urban	100.0	56.1	43.9	33.6	8.7	1.6
Rural						
nonfarm	100.0	56.7	43.3	33.2	8.8	1.2
Rural farm	100.0	58.4	41.6	29.5	10.7	1.5

[a] Limited in amount or kind of major or outside activities.
[b] Unable to carry on major activity.
SOURCE: U.S. National Health Survey, *Limitation of Activity and Mobility Due to Chronic Conditions, United States, July 1957–June 1958*, U.S. Public Health Service Publication 584-B-11, July, 1959, Table 14, p. 23. Not all percentages add to 100. See source.

were not very great (Table 5), but relatively fewer farm females and more farm males reported one or more chronic conditions than their rural nonfarm or urban counterparts. Furthermore, there was a tendency for more farm than nonfarm people of both sexes to report chronic disabilities which placed partial limitation on their activities.

Injuries involving one or more days of restricted activity or medical attendance were slightly less prevalent among farmers than among urban dwellers (Table 6). Rural nonfarm residents had the highest rates. In terms of time lost from work, however, the farmer's position does not appear so favorable. Farm men lost 3.2 days per year compared to 1.5 for rural nonfarm men and 1.8 for urban men. This suggests that injuries to farm males may be more severe.

TABLE 6. Number of Persons Injured[a] per 100 Persons per Year by Residence and Class of Accident, United States, July, 1957–June, 1958.

| Class of Accident | Residence | | | |
	All areas	Urban	Rural Nonfarm	Rural Farm
All classes	27.9	27.6	29.1	26.7
Motor vehicle	2.8	2.6	3.2	3.0
Work	4.8	4.5	5.3	5.4
Home	11.4	11.3	12.3	9.7
Other	8.9	9.2	8.4	8.5

[a] Includes only persons with injuries involving one or more days of restricted activity or medical attendance.
SOURCE: U.S. National Health Survey, *Persons Injured by Class of Accident United States, July 1957–June, 1958,* U.S. Public Health Service Publication 584-B-8, February, 1959, Table 2, p. 16.

Some information on the incidence of wounds, fractures, and other injuries is presented in Table 7. The incidence of activity-restricted injuries by residence during the period July, 1957–June, 1958, was higher among the farm (180 per 1000) than among the nonfarm population (161 per 1000). Bed-disabling injuries were also more frequent among farm people.[39]

A study conducted in Pennsylvania by Mather and Roy indicates that most farm accidents involve men and boys rather than women and girls. They found that the accident rate in terms of time was

[39] U.S. National Health Survey, *Acute Conditions, Incidence and Associated Disability, July 1958–June 1959,* U.S. Public Health Service Publication 584-B-18, June, 1960.

highest on small farms. More than twice as many accidents occurred in the afternoon as in the morning. Tractors and other machinery were involved in more than 40 percent of the accidents. The activities most often mentioned were animal chores, wood cutting and hauling, and harvesting operations. Carelessness was acknowledged by a high proportion of respondents as a personal factor contributing to accidents.[40]

TABLE 7. Incidence of Acute Health Conditions per Year by Residence, United States, July, 1958–June, 1959

Health Conditions	Total	Urban	Rural Nonfarm	Farm
All conditions	214.8	215.6	219.4	198.5
Infectious and parasitic diseases	25.8	25.6	28.0	21.4
Upper respiratory conditions	83.1	88.0	79.5	66.4
Other respiratory conditions	42.6	39.4	48.0	45.7
Digestive system conditions	11.9	12.3	11.7	10.4
Fractures, dislocations, sprains, and strains	8.3	8.3	8.0	8.6
Open wounds and lacerations	7.3	6.8	8.3	6.8
Contusions and superficial injuries	6.4	6.4	6.0	7.6
Other current injuries	6.9	6.4	6.9	9.7
All other acute conditions	22.5	22.4	22.9	22.0

SOURCE: U.S. National Health Survey, *Acute Conditions, Geographic Distribution, United States, July 1958–June 1959,* U.S. Public Health Service Publication 584-B-23, October, 1960, Table 4, p. 10.

Information collected by the U.S. National Health Survey for the period July, 1958-June, 1959 reveals a somewhat lower incidence of acute health conditions in the rural farm population than in the rural nonfarm or urban populations, Table 7).

The data presented above, with the exception of that from the Michigan survey, generally confirms the long-standing view that farm people tend to have fewer health problems than those who do not live on farms.

Medical care is much more accessible in cities and towns than in

[40] W. G. Mather and Prodipto Roy, *A Study of Accidents to Pennsylvania Farm People,* Pennsylvania Department of Public Instruction Bulletin 398, 1957.

rural areas in the United States. This advantage alone may be sufficient to offset the natural health advantages of life on an isolated farm of good water, pure air, and relatively lower exposure rates to infectious and contagious disease. These presumed advantages, of course, do not apply with equal force to farm populations residing in villages. In fact, villages in some parts of the world, as in India and Pakistan, have primitive and unsatisfactory sanitary facilities. In some crowded rural areas, human excrement is frequently used to fertilize vegetables. This practice promotes the spread of dysentery and other filth-borne diseases.

Information concerning the relative health conditions of rural and urban populations in most underdeveloped countries is practically nonexistent. The reader is cautioned that experience from western countries should not be generalized to primitive areas.

MENTAL HEALTH

Organic defects have been viewed with compassion in all parts of the world from time immemorial, but this has not been true and is still not true insofar as mental disease is concerned. The person who is afflicted with mental disease is frequently treated unsympathetically even by highly educated persons. At the present time the actual and projected future incidence of mental disease among the population is sufficiently great so that this medieval attitude may be expected to change to some extent.

Mental illnesses are ordinarily classified into psychoses and neuroses. The psychoses are much more serious; they are the mental disorders ordinarily associated with the term *insanity*. A psychotic person may have delusions of grandeur or hallucinations, exhibit weird and unreasonable behavior, or entertain private fantasies and sentiments and attitudes which are considered to be inappropriate in relation to the norms of the social system of which he is a member. Some psychoses are characterized by alternating periods of excitement and depression, others by almost complete withdrawal; some result from organic injuries whereas others, generally known as *functional psychoses*, are not attributable to any known organic cause.

The neuroses are less marked deviations from the expected norms of behavior. Some types of neuroses are hysteria, excessive anxiety, compulsive behavior, and phobias about this and that. Lundberg, Schrag, and Larson have expressed the opinion that the neuroses consist of acquired or learned behavior which is regarded as abnormal by members of a social system because it exaggerates attitudes and actions which in less extreme form are entirely appropriate.[41]

There is no reliable or valid information concerning the rural-urban incidence of either psychoses or neuroses, although it is widely believed that many of these mental disorders are attributable to the problems of role integration typical of modern urban societies. It is certain that the incidence of neuropsychiatric problems is very great. According to Menninger, 1,846,000 or 37.5 percent of the 4,828,000 men rejected by the Selective Service during the period of November, 1940, to August 1, 1945, were found unfit because of neuropsychiatric conditions detected at the time of the screening medical examination.[42] For whites there was a slightly higher rate of rejection for illiteracy and mental disease among agricultural registrants. Among Negroes the situation was reversed. In addition, it has been reported that mental disorders of one kind or another resulted in about 1 out of every 15 hospitalizations of Army personnel, and that one-third of all separations from the Army were due to this cause.[43]

At the end of the year 1903, there were 186.2 persons per 100,000 population in prolonged-care hospitals for mental disease.[44] By December 31, 1931, the rate had risen to 284.0. A peak of 407.3 was reached at the end of 1945. At the end of 1958 the rate was 357.1. The number of mental patients in prolonged-care hospitals increased from 352,000 at the close of 1931 to 612,000 at the end of 1958.[45] During 1957, there were 271,000 admissions, 207,000 discharges and 49,000 deaths.[46]

[41] G. A. Lundberg, C. C. Schrag, and O. N. Larson, *Sociology*, rev. ed., Harper, 1958.

[42] W. C. Menninger, *Psychiatry in a Troubled World*, Macmillan, 1948, p. 587.

[43] Lundberg, Schrag, and Larson, *op. cit.*, pp. 361-362.

[44] R. H. Felix and Morton Kramer, "Extent of the Problem of Mental Disorders," *Annals of the American Academy of Political and Social Science*, March, 1953, pp. 5-24.

[45] U.S. Bureau of the Census, *Statistical Abstract of the United States: 1960*, 1960, Table 94, p. 78.

[46] *Ibid*, Table 96, p. 80.

There have been few studies of the mental health of rural people. A pioneer study of the mental health of 1638 students in the public schools of Butler County, Ohio, was made in 1948-1949 by Mangus and Woodward under the sponsorship of the Division of Mental Hygiene of the Ohio State Department of Public Health, Ohio State University, the Ohio State Department of Public Welfare and the Butler County Mental Hygiene Association. The study examined the question of rural-urban differences among students in the fourth, fifth, and sixth grades. The authors of the report have the following to say: "Differences among urban-rural nonfarm, and rural farm subjects were not consistently in favor of any one of the three groups. Those living on farms excelled in the sense of personal worth and in freedom from withdrawing tendencies. Farm children also showed greater freedom from nervous symptoms, and differed favorably in school relations. They rated lowest in a sense of personal freedom."[47]

A later study of mental health needs in Miami County, a rural and semirural area of Ohio, by Mangus and Seeley also examined evidence of mental health among farm and nonfarm children and Selective Service registrants. This study revealed an amazing incidence of mental illness. They found that one out of every five elementary school children ". . . presents evidence of poor mental health of some degree of seriousness. Large numbers of these children are evidently maladjusted to a very serious degree and are in grave need of specialized guidance services to meet their mental health needs. Many are less seriously maladjusted and may somehow 'get by' without specialized help. . . ."[48]

Among those rejected for the draft in Miami County, Mangus and Seeley found that nearly 3 out of 10 were turned back because of neuropsychiatric disorders or other mental deficiencies. The rejection rate for mental disorders and defects was higher for farm workers than for other registrants.[49]

[47] A. R. Mangus and R. H. Woodward, *An Analysis of the Mental Health of Elementary School Children*, Butler County (Ohio) Mental Hygiene Association, July, 1949, p. 23.

[48] A. R. Mangus and John R. Seeley, *Mental Health Needs in a Rural and Semi-Rural Area of Ohio*, Ohio AES Bulletin 195, February, 1947, p. 23. (Mimeo)

[49] *Ibid.*, p. 19.

These authors also found that farm workers comprised 20.2 percent of all persons committed to state mental hospitals during the period 1940-1945. This was slightly less than proportionate since agricultural workers were found to comprise 22 percent of employed personnel in the county in 1940.[50]

Mangus and Seeley concluded from their evidence that personality disorders were to be found among farm people as frequently as among nonfarm residents. Their data indicated a progressive lessening of an initially more favorable position of farm children with increasing age. At both third- and sixth-grade levels they found less personal maladjustment among farm children than among those from nonfarm homes, but the differential was much smaller among the sixth graders than among the third graders. Furthermore, analysis of Selective Service records showed that there was a higher incidence of personality disorders among farm workers than among others. Summing up the results of their findings, the authors said, "This study points to the conclusion that, from the point of view of mental health, farm residence is probably an advantage for younger children, but that the advantage is lost with increasing age. Among men of military age, those in other occupations have the advantage over those concerned with farming. This may be due in part at least to migration of disproportionately large numbers of better-adjusted youths away from farms and from farm occupations."[51]

It is not possible, of course, to generalize from a study of conditions in a single county. But the findings of Mangus and Seeley should shake the complacent belief that there are few mental health problems among rural farm people.

MEDICAL CARE

In some parts of the world, medical service is provided by the government. This is particularly true in the United Kingdom and the USSR, but it is true to some extent also in other countries. In the United States, on the other hand, public health agencies provide only certain inoculations and vaccinations and supervise various aspects of sanitation. Both preventive and therapeutic medical care

[50] *Ibid.*, p. 44.
[51] *Ibid.*, pp. 12-13.

and hospitalization are generally provided on a fee basis by private physicians and surgeons.

There have been a number of studies of the availability of medical care to rural people.[52] Almost without exception these have revealed that there are fewer physicians and fewer hospitals in isolated rural areas of the U.S. The best facilities, including the most modern hospitals and the best-trained medical specialists, are to be found in urban centers.

The U.S. National Health Survey found that although the health conditions of farm people in 1957-1958 were not greatly different from those of rural nonfarm and urban people, they were less likely to visit a physician. The number of physician visits per person per year were: urban 5.0, rural nonfarm, 4.6, and rural farm 3.6.[53]

Farm people were less likely than urbanites to use hospitals (81 per 1000 compared to 101 per 1000 urban in 1957-1958), although the average length of stay (8.7 days) was not much different from that of urban patients (8.9 days).[54]

The U.S. National Health Survey also revealed that farm people were less likely to visit a dentist. The proportion who did not visit a dentist during the year ending June, 1959, was: urban 57.7, rural nonfarm 60.8, and rural farm 67.4. These residential differences were even more pronounced among school-age children and young adults.[55]

[52] See Marion T. Loftin and Robert E. Galloway, *The Use of Health Services by Rural People in Four Mississippi Counties*, Mississippi AES Sociology and Rural Life Series No. 5, 1954; Ruth M. Connor and William G. Mather, *The Use of Health Services in Two Northern Pennsylvania Communities*, Pennsylvania AES Bulletin 517, 1949; F. D. Mott and M. I. Roemer, *Rural Health and Medical Care*, McGraw-Hill, 1948; P. H. Price, *The Availability of Medical Personnel in Rural Louisiana*, Louisiana AES Bulletin 459, 1951; John F. Thaden, *Distribution of Doctors of Medicine and Osteopaths in Michigan Communities*, Michigan AES Special Bulletin 370, 1951; R. W. Roskelly, *The Rural Citizen and Medical Care*, Washington AES Bulletin 495, 1947.

[53] U.S. National Health Survey, *Volume of Physician Visits, United States, July 1957–June 1959*, U.S. Public Health Service Publication 584-B-19, August, 1960, p. 25.

[54] U.S. National Health Survey, *Hospitalization, Patients Discharged from Short Stay Hospitals, United States, July 1957–June 1958*, U.S. Public Health Service Publication 584-B-7, December, 1958, p. 14.

[55] U.S. National Health Survey, *Dental Care, Interval and Frequency of Visits, United States, June 1957–June 1959*, U.S. Public Health Service Publication 584-B-14, March 1960, p. 27.

In this connection it should not be forgotten that it is now possible for farm people with adequate means to make use of specialized medical and hospital facilities located at great distances from their places of residence.

It is certainly true that great advances have been made in sanitation and in medicine and surgery, and the benefits of some, particularly those relating to sanitation and vaccinations and inoculations for the control of contagious diseases, are available at relatively low cost to rural people as well as others. Some types of medical care, such as the treatment of cancer and heart disease, which require the services of specialists and prolonged hospitalization are beyond the reach of all except the wealthy and those whose expenses are met by a government welfare program or on a charitable basis by physicians and hospitals. To some extent, farm people along with others try to make provision for such hazards through health insurance prepayment plans. During the latter part of 1959, the U.S. National Health Survey found that rural farm people were less likely to have hospital insurance; 45.0 percent of rural farm compared to 68 percent of rural nonfarm and 71.5 percent of urban people were covered. Farm people were also less likely than nonfarm people to have surgical insurance or doctor visit insurance.[56]

The problem of adequate rural medical care includes more or less routine treatment of minor ailments plus the problem of meeting the high cost of medical care, drugs, and hospitalization. This is, of course, not different in kind from the problem which faces all residential segments of the population, but it falls with greatest impact upon low-income rural people who happen to live in relatively isolated parts of the country.[57]

One of the major remaining sources of economic insecurity in the U.S. is the hazard of disabling illness and the high cost of essential medical care. This threat weighs most heavily, of course, on the aged, because a single catastrophic illness may sweep away the savings of a lifetime, but it is also felt acutely by rural people who

[56] U.S. National Health Survey, *Interim Report on Health Insurance, United States, July–December 1959*, U.S. Public Health Service Publication 584-B-26, December, 1960, pp. 18-20.
[57] USDA, Interbureau Committee on Postwar Problems, *Better Health for Rural America: Plans for Action for Farm Communities*, 1945.

on the average have a substantially lower income than other segments of the population.

QUESTIONS FOR FURTHER STUDY AND DISCUSSION

1. Search the library for additional evidence on rural-urban differences in physical characteristics. Evaluate this evidence critically and present your own views.
2. Do you agree that it is reasonable to expect proportionately more mental defectives in rural areas? Why or why not?
3. Make up a list of farmers' personality traits on the basis of personal interviews with at least three persons.
4. Discuss the sociological implications of ill health. What solutions would you propose for meeting unmet medical needs of rural people?
5. What are the prospects that the remaining health hazards will be overcome soon?

SELECTED REFERENCES

Bertrand, A. L., ed., *Rural Sociology*, McGraw-Hill, 1958.

Hoffer, C. R., *et al.*, *Health Needs and Health Care in Michigan*, Michigan AES Special Bulletin 365, June, 1950.

Mott, F. D., and M. I. Roemer, *Rural Health and Medical Care*, McGraw-Hill, 1948.

Smith, T. Lynn, *The Sociology of Rural Life*, 3rd ed., Harper, 1953.

Sorokin, P. A., C. C. Zimmerman, and C. J. Galpin, *A Systematic Source Book in Rural Sociology*, University of Minnesota Press, 1932, vol. III.

4

Migration of Farm People

Migration involves physical movement from one geographical location to another. However, not all changes in location may be considered as migration. We should exclude the travel involved in commuting to and from work, vacation travel, and business travel.

Internal migration does include changes in residence from one county to another, one state to another, or one town to another. It also includes the movements of migratory seasonal farm laborers. International migration is discussed elsewhere.[1]

In considering migration, it should be understood that this type of movement is sometimes accompanied by social mobility either upward or downward.[2] In any case, contact with different individuals and participation in new social systems will be involved after the move. Thus, migration brings with it many problems of adjustment for a farmer and his family even though the migrant may be engaged in exactly the same type of farming.

MIGRATION TO CITIES AND TOWNS

Migration of people from farms to cities and towns has been a major source of urban growth in all countries where extensive urbanization has occurred.[3] In the United States, substantial numbers of people have moved between farms and nonfarm areas since rapid urbanization began in the nineteenth century. During the period

---

[1] See Chapter 5.
[2] See Chapter 17 for a discussion of social mobility.
[3] See P. A. Sorokin, C. C. Zimmerman, and C. J. Galpin, *A Systematic Source Book in Rural Sociology*, University of Minnesota Press, 1932, vol. III, chap. XXII.

1915-1950, more than 2,000,000 people on the average moved from
or to farms every year.[4] Except for a short period during the depression of the 1930s when the cityward trend was slowed and for
a time reversed (1931-1932), the tide has been away from farms.[5]
Since the number of farm-to-city migrants has exceeded the excess
of farm births over deaths, the farm population has shown a long-
time downward trend. In 1960, the number of people on farms was
only 15,669,000, compared to 31,855,000 in 1910.

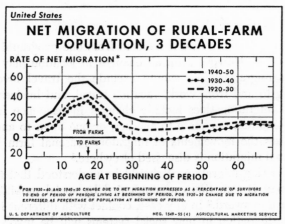

FIG. 3.   Net Migration of the Rural Farm Population of the United States, 1920-1950.

The magnitude of the net migration from the farm population has
varied materially from time to time. During the 1920s, there was a
net loss of about 6,100,000 persons who were alive at both the beginning and the end of the period. In the 1930s the net loss through
migration dropped to 3,500,000. The decade of the 1940s registered
a net loss of 8,600,000.[6] Migration from the farm population continued after 1950; during the period April, 1950–April, 1959, the net
decline in the rural farm population was 3,900,000.[7]

    [4] Gladys K. Bowles, *Farm Population Net Migration from the Rural-Farm
Population*, 1940-1950, U.S. Department of Agriculture, Agricultural Research
Service, Statistical Bulletin 176, June, 1956, p. 2.
    [5] *Ibid.*, p. 1.
    [6] *Ibid.*, p. 2.
    [7] U.S. Bureau of the Census, *Estimates of the Farm Population of the
United States, April 1950 to 1959*, Series Census-AMS (P-27), No. 26, Decem-
ber 28, 1959.

The South consistently had the highest rates of net migration from farms during the 30-year period ending in 1950. The rates for Negroes were generally higher than those for whites.[8]

A study by Gladys K. Bowles of the characteristics of those who left the rural farm population during the period 1949-1950 reveals that they were about equally divided between males and females. The study showed, however, that there were sex differences in migration rates when age is taken into account. Thus, among the migrants

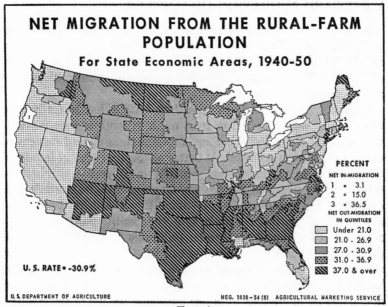

FIG. 4.

about 40 percent of the females but only 3 percent of the males were under 15 years of age in 1940.[9]

In contrast to this, males exceeded females by a considerable margin in the next three five-year age groups. For those between 30 and 34, differences were not pronounced, although a few more males than females migrated. For all other age groups except those 65 years of age and over, females exceeded males.[10]

[8] Bowles, *op. cit.*, p. 4.
[9] *Ibid.*, p. 3.
[10] *Ibid.*

There is some evidence which indicates that a considerable part of the recent movement out of agriculture may not have involved actual migration. In a study made in Alcorn County, Mississippi, Baird and Bailey found that 73 percent of those who left farming between 1954 and 1957 were still living in the same locality. Furthermore, these investigators found that part-time farming was frequently a transitional step to full-time nonfarm employment.[11]

WESTWARD MIGRATION OF SETTLERS

A tremendous volume of internal migration in the United States occurred during the period of settlement of new land which began in colonial times and continued on a large scale until about the time of World War I. As noted elsewhere, many of these settlers were from Europe.[12]

Migration of farm settlers in the United States has basically been from east to west rather than from north to south or vice versa. It was not until about 1920 that any substantial northward movement of rural population occurred. At that time the attraction of industrial employment in urban centers brought considerable numbers of rural southern migrants, particularly Negroes, into the North.[13] This movement has continued. At the same time there has been some movement of northern people into the South, particularly into areas like Florida and California. California is a special case; although located in the southern part of the United States, it is considered to be in the West rather than in the South. Its population has grown chiefly through migration, but this growth has not been dominated by migrations from any particular section of the country.

The period of drought and depression in the midsection of the continent, especially the wheat area in the Great Plains, caused a mass movement of farm people out of the area; most of them went west to the Mountain and Pacific Coast states. A further migration of people to the Far West was brought about by World War II.[14]

[11] A. W. Baird and W. C. Bailey, *Farmers Moving Out of Agriculture*, Mississippi AES Bulletin 568, October, 1958.

[12] See Chapter 5.

[13] See Lowry Nelson, *Rural Sociology*, 2nd ed., American Book, 1955, p. 133.

[14] See Paul H. Landis, *Rural Life in Process*, 2nd ed., McGraw-Hill, 1948, pp. 178-181.

This was not to any appreciable extent a movement to farms but rather to industrial employment.

Now that the land frontier is gone except for reclamation projects, it appears that the great interstate migrations of farm settlers is a thing of the past. It even appears that most of the settlers on reclamation projects do not come from afar. Straus and Parrish found that 81 percent of their sample of settlers in the Columbia Basin Irrigation Project came from one of the four northwestern states; over half were from the state of Washington.[15]

However, these migrations have left their mark on the development of American culture. The influence of the frontier has been discussed by many, including the famous historian Turner.[16] It has been suggested that the liberal tendencies observable in the Pacific Northwest may be due in part to the fact that these areas were settled by the "ultimate migrant" in the last of the great westward movements.[17]

LOCAL INTERFARM MIGRATION

There is a considerable volume of migration from one farm to another, especially in areas where a high percentage of farm operators are tenants or croppers who are not related to the owner. Smith has observed that migration of croppers from one plantation to another has been of major proportions. He regards it is an undesirable social correlate of large-scale agriculture.[18] The magnitude of this type of movement is shown by the fact that 67 percent of all changes of residence by farmers in 1949 were within the same county and 89 percent within the same state. During the 12 months ending April, 1959, 79 percent of farm migrants remained in the same county, perhaps reflecting the recession of 1958.[19]

[15] M. A. Straus and B. D. Parrish, *The Columbia Basin Settler,* Washington AES Bulletin 566, May, 1956.

[16] Frederick Jackson Turner, *The Frontier in American History,* Holt, 1921.

[17] W. L. Slocum, *Changes in Agriculture and Rural Life,* unpublished paper, 1956.

[18] T. Lynn Smith, *The Sociology of Rural Life,* 3rd ed., Harper, 1953, pp. 181-187.

[19] U.S. Bureau of the Census, *Mobility of the Population,* Series PC-14, No. 17, July, 1953; and *Mobility of the Population of the United States, April 1958 to 1959,* series P-20, No. 104, September, 1960.

CHARACTERISTICS OF MIGRANTS

Since migration from farms has been of tremendous magnitude, it is important to consider the implications of outmigration to the localities and farms involved and also to the farm population of the United States considered as an aggregate. Of course, the removal of any individual or family from a network of social interrelationships has some effect on the interactions of those who remain. If those who leave are ordinarily the better educated and the best qualified to provide leadership, the consequences may be undesirable for the area from which the migration occurred. It is certainly true that many who have left farms have attained places of distinction and leadership in the areas to which they moved,[20] but it cannot be said with any degree of certainty that they would have achieved comparable distinction had they remained on the farm in their home localities. Achievement of distinction is not wholly a matter of individual capacity, it is the result of interaction between the individual and others and is governed to a considerable degree by the existence of leadership opportunities.

If it is the adventuresome and the young who migrate, as is usually the case, an area which has experienced an outmigration for a considerable period of time will probably be characterized by excessive conservatism. By the same token, an area which has recently been settled by migrants is likely to be less conservative and more receptive to new social and economic ideas.

A famous sociologist, E. A. Ross, in 1920 viewed with alarm the migration of young people from rural areas. He suggested that the best youths were being enticed to the cities and that those who were left were not competent to provide leadership.[21]

There have been a number of efforts to find the answer to this question of qualitative depopulation, but the results have been largely inconclusive.[22] The problem is difficult if not impossible to

[20] See Landis, *op. cit.*, pp. 107-109.

[21] E. A. Ross, *The Principles of Sociology*, Century, 1920, p. 24.

[22] See Dorothy S. Thomas, "Selective Migration," *Milbank Memorial Fund Quarterly*, XVI (1938), 403-407; Carl F. Reuss, "A Qualitative Study of Depopulation in a Remote Rural District: 1900-1930," *Rural Sociology*, March, 1937, pp. 66-75, P. H. Landis, "Educational Selectivity of Rural-Urban Migration, and Its Bearing on Wage and Occupational Adjustments," *Rural Sociology*, September, 1946, pp. 218-232.

answer definitively. For one thing, the basic question involved is whether or not the more intelligent people migrate. As noted in Chapter 3, nearly all of the intelligence tests now available have been standardized on urban populations. Since those who migrate to urban areas have ordinarily made some preparation for their move, there is a biasing factor in terms of intent. Furthermore, since adult populations are rarely given intelligence tests, relatively little data has actually been systematically accumulated. Finally, in any comparison of large population segments such as rural and urban, there is such heterogeneity among the members of the respective categories that it is almost impossible to deduce valid inferences on a point of this kind. The issue is particularly clouded at the present time because of the tremendous increase in the population of the rural-urban fringe and the number of part-time farmers, and similar factors.

FACTORS ASSOCIATED WITH MIGRATION

Even though it may be impossible to learn the relative intelligence of migrants and nonmigrants, it is clear that there are certain selective factors in migration from farms. Lively and Taeuber found in the 1930s that young people were more likely to migrate to cities than older ones and that more farm women migrated than men.[23]

A comprehensive study of the demographic characteristics of rural-urban migrants from the Corn and Cotton Belts in the United States was made recently by Bogue and Hagood. Data were taken from the 1940 census which contained unusually comprehensive information on migration. The study included tests of the influence on migration of a number of occupational and educational factors. In both regions, migration was found to be selective in some manner with respect to every factor, but apparently in many different ways. Furthermore, although the pattern of selectivity was frequently found to be similar, in both the Corn Belt and the Cotton Belt there were many instances in which the intensity of selection at the various ages differed. Consequently, it appears that migration may be highly selective with respect to given characteristics in one area and selective only to a slight degree or not at all in another. This

[23] C. E. Lively and Conrad Taeuber, *Rural Migration in the United States*, WPA Research Monograph XIX, 1939, pp. 15, 106.

means that at certain times and places individuals with certain characteristics tend to migrate but not at other times and places. The authors feel that the existence of differences in selectivity is due to multiple factors including the situation in the home locality and the situation at the place to which the migrants moved.[24]

Bogue and Hagood suggest that under conditions existing in the late 1930s those who left farms for cities were not greatly handicapped in adjusting to city life if they came from prosperous agricultural communities, if they had good educational preparation, if they got some help at home while making initial adjustments, and if there were no other discriminatory factors.[25]

They found evidence that farm-city migration tends to select those who obtain the most education. Economic incentives are, of course, very important,[26] but there are evidently many other factors. Some of these are poor health, death of the farm operator, crime, divorce, marriage or the prospect of it, and the quest for higher education.

Another important conclusion from the study is that in periods of great social change, such as the rapid urbanization of the South or the settlement of a new area, the pattern of selectivity may be quite unlike the patterns which precede or follow the change. This would seem to indicate that it is not easy to predict the specific pattern of future migration.

In their words, there was evidence that

. . . the intensity, direction, and content of migration selectivity change with the age of migrants. Young migrants, many of whom are just beginning to establish their careers in the labor force or are trying to establish themselves at what they hope will be their permanent line of employment, appear to be selected primarily with respect to factors which involve adjustment to gaining a livelihood and assuming adult roles. Many other older migrants, on the other hand, appear to migrate

[24] Donald J. Bogue and Margaret J. Hagood, *Sub-Regional Migration in the United States, 1935–40,* vol. 2 of *Differential Migration in the Corn and Cotton Belts: A Pilot Study of the Selectivity of Intra-State Migration to Cities from Non-Metropolitan Areas,* Scripps Foundation Studies on Population Distribution, No. 6, 1953, p. 25.

[25] *Ibid.*

[26] See Larry Sjaastad, *Trends in Occupational Structure and Migration Patterns in the U.S. with Special Reference to Agriculture,* and Varden Fuller, *Factors Influencing Farm Labor Mobility,* papers presented at the Conference on Labor Mobility in Agriculture, Iowa State University, November 8, 1960.

as a result of failure, poor health, disaster, technological change, and many other reasons which may not influence the migration of younger people as much.[27]

REASONS FOR MIGRATION

Viewed in large perspective, it appears that the constructive innovating forces released by the industrial revolution are responsible for the urbanization of the United States. These forces gave birth to techniques and machines which made it possible to operate a farm efficiently with less labor and at the same time created a great demand for people and kept the wheels of urban industry turning. This was expressed in terms of high urban wages.

Commenting on the observed tendency for high rates of migration from the farm population to occur among young adults, Bowles offered the following explanation:

Rates are highest for persons just entering the working ages for several reasons: 1) they are in search of economic opportunities and have usually formed no or only tenuous job attachments on farms; 2) many have finished high school and will leave farm homes if they go to college; 3) most are relatively unattached as far as family responsibilities are concerned and are thus more free to roam about; 4) their sentimental attachments for farm homes and communities may not be as strong as those of the older persons; 5) many of the young people are eagerly in search of new experiences which they feel will be afforded them in nonfarm areas.

With reference to families she said,

Rates for family groups, on the other hand, are lower because of 1) less freedom of movement because of small children, 2) job attachments already made in farm communities—they may be farm owners or well established farm tenants—and 3) strong community and family attachments.

About the aged she commented,

Rates for older people, especially those of retirement age, are largely dependent on such factors as 1) death of spouse, 2) financial ability to

[27] Bogue and Hagood, *op. cit.*, p. 126.

leave the farm, or 3) customs, as for example those existing in some areas of "moving to town" when the farm is turned over to the son.[28]

There are many reasons for migration. Ordinarily there will be more than one reason for an important move like a change of residence or job. Some of these are factors which attract the individual to the new location, others cause him to wish to leave the old. The first of these may be called *attractive* forces, and the second, *repulsive* forces.[29]

Relatively little research has been done to discover the empirical significance of the various factors believed to be meaningful in terms of the relative weights which they may exercise at various times and places. Nevertheless, it may be useful and provocative of further research to consider, even if on a hypothetical basis, some of the attractive and repulsive forces that seem to be involved.

ATTRACTIVE FORCES

Of great significance in American society and culture is the long tradition of migration for economic and social advancement that began with the early settlements on the Atlantic Coast in colonial times—more than 300 years ago. These were followed by a continuous push to the west as new lands were opened. The last large geographic frontier in the continental U.S. which beckoned people to migrate westward to take up farm land came around the turn of the present century with the opening of the Rosebud territory in South Dakota and the settlement of certain previously unsettled lands in Montana and the Pacific Northwest. Since that time there have been some irrigation projects opened to settlement. A few, like the Columbia Basin Irrigation Project in the state of Washington, are open at the present time for settlement by limited numbers. Alaska has vast unsettled areas but offers little prospect for agriculture.

Along with the movement to the frontier came the growth of industry and the migration of rural people to the cities.

The essential point is that geographic migration, accompanied by the possibility of vertical mobility, is a part of the American tradition.

[28] Bowles, *op. cit.*, p. 3.
[29] See Landis, *Rural Life in Process, op. cit.*, chap. 14.

In considering reasons why a specific individual might move to a new locality, attention would normally be given to such factors as employment opportunities, living conditions, presence of relatives, and favorable climatic conditions. Climate seems to be especially important to aged persons and to those who have health problems.

REPULSIVE FORCES

In western societies, individuals located in areas subjected to severe economic depression would be interested in leaving if they thought they could improve their economic circumstances through migration. Apparently this is not a valid assumption in all societies. Davis notes that Indian villagers are extremely reluctant to move to cities even in the face of extreme poverty.[30]

In the U.S. areas like the drought bowl during the drought and depression of the 1930s, the cut-over area of the northern lake states, certain mining areas where the ore or coal has been exhausted, and parts of the South might be considered as undesirable insofar as agricultural populations are concerned. To some extent, migration might be encouraged by population pressure in areas with high birth rates and relatively limited economic resources, but it should be pointed out that there are many areas of the world with very dense populations which do not experience migrations of the type which are familiar in the United States.

Social pressure in the form of discrimination against a cultural or racial group certainly would have an effect. The Pilgrims, the Mormons, and the Mennonites may be cited as examples.

Where families are involved, the decision to migrate is probably made only after considerable discussion between husband and wife involving an evaluation of the anticipated consequences of the action.

SOCIAL ADJUSTMENT OF MIGRANTS

Once the migrant individual or family has pulled up its roots and left its farm and the community in which it resided and has taken up residence or even appeared within the new area, problems of adjustment immediately confront it. Even in the case of migration to

[30] Kingsley Davis, *The Population of India and Pakistan,* Princeton University Press, 1951, pp. 135-136.

a closely similar area, some problems exist. First of all, there is the matter of gaining acceptance by other people. This is not always easy. Established residents are sometimes inclined to be indifferent, suspicious, or even hostile.

It seems reasonable to believe that in the United States problems of social adjustment have been more severe among those who have left rural areas than among migrants from one city to another. That is because the adjustments have usually been greater. A substantial portion of those who leave farms move to towns and cities, and these are faced with not only migration and change of vocation but also the effort to move upward in the social scale.[31]

Although there have been relatively few empirical studies of the problems of adjustment faced by country-to-city migrants, the tremendous scope of the rural-urban migration and the relative absence of problems of grave maladjustment among such migrants lead to the tentative conclusion that in general most have adapted with reasonable success to their strange circumstances.[32] It should be noted, of course, that many of those who move to the city do not stay but return home and resume their places on the parental farm and in the home community.

An established farm family which has become accustomed to a particular type of agriculture in a specific locality and has worked out its *modus vivendi* with other people in that area faces a number of social and cultural adjustments when it migrates to a new area. These problems, though formidable, are not insurmountable. The principal problems involved would appear to be the following:

1. The farm operator and other members of his family are obliged to establish contact with previously unknown individuals in the new area. They must also join new social systems and work out adaptations to the customs and social norms which they find in these systems.

2. The specific agricultural practices which were successful in the old area may be unsuccessful in the new. This creates problems since farmers, like other occupational groups, tend to be creatures of habit. The adjustment to and adoption of practices which are successful in the new area may require considerable time and involve a certain

---

[31] See Landis, *Rural Life in Process, op. cit.*, chap. 15.
[32] *Ibid.*

amount of shock. This may be illustrated by Landis's statement of the problems of certain drought migrants to the state of Washington.

Since he knew nothing about the handling of water and little about many of the farming practices carried on in irrigated sections, the drought farmer experienced a new kind of farming. Fixed habits had to be discarded; old attitudes overcome. A man loses his dignity when he shifts from a quarter section, a half section, or a whole section to a ten acre tract or a five acre garden. . . . Some drought migrants who had settled on small irrigated tracts reported that they were ashamed to be seen working with a shovel and wearing rubber boots while irrigating. It was a come-down to use a shovel after having steered a tractor down a long furrow.[33]

GROUP SETTLEMENT AND ADJUSTMENT

Landis believes that interregional farm migrants tend to take their community along as far as they can, migrating if possible with friends, relatives, and neighbors.[34] Evidence from the study of drought migrants to the state of Washington seems to substantiate this hypothesis, at least in part. Kolb and Brunner also call attention to group migrations in the westward movement of farmers in the settlement of the frontier.[35]

Where this type of movement occurs, the immediate social adjustments faced by the migrants may be minimized, particularly if they are moving into an unsettled region and do not have to adapt to a lower social rank or a lower economic status than that to which they have been accustomed—as was the case with a great many of the drought migrants. But group settlement tends to encourage perpetuation of old practices in the new area, and for this reason may be regarded as a barrier to effective adjustment rather than an asset. This observation, of course, had much more significance with earlier migrants from foreign countries into agricultural areas of the United States than with present-day interregional migrants, although it is applicable today to distinctive groups which have somewhat unique cultures like the Hutterites, the Dukhobors, and the Mennonites.

[33] *Ibid.,* p. 230.
[34] *Ibid.*
[35] John H. Kolb and Edmund deS. Brunner, "Cultural Origins and Regions," *A Study of Rural Society,* 4th ed., Houghton Mifflin, 1952.

MIGRATORY FARM LABORERS

In addition to the types of farm migrants already discussed, there are perhaps as many as a million migratory agricultural workers whose principal income is earned from temporary farm employment and who migrate from one agricultural area to another in the course of a year's work.[36]

The President's Commission on Migratory Labor reported that the foremost reason for migrancy is that "many people find it impossible to make a living in a single location and had to become migratory. Technological displacement, business recession and consequent unemployment in industry, drought and crop failure, radical changes in the sharecropper system, lack of education and vocational training—these are among the basic factors responsible for migrancy."[37]

The Commission pointed out that the composition of the migrant group has changed over the years. Prior to 1917 most of the temporary seasonal farm workers in the U.S. were European immigrants. Later Japanese, Chinese, and Indians made up the bulk of the migratory labor force on the West Coast. In the 1930s the migratory labor force contained many displaced American farmers, including the "Okies," the name applied to farm people from the dust bowl in Oklahoma, Arkansas, Missouri, and Texas. Relatively few of these people were found by the Commission to be migratory agricultural workers in 1950.[38]

During the decade of the 1940s, according to the Commission, the "Texas Mexicans" emerged as the largest group in the domestic migratory labor force.

During World War II, the Office of Labor of the War Food Administration handled transportation, housing, and contract negotiations concerning wages and days of work for some interstate domestic workers and for foreign laborers brought by the U.S. government from Jamaica, the Bahamas, and Mexico under the terms of international agreements. Most of them were returned to

[36] President's Commission on Migratory Labor, *Migratory Labor in American Agriculture*, 1951, p. 1.
[37] *Ibid.*, pp. 1-2.
[38] *Ibid.*, p. 2.

their home countries at the close of each crop year.[39] During the wartime period, the state agricultural extension services assumed the responsibility for farm labor placements. The extension services also determined the need for foreign workers in specific localities. After the termination of hostilities, responsibility for labor placements, including all aspects of the foreign farm labor program, was transferred to the Employment Service of the U.S. Department of Labor and its affiliated state employment services.

The President's Commission on Migratory Labor reported that only a small proportion of the migratory agricultural labor force is employed on family farms. Most of them work on large-scale farms which produce cotton, fruits, vegetables, or sugar beets. The Commission pointed out that the revolutionary changes in labor productivity in American agriculture which have occurred in the recent past have greatly reduced the need for permanent agricultural workers.[40] On the other hand, seasonal farm labor peaks in certain crops still require substantial numbers of short-time wage hands. This, of course, means that employment opportunities for migratory workers have become less dependable. The Commission stated the problem of farm employers who require seasonal workers in large numbers: "They want a labor supply which, on the one hand, is ready and willing to meet the short term work requirements and which, on the other hand, will not impose social and economic problems on them or on their community when the work is finished. This is what is expected of migratory workers. The demand for migratory workers is thus essentially two-fold: to be ready to go to work when needed; to be gone when not needed."[41]

Some of the migratory agricultural workers are single; others are married and take their families with them from job to job. For many of the single workers, particularly the foreign nationals, migratory farm work may represent a once-in-a-lifetime experience. Such persons return to their families and home communities when they finish a season's experience as migratory agricultural workers in the United States. There have been reports that many Mexican nationals have saved sufficient funds from a single season as farm workers in

[39] Claude R. Wickard, *Report of the Secretary of Agriculture, 1943,* USDA, 1944, pp. 111-117.
[40] President's Commission on Migratory Labor, *op. cit.,* pp. 8-10.
[41] *Ibid.,* p. 16.

the U.S. to enable them to purchase land, start business enterprises, or otherwise materially improve their economic situations in their home communities.

The President's Commission on Migratory Labor suggested that further mechanization of hand tasks may eventually minimize the need for seasonal laborers; some evidence that such developments are now taking place is presented in Chapter 9. The Commission cautioned, however, that "Notwithstanding the achievements already made and the prospects of further advances, it would be unwise to suppose that machines will soon entirely replace seasonal hand labor. Many fruit and vegetable harvests—cherries and green beans, for example—will be difficult to mechanize."[42]

The implications of migratory labor for individuals, families, and communities are discussed in Chapter 16.

PROSPECTS FOR FUTURE MIGRATION

This review of the characteristics of migration in the past should make us cautious in predicting the shape of things to come. However, the trend toward equalization of the birth rates between farms, small towns, and cities indicates clearly that in the future the city will not be obliged as it was once to look primarily to farming areas for replenishment of its population. The tremendous migration of urban workers into the urban fringe adjacent to centers of population constitutes a new development on the social scene. Since many of these individuals carry on some agricultural operations, it becomes increasingly difficult, at least on the basis of generalized information collected by the Census Bureau, to identify the characteristics of those who depend upon agriculture for the whole or the major part of their livelihood.

There is considerable evidence that the movement out of full-time commercial agriculture is likely to continue, although this may not always involve migration. For some time the average size of farms has been increasing—while the basic pattern of farm organization in the United States is still the family farm, advances in technology have made it possible for families to operate much larger enterprises than previously.

[42] Ibid.

The increase in the amount of capital required to establish a "going concern" is such that entrance into full-time commercial agriculture is perhaps more difficult now than it has ever been in the history of this country. Even settlers on new lands in federally sponsored irrigation projects like the Columbia Basin are now required to have much more capital than previously.[43]

Although there is traditionally a welcome place for the stranger in rural society this cannot be taken for granted, and in the case of the new family migrating into an established area there may even be hostility if the new family is regarded as a competitor. With respect to status, the new family may be considered a threat in any of a number of different respects.

QUESTIONS FOR FURTHER STUDY AND DISCUSSION

1. During the period of first settlement of the agricultural land in the United States, the predominant movement of population was from east to west. There was relatively little north-south migration. In your opinion, what were the main reasons for this pattern of migration? What are the consequences of it?

2. Kolb and Brunner indicate that the idea of "rugged individualism" may be a product of westward migration. Comment on this idea, indicating whether you believe it is a reasonable assumption and giving a justification for your position.

3. Interstate migration of farm and nonfarm people continues according to census reports. What categories of farm people are most likely to migrate to towns and cities? to other farms? What categories of urban people are most likely to migrate to farms? To other cities or towns?

4. Discuss the influence of migration on the social training of children.

5. Discuss the impact of technology and industrialization on the migration of farm and nonfarm people.

6. Kolb and Brunner believe that rural-urban migration has benefited the cities. Do you feel that this migration has also impoverished the farms? Explain your stand.

7. Trace the moves of your family or some other family well known to you as far back as you can. What were the motives for each move?

8. Many years ago, Dr. E. A. Ross said, "The continual departure [from

---

[43] Announcement by the U.S. Bureau of Reclamation, November, 1956, with respect to capital requirements of veterans desiring farm units in the Columbia Basin.

rural areas] of young people who might in time have become leaders
results eventually in a visible moral decline of the community." Comment critically on this idea, stating what influence you think the
migration from farms to towns and cities has had upon rural community life.
 9. What contributions, other than economic, have farm migrants made
    to urban centers?
10. Describe the recent mobility of the rural American Negro and com-
    ment on the social implications of this movement.
11. What are the prospects for improving the economic and social con-
    ditions of migratory farm laborers?

SELECTED REFERENCES

Bogue, Donald Jr., and Margaret J. Hagood, *Sub-Regional Migration in
    the United States, 1935-40,* vol. 2 of *Differential Migration in the
    Corn and Cotton Belts: A Pilot Study of the Selectivity of Intra-State
    Migration to Cities from Non-Metropolitan Areas,* Scripps Foundation
    Studies on Population Distribution, No. 6, 1953.
Landis, Paul H., *Rural Life in Process,* 2nd ed., McGraw-Hill, 1948,
    chaps. 12-17.
Nelson, Lowry, *Rural Sociology,* 2nd ed., American Book, 1952, chaps.
    7, 12.
President's Commission on Migratory Labor, *Migratory Labor in Amer-
    ican Agriculture,* 1951.
Smith, T. Lynn, *The Sociology of Rural Life,* 3rd ed., Harper, 1953,
    chaps. 9, 24.

II

CULTURE: THE HERITAGE
OF THE PAST

All of the members of a society share in a common cultural background
which is so familiar to them that it is almost as unnoticed as the air
they breathe; it is taken for granted. Ordinarily we become fully
aware of the distinctive characteristics of our way of life only
when we come into direct contact with people who have been reared
in another society. Such individuals, to our eyes, behave strangely.
They have unfamiliar values, sometimes wear strange clothes, frequently
worship strange gods, and rear their children in queer ways.

Within our general heritage there are variations in values and
behavior norms which are associated with local or regional traditions,
ethnic backgrounds, religious affiliations, occupations, family
backgrounds, and other factors. Many of these variations in culture are
relatively minor, but some are pronounced. It is in contrast to the general
norms of the society that variations take on significance.
Consequently, it will be helpful to keep the general heritage
of the past in mind as we proceed.

5

The Contribution of Immigrant
Nationality Stocks

It is well known that the United States of America was peopled
principally by European immigrants and their descendants. It
has been estimated that more than 39,000,000 immigrants entered
the country between 1820 and 1950, mostly from the British Isles
and Europe,[1] and that of these approximately 32,000,000 remained[2]. According to the Census Bureau, 40 percent of the
white population in 1920 was of English ancestry, 16 per cent of
German origin, and 11 percent of Irish descent. The remaining
third of the people were nearly all from other European countries
and Canada.[3] Between July 1, 1950, and June 30, 1959, 2,251,000
immigrants entered the U.S.,[4] as in previous periods mainly from
Europe.

During the period of principal agricultural settlement prior to
1900, most of the immigrants came from northern European countries; after that year there was a large influx of immigrants from
southern and eastern Europe. Most of the later immigrants came
from farms, but there were few attractive opportunities in farming
for penniless immigrants when they arrived, and for the most part
they joined the ranks of industrial laborers in urban areas.

The native Indians of North America were predominantly no-

[1] P. H. Landis and P. K. Hatt, *Population Problems,* 2nd ed., American
Book, 1950.
[2] U.S. Immigration and Naturalization Service, *1950 Annual Report,* 1950.
[3] U.S. Bureau of the Census, *Mother Tongue of the White Population:
1940,* Series P-15, No. 4, September 22, 1942.
[4] U. S. Immigration and Naturalization Service, *1959 Annual Report,* 1959.

madic hunters.[5] Except those in the southwest, few had any agricultural technology of any consequence, in spite of the legend that Squanto taught the Virginia colonists how to fertilize corn by putting a dead fish in each corn hill. Today most Indians live on reservations located in areas of low agricultural potential. They eke out a subsistence by means of rudimentary agriculture, herding, and various allowances from the federal government.

Immigrants from Europe brought domesticated animals for both meat and power, the seeds of domesticated plants, and well-developed agricultural implements and practices. As noted elsewhere in the discussion of advanced plow culture, they brought with them a considerable agricultural tradition of practices developed gradually through centuries of trial and error, which with some modifications to suit the new habitat provided a basis for a successful agriculture.

The original 13 colonies were settled mainly by immigrants from various parts of the British Isles. Early settlements were made in Virginia in 1607, the Massachusetts Bay area in the 1620s, Maine and New Hampshire in 1623, Maryland in 1632, Connecticut in 1635, Rhode Island in 1636, Pennsylvania in 1681, and Georgia in 1682. In 1664, the English captured the Dutch settlement of New Amsterdam and renamed it New York.

During the colonial period most of the foreign-born immigrants continued to come from the British Isles, although a substantial group of Germans settled on Pennsylvania farms. A considerable number of Negroes were imported from Africa during this period to serve as slaves on the southern plantations.

It was not until about 1832 that really large numbers of foreign immigrants started arriving. In that year there were 60,482. Between 1830 and 1870 more than 7,225,000 immigrants entered the United States. Even during the period of the Civil War immigration exceeded 90,000 every year. Immediately after the War the railroads and steamship companies vigorously promoted foreign immigration in an effort to settle the frontier rapidly; 11,746,000 immigrants appeared between 1870 and 1901, and during the period from 1901 to 1910 there were 8,795,000.[6] Not all of these settled on farms.

[5] See Clark Wissler, *Indians of the United States: Four Centuries of Their History and Culture,* Doubleday Doran, 1940.
[6] *1950 Annual Report, op. cit.*

Many of the later ones went directly to the cities where they took industrial or other unskilled labor jobs. Some returned to their native lands, but most stayed in America, and many settled on farms.

The settlement of the far western part of the United States was accomplished principally by the native-born. Many of these, of course, were of foreign or mixed parentage. There were also some foreign-born immigrants but their numbers were not great; the proportion of foreign-born in the population of the state of Washington, for example, never exceeded 20 percent.[7]

The southern states east of the Continental Divide were settled principally by native-born Americans of native stock. The great bulk of these came from the southeastern states. Other notable ethnic stocks in the South include the French in Louisiana and the Spanish Americans in Texas, Arizona, and New Mexico. In addition there were some local settlements or "cultural islands" involving other stocks.

The great flood of foreign immigration was cut off by the outbreak of World War 1. By that time, however, almost all the available agricultural land had already been settled. Although a substantial number of immigrants still enter the United States every year (260,689 in 1959), for all practical purposes the movement of foreign-born to American farms may be regarded as completed.

MAJOR ETHNIC STOCKS

Systematic anthropological and sociological studies of various ethnic stocks and subcultural groups are relatively sparse. Most of the information about ethnic folkways available in the literature, even in historical accounts, is based on personal impressions rather than on empirical data collected systematically. Futhermore, differences may exist within a given ethnic stock (e.g., between Catholic and Protestant Germans). In spite of these deficiencies, authorities agree that meaningful ethnic folkways do exist.

Unfortunately, no comprehensive nationwide map of the locality pattern of concentrated ethnic settlements has been prepared,

[7] Vernon Davies, *Farm Population Trends in Washington*, Washington AES Bulletin 507, 1949.

though the interested student may be able to find state or area maps in some states.[8]

NATIVE AMERICAN STOCKS

During the period of over 200 years that elapsed between the time that the first English colonies were established and when the great European immigration commenced in 1830, there evolved at least three major subcultural groups from three particular subcultural groups within the English stock. These were (1) the *Yankee*, the lineal descendant of the Puritans, the Pilgrims and other Protestant yeomen who settled in New England and New York; (2) the *planter*, a cultural descendant of the aristocratic Cavaliers; and (3) the *southern small farmer*, sometimes called a "redneck," "poor white," or "cracker," who was a descendant of immigrants from the lower classes of the British Isles, many of whom came to the new world as indentured servants.

Although the rate of population increase was high during colonial times, the total population remained relatively small. The first census, in 1790, recorded a total population of less than 4,000,000.[9] A large part of the population growth that occurred during colonial times was due to natural increase (the excess of births over deaths). There was relatively little migration from one section of the Atlantic seaboard to another; as a consequence, distinctive subcultural groups developed. The area directly west of the Appalachians and Alleghenies was settled initially by people from the coastal areas —relatively few foreign-born immigrants were involved.

THE YANKEES. Many writers have called attention to the distinctive characteristics of the Yankee. The general picture that emerges is that of a restless, industrious, practical-minded people imbued with a deep sense of moral propriety. Some of the distinctive Yankee folkways were an ambition to engage in public service; strict observance of Sunday, emphasis upon temperance; the tradition that every young man should receive enough education to make

[8] See W. L. Slocum, *Ethnic Stocks as Culture Types in Rural Wisconsin*, unpublished Ph.D. thesis, University of Wisconsin, 1940, Fig. 1, p. 22; A. L. Bertrand, *The Many Louisianas, Rural Social Areas and Culture Islands*, Louisiana AES Bulletin 496, June, 1955, Fig. II, p. 21.

[9] U.S. National Resources Committee, *The Problems of a Changing Population*, May, 1938, p. 21.

his way in the world; and shrewdness in business relationships.[10]

With particular reference to agriculture, the farming practices utilized by the early Yankee apparently were generally exploitative rather than soil-conserving. He was likely to mine the soil. He assumed that there was plenty of good land farther west and he was ready to move and did move to new frontiers when his soil was exhausted to the point where yields declined.[11]

THE PLANTERS. The planters did not make up the bulk of the population of the southern colonies at any time, although they had the lion's share of the most productive land under their control; because they were the managers of large estates, their influence was greater than their numbers, particularly with reference to political affairs and agricultural practices.[12]

The social life of the aristocracy of the old South has been the subject of several novels, including *Gone with the Wind* by Margaret Mitchell. Less well publicized but of great importance in the development of farming was the plantation system of agriculture, to a great extent developed around tobacco and cotton with Negro slaves as the source of manpower. The old-style plantation was largely a self-sufficient economic enterprise. Basic policies were determined by the landowner and his family. Relationships with the labor force were carried out through intermediaries—the managers or overseers.

THE SOUTHERN SMALL FARMERS. Less influential than the planters but much more numerous and of considerable signficance in the development of the South were the southern small farmers. These people existed largely outside of the plantation system and were negatively influenced by it in that they were usually obliged to subsist on the poorer land. Records concerning the southern small farmers are scanty. Most of the literature pertaining to the South deals with either the planters or the Negroes or both, although there is some literature relating to the activities and presumed characteristics of the "poor white," like Steinbeck's *Grapes of Wrath* and Gibson's *Hound Dog Man*. Some early writers characterized

[10] See Slocum, *op. cit.*, pp. 35-38.

[11] Joseph Schafer, "The Yankee and the Teuton in Wisconsin," *The Wisconsin Magazine of History*, VI, no. 2 (1922), 13, 21.

[12] See T. Lynn Smith, *The Sociology of Rural Life*, 3rd ed., Harper, 1953, pp. 304-319.

the poor whites as indolent and immoral, but this stereotype is far from generally applicable—many of these people were of Scotch-Irish origin and quite religious.[13] Even today the rural South is sometimes called the "Bible Belt."

T. L. Smith, who has made a study of this stock, considers that the role of the southern small farmer has been of prime importance in American agriculture,[14] and this evaluation is undoubtedly correct. Southern small farmers have not been in the forefront of commercial agriculture, but even in 1950 their descendants were far more numerous in rural areas than those of any other ethnic stock; the southern states, including Texas, contained more than half the white farm population. There were few non-English-speaking immigrants in the South. In 1950 only Texas and Florida of the southern states reported as high as 2 percent of their population to be foreign-born.

THE GERMANS

A few German immigrants reached Philadelphia in 1683, and between 1710 and 1720 settlements were made in New York and Pennsylvania. The Pennsylvania farming settlements were concentrated in the southeastern counties of Lehigh, Montgomery, Berks, Chester, Lancaster, and York. It has been estimated that at the time of the Revolution 100,000 or about a third of the population of Pennsylvania was of German extraction. This area is still known as "Pennsylvania Dutch" country.[15] During the colonial period, Germans also settled on farms in Delaware, Maryland, New Jersey, Virginia, and North and South Carolina.[16] Kolb and Brunner have commented on the tenacity with which these early Germans clung to their traditions, language, and religion;[17] Cunz says that the

[13] See Frederick Jackson Turner, *The Frontier in American History*, Holt, 1921, pp. 104-106; J. R. Commons, *Races and Immigrants in America*, Macmillan, 1907, pp. 31-38.

[14] Smith, *op. cit.*, pp. 55-59.

[15] See Ralph Wood, ed., The Pennsylvania Germans, Princeton University Press, 1942; Dieter Cunz, "German Americans," in F. J. Brown and J. S. Roucek, eds., *One America*, 3rd ed., Prentice-Hall, 1952, pp. 104-120.

[16] Dieter Cunz, "German Americans," in Brown and Roucek, eds., *op. cit.*, p. 107.

[17] John H. Kolb and Edmund deS. Brunner, *A Study of Rural Society*, 4th ed., Houghton Mifflin, 1952, pp. 13, 14.

Pennsylvania Dutch farm community still maintains its distinctive ethnic character.[18]

Between 1820 and 1950, more than 6,248,000 additional German immigrants entered the U.S. The greatest number (4,807,000) arrived during the period 1850-1900.[19]

The Germans had a tendency to arrive in groups and to settle near other Germans. Most of those who came prior to the Civil War were peasants who settled on farms. A higher percentage of those who came later were businessmen and craftsmen who had a tendency to locate in the cities.[20]

There are heavy concentrations of German stock in various parts of the Midwest. The census of 1910 reported 832,000 rural residents who had been born in Germany. The approximate numbers in the leading states were as follows:

Wisconsin	111,600	Nebraska	40,000
Illinois	78,600	New York	40,000
Iowa	71,900	Pennsylvania	40,000
Minnesota	69,900	Texas	30,400
Michigan	52,300	Missouri	26,400

In addition, there were lesser numbers in other states. In North and South Dakota, for example, there is an 11-county area of heavy settlement of Russian German farmers. These people had migrated from Germany to Russia under promises from Catherine the Great and Alexander I of exemption from military service. When these promises were broken, after 1848 a mass migration to the U.S.A. occurred.[21]

There is remarkable agreement concerning the nature of the immigrant German farmer's values and agricultural folkways which various writers consider to have influenced the conduct of his posterity whether found in Pennsylvania, Texas, Wisconsin, or elsewhere in the United States:

1. He looked for good land, preferring such as was already slightly improved.

[18] Cunz, *op. cit.*, p. 115.
[19] *1950 Annual Report, op. cit.*, Table 11.
[20] Cunz, *op. cit.*, pp. 110-111.
[21] Rev. H. Joachim, *The Russia-Germans*, unpublished paper, 1941, p. 70.

2. His methods of farming were those of thoroughness and patient labor. He would clear the land carefully of stumps and stones, and aim at producing the largest possible yield per acre. He believed in a rotation of crops, so as not to exhaust the land, for he planned for the future, and with a view to permanent possession.

3. The native American farmer was wasteful; the German invariably economical. . . . If his standard of living was lower than that of the native population, it was best fitted to insure success in farming.

4. He was very considerate of his livestock, feeding his horses and cattle well, and housing them instead of letting them run wild. In the winter he kept them warm in barns or stables. He kept them hard at work, but never overworked them.

5. Everything about his place was in good order, fences, houses, gardens, and agricultural implements. He first built a great barn to keep his grain. The barn was more imposing than the house, and the particular architectural style of German barn, built first in Pennsylvania, made its way down the Ohio, and can be seen in Wisconsin or wherever the German abides. . . . The house of the German farmer was constructed of stone for permanent occupancy, though for reasons of economy it generally took a second generation to build it. This characteristic is noticeable today in Wisconsin, where the dwelling of the farmer is very often built of light colored brick.

6. The German farmer did most of his work with his own hands and was assisted by his wife and children. Large families on the farm were therefore a source of prosperity, and this economic fact had a tendency to produce large families.

7. The Germans made it a matter of pride to keep their farms in their own families, generation after generation. This is as true of the Mennonites of Lancaster County, Pennsylvania as of the German immigrants of the 19th Century in Wisconsin.[22]

The Wisconsin historian Joseph Schafer is in substantial agreement with the points of view expressed in the above quotation. In addition, he points out that most of the Germans who settled on Wisconsin farms had been small holders at home who lived in villages and were habituated to intensive modes of cultivation. He

[22] Albert B. Faust, *The German Element in the United States,* Houghton Mifflin, 1909, II, 29 ff. Faust acknowledges his indebtedness to an early writer, Dr. Benjamin Rush, who in 1789 wrote an essay entitled "An Account of the Manners of the German Inhabitants of Pennsylvania." Sixteen agricultural characteristics of the Germans listed by Dr. Rush are cited in vol. I of the above work, pp. 131-138.

considered their farming habits to be most nearly comparable to those of a modern truck farmer, although he points out that they were not "one-crop" farmers, that they fertilized their land, and that, above all, they were persistent.[23]

These habits of industry and persistence were part of a configuration apparently integrated around a central dominating idea, that of perpetuating the family line on the land. Von Skal has said that the German "loved the soil as he loved his family. . . . They farmed not for one harvest, but forever."[24]   *1 0 9 4 6 6*

Writers concur that the influence of the agricultural folkways of the Germans was not soon exhausted but passed on to succeeding generations. Skal wrote in 1908, "We find the traits that distinguish the first settlers still in existence; a strong desire for independence, . . . the untiring industry, strongly marked honesty, frugality, and the inclination to take life seriously. All these qualities have produced a conservatism which has kept them and their offspring on their farms."[25] Even as late as 1935, the German farmers in Wisconsin were found to have a tendency to act, in agricultural matters, according to common standards. "Germans have had, in the past, and evidently continue to have, rather consistent patterns of behavior in respect to the aspects of man-land adjustment, reflected by the data of the study." Furthermore, the patterns of husbandry thus transmitted have generally been superior, within the range of behavior studies, to the patterns of other ethnic groups in Wisconsin.[26]

Kollmorgen reported in 1941 on the differences between people of German descent and Georgia "crackers" who had lived side by side in Cullman County, Alabama, for nearly a century. During this period the Germans had lost much of their old world culture and become more nearly like their cotton-growing neighbors, but their agricultural folkways and practices had survived to a significant degree. Furthermore, the Germans were generally more successful than their neighbors: "They give more stress to diversifica-

[23] Joseph Schafer, "A History of Agriculture in Wisconsin," in *Wisconsin Domesday Book*, Wisconsin State Historical Society, 1922, vol. I.
[24] George von Skal, *History of German Immigration in the United States*, New York, privately published, 1908, p. 16.
[25] *Ibid., pp.* 16-17.
[26] Slocum, *op. cit.*, p. 83.

tion, and live more adequately at home, than do their neighbors, and they are still chiefly Lutheran or Catholic, but they are no longer the supremely confident German peasant farmers that they were when they came South. Many of the Germans carry an air of having been beaten, and most of them did take a beating during their early years in the South."[27]

The non-German informants in Cullman County generally credited the success of the Germans largely to their characteristic persistence and hard work.[28]

Kollmorgen also studied a settlement of farmers of German-Swiss ancestry in Franklin County, Tennessee; and concluded that their agricultural practices were determined in a very large measure by their cultural backgrounds. He stated that by following practices that build up and maintain soil fertility, the German-Swiss had established themselves as constructive farmers and had realized more adequately than farmers of different ethnic backgrounds the potentialities of agriculture in the locality.[29]

THE SCANDINAVIANS

Denmark, Norway, and Sweden contributed large numbers of farm immigrants to the U.S. The immigration statistics show that 340,000 Danes, 814,950 Norwegians, and 1,228,000 Swedes entered this country between 1820 and 1950, large numbers of whom settled on farms, especially in the Midwest.

Concentrated settlements of Norwegians were made in south and central Wisconsin, northern Iowa, Minnesota and North and South Dakota. Montana, Oregon, and Washington also received large numbers. Hovde reports that few returned to Norway and that assimilation of the Norwegian Americans has been rapid.[30] Slocum found little evidence of distinctive Norwegian agricultural folkways among Wisconsin Norwegian Americans,[31] though Nelson

[27] W. M. Kollmorgen, *The German Settlement in Cullman County, Alabama,* U.S. Department of Agriculture, Bureau of Agricultural Economics, June, 1941, p. 63.
[28] *Ibid.,* p. 64.
[29] W. M. Kollmorgen, *The German-Swiss in Franklin County, Tennessee,* USDA, Bureau of Agricultural Economics, June, 1940, p. 106.
[30] B. J. Hovde, "Norwegian Americans," in Brown and Roucek, eds., *op. cit.,* pp. 66-72.
[31] Slocum, *op. cit.,* p. 85.

found that Norwegians in Wright County, Minnesota, were more likely to marry members of other ethnic stocks than persons of Norwegian descent.[32]

Swedish immigrants also settled in the Midwest with heavy concentrations in Minnesota and Illinois.[33] Large numbers also settled in Nebraska, the Dakotas, and the Pacific Northwest. Like the Norwegians, the Swedes readily adjusted themselves to American life and few returned to Sweden. Benson reports that 92 percent of Swedish men who had been in the United States five years or more in 1910 either were citizens or had taken out their first papers.[34]

Many of the Danes also settled on farms in the Midwest. Concentrated settlements were made in Iowa, Minnesota, Nebraska, Wisconsin, and the Dakotas. Like the Swedes and the Norwegians, the Danes and their descendents have been rapidly assimilated.[35]

All of the Scandinavians were Protestants, most of them Lutherans. During the early period of settlement, church services were conducted in the language of the settlers rather than in English. J. P. Johansen has presented information for Norwegian Lutheran congregations in South Dakota which shows that the percentage of preaching services in Norwegian dropped from 93 percent in 1905 to 13.6 percent in 1935. Commenting on the importance of language, he observed:

One of the most important elements in culture is language and every European church in America, save those whose native tongue was English, has been required to make its accommodation to this factor. The language question has been one of the most difficult problems with which the immigrant churches have had to deal, for it involved the problem of rebirth in a new civilization. Conservatives in these churches have always maintained that the abandonment of the old European tongue and the adoption of English as the language of worship and instruction involved the abandonment of all the ways of the fathers and the introduction of a

[32] Lowry Nelson, "Intermarriage Among Nationality Groups in a Rural Area of Minnesota," *American Journal of Sociology*, March, 1943, pp. 585-592.

[33] O. A. Benson, "Swedish Americans," in Brown and Roucek, eds., *op. cit.*, pp. 73-77.

[34] *Ibid.*, p. 75.

[35] Paul M. Gustafson, "Danish Americans," in Brown and Roucek, eds., *op. cit.*, pp. 77-83.

new "English or American religion." Their intuitions have usually been correct, for the adoption of the native tongue is only the most obvious symptom of the assimilation of the native culture as a whole.[36]

THE POLES

Approximately 422,000 Polish immigrants entered this country during the period 1820 to 1930 according to the U.S. Immigration and Naturalization Service,[37] but these figures understate the Polish immigration grossly: many Poles came with passports from Prussia, Austria, and Russia. Figures ranging from two million to five million Polish immigrants have been published.[38] The peak of the mass immigration came during the period between 1900 and the outbreak of World War I in 1914.[39] Polish farmers are to be found in Wisconsin, Michigan, New York, Pennsylvania, Minnesota, Massachusetts, and Connecticut.

The Polish immigrants were Catholics, and in large part peasants. First-generation Polish farmers have been quite successful economically because of their willingness to work extremely hard and at the same time to be content with a poorer level of living than was customary among other American farmers. The Poles tend to be ethnocentric and have not been assimilated as readily as the Scandinavians or the Germans.

The Poles have been successful truck farmers near large cities. The influx of Polish immigrants to worn-out New England farms has resulted in a revival of agriculture in that area.[40] By holding down their standard of living, they were able to increase their holdings and reclaim many New England farms which had been abandoned.

Many Polish people who came first to Chicago and Milwaukee were induced to settle on submarginal lands in the cutover areas

[36] John P. Johansen, *Immigrant Settlements and Social Organization in South Dakota*, South Dakota AES Bulletin 313, June, 1937, p. 54.

[37] *1950 Annual Report, op. cit.*

[38] R. A. Schermerhorn, *These Our People*, Heath, 1949, p. 266; J. V. Swastek, "Polish Americans," in Brown and Roucek, eds., *op. cit.*, pp. 144-146.

[39] Swastek, *op. cit.*, p. 146.

[40] See Edmund deS. Brunner, *Immigrant Farmers and Their Children*, Doubleday Doran, 1929, p. 216.

of Wisconsin, Michigan, and Minnesota. In spite of their willingness to work hard, they found it difficult to make a satisfactory
adjustment to this inhospitable environment.[41]

THE CZECHS AND SLOVAKS

In 1930, according to the U.S. Census, there were 491,000 foreign-
born Czechoslovaks in the U.S. and 890,000 of Czechoslovak descent; 707,000 of the latter reported that both of their parents were
foreign. According to Schermerhorn, most of the Czechs settled on
farms, whereas most of the Slovaks settled in cities or became
miners.[42]

The immigration of the Czechs began in the 1850s, early enough
for them to take advantage of the Homestead Act which provided
160 acres free to a person who would live on it for five years. Most
of the Czech immigrants brought their families with them.[43] A study
of a Czech neigborhood in the cutover area of northern Wisconsin
in the 1930s showed that the people had low levels of living but
had nevertheless worked out a pattern of life that was satisfactory
to them in many ways.[44]

Brunner found that the hard work of members of a Czech
colony in Virginia enabled them to achieve economic successes
comparable to those of the Polish in New England. However,
social distance between the Czechs and the aristocratic Virginians
was still great even in the third generation. Little intermarriage
had occurred.[45]

A study by Lynch of a Czech settlement in Oklahoma revealed
that the Czechs had made a much more satisfactory economic
adjustment than others in the locality. They had greater residential
stability, a higher percentage of ownership, larger farms, and greater
incomes. Lynch concluded that the cultural backgrounds of these

[41] See Brunner, op. cit., chap. 2; B. J. Przedpelski et al., New Approaches for
Agricultural Extension in Problem Areas, Wisconsin Extension Bulletin 1, September, 1952, pp. 1-2.
[42] Schermerhorn, op. cit., pp. 299, 313.
[43] Ibid., pp. 300-301.
[44] See Geo. H. Hill, Walter Slocum, and Ruth O. Hill, Man-Land Adjustment, Wisconsin AES Research Bulletin 134, February, 1938, pp. 29-36.
[45] Brunner, op. cit., pp. 183-212.

farmers had contributed to their success in meeting the problems of agriculture in the area.[46]

THE JAPANESE

Japanese immigration to the Pacific Coast began during the 1890s after the Chinese were officially excluded in 1882. Approximately 279,000 had entered the United States up to June 30, 1950. However, a very large proportion of these returned to Japan.[47] In 1950, the number of foreign-born Japanese in the 48 states was estimated by the U.S. Bureau of the Census at 127,000.

Quite a number of the Japanese were engaged in agriculture prior to World War II; in 1940 about 20,000 of those who were gainfully employed in the state of California were farmers or agricultural workers.[48] Their knowledge of intensive agriculture and their industry, persistence, and relatively low standard of living made them very successful truck gardeners. They were not, however, readily assimilated because of their skin color, customs, and low social rank. Furthermore, they were suspected by the military as possible sources of subversion, and soon after Japan attacked the United States they were evacuated from the Pacific Coast states and placed in relocation centers in other parts of the United States. Most of them were held until the end of World War II, and only 55 percent then returned to the Pacific Coast.[49] Information is not available concerning the extent to which the Japanese Americans have returned to agriculture.

THE SPANISH AMERICANS

In the southwestern states, especially in Texas and New Mexico, there are considerable numbers of Spanish-speaking farm people. Exact figures are not known, but it has been estimated that more than 200,000 people or about half the population of New Mexico and 1,100,000 to 1,300,000 of the population of Texas in 1948 were

[46] R. W. Lynch, "Czech Farmers in Oklahoma," Oklahoma A & M College Bulletin, June, 1942, pp. 104-105.

[47] *1950 Annual Report, op. cit.,* Table 11.

[48] J. S. Roucek, "Japanese Americans," in Brown and Roucek, eds., *op. cit.,* p. 324.

[49] Schermerhorn, *op. cit.,* pp. 199 ff; Roucek, *op. cit.,* pp. 319-334.

Spanish-speaking.[50] Spanish-Americans are of swarthy complexion, generally poor, and considered by the "Anglos" (white Americans) to be of low social rank. They have not been assimilated to any appreciable extent even though many of them have been residents of the United States all of their lives. Leonard and Loomis studied a Spanish American agricultural community in New Mexico in 1940. They reported that traditional land inheritance patterns had been followed with the result that the land had been divided and subdivided into holdings in some cases so small that it was difficult for the owners to know exactly where the boundaries were. Leonard and Loomis also reported that traditional agricultural practices were followed to a very large extent: "Sons have truly followed in the footsteps of their fathers, and their sons in turn have followed after them. An early Colonist, returning to El Cerrito today, would find little change in crops grown or methods of cultivating and harvesting."[51]

The dominance of the idigenous Spanish American values and customs including the language has made the problem of acculturation very difficult.[52] The resistance of members of this ethnic stock to the English language has impeded diffusion to them of improved agricultural technology.[53]

THE LOUISIANA FRENCH

The southern part of Louisiana had been settled by the French before the Louisiana Purchase in 1803. Bertrand reports that their descendents, who comprise 40 to 50 percent of the people of Louisiana, have been remarkably successful in preserving their language and other aspects of French culture. All are Catholics and fertility is high. Many are farmers who live in the southern section which Bertrand has called "French Louisiana."[54]

[50] Lyle Saunders, *The Spanish-Speaking People of Texas,* University of Texas Press, December, 1949, pp. 8, 12.

[51] Olen Leonard and C. P. Loomis, *Culture of a Contemporary Rural Community: El Cerrito, New Mexico,* USDA, Bureau of Agricultural Economics, Rural Life Studies No. 1, November, 1941, p. 24.

[52] See George I. Sanchez, *Forgotten People: A Study of New Mexicans,* University of New Mexico Press, 1940, pp. 31-32.

[53] Glen Grisham, "Meeting Today's Needs in the Land of Mañana," *Land Policy Review,* III (1940), 32-36.

[54] Bertrand, *op. cit.,* p. 20.

Smith reports that the principal form of agricultural settlement in this area is the line village with long rectangular fields. Some of these were located along river fronts.[55]

OTHER ETHNIC STOCKS

There are, of course, other ethnic stocks which are important in specific localities but which because of limited numbers and lack of specific information will not be discussed here. These include Finns, Dutch, Italians, Austrians, Hungarians, and others.[56]

ETHNIC ORIGINS, CULTURAL DIVERSITY, AND INTEGRATION

Does great diversity still exist between ethnic stocks in American agriculture? To what extent has cultural integration occurred? What are the prospects?

The answers to these questions cannot be given without qualification. Nationwide systematic studies have not been made. Nevertheless, penetrating insights have been provided by scholars who have made detailed studies in various parts of the country.

Before proceeding further, we should define *cultural integration*. We may regard it as an organization or accommodation of culture elements into a working relationship or pattern which is considered to be "right" by the social system involved. It does not necessarily mean homogeneity.[57] Furthermore, a culture may be integrated even though it contains conflicting elements.[58] However, no culture is ever perfectly integrated because change is continuous.[59]

It seems obvious that much integration has occurred. For example, nearly all immigrants are citizens. Relatively few persist in using the original mother tongue rather than English, notable exceptions being the Pennsylvania Dutch, the Louisiana French, and

---

[55] Smith, *op. cit.*, pp. 236, 253, 255.

[56] See Bertrand, *op. cit.*; John I. Kolehmainen and George W. Hill, *Haven in the Woods: The Story of the Finns in Wisconsin*, Wisconsin State Historical Society, 1951; Brown and Roucek, eds., *op. cit.*; Schermerhorn, *op. cit.*

[57] See A. L. Kroeber, *Anthropology*, Harcourt Brace, 1948, pp. 286-287; J. L. Gillin and J. P. Gillin, *Cultural Sociology*, Macmillan, 1948, pp. 551-556.

[58] Ralph Linton, *The Study of Man*, Appleton-Century, 1936, p. 358.

[59] *Ibid.*, p. 357.

the Spanish Americans of the Southwest. As far as agricultural technology is concerned, integration is far advanced. Culture elements from diverse sources have been organized into workable patterns or sets of practices which are applied to major commercialized farm enterprises.

In the process of cultural integration, some of the agricultural folkways of the foreign groups have been adopted by others, but the more important change that has occurred has been the evolution of a new and common set of practices. In the commercial farming areas of the country, these have been influenced to a marked degree by the results of agricultural research and invention.

The influence of the dominant American culture in the agricultural practices of specific ethnic groups has been acknowledged by a number of students. Writing about the acculturation of Finns in northern Wisconsin, Hill has said; "New farm practices are being introduced into Brantwood, for example, by the few boys enrolled in the 'ag' course and the few immigrants who have enough intellectual curiosity to read agricultural bulletins."[60] Whetten and Green commented about a Finnish settlement in Connecticut, "Both informal mutual aid and the *talkoo* appear to be swiftly passing."[61] Leonard and Loomis indicated that some cultural changes were beginning to occur among the Spanish Americans in the locality of El Cerrito.[62]

Cultural integration of agricultural practices does not necessarily mean, however, that nationality and ethnic origins are of no consequence in farming localities. As Williams has correctly pointed out, subtle ethnic influences may persist for generations even after the distinctive ethnic culture has almost entirely disappeared.[63]

Marshall has taken issue with the assumption that the various nationality stocks have been fully integrated or amalgamated. He holds that, particularly in the Midwest, there is a mosaic of cultures in which, however, the original value and idea systems of particular nationality groups have been greatly modified. He feels

[60] Kolehmainen and Hill, *op. cit.*, p. 89.
[61] Nathan L. Whetten and Arnold W. Green, *Ethnic Group Relations in a Rural Area of Connecticut*, Storrs AES Bulletin 244, January, 1943, p. 38.
[62] Leonard and Loomis, *op. cit.*, p. 70.
[63] R. M. Williams, "Unity and Diversity in Modern America," *Social Forces*, October, 1957, pp. 1-8.

that most of the modifications are attributable to modern transportation and communication, although he concedes that to some extent it has been due to the fact that people of different ethnic backgrounds have lived adjacent to each other for 40 years or more.[64] Nelson also takes the view that ethnic differences are quite persistent in rural areas. He contrasts the rural situation with the apparent tendency for urban ethnic groups to lose their identity by the third generation.[65] He presents evidence of ethnocentrism from a study in Wright County, Minnesota; two-thirds of the sample adults had married persons of the same nationality stock. However, he also commented that there was little apparent difference in behavior between ethnic groups like the Finns, Germans, Swedes, French, English, Irish, and native Americans.[66]

Anastasio recently found evidence in a rural Washington community that ethnic ties continue to be significant among persons of Norwegian descent, although less important that previously. He reported: "Ethnic differences were once very important in Port Haven. While this situation is changing, the population is still predominantly Norwegian. . . . Port Haveners have acquired the reputation of being clannish, unfriendly, cold, and indifferent to anyone who is not Norwegian or at least Scandinavian. Many people today hold to this view. A careful analysis shows that, like many stereotypes, this is partly true and partly false."[67]

Further cultural integration and the eventual disappearance of ethnic origins as a factor of great significance in social relationships in rural America may be anticipated. However, it is likely that certain racial or large ethnic stocks such as the Louisiana French, the Pennsylvania Dutch, and the Spanish Americans and small ethnoreligious groups which operate closed social systems such as the Hutterites, the Amish, and the Dunkards will persist for an indefinite period.[68]

[64] Douglas Marshall, "Nationality and the Emerging Culture," *Rural Sociology*, March, 1947, pp. 40-47.
[65] Lowry Nelson, *Rural Sociology*, American Book, 1952, p. 192.
[66] *Ibid.*, p. 198.
[67] Angelo Anastasio, *Port Haven, A Changing Northwestern Community*, Washington AES Bulletin 616, May, 1960, pp. 14-16.
[68] See Chapter 12 for a discussion of assimilation.

It is clear from the foregoing discussion that a considerable degree of cultural integration has occurred in both rural and urban sections of the U.S. Similar results have been achieved in the English-speaking portions of Canada. In both cases, the major values appear to have been derived from the Christian ethics common to all the countries of Western Europe.

Common values and forms of social organization of ethnic origin have generally been developed from the English heritage. Australia, New Zealand, and English-speaking areas of Canada have had a similar experience. This does not appear to be true of French Canada, of India, or of many other parts of the former British Empire. The reasons for these differences are complex and not fully understood. The subject is discussed at greater length in the section on assimilation which is closely related to the subject of cultural integration.

QUESTIONS FOR FURTHER STUDY AND DISCUSSION

1. Discuss the concept of cultural integration. Describe the situation with respect to ethnic diversity and integration in a rural locality with which you are familiar.
2. Assume that you are an agricultural agent in a county which contains a "cultural island" of farm people of some particular nationality stock. Tell how you would proceed in your attempt to gain the confidence and cooperation of these people in your 4-H Club program.
3. Many of the farms of the northern United States were settled by immigrants from northern European countries. How do you account for the fact that there are no large areas in the North populated by people who speak their original mother tongue as do the French Canadians?
4. Which ethnic stocks were most important in terms of their influence on current American patterns of rural life? Explain the basis of your rankings.
5. Kolb and Brunner have pointed out that American forms of local government have persisted. How do you account for this in view of the large number of foreign-born settlers?
6. How do you account for the persistence of ethnic orientations among the Pennsylvania Dutch, the Louisiana French, and the Spanish Americans?

SELECTED REFERENCES

Brown, F. J., and J. S. Roucek, eds., *One America*, 3rd ed., Prentice-Hall, 1952.

Schermerhorn, R. A., *These Our People*, Heath, 1949.

Warner, W. L., and Leo Srole, *The Social Systems of American Ethnic Groups*, Yale University Press, 1945.

6

Patterns of Settlement

The farm people of a highly industrialized country like the United States may seem emancipated from the bonds of locality and hence unaffected by the physical patterns of settlement. In many ways this is true. Due to rapid communications systems the American farmer is in constant touch with national and international events; the automobile and the airplane and other transportation facilities make it possible for him to carry on business and social relationships on a face to face basis with people in far places.

But in spite of all these improvements, the physical location of the farm buildings in relation to the farm and to the shopping center is still important. Tractors do not travel so fast as automobiles. Heavy farm products cost time and money to transport. Animals do not move any faster on their own legs than they ever did. And it takes time to go to town even in a fast car on good-hard surfaced roads. These problems are accentuated where severe winters are common.

In the less developed areas of the world where few farmers have motorized transport and depend instead on their own feet or on slow animals to get from place to place, the settlement pattern has more significance yet. Even in an Indian or Pakistani village, however, social distance is of greater importance than physical distance in regulating relationships between people.

Settlement patterns of concern in agriculture include not only the ways in which farm dwellings are arranged on the face of the land but also the physical relationship of farms to larger aggregations of population, because many of the products of farms are consumed in towns and cities; they in turn supply farmers and their families with most of the manufactured products they use. Furthermore, towns and cities are increasingly important as sources

111

of intellectual stimulation and social contact for farmers. Finally, the city is spilling over into the country so that urban workers may live next to full-time farmers.

Settlement patterns are traditional in origin and tend to change slowly because of the relative durability of the materials used in buildings and other structures. Consequently, the patterns of settlement are not always clearly preceived to be an aspect of culture. The relationship of settlement forms to forms of social organization can be seen better by considering the changing history of settlement patterns in a given area of land over a long period. Prior to the coming of the white man, for example, North America was inhabited by nomadic Indian tribes most of which had no fixed abode but moved from place to place within a general area living in tents or other temporary structures. The current pattern of dispersed farmsteads surrounding a trade center found in most rural parts of the United States was established at the time of initial settlement and has been changed little since except as urban centers, military reservations, and irrigation projects have influenced the situation. In pre-Communist eastern Europe and in much of Asia including India and Pakistan the prevalent rural settlement pattern is the agricultural village rather than the dispersed farmstead of western Europe and England as well as most of the United States.[1] The Communist Chinese are evidently disrupting the traditional village system, but as yet we have little concrete information about the extent of the change.[2]

The pattern of settlement is never completely fixed; as noted above, changes tend to occur gradually and the pattern established at the time of initial settlement usually persists for a considerable length of time. Perhaps the most important contemporary change in American settlement patterns is the infiltration of rural residents and part-time farmers into areas which once were populated only by full-time farmers. Another trend of some significance is farming land but not residing on it.[3]

[1] See P. A. Sorokin, C. C. Zimmerman, and C. J. Galpin, A Systematic Source Book in Rural Sociology, University of Minnesota Press, 1930, I, pp. 266, 273.

[2] John Strohm, "An American in Red China," Look, April 28, 1959.

[3] See J. C. Belcher, "The Nonresident Farmer in the New Rural Society," Rural Sociology, June, 1954, pp. 121-136.

MAJOR FORMS OF RURAL SETTLEMENT

More farmers live in agricultural villages than in any other type of settlement.[4] It is the dominant form in northern and eastern France, southern Belgium, most of Germany, Denmark, southern Sweden, southern Italy and Sicily, India and Pakistan, Java, Japan, and Korea, and was predominant in pre-Communist Russia and China.[5]

The dispersed dwelling, where the farm operator and his family live on the farm, is most common in North America. It is also the principal type of settlement in many other parts of the world, including Great Britain, about two-thirds of France, areas in Germany, Belgium and the Netherlands, the Po Valley of Italy, in Finland, in northern Sweden and Norway, and in some parts of Central and South America.[6]

The collective farm is a socialistic or communistic form of settlement found principally in Communist Russia and China. Some collective settlements are also found, however, in the U.S. and other countries; most of these are commonal religious groups like the Amanas in Iowa, the Hutterites in South Dakota, and the Dukhobors in Canada.[7]

Other settlement forms of local importance in certain parts of the world are the large farm, the part-time farm, the rural residence, and the nomadic camp.

SETTLEMENT PATTERNS IN THE UNITED STATES

The early American colonists from England brought with them, among other things, the two basic land settlement patterns then existing in England—the agricultural village and the manorial or plantation system. The agricultural village became the dominant pattern of settlement in New England and the plantation system in the Southeast.

[4] T. Lynn Smith, *The Sociology of Rural Life*, 3rd ed., Harper, 1953, p. 201.
[5] Sorokin, Zimmerman, and Galpin, *op. cit.*, p. 263.
[6] *Ibid.*
[7] See Lowry Nelson, *Rural Sociology*, 2nd ed., American Book, 1955, pp. 63-64.

The colonists who settled in New England were recruited principally from the peasant and yeoman classes and came, in most cases, directly from agricultural villages, and it was natural for them to establish in the new world the form of settlement with which they were familiar in the old. The proprietors of the colonies encouraged this type of settlement for reasons of defense and social control and probably because tradition and familiarity led them to consider it the right form. Agricultural villages were established as the basic pattern of settlement throughout New England and to some extent in New York and New Jersey and in the early colonization of Pennsylvania.

Inasmuch as the agriculture of the northern half of the United States has been greatly influenced by the culture patterns of the original New England settlers, we may well question why the initial village pattern of settlement was not perpetuated and extended; with the exception of New England and the Mormon settlements in Utah and Idaho, the pattern of the isolated farmstead served by one or more trade centers dominates the entire northern United States. The answer seems to be that the agricultural village did not prove to be well suited to North America. The village had ceased to be a compelling pattern some time before the settlement of the land beyond the Atlantic seaboard began; there are indications that the system of agricultural villages was not entirely successful or universal even in the New England area.[8]

It is not possible to identify all the diverse factors that were involved in the breakdown of the pattern, but it seems highly probable that the major influences were (1) the requirements of farm enterprises involving daily care of domestic animals, and (2) the ease of land acquisition which promoted larger holdings than could be efficiently managed from a village residence at that time.

Nelson has attributed great importance to the nature of the land settlement laws established by Congress.[9] The first law he cites was the rectangular survey law of 1785 which provided for division of land into townships consisting of 36 sections of 1 square mile each which were in turn subdivided into quarter-sections of

[8] William B. Weeden, *Economic and Social History of New England, 1620-1789*, Houghton Mifflin, 1890, p. 73.
[9] Lowry Nelson, *op. cit.*, p. 51.

160 acres each, thereby establishing a square pattern. The second was the requirement made by the Pre-emption Act of 1841 that a settler had to establish residence on the land as a prerequisite to obtaining title or securing a patent.

It seems reasonable to suppose that these laws had considerable influence on the settlement which occurred after their enactment, but developments which had occurred previously had unquestionably taken the direction of the isolated farmstead pattern of settlement. It is doubtful whether the rectangular system of survey would have been adopted had there been strong public sentiment for the preservation of the village plan of settlement.

The Plantation

The leaders in the settlement of Virginia and the other southern colonies were English aristocrats or oriented toward their values. They were accustomed to the management of large estates, had considerable capital, and were able to obtain large grants of land on which they established plantations. These holdings were relatively self-contained with sufficient specialized manpower to perform the necessary occupational roles involved in producing and processing cotton and tobacco for sale as well as food and clothing for use on the plantation. Once established, the plantation system flourished and thrived, utilizing first indentured servants and later Negro slaves as the source of manpower.[10] Smith has pointed out, however, that the plantation had a village form of settlement with its buildings concentrated in one area. He also observes that there were some agricultural villages in North Carolina, South Carolina, and Georgia during colonial times.[11]

Although the plantation system was of great importance in the social and economic life of the old south, it was not by any means the only system. The "poor whites" established isolated farmsteads on the poorer land. Smith feels that these small farmers have made a much larger contribution to the settlement and development of the South than they have ordinarily been given credit for doing,[12] one reason being that the many descendents of their large families

[10] N. L. Sims, *Elements of Rural Sociology*, 3rd ed., Crowell, 1940, pp. 54-55.
[11] Smith, *op cit.*, p. 230.
[12] *Ibid.*, pp. 56-59.

have constituted a majority of rural white people in the South.

The plantation system faced a major crisis after the conclusion of the Civil War and the subsequent emancipation of the slaves, but a new type of sharecropping arrangement maintained the plantation in substantially the same manner as before. This accommodation left the authority of the planter much less absolute than previously, the bond being primarily economic rather than legal, as was previously the case under the system of slavery.

A substantial number of plantations are found at the present time in various sections of the South.[13] These are interspersed with isolated farmsteads operated by small holders, and in some sections, notably Louisiana and the Southwest, a few agricultural villages are to be found. The plantation as a social system will be discussed in Chapter 15.

THE ISOLATED FARMSTEAD AND THE FARM TRADE CENTER

The typical pattern of agricultural settlement in the United States involves isolated farmsteads surrounding a trade center. The family lives on its own farm in a house ordinarily surrounded by outbuildings including the barn, machinery shed, chicken houses, or other structures as required by the type of farm enterprise. In very large areas of the country, particularly in the agricultural Middle West, isolated farmsteads are laid out in a rectangle. In other sections, like the Pacific Northwest, where the topography is such that it is not possible to lay out roads along a rectangular plan, isolated farmsteads are nevertheless to be found but their boundaries are not necessarily rectangular and roads tend to follow the water courses and other dominant features of the terrain.

Most American farm trade centers were established prior to the advent of the automobile and improved roads. Consequently, in areas of good land and concentrated agricultural settlement, trade centers were usually only 8 to 10 miles apart so as to be readily accessible to farmers whose principal means of transportation were horse-drawn vehicles. Many of the smaller centers have disappeared since good roads and automobiles have made it possible for farmers to travel greater distances for goods and services.

[13] *Ibid.*, p. 308.

Fig. 5.   Scattered Farmsteads and Trade Centers in Walworth County, Wisconsin. (C. J. Galpin, *The Social Anatomy of an Agricultural Community*, Wisconsin AES Bulletin 34, 1915.)

These trade centers perform several important functions to farmers who live on dispersed holdings. First, they serve as primary markets for farm products. Second, they supply goods which the farmers need. Third, the professional people and artisans who provide many social services required by the farm population make their homes in the trade centers. Fourth, the centers provide convenient meeting places for farm organizations.

An important feature of the American pattern of dispersed settlement is the larger centers to which the primary trade center is itself subsidiary and which in turn maintain trade relationships with regional and national metropolitan centers. It is true, of course, that a farmer can and does maintain independent business and social relationships with firms and individuals in large cities.

The prosperity of an agricultural trade center is largely dependent on the prosperity of the farmers who live in its territory and on the extent to which they channel their purchases and sales through the merchants and service agencies in the center. Many smaller centers have lost trade to larger centers. Lack of patronage, if long continued, brings about business failures and eventual decay of the economic services of the center.

Various writers have commented on the existence of conflicts and misunderstandings between farmers and townspeople. These have been accentuated in some areas by the system which erects a legal barrier at the city limits and provides a separate legal existence for the town in which the farmer has no voice. In many parts of the country consolidated school districts have removed one of the major sources of town-country misunderstanding.[14] They provide an opportunity for both farmers and villagers to participate in the management of schools and bring their children into daily contact with one another.

Brunner found that during the decade of the 1940s hamlets with a population of less than 250 continued to decline in numbers as did villages with less than 1000 located in nonsuburban areas in the Midwest. Small villages between 250 and 1000, however, tended to be stable, registering relatively little gain or loss.[15]

Advantages and Disadvantages of Dispersed Farmsteads

The isolated farmstead is not without advantages. Upon it the farm family is close to its work, which means there is relatively little loss of time in getting from the house to the fields. This facilitates caring for livestock and poultry, and makes it possible for the farmer to keep his machinery relatively close to his house where he can protect it more readily. The physical isolation of the farm family is not necessarily a disadvantage in all respects, for it may promote

[14] See Paul H. Landis, *Rural Life in Process*, 2nd ed., McGraw-Hill, 1948, pp. 24-27; John H. Kolb and Edmund deS. Brunner, *A Study of Rural Society*, 4th ed., Houghton Mifflin, 1952, pp. 181-208.

[15] See Edmund deS. Brunner, "The Small Village: 1940-50," *Rural Sociology*, June, 1952, pp. 127-131.

closeness between various members of the family. Improved transportation allows farm people to maintain close social relationships with other farm people located at considerable distances and with nonfarm people as well. The consolidated schools established in many sections of the country make it possible for farm children to have substantially the same type of education as those who live in villages, towns, and cities. Children from dispersed farms who attend consolidated schools must of course spend some time commuting to and from these schools, though in many cases the time may not be greater than the time it takes town children to reach metropolitan schools.

Some of the supposed disadvantages of isolated settlement no longer exist, although they may have been real drawbacks during the days when the primary mode of transportation was the horse and buggy. The contemporary American farmer and his family usually are not socially isolated because of location. They maintain intimate interpersonal relationships with both farm and nonfarm people. Furthermore, they are as able as the city man to keep in touch with developments on the national and international scene through the mass media of the radio, television, and newspapers and magazines.

The disadvantages of the isolated farmstead are primarily social, and the greatest impact is on the social training of the preschool child. On the other hand, it is possible that a person who is reared on an isolated farm may develop more initiative than someone who lives in a group settlement, though independence in decision-making is more likely to be effected by the specific traditions of the family than by the physical form of settlement.

Both Nelson and Smith have argued that one of the disadvantages of the isolated form of farm settlement is that road costs are high.[16] This may be true in an underdeveloped country, but it should be pointed out in this connection that good roads are essential to permit access to the land if it is to be farmed with modern machinery.

AGRICULTURAL VILLAGES

As noted above, farm villages are common in many parts of the world, including Asia and parts of Europe, Africa, and South Amer-

---

[16] Nelson, *op. cit.*, p. 54; Smith, *op. cit.*, p. 222.

ica. In this form of settlement farmers' residences are clustered together rather than being situated on dispersed farms.

The principal agricultural village settlements in the United States
at the present time are those of the Mormons in Utah and Idaho, the
Spanish Americans in Texas and New Mexico, and the French Americans in Louisiana. A few New England villages also have maintained part of their original farm settlement layouts.

The New England Village

The typical colonial New England village had a compact form of
settlement. Houses and lots were owned by individuals with common fields outside the village. There was also an outlying tract of
undivided land which was used for pasture and woodland under
regulations set up by the town.[17]

The division of labor which accompanied this form of settlement
included herdsmen who had charge of cattle, livestock, and poultry
as they were pastured on the common land, and it was characterized
by intimate social and work relationships. During colonial times the
village was relatively self-sufficient in respect to food, clothing, and
shelter, being dependent upon trade only for essential commodities
which could not be produced in the locality.

The Mormon Village

The Mormons began settling in the intermountain West in 1847.
By this time the isolated farmstead was common in many parts of
the United States.

Nelson states that the main reason for their departure from the
prevalent pattern of settlement is to be found in their religious
ideology, which held among other things that a second coming of
the Savior was imminent and the city of Zion was to be rebuilt as
his headquarters during his reign on earth. This design was used
as the basic plan for all Mormon settlements.[18]

The initial plan of the Mormon agricultural village featured small
allotments with an equal distribution among the families of land and

[17] Anne B. Maclear, *Early New England Towns*, Columbia University Studies
in Economics, History, and Public Law, XXIX, No. 1, cited by Sims, *op. cit.*,
p. 56.
[18] See Lowry Nelson, *Some Social and Economic Features of American
Folk, Utah*, Brigham Young University Studies No. 4, 1933, pp. 9-10; and
The Mormon Village, University of Utah Press, 1952, chap. IX.

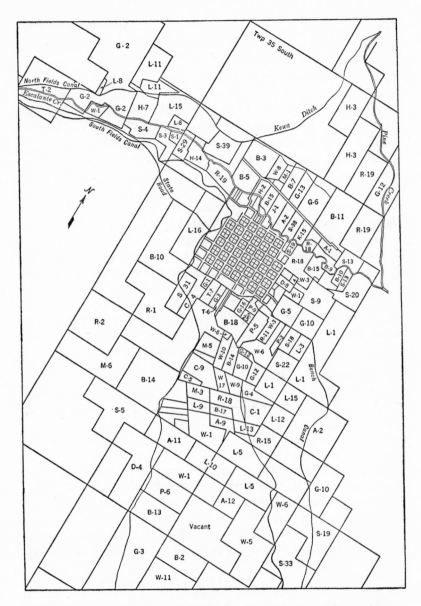

FIG. 6. Fragmentation of Holdings in a Mormon Village. (Lowry Nelson, *The Utah Farm Village of Ephraim*, Brigham Young University Studies 2, 1928.)

irrigation water. Nelson attributes this pattern of land allocation to an early Mormon doctrine of economic equality which engendered "a species of communism." He notes that ". . . the actual practice of this doctrine was attempted, but without great success and the institution was officially abandoned."[19] This initial land distribution has had a continuing effect on Mormon agriculture since the allotments were inadequate for economic farm operations and it was not always possible for a farmer to get adjacent tracts. This has led to inefficient farm layouts, some farmers owning widely separated tracts. Nelson cites an extreme case in Ephraim, Utah, where one farmer owned twelve different tracts only two of which were contiguous, and even these were separated by a railroad right-of-way.[20]

In the Mormon type of farm village, each family has about one and a quarter acres in the village on which the house and barn are built,[21] so that forage crops must be transported to the village and either the livestock must be kept in the village throughout the winter months or someone must drive out to the farms daily to feed and water them. Further, during the growing season a farmer must commute daily between his village home and his farm, an average distance of two miles. This illustrates very clearly some of the disadvantages of the agricultural village from the standpoint of the farm enterprise.

On the other hand, of course, it must be acknowledged that the close physical proximity of the villagers facilitates social interaction, which is particularly important in the social training of the children.

The Louisiana French Village

In the agricultural village of Louisiana, farmsteads are concentrated along a road, riverfront, or lakefront with the farming lands in long strips behind them. Smith, who has studied this form of settlement extensively, attributes its presence in the United States principally to French culture.[22] In southern Louisiana, which Bertrand calls French Louisiana,[23] the line village is the principal type

---

[19] Nelson, *Some Social and Economic Features, op. cit.*, p. 26.

[20] Lowry Nelson, *The Utah Farm Village of Ephraim*, Brigham Young University Studies No. 2, 1928; and *The Mormon Village, op. cit.*, chaps. VI, VIII.

[21] Nelson, *Rural Sociology, op. cit.*, p. 59.

[22] See Smith, *op. cit.*, pp. 235-237.

[23] See A. L. Bertrand, *The Many Louisianas, Rural Social Areas and Culture Islands*, Louisiana AES Bulletin 496, June, 1955.

of settlement. Smith notes, however, that line villages have been established by other ethnic groups as well as the French, though such settlements are evidently not numerous.[24]

Spanish American Villages

A comparison of a plot of a village in New Mexico with villages in certain South American and Latin American countries led Smith to the conclusion that there was a strong resemblance between these settlements.[25] This resemblance is unquestionably due to the common cultural origin of the original Spanish settlers.

Leonard and Loomis have described the structure of one such agricultural village located in New Mexico.

The physical structure of the community is also a significant factor in the integration and stability of the village. The houses are compactly located to form the perimeter of a circle, with barns and corrals in the rear. Although such an arrangement interferes with efficient farming, it greatly facilitates living. The house is farther from fields and pastures but is closer to school, church, and neighbors. Such proximity of living has developed a sociability and an integration of group life that would be difficult, if not impossible, to duplicate in any other type of arrangement. Seldom does a day pass when a farmer does not converse with a number of his neighbors. Children are seen playing together, after the chores are done, both night and morning. Childhood associations are almost as close between playmates as between members of the same family. They grow up to know each other almost as well as if they had been reared under the same roof.[26]

PROSPECTS FOR CHANGE IN SETTLEMENT PATTERNS

Once established, settlement patterns are very persistent, but it is clear from a review of history that changes do occur. In Communist countries, changes have been brought about by state action. In the USSR, both agricultural villages and dispersed family farms have largely been superseded by agricultural collectives. At present, at-

[24] See Smith, *op. cit.*, pp. 236-237.
[25] *Ibid.*, p. 233.
[26] Olen Leonard and C. P. Loomis, *Culture of a Contemporary Rural Community: El Cerrito, New Mexico*, U.S. Department of Agriculture, Bureau of Agricultural Economics, Rural Life Studies No. 1, November, 1941, p. 8.

tempts are being made to replace the Chinese village with the commune.

In the United States the form of rural settlement is in the process of changing in areas adjacent to population centers. Hundreds of thousands of full- and part-time urban workers now live in the country, some operating farms and others simply residing on rural acreages because of a preference for rural living. Other changes have taken place as a result of changes in type of farming or because of the encroachment of nonfarm activities such as military reservations, recreational facilities, superhighways, and atomic energy installations.

The results of governmental efforts to influence settlement patterns in the Columbia Basin Irrigation Project are interesting as a case study of the limited potential influence of conscious governmental planning which runs counter to business interests in the U.S.

The Columbia Basin Irrigation Project is located in central Washington and covers approximately 600,000 acres of land which previously was very sparsely populated because of the small rainfall in the area.

This project was developed under the supervision of the Bureau of Reclamation of the United States Department of Interior. In establishing farm units the Bureau was guided by the basic legislation of the Reclamation Act which limited the number of acres a family could own although no comparable limitation was placed on the number of acres that could be operated. The farm units were established largely on the basis of the recommendations of agricultural economists. Prior to settlement the Bureau of Reclamation owned approximately 20 percent of the land area; the remainder was privately owned. After water was brought to the land, however, the original owners were required to divest themselves of all but 160 acres. Federal legislation enacted in 1957 increased the number of acres to conform to experience in the area which indicated that larger-sized farms were essential for efficient farm operations.

The establishment of this irrigation project with approximately 5000 farm units controlled by a central planning organization appeared to present a splendid opportunity for the introduction of settlement patterns which would be both economically efficient and sociologically sound. The Bureau of Reclamation enlisted the aid of the State College of Washington and other agencies including the United States Department of Agriculture and conscientiously sought information upon which to base such plans. Insofar as the farms themselves are concerned, the settlement pattern in the Columbia Basin conforms reasonably well to the plans established by the Bureau. Most of the farmsteads are located along the highways and are sufficiently close together so that community water systems have been established in many areas of the Basin. This, of course, is in part a matter of economic necessity since adequate drinking water was not available except from deep wells which are expensive.

The Bureau of Reclamation established a community development division which investigated the pattern of town-country relationships and service and trade centers in a number of roughly comparable irrigation areas including the Yakima valley and sections of Idaho, Montana, and Wyoming. On the basis of these studies,[27] the Bureau concluded that at least 1000 farm families were required for adequate support for the most desirable type of local shopping center, although it was recognized that a smaller number might be reasonably satisfactory if distance or other considerations limited the trade area. The Bureau report also considered the spacing which would be desirable for trade centers in the Columbia Basin area. Land was set aside for the establishment of at least two entirely new trade centers which were then laid out by the Bureau, but the opposition of merchants in established trade centers forced the Bureau to abandon its plans. Consequently, there has been an expansion of the facilities of already existing centers, some of which were very small at the time active irrigation development commenced.

The experience of the Bureau of Reclamation in the Columbia Basin Project and earlier experiences of the Resettlement Administration indicate that at least as far as the United States of America is concerned, the ability of governmental agencies to establish planned communities involving new patterns of settlement is very limited. It appears that planned communities can expect little support except under unusual circumstances such as those involved in the location

[27] See Columbia Basin Project, Washington, *Towns and Villages,* Joint Investigations, Problem No. 18, U.S. Dept. of Interior, Bureau of Reclamation, Boise, Idaho, June, 1947, pp. 121-122.

of residence and service centers for workers at atomic plants and on military reservations. A successful settlement of this type is found at Richland, Washington, where the families of workers at the Hanford atomic energy plant are located.

QUESTIONS FOR FURTHER STUDY AND DISCUSSION

1. Discuss the Mormon form of settlement, indicating the importance of religious culture. What are the advantages and disadvantages of this form of settlement at present? (See Lowry Nelson, *Rural Sociology,* Chapter 4.)
2. Discuss the history of collective settlements in the U.S. Why has this form of settlement failed to attract many adherents? (See Nelson, *ibid.*)
3. Discuss the importance of highway development to rural-urban patterns of settlement in the U.S. (See Loomis and Beegle, *Rural Social Systems,* Chapter 7.)
4. Discuss the advantages and disadvantages of dispersed versus concentrated settlement.

SELECTED REFERENCES

Loomis, C. P., and J. A. Beegle, *Rural Social Systems,* Prentice-Hall, 1950.
Nelson, Lowry, *The Mormon Village,* University of Utah Press, 1952.
Nelson, Lowry, *Rural Sociology,* 2nd ed., American Book, 1954.
Sims, N. L., *Elements of Rural Sociology,* Crowell, 1946.
Smith, T. Lynn, *The Sociology of Rural Life,* 3rd ed., Harper, 1953.
Sorokin, P. A., C. C. Zimmerman, and C. J. Galpin, *A Systematic Source Book in Rural Sociology,* University of Minnesota Press, 1930, vol. I.

7

Regional Patterns of Agriculture

All who are familiar with agriculture are aware of the fact that there are variations in the dominant type of agricultural enterprise from one geographic area to another. Particular methods of cultivation may be more effective in one area than another. Tropical agriculture differs markedly from that practiced in the far north, for the obvious reason that climatic conditions and soils are major limiting factors. Crops adapted to warm humid regions either cannot be grown at all or do not do well in the arid regions with short growing seasons. Cotton, for example, cannot successfully be produced in the northern plains, and fruits and vegetables require special soils and climate which may be found in optimum combination only in specific geographic regions or areas.

In spite of their importance, however, it seems correct to regard physical factors predominantly as negative or limiting. In some cases these limits preclude successful agriculture. Perpetual ice and snow, barren rocks, steep terrain, desert conditions, marshes, excessive salts, and excessive heat are all conditions inhospitable to agriculture. On the other hand, most geographic areas which are arable can be farmed in more than one way. Man is the dynamic factor, and it is culture which provides him with the methods, social organization, tools, and ideas which enable him to subjugate the land. The American Indians had a predominantly hunting and fishing culture, for example, and with the exception of a few tribes, mostly in the southwest, were not able to utilize for agricultural purposes the farm lands of the North American continent which now yield such bountiful crops.

PHYSIOGRAPHIC REGIONS

The continental United States may be divided broadly into a few great physiographic regions[1] (Fig. 7). It should be understood that great variations in soil, topography, and climatic conditions may exist that limit agricultural operations from one locality to another within a region.

Along the Atlantic seaboard from New York southward to northern Florida is a coastal region between the foothills of the Appalachian highlands and the Atlantic Ocean sometimes known as the Atlantic plain. Some productive farms are found in this area, but in many places drainage is poor and large areas are occupied by swamps and marshes, pine barrens, and other wastelands.

The Atlantic coastal plain merges with the Gulf coastal plain. This region includes east Texas, Louisiana, southern Arkansas, Mississippi, part of Tennessee, southern Alabama, southwestern Georgia, and nearly all of Florida. It has a warm, humid climate and the land is fairly level. This region includes most of the Cotton Belt, fast-growing forests of southern pine, sugar cane, rice, and various types of citrus fruits. In recent years livestock production has become important in some sections.

The Appalachian Mountain region reaches from Maine southwestward to northern Georgia and Alabama. The area contains a number of fertile valleys including the Lehigh, the Lebanon, the Cumberland, and the Shenandoah as well as the valley of eastern Tennessee. Variations in growing seasons are, of course, very great from the southern extremity of the Appalachians with a growing season of from 180 to 210 days to northern Maine which has less than 90 days. The major types of farming include dairying, found principally in New York, New Hampshire, and eastern Pennsylvania, potatoes in Aroostook County, Maine, and a substantial number of subsistence farms.

The central plains and the Great Plains comprise a great region which embraces most of the central section of the United States from the Appalachian Mountain region to the Rocky Mountains. It extends from Texas to Montana, North Dakota, and Minnesota and from

[1] See "The USA, Its Land, Its People, Its Industries," in *Compton's Pictured Encyclopedia,* Compton, 1956, pp. 287-387.

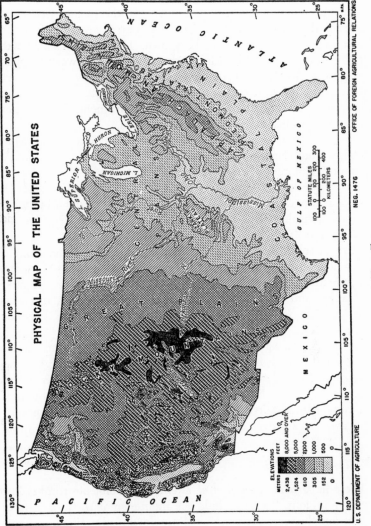

PHYSICAL MAP OF THE UNITED STATES

FIG. 7.

U. S. DEPARTMENT OF AGRICULTURE

OFFICE OF FOREIGN AGRICULTURAL RELATIONS

NEG. 1476

Wyoming and Montana eastward to Ohio. The Black Hills and the Ozark-Ouachita Mountains are the only important mountains within this vast area. The rainfall is quite heavy in the eastern plains and gradually decreases westward. This, of course, greatly affects the type of vegetation which can be grown. The eastern plains were initially heavily forested with deciduous trees. The western plains were mostly treeless except along the water courses. The north central plains are now the location of the Corn Belt. North of this is an important dairying area. The western plains include wheat areas and some portions of the range livestock area.

West of the Great Plains is a large mountainous area which stretches from Canada to Mexico extending from western Montana, Wyoming, Colorado, New Mexico, and east and west Texas on its eastern border and the Cascades and Sierra Nevadas in the west. The mountain ranges are interspersed with plateaus and basins which support a considerable agriculture. They include many large livestock ranches, the fruit areas of Washington, the Palouse wheat-pea country in southeastern Washington, the Columbia Basin irrigated area which produces vegetables, sugar beets, alfalfa, and other crops, the irrigated areas of Idaho and Utah which produce potatoes, vegetables, and sugar beets, and irrigated portions of Arizona and New Mexico which produce citrus fruits, cotton, and various specialty crops.

The Pacific Coast stretches from British Columbia southward to Mexico and includes the coastal areas of Washington, Oregon, and California. Near the ocean is the coast range. East of this are the Cascade and Sierra Nevada ranges. Rainfall is variable and agriculture ranges from dairying and vegetables in western Washington to extensive citrus groves and specialty crops in California.

CULTURE AREAS

There have been a number of attempts to delineate rural culture areas or regions. These include the monumental work of Howard Odum and his associates who delineated and described six major regions (the Southeast, the Northeast, the Middle States, the Northwest, the Southwest, and the Far West) and the work of A. R. Mangus and his associates in outlining rural cultural regions. In addition there have been attempts to establish rural social subareas or culture areas by Lively and Almack in Ohio and by Lively and others in Missouri. Bertrand has also defined rural cultural areas in Louisiana.[2]

There is no doubt that it may be useful for certain purposes to delineate regional patterns where these exist. The sweeping criticism of the culture area concept by Sorokin, Zimmerman, and Galpin that "any attempt to apply the concept to relatively complex societies is entirely hopeless and useless"[3] is difficult to defend. Judgment of usefulness cannot be rendered in the abstract but must be made in connection with specific ventures. However, investigation of the problems involved in identifying culture areas by the use of statistical indices has convinced the writer that broad so-called culture areas or regions of the type defined by Odum and Mangus have limited utility because of the great heterogeneity existing within the boundaries.[4] For the purpose at hand of examining regional patterns in agriculture, the regional distribution of major types of farming seems to be of greater value.[5]

REGIONAL DISTRIBUTION OF MAJOR TYPES OF FARMING IN THE UNITED STATES[6]

Within American agriculture today there are distinct regions or area concentrations of certain types of farming. These have been mapped by the U.S. Department of Agriculture (Fig. 8). The boundaries of some of these concentrations are established by

[2] A. L. Bertrand, *The Many Louisianas, Rural Social Areas and Culture Islands,* Louisiana AES Bulletin 496, June, 1955.

[3] P. A. Sorokin, C. C. Zimmerman and C. J. Galpin, *A Systematic Source Book in Rural Sociology,* University of Minnesota Press, 1931, II, 378, n. 79.

[4] W. L. Slocum, *Ethnic Stocks as Culture Types in Rural Wisconsin,* unpublished Ph.D. thesis, University of Wisconsin, 1940.

[5] It is true that Mangus used regional-type farming data as one of the components of his definitions of rural cultural regions. Nevertheless, his rural culture regions of the United States and the regional distribution of types of farming do not correspond to any great degree. There is no simple explanation for the differences. This is not to say that the rural culture regions of Mangus have no utility but only that they do not seem particularly valuable for the present purpose.

[6] Much of the factual information presented in this discussion has been drawn from Carl C. Taylor *et. al., Rural Life in the United States,* Knopf, 1949, part IV, "Rural Regions."

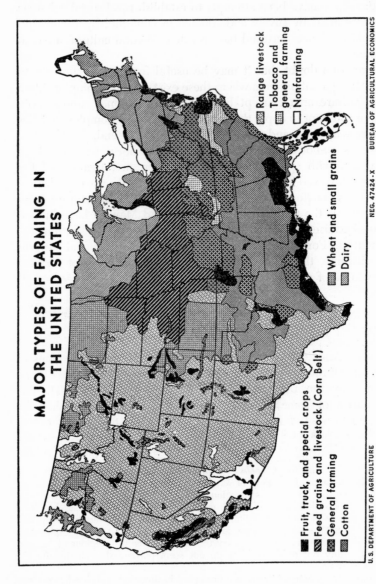

MAJOR TYPES OF FARMING IN THE UNITED STATES

Legend:
- Fruit, truck, and special crops
- Feed grains and livestock (Corn Belt)
- General farming
- Cotton
- Wheat and small grains
- Dairy
- Range livestock
- Tobacco and general farming
- Nonfarming

U. S. DEPARTMENT OF AGRICULTURE NEG. 47424-X BUREAU OF AGRICULTURAL ECONOMICS

FIG. 8.

topographic features, soil, or climate, most often separated by zones of transition rather than sharp boundaries. The presence of a specific type of agriculture in a country and the area concentration of its use may be regarded as predominantly due to physical factors, culture, history, and social organization. The agriculture practiced in irrigation projects, for example, requires a special type of social organization because of the great cost involved in building dams, storage facilities, and distribution networks; the technique of irrigation farming can be regarded as an aspect of culture.

The primary sociological significance of area concentrations of types of farming is the fact that within these major types the social influence of the organization of farm work is roughly similar. It should not be overlooked, however, that within all of the types there are local variations of considerable magnitude, some due to physical factors, others to unique historical events, and still others to proximity of markets or other economic considerations. In addition, there are, of course, substantial organizational differences from farm to farm in a given type of area. For example, dairy farms within a dairy area may range from simple nonmechanized operations where the cows are milked by hand to modern automated establishments with milking parlors and machines from which the milk is piped to central cooling tanks from which in turn it is collected in glass-lined tank trucks and transported to a central processing plant. Furthermore, not all farmers in the dairy areas are dairy farmers. Some raise vegetables and others grain, and still others are part-time or subsistence farmers.

The major types of agriculture which display distinctive area concentrations within the United States are corn, cotton, dairying, wheat, livestock ranching, vegetables and other specialty crops like citrus fruits, and the general and self-sufficing type of farming. The significance of these categories in terms of the organization of daily work and the influence of such patterns on the social relationships of the farmer and his family are of particular interest in this book. As we consider these matters, we should not lose sight of the fact that, in this aspect of human life as in all others in modern transitional society, substantial changes are under way. Furthermore, other types of agriculture such as the production of tobacco, poultry, mink, or rabbits may be of great importance in particular localities.

THE CORN BELT

The Corn Belt is a vast area consisting of 469 counties which lie within the boundaries of eleven states—Ohio, Indiana, Illinois, Iowa, Michigan, Wisconsin, Minnesota, South Dakota, Nebraska, Kansas, and Missouri, and includes approximately 900,000 farms, most of which are family-sized and family-operated. The most productive part of the Corn Belt has the heaviest concentration of the typical corn-hog farm enterprise; this is to be found in Iowa, Illinois, Ohio, and Indiana.

Corn Belt farms generally have fertile soil and reasonably dependable rainfall. Coupled with a favorable growing season this provides a combination of physical conditions which is conducive to the production of corn. The area has not, of course, always been used for this purpose; the native American Indians in the area did not practice agriculture.

The seasonal pattern of work on the typical Corn Belt farm is dictated to a considerable extent by seasonal variations in climate. Thus, during the winter while the ground is covered with ice and snow, emphasis is upon the feeding of livestock. Little or no field work is possible, and traditionally winter is the time of maximum social activity among the Corn Belt farmers. With the coming of spring, attention is given to the preparation of the fields and seeding of crops. During the early summer comes haying and cultivation of the growing corn to control weeds and conserve moisture. In late summer there is a period of slack activity after the small grain harvest and prior to the corn harvest. In the fall the corn is gathered and certain crops are seeded. Although some seasons are busier than others, the Corn Belt farmer who raises livestock has a year-round seven-day week—animals must be cared for on Sunday as well as on other days.

In earlier times the daily rhythm of work on a Corn Belt farm was tied to a considerable extent to the capabilities and requirements of the livestock. During the rush seasons, the farmer and his family were out of bed early, perhaps by 5 or 6 A.M. First came the chores, then breakfast, after which the farmer would harness the horses and go to the fields. At noon there would be a break of a couple of hours, primarily to rest the horses, after which there was more field work until 5 or 6 P.M. Then came more chores and supper. This schedule has, of course, been greatly modified with increasing mechanization. During the rush season some farmers operate their machinery on a 24-hour basis. The working day, while still somewhat longer than that of a factory worker, is much shorter than it was a generation ago, and because of good all-weather roads and dependable automobiles, Corn Belt farmers are able to participate more readily in groups and events which are of concern to them.

Farmers of the Corn Belt are relatively prosperous in relation to their agricultural colleagues elsewhere. This has always been true. However, their prosperity has been achieved by careful management and unremitting toil rather than as a gratuitous result of geographic factors. Perhaps more than most other American farmers they have been caught in the "cost-price squeeze," a term used to describe the fact that the prices of manufactured products keep rising but the prices of farm products do not keep pace, because their major source of income is not corn but meat, which has never had government price supports as corn has had from time to time. This unrelenting economic pressure has doubtless contributed to the Corn Belt farmer's constant search for more productive crops and livestock and for more efficient farming practices. At any rate, the agricultural practices of Corn Belt farmers have undergone marked changes, and the changes are continuing. Such great diversity exists that it is hardly possible to describe a typical corn-hog operation. The range in farm organization is from low mechanization to intensive automation, from one-man farms to virtual agricultural factories.

Taylor has given an interesting description, drawn partly from personal experience, of farming operations and organization in the Corn Belt of 20 to 30 years ago. The farm family is pictured as a closely knit, cooperative, extremely industrious work group directed in its activities by the husband-father. The daily round of activities was related to the requirements of farm animals and to the exigencies of the seasons.[7]

The evolution of agriculture in the Corn Belt shows clearly the influences of culture and social organization. During Indian times, as noted earlier, little agriculture there was. The early white settlers were general farmers who farmed mainly for subsistence with wheat

[7] Taylor *et al., op. cit.,* p. 367.

and some livestock as principal sources of cash income. Corn became established around the middle of the nineteenth century. Associated with corn is the raising and finishing of meat animals, especially hogs and beef cattle. This is still the basic agricultural pattern. There have been technical improvements, however, which constitute a virtual agricultural revolution. Mechanization, the production of hybrid corn, heavy use of fertilizers, and the introduction of other farm chemicals are some of the more dramatic aspects of these changes.

Through all of these changes the family farm has remained the predominant form of farm organization. At present on most Corn Belt farms the operator constitutes the main labor force, his activities being supplemented by unpaid family help and from time to time by paid farm laborers.

Great changes have also been taking place in the social systems and associated culture in which the Corn Belt farmer and his family participate. The nature of his social life has obviously been greatly affected by urbanization in the region. Improved roads and better communication facilities have brought him into touch with urban markets and shopping centers. Many great cities lie either in the Corn Belt or on its margins, among them Chicago, Omaha, Indianapolis, Des Moines, Sioux City, Minneapolis and St. Paul, St. Louis, and Kansas City.

In many Corn Belt localities the distinctive open-country church and the one-room school have been superseded by village churches and consolidated schools. The open-country neighborhood as a typical and ubiquitous informal social system has lost ground to the town-country community and to the many interest groups which have been organized to achieve special purposes.

While the Corn Belt farmer may have lost his keen sense of identification with local issues and interests to some extent, he has at the same time been drawn increasingly into broader, even international, spheres of interest. Education is highly valued now and farm dwellers associate freely and on equal terms with nonfarm people.

The Wheat Areas

The main wheat areas are the Great Plains and southeastern Washington, northeastern Oregon, and north central Idaho with scattered concentrations elsewhere. Though wheat can be raised almost anywhere in the U.S., it is the most profitable crop which can be produced in these areas.

For the most part the wheat lands have relatively low rainfall, and except in eastern Washington, central Idaho, and northeastern Oregon the risk of crop failure is considerable.

The sections of the Great Plains which are devoted to wheat production were used by the first white settlers for raising range livestock. The early cattle and sheep men resisted settlement by the homesteaders who moved into the area in the period between 1870 and 1914 and took up land under the Homestead Act. As Taylor has pointed out,[8] many of the early homesteaders were unsuccessful and soon left. These early farmers attempted to grow corn and generally to use the methods of humid agriculture with which they were familiar, but the techniques proved to be ill adapted to the semiarid conditions in the wheat areas. The development of a satisfactory pattern of agriculture took a considerable period of time, particularly in the marginal areas where humid-area crops can sometimes be grown successfully.

As in the Corn Belt, mechanization of farming operations in the wheat areas has proceeded at a rapid pace. On the bigger farms extremely large-scale machinery is utilized. It is not unusual for wheat ranchers in eastern Washington and northeastern Oregon to own machinery valued at more than $50,000.

In the Plains area, a succession of developments in farm machinery has caused great changes in farming practices. The scythe and the cradle were superseded by the reaper, then by the self-binder and the header, and finally by the combined harvester-thresher, known as the combine.

Prior to development of the combine, as many as 250,000 migratory agricultural workers followed the wheat harvest northward from Texas into Canada. These have been succeeded to some extent by migratory combines, but larger operators often own their own machinery. This pattern of migratory labor and machines has never been characteristic of the intermountain wheat country. Here large-scale machinery was apparently typical from the first, and 20 to 35 horse teams were not unusual prior to the introduction of big tractors in the 1930s.

In all the wheat areas production is influenced by government

[8] *Ibid.*, p. 387.

price support and acreage control programs. Each wheat farm has a "wheat base" which is determined by historical events on the farm and is not necessarily proportional to the actual size of the farm. Government price supports for wheat are considered by most wheat farmers to be essential since even with restricted acreage the production is so great that the price would probably drop to disastrous levels if the supports were suddenly removed. Administration of the acreage controls at the farm level is placed in the hands of local officials, some of whom are elected and others appointed under the authority of the federal legislation which provides for the price support–acreage control program.

Because of the restriction of the wheat base, many farms which would perhaps be more efficiently operated if devoted entirely to the production of wheat are also used in part for other crops and livestock.

Although there are some corporation wheat farms, most holdings are actually operated as family enterprises. The large-scale machinery now available makes it possible for a very small labor force to work extensive acreages. During the rush seasons when the seedbed is prepared and the crop is planted and again during the harvesting period, machinery equipped with headlights may be operated nearly 24 hours a day. Farms which are operated exclusively for the production of wheat have substantial periods when there is little or no work, which enables wheat farmers to take long vacation trips if they are prosperous, and also makes it convenient for some of them to live in town rather than on the farm. In some areas of the country, according to Belcher,[9] this is becoming a typical pattern. Where it has been developed it greatly reduces the cost of maintaining schools, churches, and other social services.

The relatively sparse settlement of the wheat areas obviously has an influence on both informal and formal social systems. However, the residents have adjusted themselves to the concept of greater land expanses and do not hesitate to travel distances which to a Corn Belt farmer or a city dweller might seem excessive. Even so, the fact that the nearest farm family may be located miles away necessarily makes for close and intimate relationships with family

[9] J. C. Belcher, "The Nonresident Farmer in the New Rural Society," *Rural Sociology*, June, 1954, pp. 121-136.

members to the relative exclusion of others. Sparse settlement also makes it difficult to maintain open-country schools and churches, fire departments, and other social services.[10] School consolidation and the development of village churches have to some extent overcome these probems, and, as noted above, many wheat farmers have taken up residence in towns and villages.

The initial settlement of the wheat areas in the Great Plains was accomplished to a considerable extent by foreign immigrants. Among these the Scandinavians and the Russian Germans were especially numerous.

There are numbers of interest groups of various kinds in the wheat areas, although perhaps not so many as in the more populous Corn Belt. The wheat areas are not located as near to urban centers as the Corn Belt, although all are close enough to be influenced by urban development. The wheat farmers who survived the economic difficulties of the drought-depression era generally operate farms of substantial size, and many have very good incomes. Some are world travelers. Education is highly valued. An international outlook is perhaps even commoner among wheat farmers than Corn Belt operators, since their present markets are to a considerable extent found in foreign countries.

THE COTTON BELT

Cotton is a hot-weather plant which requires adequate rainfall and a growing season of more than 200 frost-free days. It is the dominant crop in the southeastern United States. The area delineated as the Cotton Belt includes 690 counties stretching from Texas to North Carolina. Much of this area was originally relatively fertile but subject to heavy water erosion. Drought is frequent and floods are also a serious problem in many sections, particularly along river bottoms. Heavy applications of commercial fertilizer are necessary, particularly in the eroded eastern uplands.

Other crops which are grown in the Cotton Belt include corn, sorghum, tobacco, rice, fruits, and vegetables. The growth cycle of the cotton plant is such, however, that it requires a great deal of

[10] See Carl Kraenzel, "Sutland and Yonland Setting for Community Organization in the Plains," *Rural Sociology*, December, 1953, p. 357.

attention at the same time as competitive crops, which has tended to crowd out diversification.

Mechanization has proceeded more slowly in the Cotton Belt than in other commercial farming operations. In 1949 Raper was able to say that most cotton was produced with one-horse implements and hand labor,[11] but since then mechanization has been proceeding at a very rapid rate, particularly in the Southwest.[12]

The pattern of farm organization in the Cotton Belt has been influenced to a material extent by the plantation, which is described in some detail elsewhere in this book (see Chapters 6 and 15). This system features the sharecropper who is actually an agricultural laborer. He is paid in kind, provided with equipment and work stock, and advanced credit for the food and clothing required while he is producing the crop.

The low rate of mechanization of cotton farming operations in the past resulted in small farming units. Plowing was generally accomplished by a one-bottom plow pulled by one or two mules, and the cotton plants were thinned and kept free of weeds by hoeing. Nearly all cotton produced under this type of technology was also picked by hand. Mechanical cotton pickers, improvements in ginning equipment, use of flamethrowers for the eradication of weeds, and other technological developments are now being adopted at a fairly rapid rate.

The number of cropper units decreased from 776,000 in 1929 to 273,000 in 1954 and to 121,000 in 1959. According to McElveen, this represents a reorganization of plantation operations to use more machinery and systems of farming that require less labor or change the status of croppers to hired workers.[13] As a result a substantial part of the farm labor force has been released and has migrated from farms to cities. Along with these developments has come an increasing emphasis on growing alternate crops and, in some areas, on raising livestock.

[11] Arthur F. Raper, "The Cotton Belt," in Taylor *et al.*, *op. cit.*, p. 344.

[12] A. L. Bertrand *et al.*, *Factors Associated with Agricultural Mechanization in the Southwest Region*, Arkansas AES Southwest Regional Bulletin 6, February, 1936.

[13] J. V. McElveen, *Family Farms in a Changing Economy*, U.S. Department of Agriculture, Agricultural Research Service, Agricultural Information Bulletin 171, March, 1959, p. 35.

The production of cotton is characterized by a distinctive cycle of activities in the planting, cultivating, harvesting, and marketing of the crop. There is a busy season in the spring when the seedbed is prepared and planted. Heavy labor demands continue during the period when the fields are cultivated to control weeds. In the past this was ordinarily done by women and children with hoes. In midsummer there is a slack period. The cotton picking season begins in the early fall and may continue, in areas with good yields, until well into the winter. In contrast to the wheat region where the ripe grain must be harvested almost immediately or be lost, the cotton harvest can be fairly leisurely.

The Cotton Belt has always been an area of relatively low per capita income. A recent survey of 40 large cotton plantations in Mississippi revealed that the per capita cash income of all plantation households in 1958 was only $845.[14] Cotton farmers have doubtless shared to some extent in the general increase in prosperity, but information collected from time to time by the U.S. Bureau of the Census and the agricultural experiment stations in the region indicate that the economic position of farm families in the area is still far below the national average (see Chapter 8, "Standards and Levels of Family Living").

With respect to social organization, the situation in the Cotton Belt is complicated by the traditional social stratification associated with the plantation system and by the racial problem introduced by the early planters who imported slaves from Africa.[15] The nature of the organization of work on cotton plantations prior to the mechanization of operations preserved the social distinctions between the sharecroppers and wage hands and the members of the managerial class.

Throughout the South, separate schools, churches, and other local institutions have been maintained for Negroes and for whites. The existence of these "separate but equal" facilities has been challenged by the 1954 Supreme Court decision which requires integration of the schools. The transition is accompanied by a high degree of emotion in many sections of the South, and progress toward actual

[14] Nelson L. LeRay, G. G. Wilber, and Grady B. Crowe, *Plantation Organization and the Resident Labor Force, Delta Area, Mississippi*, Mississippi AES Bulletin 606, October, 1960, p. 4.

[15] For a discussion of the social organization of the plantation, see Chapter 15.

intergration has been relatively slow, particularly in the states which were the center of the plantation system.

Like wheat, cotton is one of the major crops under the price support–acreage control program administered by the United States Department of Agriculture.

Because of the relatively inefficient use of labor in the past, the Cotton Belt has been characterized by an excess population in relation to land, capital, and customary technology; the area contains a disproportionate part of the U.S. farm population, 30 percent of which was located in the 690 counties delineated as the Cotton Belt in 1940. In addition, the birth rate has been relatively high.

However, great changes in farm organization and technology are taking place in the Cotton Belt. During the 1950s the number of farms in the region declined drastically. Seventy per cent of the national decrease of 1,079,000 farms in the last half of the decade occurred in the 16 southern states.[16] These changes have been accompanied by the appearance of nonfarm employment opportunities in industries newly located in southern communities.

THE DAIRY AREAS

Dairy farms are found in all sections of the United States, but the heaviest concentrations are in the north and east, on the West Coast, and adjacent to large concentrations of population. The high consumption of milk and milk products by American families provides a ready and ever-expanding market. Although surpluses have been encountered from time to time, these have apparently now largely disappeared.

Areas best suited to dairying from the physical point of view include farms with good pastures and fertile land upon which supplemental feed can be produced. However, the economics of the dairy industry are such that it is frequently advantageous to transport feed longer distances than milk. This has stimulated the development of dry-lot dairies adjacent to urban centers where little or no natural pasture is available.

Dairy farmers have been in the foreground in adopting mechaniza-

[16] U.S. Bureau of the Census, *1959 Census of Agriculture—Preliminary,* Series AC59-1, January, 1961.

tion and other scientific agricultural practices. This is, of course, particularly true of the larger and more prosperous operators. At the present time the character of the dairy industry is changing rapidly. Highly mechanized farms with large capitalization are displacing the traditional family-type, low-capacity operations which emphasized self-sufficiency and extensive use of unpaid family labor. These developments have been stimulated by sanitary requirements imposed by the health departments of the cities in which fluid milk is sold. The regulations call for strict compliance with rigid sanitary standards which are enforced by frequent inspections.

The traditional dairy farm was operated by the farm operator and his family and consisted of ten to twenty milk cows which were milked by hand. This was largely a self-sufficient enterprise, as we have said: family members normally supplied all labor needs, the farm provided feed and pasture, and the manure produced by the dairy herd was used to maintain the fertility of the fields and pastures.

The advanced dairy farms of the present, on the other hand, are characterized by extremely high capitalization and advanced mechanization. They feature milking parlors and expensive equipment such as large cooling tanks and milking machines; all equipment which is used in the handling of milk is carefully sterilized. While these enterprises may be owned by individual families, they are different in many essential respects from the typical family-type dairy farm briefly described above.

The traditional dairy farmer who did not produce fluid milk for sale to a processing plant or to individual customers manufactured cream which was sold for butterfat content and was then processed into butter. Competition from the vegetable-oil product oleomargarine, which has gained wide acceptance among urban dwellers, has brought about a shift in emphasis from butterfat to the nonfat dry milk component. This in turn is likely to have an important effect on the demand for and marketing practices of fluid milk, since nonfat dry milk is a direct competitor of fresh fluid milk.

The characteristic rhythm of the dairy enterprise is linked closely to the daily, seasonal, and annual requirements of dairy animals as defined by the culture. Cows must be fed and watered at specific intervals daily. Ordinarily they must be milked at least twice a day.

In order to maintain milk production, the cows must be bred once each year.

The requirements of the dairy animal have produced a characteristic pattern of chores which dominate the daily activities and the social life of the farm operator and the members of his family who are actively engaged in the farming operation. In dairy areas, farm meetings have to be scheduled at a time when they will not conflict with the requirements of the dairy enterprise.

More than most other farmers, dairy farmers have turned to cooperative activities to advance their interests. These cooperatives include farmer-owned cheese factories, creameries, and dairy herd improvement associations among others. Dairy farmers have also been receptive to the activities of agricultural extension services, and 4-H Clubs have found ready acceptance in most areas. Another indication of the extent to which dairymen welcome technological developments is their ready acceptance of artificial insemination as a means of improving herd quality. At the same time, according to Raper, they have emphasized local control of schools and governmental functions as far as possible. Dairy farmers tend to participate actively in local organizations and associations.[17]

Dairy farmers' social organization and activities have been intensively studied by the Departments of Rural Sociology at the University of Wisconsin and at Cornell University, Ithaca, New York. Thus, the neighborhood studies of Kolb and Sanderson and their associates can be regarded as studies of the locality forms of organization of dairy farmers. As noted elsewhere in this book, the locality emphasis has been changing with the introduction of more and more special interests and the constant improvement of transportation and communication facilities.[18] Nevertheless, it is undoubtedly true, as Raper suggests, that the dairy areas have been and are characterized by a high degree of stability in residence and occupational activity which permeates all relationships.[19] Dairy farming is not inherently a high-risk proposition, and satisfactory returns, at least under earlier conditions of mechanization and capitalization, could be obtained through hard work and careful attention to detail. This may be

[17] Raper, *op. cit.*, p. 424.
[18] See Chapters 19 and 20.
[19] Raper, "The Dairy Areas," in Taylor, *op. cit.*, p. 428.

contrasted with the risk involved in such enterprises as onions, wheat, hogs, or potatoes.

The Range Livestock Areas

The major range livestock area extends from the Canadian border to Mexico and from the Sierra Nevada and Cascade Mountains to the eastern foothills of the Rockies in Colorado. Other areas include the Sandhills area of northern Nebraska, western South Dakota, and east central Montana.

The topography is generally rough. Rainfall is characteristically low and not dependable. In mountain valleys which are too high for crops there is summer grazing, and livestock are pastured in vast areas of the public forests. Along the western fringes of the Great Plains, livestock and wheat production are interspersed, and some farmers produce both wheat and range livestock.

The adventures of the cattle ranchers of the early frontier provide the basis for many of the legends of the region. The so-called Western movies tend to keep these legends alive, and there is a distinctive type of Western cowboy music which is quite popular with many people.

As in other types of farming, there are definite work rhythms, which are related to the physical needs of the animals and affected by seasonal variations and climate. The activities associated with lambing, shearing, and culling for market on sheep ranches come at definite periods of the year, as do the calving, branding, and identification and separation of cattle for shipment to market on cattle ranches. The daily routine is also affected by the season. In the winter herds must be fed. Wells and other sources of water supply must be checked periodically, salt distributed, fences inspected, and predators controlled. In addition, the production of hay and forage for winter feed requires agricultural operations which follow a seasonal pattern.

The outdoor work on a livestock ranch is almost exclusively done by men. Women have little if any part in the manual labor involved in ranching; their activities are generally confined to the ranch headquarters. Children are not of much help either until they are old enough to ride horses. There are relatively few chores on a ranch as distinguished from a dairy or general farm.

It is said that livestock ranchers are more inclined to be individualistic than other farmers. They have vigorously resisted attempts to apply federal price supports and controls.

As is the case with other types of agriculture, there are wide variations in size and type of enterprise within the range livestock areas. But because the industry is located in areas where the productivity of the land is not high, ranches are usually large in size. The population is sparse, which of course has made it difficult for the people to maintain social institutions and services which are taken for granted by the farm population in more thickly settled areas.[20] Because of the sparse settlement and the long distances to substantial population centers, people who live on livestock ranches may travel hundreds of miles for specialized shopping. Ranchers routinely travel greater distances than most other farmers.

General farmers' organizations such as the Grange, the Farmers Union, and the Farm Bureau have not been particularly active in the range livestock areas, though from the early days of settlement cattlemen's and sheepmen's associations have been well supported. In these areas there are also cooperatives, shipping and marketing associations, grazing associations, soil conservation districts, and, of course, the Agricultural Extension Service.

Operations on livestock ranches have been somewhat less susceptible of mechanization than operations involved in intensive agriculture. However, ranchers are receptive to mechanization and other improved farm practices where these are applicable. Supplementary crop production and haying are highly mechanized and supplemental irrigation may be utilized to increase yields. In addition, some enterprising ranchers use helicopters or small aiplanes to patrol their extensive ranges.

THE GENERAL AND SELF-SUFFICING FARM AREAS

These areas are located in the east central part of the United States where the country is rugged and not conducive to highly developed commercialized agricultural operations. Most farms in the Appalachian Highlands and the Ozark-Ouachita areas are

[20] See Kraenzel, *op. cit.*, p. 357.

general or self-sufficing. Operations on the general farm have been mechanized less completely than on other major types of farms. Acreages are usually small and fields are irregular in shape and size. Farm incomes are relatively low, on the main even lower than those of the Cotton Belt. However, since emphasis is upon self-sufficiency and production for home use rather than for the market and there is a high rate of off-farm work, many enjoy a higher level of living than their income from farm sales alone would permit.

The daily and seasonal cycle of activities on farms in these areas is probably similar in many respects to the Beech Creek families reported by Brown.[21] Studies of social organization indicate that locality groups are still very important. Travel is difficult because of natural physical barriers like mountains and streams, and contacts traditionally tend to be restricted to persons in the immediate locality. Even this, of course, has been greatly modified in recent years, and the distinctive character of rural life in these previously isolated areas is undergoing substantial change.[22]

THE SPECIALTY CROP AREAS

There are a number of locales in the United States devoted to the production of specialty crops like fruits, nuts, vegetables, or herbs. The heaviest concentration of such farms is in the state of California, but Arizona, Utah, Idaho, Washington, and Oregon also have substantial areas, as does Florida with its citrus groves and vegetable farms. Some parts of Texas produce vegetables and citrus fruits. Along the eastern seaboard and in the vicinity of the Great Lakes are vegetable crop regions. Pecans and other nuts and certain fruits such as peaches and pears are grown in Georgia.

Specialty crop areas are generally chosen for their favorable soils, topography, and climatic conditions.

The type of farm organization may vary greatly from one kind of specialty crop to another and from one region to another. The family-type general farm tends to prevail in Utah and Idaho, whereas in California many specialty crop areas are dominated by corporation farms.

---

[21] See Chapter 14 for selections from his study.
[22] Taylor *et al., op. cit.,* chap. 26.

The specialty crops have one common characteristic: all are labor-intensive crops which require relatively large numbers of hired hands at certain seasons of the year. These labor needs have historically been met by the use of seasonal migratory laborers, both foreign and domestic.

Formal organizations associated with agriculture are generally designed to promote the interests of suppliers of specific agricultural products. Thus, each specialty crop usually has its own group, most often distinctively identified by the name of the commodity. In addition, buying and selling cooperatives are plentiful, and many farmer-operators take an active part in nonfarm service clubs, civic organizations, veterans' groups, and social clubs. The wives also participate actively in social and recreational activities with nonfarm people. Incomes of operators and owners are frequently high and are reflected in their standards and levels of living. They are well educated, mobile, and active in leadership roles in interest groups and social organizations. Through their commodity organizations they are able to make their wishes known to legislatures and public administrators.

Because of the intensive character of their operations and the high productivity per unit of land, specialty crop farmers are extremely receptive to improvements in farm practices and products which offer the prospect of increasing the farm income. Many phases of production and marketing operations are highly mechanized, a trend that will doubtless continue in the future.

QUESTIONS FOR FURTHER STUDY AND DISCUSSION

1. Evaluate the relative importance of physical and cultural factors in the development of agriculture in a particular region.
2. Have each member of the class visit a particular type of farm located in the immediate area. The report on the visit should evaluate the extent of mechanization observed as compared with the maximum possibilities in that type of farming.
3. Compare and contrast wheat farming with dairy farming in respect to farm organization, division of labor, and effect on the social life of the family.
4. Evaluate the probable future of area concentrations in particular types of agriculture within the United States.

5. Discuss the impact of international developments on particular types of farming.

SELECTED REFERENCES

Bertrand, A. L., *et al.*, *Factors Associated with Agricultural Mechanization in the Southwest Region*, Arkansas AES Southwest Regional Bulletin 6, February, 1936.

Mangus, A. R., *Rural Regions of the United States*, Federal Works Agency, Works Projects Administration, 1940.

Odum, Howard W., *Southern Regions*, University of North Carolina Press, 1936.

Taylor, Carl C., *et al.*, *Rural Life in the United States*, Knopf, 1949.

8

Standards and Levels of Family Living

The goods and services consumed by farm families constitute the level of living. The level of living reflects the standard of living, which consists of the norms by which achievement is evaluated. It is what people want. Among the very wealthy, the two may be the same, but usually there are enough unsatisfied desires so that the standard is somewhat different from the attained level of living evidenced by the consumption or possession of specific culture objects of different makes and models.

The standard of living is, of course, greatly affected by the level of living. Like other cultural norms, it is a product of interpersonal relationships and influences. What is customary in one's reference groups tends to be his standard.

Differences exist between societies and between lesser social systems with respect to the value placed on different consumption items or practices. Among the Kwakiutl Indians of the Pacific Northwest, for example, conspicuous and wasteful consumption of expensive items had a high value.[1] Among members of certain religious orders, on the other hand, self-denial and renunciation of worldly possessions is the standard. The existence of such differences is of major importance in cross-cultural comparisons.

Living standards are relative—they derive their significance from their interrelationship with other aspects of the culture associated with a society or smaller social system. It cannot be said flatly, for example, that the American standard of living is higher or better than that of the ancient Aztecs or Incas, but only that it is different. If there is agreement on certain goals or values (i.e., the standard),

[1] Robert H. Lowie, "American Indian Cultures," *American Mercury*, July, 1930, pp. 263-264.

then it is possible to evaluate comparatively the level attained.

When the American level is compared to the farm norm in most other countries, it is frequently described as high. This is usually intended to mean that the number and quality of the material possessions used in the daily business of living are superior—that American farmers drive more and better cars, have more and better clothes, food, gadgets, home appliances, and conveniences, and live in newer houses.

The possession of various combinations or patterns of such items characterizes the contemporary style of life and may be conceptualized as the level of living. Generally speaking most Americans, farmers included, aspire to having as many consumption items of as high a quality as their incomes allow, consistent with the attainment of other values. For example, Americans tend to evaluate their cars in terms of the newest car of the most luxurious and expensive make owned by those with whom they compare themselves. Discrepancies generate discontent and motivate consumers to raise their levels. This principle is the basis for frequent style changes in clothing, home appliances, and automobiles, and is widely used by advertisers.

The influence of tradition is so strong that customary standards tend to govern behavior even in the few areas of consumption where scientific standards are available. For example, few farm families, even in science-minded countries, apply scientifically established nutritional principles in planning family menus.

At the same time, it is evident from recent history that the living standards and levels of farm people can be changed. Contact with city dwellers has so influenced the ways of life of American commercial farmers that their standards and even their attained levels of living are now little if any different from the urban. This apparently is fairly exceptional; the limited empirical evidence available on the subject indicates that in most parts of the world, including Europe, the living standards of farm people differ markedly from those of city people. A world traveler finds much similarity among the consumption standards of city people the world over, with the dominant theme even in Asia being eager acceptance of many aspects of western culture. The farm populations generally continue to be bulwarks of conservatism.

In any social system, certain items like dress, housing, and manner of transportation—whether it be by coach and four, elephant, or expensive automobile—tend to become status symbols, the difference in type depending on the specific culture.

CONSUMPTION LEVELS

The traditional peasant or subsistence farmer does not enjoy a very high material level of living. He and his family produce much of their food, clothing, and shelter on the farm. The emphasis is upon production for use, not production for sale. In America, the increase in commercial farms and the decline of subsistence farming has been accompanied by an increasing emphasis upon consumption. An important goal for both full- and part-time farmers is the earning of sufficient income to purchase the culture objects which are part of the "American standard of living."

Studies of the level of living based upon census reports show that there has been a tremendous increase in the number of farm families who own all or nearly all the important labor-saving devices like automatic washing machines and mechanical refrigerators. American farm homes also generally now have electricity. A high percentage have television; nearly all have automobiles or trucks (Table 8).

TABLE 8.   Selected Items or Services Reported
by American Farm Families, 1959

Item	Percent
Motor truck	58.6
Automobile	79.7
Telephone	64.9
Electricity	96.0[a]
Home freezer	55.7
Television	76.0

[a] USDA, Rural Electrification Administration, Mimeo news release, Washington, January 5, 1960.
SOURCE: U.S. Census Bureau, *1959 Census of Agriculture, Preliminary, Summary for the 48 States*, Series AC59-1, January, 1961; and *Current Housing Reports, Households with Television Sets in the United States, May 1960*, Series H-121, No. 7, August 30, 1960.

Indexes based upon the possession of such culture objects by farmers indicate that there has been a marked increase in the level of living of farm families since 1930:

Year	Index
1930	75
1940	79
1945	100
1950	122
1954	140

Source: M. J. Hagood, G. K. Bowles, and R. R. Mount, *Farm-Operator Family Level of Living Indexes for Counties of the United States, 1945, 1950 and 1954,* USDA, Agricultural Research Service, Statistical Bulletin 204, 1957.

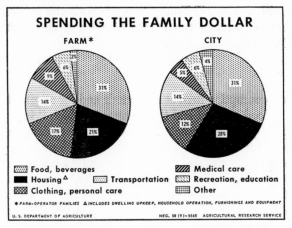

Fig. 9.   Differences in Farm and Urban Patterns of Spending.

Such a high level of affluence has been attained that the emphasis in prosperous homes is not upon possession of a particular item but upon its quality or upon the possession of multiple items—a family may own several radios, and its members may aspire to own a new model of an expensive car rather than an old model of a cheap car.

The family consumption patterns of farm and city families are alike in some ways but different in others. A 1955 study reported by the U.S. Department of Agriculture shows that families in both residential categories spent the same proportion of their consumption budgets for food, transportation, recreation, reading, and education (Fig. 9). Farm families spent relatively more for clothing and medical care but relatively less for housing, upkeep, household operation, furnishings, and home equipment.

Substantial regional differences in levels of living of farm families are revealed by indexes for 1954 prepared by the U.S. Department of Agriculture (Fig. 10). The highest region was the Northeast, followed closely by the Pacific division and the North Central region. The South was far below other areas, although Hagood, Bowles, and Mount reported that the greatest percentage increases between 1940 and 1954 occurred in the South.[2]

Other agricultural areas besides the South with moderate to serious poverty and low levels of family living include the cutover area of the lake states, parts of the Pacific Northwest, and part of New Mexico (Fig. 11).

Food

A major consumption item at all periods and for all people is food. The type of food utilized and the manner in which it is prepared is affected greatly by the practices which are prevalent in a given culture area. It is well known, for example, that there are substantial differences between the diets of Japanese and American families. In some culture areas, like Mexico and India, highly spiced and seasoned foods are common, whereas in others, like the United States and Great Britain, much less seasoning is generally used. Even within a major culture area like the United States, however, there are regional differences and variations associated with the ethnic backgrounds of particular families or groups of people. And there are, of course, gradations in the quality of given items—there is a substantial difference between a choice T-bone steak from a grain-fattened steer and a steak from an old bull or a milk cow. In addition, nutrition experts consider that variations in methods of preparation affect food value.

[2] M. J. Hagood, G. K. Bowles, and R. R. Mount, *Farm-Operator Family Level of Living Indexes for Counties of the United States, 1945, 1950 and 1954*, U.S. Department of Agriculture, Agricultural Research Service, Statistical Bulletin 204, 1957.

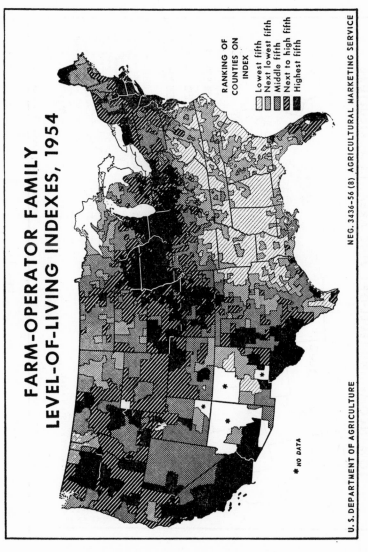

FARM-OPERATOR FAMILY
LEVEL-OF-LIVING INDEXES, 1954

RANKING OF
COUNTIES ON
INDEX

Lowest fifth
Next lowest fifth
Middle fifth
Next to high fifth
Highest fifth

* NO DATA

U. S. DEPARTMENT OF AGRICULTURE

NEG. 3436-56 (8) AGRICULTURAL MARKETING SERVICE

FIG. 10.

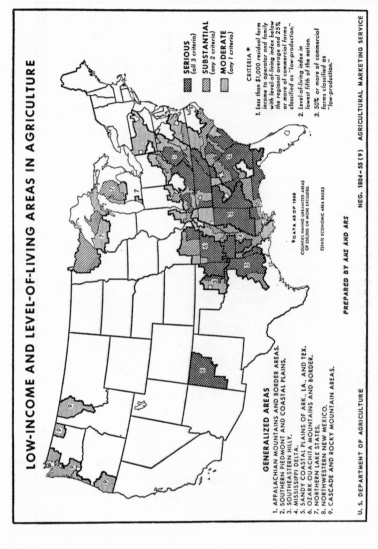

LOW-INCOME AND LEVEL-OF-LIVING AREAS IN AGRICULTURE

SERIOUS
(all 3 criteria)

SUBSTANTIAL
(any 2 criteria)

MODERATE
(any 1 criteria)

CRITERIA *

1. Less than $1,000 residual farm income to operator and family with level-of-living index below the regional average and 25% or more of commercial farms classified as "low-production."

2. Level-of-living index in lowest fifth of the nation.

3. 50% or more of commercial farms classified as "low-production."

*DATA AS OF 1949

COUNTIES HAVING URBANIZED AREAS OF 250,000 OR MORE EXCLUDED.

(STATE ECONOMIC AREA BASIS)

GENERALIZED AREAS

1. APPALACHIAN MOUNTAINS AND BORDER AREAS.
2. SOUTHERN PIEDMONT AND COASTAL PLAINS.
3. SOUTHEASTERN HILLY.
4. MISSISSIPPI DELTA.
5. SANDY COASTAL PLAINS OF ARK., LA., AND TEX.
6. OZARK-OUACHITA MOUNTAINS AND BORDER.
7. NORTHERN LAKE STATES.
8. NORTHWESTERN NEW MEXICO.
9. CASCADE AND ROCKY MOUNTAIN AREAS.

PREPARED BY AMS AND ARS

U. S. DEPARTMENT OF AGRICULTURE   NEG. 1804-55 (9)   AGRICULTURAL MARKETING SERVICE

FIG. 11.

Nutritional research has influenced standards to some extent. Much extension work in the field of food is aimed at establishing higher standards of nutrition on the basis of scientific research.

Recent developments in food processing have greatly influenced food preparation procedures in American farm as well as nonfarm homes. The home freezer, for example, has revolutionized the storage of meats and vegetables on the farm. The widespread use of cake mixes and other partly prepared foods has reduced kitchen work to a marked extent, and there has been a subtantial decline in the extent to which farm families depend on their own gardens, flocks, and herds for their food.

Clothing

Comparison shows that there are great differences between major cultures in respect to clothing as well as occupational and sex differences. Some of these differences may be utilitarian in origin, but to a considerable degree they are traditional in nature. Thus, males in western societies ordinarily wear trousers, but except for some sports clothes, females do not—they wear dresses, skirts, blouses, and similar garments. Rural West Pakistan provides a contrast: there men wear a sort of skirt while women wear a kind of trousers. The clothing styles of the Japanese traditionally provided that a kimono, a gownlike garment, be worn by both sexes, with subtle variations in style and color distinguishing the garments considered appropriate for the wearer's age, sex, and class. The kimono has now virtually been supplanted by western dress, especially in cities.

Distinctive clothing is still associated with specific occupational roles to some extent in contemporary American society, where farm workers, the military, policemen, firemen, nurses, bellhops and others are identifiable by their characteristic work attire. But when the same individuals are engaged in recreational and social pursuits, there are few if any distinguishing characteristics in wearing apparel on the basis of occupational status or class orientation. Sex-associated differences in clothes do persist, and there are subtle variations in quality concomitant with possession of wealth and membership in certain social classes. Thus, the wealthy socialite may wear an original gown by a noted Paris designer and own an expensive mink stole. At the same time, however, the wife of a farmer may have clothing which looks almost identical even though mass-produced and consequently much less expensive.

Farmers usually wear inexpensive durable clothing suitable for outdoors while actually engaged in farming operations, but their nonwork clothes do not differ in any distinguishable respect from what is worn by other American males of the same age.

HOME APPLIANCES

The great proliferation of home appliances of various types designed to lighten the task of the homemaker is a characteristic of the American city and country alike. In most cases these appliances were not specifically designed with either the urban or the rural home in mind. However, because farms were generally electrified later than towns and villages, the farm homemaker's acquisition of many farm appliances occurred later, though the rapidity with which farm families acquired modern conveniences after World War II indicates that they were included in the standard of living of farm families even before acquisition.

On the basis of a study of farm families in Oklahoma during the 1930s, Sewell established a scale for rating farm families according to the level of living as reflected in the possession of various appliances and some related items.[3] This scale has been modified by Belcher in relation to information from Oklahoma farm families on later developments.[4]

In many parts of the country, however, farm families have now acquired so many of the items included in the Sewell level-of-living scale that its further use seems questionable; the distinguishing characteristic now, as we have said, is not possession but rather the quality and in some cases the number of a given item which a family owns.

[3] W. H. Sewell, *The Construction and Standardization of a Scale for the Measurement of the Socio-Economic Status of Oklahoma Farm Families*, Oklahoma AES Technical Bulletin 9, April, 1940.

[4] J. C. Belcher and E. F. Sharp, *A Short Scale for Measuring Farm Family Level of Living: A Modification of Sewell's Socio-Economic Scale*, Oklahoma AES Bulletin T-46, September, 1952.

RECREATION

Recreation as a factor in the lives of American farm families has undergone tremendous changes since the turn of the century. The early farm family did not participate to any appreciable extent in recreational activities which involved the purchase of expensive culture objects or other expenditures. Most recreational activities were not commercialized.

To some extent this is still true, but American farm families like urban dwellers now pursue activities which cost substantial sums of money. These include family vacation trips; ownership of television sets, boats with motors, hunting, fishing, and camping equipment; and attendance at football games, baseball games, and moving pictures.

TRANSPORTATION

Like recreation, transportation was not a major item of expense for the farm family prior to the days of the gasoline engine and the automobile. Farmers simply did not travel to any appreciable extent; travel was slow and uncomfortable. All this has been changed, of course, with the advent of improved roads and dependable automobiles. Most American farm families now own at least one automobile or truck and their range of travel is often quite similar to that of nonfarm dwellers, with the exception that most full-time farmers do not commute to work. Even here there are exceptions, particularly in the case of farmers who live in farm villages such as those of Utah and Idaho and the wheat farmers of some midwestern states. A high proportion of the latter now live in towns and villages rather than on their farms.[5]

HOUSING

Because of the greater amount of money invested in farm homes, the type and quality is less subject to change than other items included in the material level of living. Most existing farms have dwellings many of which were constructed a considerable number

[5] See J. C. Belcher, "The Nonresident Farmer in the New Rural Society," *Rural Sociology*, June, 1954, pp. 121-136.

of years ago. To some extent, these homes have been modernized with running water, indoor bathrooms, electricity, and other changes. In some cases, older houses have been replaced by dwellings which meet substantially the same standards as those found in nonfarm locales. In open country adjacent to metropolitan centers where there has been an influx of urban people, there has been a great deal of building. Some farmhouse building occurs every year. The 1950 *Census of Housing* found nearly 1,000,000 dilapidated farmhouses; in the South 35 percent were so classified. This indicates a need for more building.

A study of factors involved in farmhouse building in North Carolina indicates that to an appreciable extent, at least in that state, structure is usually influenced by traditional standards rather than by the standards advocated by architects.[6]

In the Palouse area of the state of Washington, on the other hand, where farms are large and the farmers relatively prosperous, much of the building since World War II has taken advantage of architectural principles. These houses are fully modern in every way, and in many cases are superior to contemporary homes built by nonfarm families in the same area. The Agricultural Extension Service in some states employs architects who attempt to influence the housing standards of farm families by making them aware of the living needs of their families as related to house design.

An important factor in regard to the quality of housing is whether the occupants are owners or tenants. Tenants frequently take little or no interest in maintaining their premises, whereas the home owner has a greater incentive to maintain housing in accordance with contemporary standards.

The size of the farm home may have little or no relationship to the actual space needs of the occupant's family. In some parts of the United States, for example Iowa, many farm homes are very large because they were constructed for bigger families than those which now occupy them. However, census data indicates that in general farm homes compare unfavorably in number of rooms per person with urban and rural nonfarm dwellings. Three times as large a proportion of farm homes in 1950 had more than 1.5 persons per

[6] See James W. Green, *House Building by Farm Owners in North Carolina,* North Carolina AES Bulletin 391, 1954.

room than was true of urban homes.[7] In a 1942 study of farm housing in Pennsylvania, Howard Cottam found a relationship between size of house and size of family, but ". . . the relationship was a reverse order to that which is commonly advocated by child welfare workers. That is, the largest families had the poorest housing."[8]

FACTORS THAT INFLUENCE LIVING STANDARDS

The style of life of any population is affected by many factors, but according to the findings of anthropologists, archaeologists, and historians the most important and pervasive influence is the nature of the general culture associated with a given society at a particular time. The standards of living of the ancient Aztecs and Incas were vastly different from those of contemporary South Americans. By the same token, the living standards of contemporary residents of India and Pakistan differ in important ways from the standards of modern-day Japanese, and these, in turn, contrast materially with American norms. It is probable, however, that there are greater similarities between societies today than was true in earlier times when there was less communication between the members of different societies.

Superficial similarity in certain culture objects, such as automobiles, modern farm machinery, radios, and television, does not necessarily mean that standards are the same. Material objects may be associated with distinct sets of values and thus have different meanings for the members of different societies. For example, radio and television in the United States are regarded chiefly as entertainment media and are supported by advertisers who seek to influence listeners and viewers to purchase their products. In the Soviet Union, on the other hand, these media are utilized by the state for ideological indoctrination and as agencies of social control.

INFLUENCE OF REFERENCE GROUPS

The living standards of a particular individual are influenced appreciably by his internalization of the style preferences and

[7] U.S. Bureau of the Census, *U.S. Census of Housing, 1950,* vol. I, part 1, 1953.

[8] Howard R. Cottam, *Housing and Attitudes Toward Housing in Rural Pennsylvania,* Pennsylvania AES Bulletin 436, December, 1942, p. 15.

other norms of important reference groups to which he belongs or with which he identifies himself psychologically.[9] Thus, in societies organized on the basis of a caste system, members of specific castes or classes are expected to conduct themselves in specific ways and to give objective manifestation of their identification with the caste or class by possessing culture objects of particular types. For example, in some parts of the world, peasants can be identified by their characteristic clothing even when they are not in their fields. In the contemporary United States, such class differences as exist in the possession of material or culture objects are usually subtle.

The standard of living of a particular family group may be greatly influenced by unique family values. The possession of material objects may be relegated to a secondary position and income diverted instead to education or travel for family members. Some families emphasize saving for the purchase of income-producing property which will provide greater economic security in old age or greater income at a later date; others prefer to spend as they earn and may mortgage future income by buying desired consumption items on the installment plan. In contemporary America this philosophy of immediate gratification of wishes is evidently quite prevalent as evidenced by the tremendous use of installment credit for purchasing both necessities and luxuries. It seems to be fairly rare now for individuals to deprive themselves and their families of the immediate enjoyment of culture objects which are regarded as part of the American "standard of living" for the purpose of attaining distant goals.

During the initial settlement of much of the farm land of the United States, farm families were much more likely to "do without." Deprivation was rationalized on the basis of the great importance then attached to obtaining debt-free title to the land. But this attitude does not seem to have persisted. In his study of the adjustment of settlers to the Columbia Basin, Murray Straus raised this question specifically with respondents. "A number of the farmers interviewed," he says, "commented that not only did they think it unnecessary to have to accept a lower level of living for a few years, but they thought it undesirable for anyone to have that expectation.

[9] See Chapter 11 for a further discussion of reference groups.

Some even stated that, if that were to be the case, they would not have come to the Columbia Basin."[10]

MONEY INCOME

The level of living attained as distinguished from the standard in a market economy is, of course, greatly influenced by the money income and associated credit available to a family, and doubtless the standards are also affected to some extent. Some families with low incomes may feel that a higher level of living is unattainable while others may strive to increase their incomes in an effort to achieve their aspirations.

The actual level a given individual or family attains unquestionably has a great impact upon the standards used by that individual or family in evaluating existing and potential future levels of living.

Farm income is such that in many cases the quality of the culture objects owned by farm families must be lower or the quantity smaller than comparable objects owned by nonfarm families. In 1958, the median farm family income was $2,747 compared to $5,338 for urban and rural nonfarm families.[11] This is offset to some degree by the fact that many farm families produce part of their food and fuel themselves.

Thus, many a farm family's ability to acquire the material objects associated with the concept of the American standard of living is effectively limited by its level of attained income. This is a matter of concern to the family itself, to those who are directly interested in its welfare, and, since low income curtails consumption of the products of industry, to industrial segments of the economy as well.

Information from census and other sources shows clearly that with the exception of a period immediately after World War II, the average per capita income of farm people has always been lower than that of nonfarm families (Table 9). A special nationwide sample study of 1950 census data by the Department of Agriculture and the Census Bureau throws some light on the influence of

[10] M. A. Straus and B. D. Parrish, *The Columbia Basin Settler,* Washington AES Bulletin 566, May, 1956, p. 18.

[11] U.S. Bureau of the Census, *Slight Rise in Family Income in 1958,* Series P-60, No. 32, October 22, 1959.

TABLE 9. Per Capita Income of Farm and Nonfarm Population,
United States, 1934-1959 (in Dollars)

Year	Farm Population Agricultural Sources	Nonagricultural Sources	All Sources	Nonfarm Population All Sources
1934	106	59	165	468
1935	182	62	244	517
1936	156	72	228	592
1937	216	80	296	642
1938	165	74	239	589
1939	168	81	249	626
1940	174	88	262	685
1941	246	103	349	823
1942	379	130	509	1034
1943	497	157	654	1240
1944	524	172	696	1328
1945	554	166	720	1312
1946	644	162	806	1295
1947	644	181	825	1394
1948	765	197	962	1534
1949	567	200	767	1511
1950	626	212	838	1585
1951	751	232	983	1763
1952	711	251	962	1849
1953	666	265	931	1902
1954	660	265	925	1849
1955	610	284	894	1975
1956	602	301	903	2056
1957	658	309	967	2082
1958	740	299	1039	2082
1959	644	321	965	2216

SOURCE: USDA, Agricultural Marketing Service and Agricultural Research
Service, *Agricultural Outlook Charts,* 1959, November, 1960.

income.[12] The poorest commercial farm families (Class VI) had the worst housing, and relatively fewer had electricity, running water in the house, or telephones. These farmers were older than other operators and had less formal education; they were most numerous in the hilly upland sections of the South and in the Mississippi Delta. Many of these Class VI farms are subsistence farms which produce a large portion of the food consumed by the family.

At the other end of the scale, the more prosperous farmers in economic Classes I and II were reported to have superior housing and home facilities and to produce less of their own food. Owners generally had better housing and fixed equipment than tenants, but there was little difference between owners and tenants with respect to equipment that was not attached to the house.[13]

EDUCATION

Formal education is clearly a very important factor in the molding of standards of living because, among other reasons, an educated person is exposed to a much larger range of stimuli. Consequently, the standards which are internalized as a result of direct participation in important reference groups are challenged to a greater degree.

Viewed broadly, many stimuli communicated through mass media may be regarded as educational influences. Some operate indirectly; others, like the conscious persuasive efforts of advertisers, attempt directly to change the standards of those exposed to their material. People have to be persuaded that a new product is better than an old one, and taught to desire things which do not replace anything. The market for new consumer goods is developed chiefly through the promotional efforts of manufacturers and retailers.

The adult education programs of the Agricultural Extension Service aim specifically at introducing change. This can only be accomplished through the internalization by farm people of the standards advocated by Extension workers, a process that will be discussed in Chapter 10.

[12] U.S. Bureau of the Census, *Farms and Farm People—Population, Income and Housing Characteristics by Economic Class of Farm*, 1952.
[13] *Ibid.*, pp. 70-71.

OPINION LEADERS

Within major culture areas certain innovators, such as Paris dress designers, have a tremendous influence on the establishment of standards of living; in local social systems there is also a tendency for specific individuals to attain the status of opinion leaders. Others are quite likely to imitate the styles of life these individuals accept. This, of course, is well known by advertisers, who use testimonials by athletic stars, TV and movie actors, and other figures of prestige in an effort to obtain acceptance of their products.

EMPIRICAL STUDIES OF STANDARDS OF LIVING

Most of the empirical studies of family living standards and levels, including those by rural sociologists, have concentrated on the economic aspects of family consumption. The focus has been mainly on levels of living, and little attention has been devoted to the sociological and psychological aspects of the decisions involved.

The early case studies of LePlay in Europe took many aspects of family life into account. He lived with selected families and carefully observed their consumption patterns. This case approach has been largely replaced by the statistical study, which was initiated in 1886 by Engel.[14]

In the United States a significant nationwide statistical investigation of farm family living was made by E. L. Kirkpatrick in 1922-1924. This was followed by much local research by rural sociologists at various land-grant institutions.[15]

In 1935-1936, a study of families living on farms and in villages, towns, and cities was made by the National Resources Committee.[16] Since that time, numerous local studies have been made by various agricultural experiment stations. A countrywide study made by the Department of Agriculture and the Census Bureau in 1956 showed that the total family living expenditures of farm operator families

[14] See C. C. Zimmerman, ed., *Research in Farm Family Living—Scope and Method*, Social Science Research Council Bulletin 11, April, 1933, pp. 48-56.

[15] See John H. Kolb and Edmund deS. Brunner, *A Study of Rural Society*, 4th ed., Houghton Mifflin, 1952, p. 288.

[16] U.S. National Resources Committee, *Consumer Expenditures in the U.S.*, March, 1939.

averaged $3309 in 1955.[17] Housing costs were $868 or 26.3 percent of the annual figure while food costs were $833 or 25.2 percent. The value of home-produced food consumed on the farm was not included, meaning a considerable understatement in the value of food consumed. A Department of Agriculture survey made in the spring of 1955 revealed that farm families produced about two-thirds of the milk and milk products, half of the meat, and two-fifths of the vegetables and fruits used during the survey week.[18] In 1955 clothing expenditures were $427 (12.4 percent) and transportation $378 (13.2 percent). Medical expenses came to $240 (7.5 percent) and cash gifts to $110 (2.6 percent). All other expenditures for family living totaled $453 (14 percent).

These empirical studies are of value to sociologists principally as indicators of the standards existing at various times. They do reflect changing consumer preferences, but few probe into the factors involved in changing standards. This is a challenging area for future studies.

QUESTIONS FOR FURTHER STUDY AND DISCUSSION

1. Distinguish between the terms *standard of living* and *level of living*. How are family living *standards* developed?
2. Governmental activities of various kinds have influenced levels and standards of farm family living. Name the most important. What is your opinion on the desirability of such governmental action?
3. Comment critically on the LePlay case history approach to the study of living standards.
4. What are the principal factors that determine family spending behavior?
5. What is the significance of the fact that the farm level-of-living index is lowest in the Southeast and highest in the Corn Belt? Cover both causes and consequences.
6. What was the comparative status of farm and urban housing in the U.S. and in a selected state in 1950? (Data to answer this question can be obtained from the *Census of Housing*.) What, if anything, should be done by society to improve these conditions?

[17] See U.S. Bureau of the Census, *Farmers' Expenditures,* vol. III, Special Reports, part 11, of *U.S. Census of Agriculture: 1954,* 1956.

[18] USDA, Agricultural Marketing Service and Agricultural Research Service, *Agricultural Outlook Charts, 1959,* November, 1958.

7. What family factors should be taken into account in planning a new farmhouse?

SELECTED REFERENCES

Kolb, John H. and E. deS. Brunner, *A Study of Rural Society*, 4th ed., Houghton Mifflin, 1952, chap. 17.

Nelson, Lowry, *Rural Sociology*, 2nd ed., American Book, 1955, chap. 16.

Taylor, C. C., *et al.*, *Rural Life in the United States*, Knopf, 1949, chap. XVII.

9

Culture Change: From Folklore to Science in Farm Technology

The beginnings of agriculture are lost in the dim past of prehistoric times. Gras has stated that prehistoric man was not a farmer and that agriculture is a comparatively recent development,[1] but archaeological investigations in various parts of the world show that some prehistoric people had domestic animals and many knew at least the rudiments of cultivation. It is not necessary for our purposes to trace the slow development of agricultural implements and practices from prehistoric to modern times. We can say briefly that not all societies have passed through all of the stages of increasing complexity of agricultural technology, and some have skipped some stages entirely.[2] Others are still in a relatively primitive stage. Change is occurring rapidly in some areas and slowly in others.

Due chiefly to the application of science, agricultural production of the United States has enjoyed phenomenal increases, especially in the last 30 years (Fig. 12). These have been accompanied by a substantial decrease in the farm population and tremendous farm surpluses. In 1945, each American farm worker produced enough agricultural products to support 14 persons compared with 10 persons in 1920 and 4 in 1820.[3] In 1959, one farm worker supported

[1] R. S. B. Gras, *A History of Agriculture in Europe and America,* Crofts, 1940, p. 3.

[2] John Lewis Gillin and John Philip Gillin, *Cultural Sociology,* Macmillan, 1948, p. 172.

[3] Martin R. Cooper, Glen T. Barton, and Albert P. Brodell, *Progress of Farm Mechanization,* U.S. Department of Agriculture, Miscellaneous Publication 630, October, 1947.

23 others.[4] This does not mean, however, that all farms are efficient; in 1954, 58 percent of all farm products marketed in the U.S. were produced by only 12 percent of the farms.[5]

To an extent not generally understood, receptivity to and active encouragement of such changes has been based upon the form of social organization and culture in America. It is no accident that the American farmer is in the vanguard. Farm labor has always been relatively expensive, which has put a premium on machines.

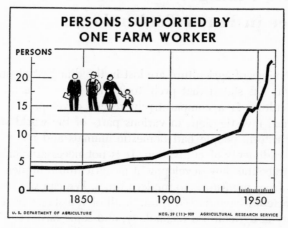

PERSONS SUPPORTED BY ONE FARM WORKER

U. S. DEPARTMENT OF AGRICULTURE   NEG. 59 (11)- 909   AGRICULTURAL RESEARCH SERVICE

Fig. 12. Since 1850, increases in productivity have more than quadrupled the number supported.

American farmers produce for the market; consequently, they value products and techniques which increase income. They are members of a science-oriented society and share the general values of that society. At the present time, underdeveloped countries are being provided with technical assistance by the ICA and various United Nations agencies in their efforts to modernize farm technology and thus increase production.[6]

[4] USDA, Agricultural Marketing Service and Agricultural Research Service, *Agricultural Outlook Charts, 1959,* November, 1958.

[5] J. V. McElveen, *Family Farms in a Changing Economy,* USDA, Agricultural Research Service, Agricultural Information Bulletin 171, March, 1959, p. 12.

[6] See Lyle W. Shannan, ed., *Underdeveloped Areas,* Harper, 1957, chap. IV.

PATTERNS OF AGRICULTURAL TECHNOLOGY

As a background for the systematic consideration of changes in agriculture, we will outline certain major patterns of agricultural technology. These include only patterns which involve the seeding and harvesting of plants and exclude hunting and fishing and nomadic herding.

RIVERBANK PLANTING

Riverbank planting consists of dropping seeds in the mud left as a stream recedes after flood stage and finally harvesting the crop. No implements or tools are involved and little labor is needed since the seedbed is prepared by the water. Smith calls this the most elementary form of agriculture.[7]

Today hundreds of thousands of people depend on this type of agriculture, which is found in South America along the Amazon and Orinoco Rivers. Smith states that "transportation on the farm is limited to the back or head of woman herself,"[8] indicating that women do most of the work.

FIRE AGRICULTURE

In this system, existing vegetation, including trees, is destroyed by fire. The trees are cut with an ax or machete if need be so that they can dry out enough to burn. After the burning, seeds are planted in the ashes. A digging stick, a hoe, or a big toe may be used in planting; few other tools are used. There is no cultivation during the growing season.

Two or three crops may be grown after which the land is abandoned and the process is repeated in another area. Smith says that millions of people in Central and South America, Africa, Asia, and Oceania use this system. It is a highly wasteful pattern because it involves destruction of timber and a great amount of labor in felling the trees.[9]

[7] T. Lynn Smith, *The Sociology of Rural Life*, 3rd ed., Harper, 1953, p. 332.
[8] *Ibid.*, p. 333.
[9] *Ibid.*, pp. 334-336.

People are the principal sources of power. Boats, rafts, and pack animals are sometimes used for transportation.

HOE CULTURE

A more complex system involves the hoe, used by hundreds of millions of people to extract their living from the soil. Smith believes that the hoe was probably developed by fastening a piece of bone on the digging stick; metal blades are now generally used.

The hand sickle is used for harvesting. Humans are the principal labor source, although pack animals may be used to some extent.[10]

RUDIMENTARY PLOW CULTURE

Crude plows drawn by oxen were the chief reliance of agricultural people in ancient Egypt and Mesopotamia.[11] These implements merely stirred up the soil instead of cutting and turning it like the moldboard or disk plow.

Few horses were used on such plows. This, says Smith, is still true. Camels, bullocks, and buffaloes are used for draft animals. At present, according to Smith, this system is used by the majority of agriculturists in the world. He cites especially India and China but also notes that the method is to be found in southern and eastern Europe, Oceania, and much of Latin America.[12] As in much of India today, crops are generally harvested with a hand sickle. Threshing is accomplished by primitive methods too, among them using the flail or driving animals over the straw.[13] This type of agriculture is largely subsistence farming.

Crude two-wheeled carts drawn by bullocks or buffaloes are used for some purposes. There is much lifting and heavy physical labor.

Traditional practices are likely to have near-sacred status and change is generally accepted slowly if at all.

[10] *Ibid.*, pp. 338, 341, 342.
[11] E. B. Taylor, "On the Origin of the Plough, and Wheel-Carriage," *Journal of the Anthropological Institute of Great Britain and Ireland,* X (1881), 74-82, cited by Smith, *op. cit.,* p. 342.
[12] Smith, *op. cit.,* p. 343.
[13] See S. C. Dube, *Indian Village,* Routledge & Kegan Paul, 1955, pp. 79-82.

ADVANCED PLOW CULTURE

Advanced plow culture, involving the moldboard or turning plow and the use of horses as draft animals, was developed in northwest Europe.[14] It developed there rather than elsewhere because the necessary cultural elements were available.

The early colonists, who came principally from the British Isles, brought with them the agricultural practices which were then prevalent in their home localities. Along with use of the plow and other implements for tilling the soil, they had some knowledge of fertilization, although not very much, and used domesticated animals for meat and farm power. Both oxen and horses served as draft animals. There was evidently some crop rotation, and naked fallow was followed to a limited extent as one phase in the rotation.[15]

This type of agriculture was not very different from that which had been practiced in Great Britain for centuries, and it persisted in America for a long time. The changes that occurred between the early settlement of the colonies and the beginning of the twentieth century were so slight that a farm boy of George Washington's time would have been quite at home on a farm of 1900. It was not until 1903 that the first gasoline traction engine was produced commercially and chemistry had not yet brought forth the pesticides, insecticides, and chemical fertilizers which are so familiar and useful to the contemporary farmer. Nevertheless, the changes in agricultural technology which have been made since the beginning of the twentieth century stemmed from earlier developments in agriculture and industry.

During colonial times and earlier, farmers, not knowing the causes of proven successful practices worked out by their predecessors, would repeat them in their entirety. In agricultural communities in an earlier time success or failure was frequently attributed to the degree to which certain magical procedures were followed. Sims calls this the magical stage. He cites a number of examples of agricultural superstition directly connected with production, and alleges that similar superstitions are more or less

[14] Smith, *op. cit.*, p. 344. Smith attributes a great deal of importance to the invention of the horse collar as a pivotal innovation in the use of horsepower.

[15] Gras, *op. cit.*, pp. 288-290.

seriously believed in and followed by some American farmers everywhere.[16]

Sims also identifies an intermediate stage between magical practices and reliance upon science. This he has called the *practical*, which in essence means practices which have met the test of time.[17] Emphasis is upon high production, and rational rather than superstitious elements tend to influence decisions about technology.

Although there have been no comprehensive nationwide studies of the extent to which magical, practical, or scientific methods of farming are followed by American farmers, it is evident that the magical or superstitious attitude is on the wane. The practical basis is believed to be still predominant, but more and more commercial farmers are clearly taking advantage of the results of scientific research conducted by agricultural experiment stations and other agencies and individuals engaged in developing new crop varieties, breeds, and agricultural practices.

Marked changes in farm technology and organization occurred during the last half of the decade of the 1950s. According to the U.S. Census Bureau, specialization of farm production on larger producing units proceeded at a faster rate in the period 1954-1959 than during any previous five-year period in history. Farms having 3,200 or more chickens, for example, increased 125 percent, and those with 50 or more milk cows increased 41 percent. At the same time many producers withdrew from competition, as the following tabulation shows:

	Percent Decrease in Farms Reporting
Milk cows	39
Chickens	36
Turkeys	49
Eggs for sale	37
Vegetables for sale	35
Irish potatoes	52
Cotton	41

SOURCE: U.S. Bureau of the Census, *1959 Census of Agriculture—Preliminary*, Series AC59-1, January, 1961.

[16] N. L. Sims, *Elements of Rural Sociology*, 3rd ed., Crowell, 1940, pp. 398-401.

[17] *Ibid.*, p. 400.

DEVELOPMENT OF NEW FARM PRACTICES

Agricultural experiment stations now develop many new farm practices by the application of principles discovered through scientific research and experimentation. Some are the result of trial and error by individual farmers on their own farms. Others come from nonfarm sources. Still others are supplied by chemical firms, farm implement companies, and other business organizations.

Inventions, according to Linton, consist of new applications of knowledge developed by specific individuals.[18] But inventors must proceed within the framework of the existing culture;[19] and greater opportunities for invention are found in a society with a rich culture. Furthermore, the type of inventions which appear will depend upon the values of the society. Thus, technological inventions in agriculture have occurred in the United States but not to any appreciable extent in India or other economically underdeveloped countries.

Linton has offered a useful distinction between basic inventions and improving inventions.[20] The former involve new principles or at least new combinations of existing principles, while the latter consist of modifications of existing practices or culture objects. Thus, the gasoline tractor may be regarded as a basic invention whereas the diesel crawler tractor, on the other hand, would be an improvement.

Many of the earlier agricultural inventions made in America were not systematically planned, but arose from the imagination and ingenuity of independent inventors. The general culture was apparently favorable for technological innovation.

Technological innovation in agriculture no longer depends primarily upon relatively isolated individual inventors. Organizations now exist which are designed to exploit systematically the possibilities of applying scientific principles to agriculture. Perhaps the most important of these are the agricultural experiment stations, which were established at the land-grant colleges of the several states under the authority of the Morrill Act of 1862.[21]

[18] Ralph Linton, *The Study of Man*, Appleton-Century, 1936, p. 306.
[19] *Ibid.*, p. 319.
[20] *Ibid.*, p. 316.
[21] See Chapter 22.

The research work of agricultural scientists has led to the improvement of tillage practices and weed control; to the development of improved varieties and breeds of plants, fruit trees, livestock, and poultry; to improved practices of animal management and nutrition; and to the isolation and successful combating of diseases, insects, and pests which affect farm production. The field of mechanization has been relatively little exploited by governmental agencies, most of the inventions having been made by private inventors or agricultural implement concerns. Agricultural experiment stations also conduct some research in farm management and other aspects of the economics and sociology of agriculture. Some work is also carried on in human nutrition and other phases of home economics.

MECHANIZATION

Developments in mechanization have had perhaps the greatest influence on farm organization and management. These changes have affected the nature of the relationships between the farm operator and members of his family, his hired help, and his neighbors.

In most cases, new agricultural machines were not invented by farmers. A problem existed and some enterprising inventor worked out a solution. The need was sometimes very clearly felt, as for a plow that would scour in the black soils of the Ohio Valley, a problem solved by the invention of the steel plow. But often the need was not as apparent and the consequences of new innovations were not fully understood.

Some of the great advances in mechanization which have profoundly influenced the character of farm life are the following:[22]

1. In 1793 Eli Whitney invented the cotton gin. This development induced the planters of the South to devote a large portion of their efforts to the production of cotton, which in turn required a large, cheap labor force. The importation of African slaves was stepped up to meet this demand. Thus, the invention had far-reaching consequences, for it brought about an increase in the Negro

[22] See Bert S. Gittins, *Land of Plenty*, 2nd ed., Chicago, Farm Equipment Institute, 1959. This publication contains a list of major inventions in farm mechanization up to 1958.

population and greatly influenced the nature of southern agriculture for more than a century.

2. John Deere's invention of the steel plow in 1837 opened up the Ohio Territory and other areas to more rapid settlement, undoubtedly greatly accelerating the settlement of American farms. This plow made it possible to work land which had not proved amenable to cultivation by previously existing implements.

3. The invention in 1873 of the reaper by Cyrus McCormick eventually made it possible to harvest crops with a greatly reduced labor force. Further improvements on this basic invention led to the combined harvester-thresher known as the *combine*. These inventions made it possible to enlarge the size of farms, which, of course, had an important effect upon farm organization and management.

4. Mechanical power was introduced and came to replace animal power in large measure. The first tractor was not commercially produced until 1903, and its development and acceptance was a relatively gradual matter. However, at the present time, the draft horse and the mule have been virtually superseded by tractors on American commercial farms (Fig. 13). This has released for other uses vast acreages formerly devoted to pasture and the production of horse feed.

5. Motor transport replaced horse-drawn. Along with the development of trucks and passenger automobiles, of course, have come hard-surfaced roads which facilitate the efficient use of these vehicles.

Recent developments involve the use of still more complicated machines which require even less human muscle (Fig. 14). On the modern dairy farm, milk is extracted from the cows by milking machines, piped to a cooling tank, picked up by a glass-lined refrigerated tank truck, and delivered to a milk processing plant without having been handled physically by humans. Poultry and egg production is also mechanized to the point where one man can easily handle thousands of birds. Fruits, nuts, and vegetables traditionally have required large amounts of hand labor, but recently agricultural engineers have devised machines which will greatly reduce the labor requirements for harvesting. Even soft fruits like peaches and apricots can be harvested mechanically.

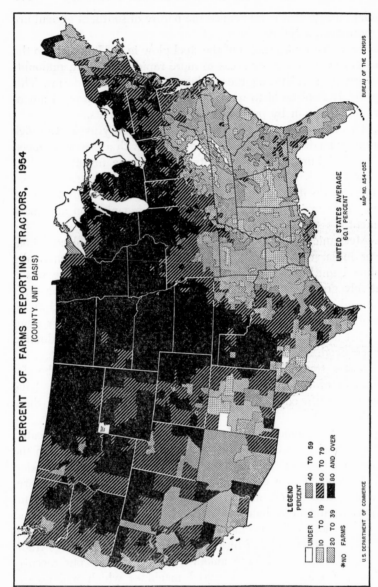

PERCENT OF FARMS REPORTING TRACTORS, 1954
(COUNTY UNIT BASIS)

LEGEND
PERCENT

UNDER 10 40 TO 59
10 TO 19 60 TO 79
20 TO 39 80 AND OVER
*NO FARMS

UNITED STATES AVERAGE
60.1 PERCENT

U.S. DEPARTMENT OF COMMERCE

MAP NO. A54-052

BUREAU OF THE CENSUS

FIG. 13.

Some farmers are even beginning to plan their farm operations for maximum profit by means of linear programming. This is a mathematical technique developed by farm economists which takes into account such variables as soil, climate, fertilizer, and probable prices for various alternative commodities. Some farmers have set up livestock feeding operations virtually on a push-button production line basis with as many as 30,000 animals in a single location.[23]

These developments have brought farmers into more frequent contact with nonfarm people and greatly expanded their range of

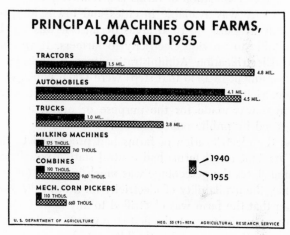

FIG. 14.

business and personal relationships. Mechanization has reduced the need for human labor in agriculture, thereby changing the nature of farm organization and releasing the surplus population to non-farm employment.

Cooper and associates have summarized some of the more important results of farm mechanization:

Modern mechanization has made the farm a better place to live and to work. Modern farm and home facilities have improved farm sanitation and health conditions of the farm family. They have made farm and home

[23] See "Farm Automation," *Newsweek*, Pacific ed., March 9, 1959, pp. 58-63; USDA, *Power to Produce: The Yearbook of Agriculture, 1960*, 1960, pp. 416-426.

work easier by reducing hand labor and human drudgery. Farm machines and facilities have reduced sizes of crews needed to perform some of the major, labor-consuming farm jobs, and made possible greater use of older and younger workers. Electric lights, piped running water, television, and radio, have provided satisfying influences in keeping good hired hands, and they have aided the farm family in conducting its business, and its educational and social affairs.[24]

ELECTRIFICATION

Large-scale electrification of farms is a relatively recent development. Electricity was available in cities and towns long before it was generally available in rural areas because it was not believed to be profitable to provide electricity to farmers. It was not until the Rural Electrification Administration was established by the federal government in 1936 that steps were taken which eventually brought electricity within reach for nearly all American farms. This *social* change was made for the purpose of promoting a *culture* change desired by public policy-makers.

By 1960 the electrification of farms had proceeded to the point where 97 percent of all farms had central station power available, and in some states the percentage was much higher[25] (Fig. 15).

Of course, the availability of electricity on a farm did not necessarily mean that the farm was electrified to any appreciable extent. In many cases, perhaps most, the first step was to utilize it for lighting purposes in the house and outbuildings. Subsequently, however, a great variety of electrical appliances have made their appearance in farm homes and electric motors of various types have been adopted as motive power for many stationary farm machines.

Some of the more important labor-saving devices in fairly common use on American farms are milking machines, electric welders, electrified feed grinders, electric fans for use in drying hay, electric pig brooders, water pumps for domestic irrigation and drainage purposes, electric washing machines, clothes dryers, and electric sewing machines. This is only a partial list, but it serves to illustrate the great change which electricity has made possible in banishing drudgery from farm and home tasks.

---

[24] Martin R. Cooper et al., "Farm Machinery and Facilities," in U.S. Bureau of the Census, *Agriculture, 1954, A Graphic Summary,* vol. III, Special Reports, part 4, of *U.S. Census of Agriculture, 1954,* 1956, p. 113.

[25] *Power to Produce: The Yearbook of Agriculture, 1960, op. cit.,* p. 69.

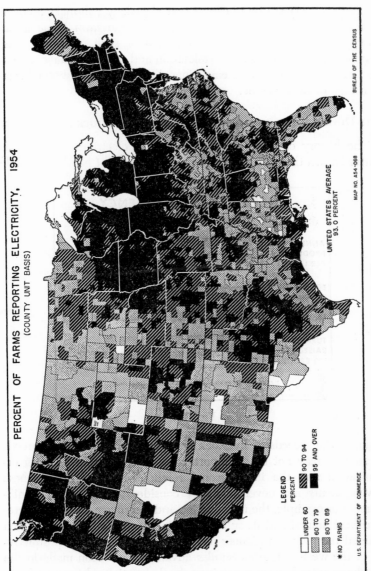

PERCENT OF FARMS REPORTING ELECTRICITY, 1954
(COUNTY UNIT BASIS)

LEGEND
PERCENT
UNDER 60
60 TO 79
80 TO 89
90 TO 94
95 AND OVER
* NO FARMS

UNITED STATES AVERAGE
93.0 PERCENT

U.S. DEPARTMENT OF COMMERCE

BUREAU OF THE CENSUS

MAP NO. A54-'068

Fig. 15.

There is every reason to expect that electricity will make an ever-increasing contribution to agriculture and the farm home as an energy source. Moreover, the expansion of such electronic mass communication devices as the television and radio will have a great impact on the work, living conditions, ideas, values, and social relationships of farm people.

THE DEVELOPMENT OF IMPROVED BREEDS OF LIVESTOCK AND POULTRY

The history of farm mechanization and electrification is much better known than the history of the advances that have been made

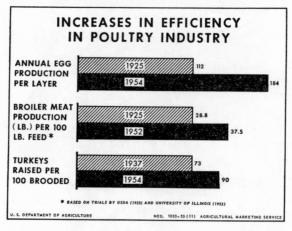

FIG. 16.

in improving breeds of livestock and poultry. While better breeds of animals may not be as important as mechanization to farm organization and the interpersonal relationships of farmers, these developments are nevertheless of considerable economic significance. For example, the introduction and improvement of the Hereford beef animal and its substitution for the Texas longhorn which roamed the plains in pioneer days greatly increased the productivity of the western ranges. Similar advances have been made in the development of high-grade dairy animals, specialized types of hogs, broad-breasted turkeys, and certain breeds of chickens.

A recent development of great significance to both farmers and consumers has been the growth of the broiler industry. In 1947, a fourth of the supply of chicken meat came from broilers. By 1955, this had increased to three-fifths.[26] Improvements in the efficiency of poultry enterprises are shown by Figure 16.

Livestock breeding experiments have been carried on by agricultural experiment stations and by private individuals. There is no doubt that systematic research can bring additional advances in livestock.[27]

IMPROVED CROP VARIETIES

The crop varieties utilized on American commercial farms are considerably different in most cases from those that were being used at the turn of the century or even 10 years ago. Great advances have been made in developing varieties which are resistant to smuts, rusts, and other diseases. Special-purpose crops have been developed. In addition, as with hybrid corn, new varieties of grains have made it possible to double and sometimes triple the yields obtained.

As in the improvement of livestock but to an even greater degree, the agricultural experiment stations have participated in developing new crop varieties. Individual farmers are also to be credited for contributions to these advances.

Fruits, Nuts, and Vegetables

Comparable developments have occurred in the creation of improved varieties of fruits, nuts, and vegetables. The propagation and care of such products is highly complex. Leadership in the development of new varieties has been taken by commercial nurseries and seed houses.

FARM CHEMICALS

Effective chemical fertilizers, pesticides, and insecticides have given the farmer a powerful ally in protecting and nurturing the welfare of his crops.

Chemical fertilizers have in many cases proved to be much more efficient than the natural manures utilized for centuries, and have

[26] *Agriculture, 1954, A Graphic Summary, op. cit.,* p. 56.
[27] T. C. Byerly, "The Biological Sciences," *Journal of Farm Economics,* December, 1958, pp. 1037-1048.

greatly increased crop yields. In 1954, chemical fertilizer was applied to 123,000,000 acres, half of them in the Corn Belt, the Great Plains, and the western states. In 1930 these areas accounted for only a sixth of the much smaller amount spent by farmers for commercial fetrilizer.[28] Between 1954 and 1959 there was an increase of 8 percent in the acreage fertilized.

Insecticides and pesticides have been developed which, when applied by airplane or other means, have given farmers a degree of control over weeds, insects, and other pests never before possible.

Farm chemicals have greatly increased the productivity of American farms and have, because of the special nature of the materials involved, created a demand for agricultural specialists who offer their services to commercial farmers on a contract or fee basis. From the standpoint of the social organization of agriculture, this is a new development of considerable significance.

SCIENTIFIC FARMING

Scientific farming can be regarded as an emerging culture pattern; it is a combination of interrelated ideas and practices. It is affected no less by cultural history than earlier patterns; it differs from other patterns chiefly in its orientation toward science as the source of its productive technology and in its emphasis upon rationality in economic decision-making. As such, it is part and parcel of the prevailing emphasis, societywide and individual, upon science and economic rationality in modern industrial production.

QUESTIONS FOR FURTHER STUDY AND DISCUSSION

1. Discuss the differences between herding and farming from the standpoint of sociology. (See Gillin and Gillin, *op. cit.*, pp. 170-171.) Contrast herding with livestock ranches in the western U.S.
2. Describe the early development of advanced plow culture in northern Europe. (See Smith, *op. cit.*, chap 14.) Why did this pattern develop in northern Europe and not in India or China?
3. Describe the agriculture of a specific rural locality. Characterize the patterns in terms of Sims's three-fold classification.

[28] *Agriculture, 1954, A Graphic Summary, op. cit.*, p. 45.

4. Visit a modern dairy or poultry farm. Try to find out what practices, if any, are unique to this farm and what practices are generally followed by other farmers in the locality.

SELECTED REFERENCES

Cooper, M. R., Glen T. Barton, and Albert P. Brodell, *Progress of Farm Mechanization*, USDA, Miscellaneous Publication 630, October, 1947.

Gillin, John Lewis, and John Philip Gillin, *Cultural Sociology*, Macmillan, 1948.

Gittins, Bert S., *Land of Plenty*, 2nd ed., Chicago, Farm Equipment Institute, 1959.

Sims, N. L., *Elements of Rural Sociology*, 3rd ed., Crowell, 1940.

Smith, T. Lynn, *The Sociology of Rural Life*, 3rd ed., Harper, 1953.

USDA, *Power to Produce: The Yearbook of Agriculture 1960*, 1960.

10

Culture Change: Diffusion of Improved Agricultural Technology

Although great progress has been made in the diffusion of improved agricultural practices in the United States, studies have shown that many farmers do not use modern practices but cling instead to outmoded and discredited methods. This is, of course, even more true of farmers in most other parts of the world.

For the purposes of this discussion, we will consider changes in agricultural technology, including machinery, new breeds of livestock, new varieties of crops, new farm chemicals, or new techniques of cultivation, to be improvements if they increase yield or cut production costs.

The diffusion of new agricultural technology from innovators to users was slow and rather haphazard in America as elsewhere until the last 25 or 30 years. At present, however, the situation in the U.S. is very different. Channels of communication now exist which make it possible for new agricultural information to reach interested farmers rapidly. Some farmers are so keenly interested in new technology that they keep in personal touch with agricultural experiment station workers. Some conduct their own experiments, and are even said to be technologically more advanced than AES scientists.

It has generally been assumed by agricultural specialists that rapid diffusion of more efficient farm practices and more productive varieties of crops or breeds of livestock is a desirable goal for individual farmers and for society. Recently, however, it has become evident that, in this country at least, the rapid growth of farm techology creates problems. Farmers who adopt a successful new

practice early may reap significant gains in income. Others, however, may be forced to use it simply to stay in business, and when
substantially all producers have adopted the practice, production
may outstrip effective demand to the point where prices and farm
incomes fall. At the same time appropriations for price supports to
bolster farm incomes may increase while unwanted commodities
pile up in warehouses.

THE ADOPTION PROCESS

There are, of course, many types of new agricultural and home
technology, some of which are merely improvements in already
existing practices. Others represent qualitative changes, more difficult to make and possibly with major consequences for farm organization or family life.

STAGES IN THE ADOPTION PROCESS

The decision to adopt a new practice can be broken down into a
sequence of five stages, according to a committee of midwestern
rural sociologists:

1. *Awareness:*   At this stage the individual learns of the existence of the
   idea or practice but has little knowledge about it.
2. *Interest:*   At this stage the individual develops interest in the idea.
   He seeks more information about it and considers its general merits.
3. *Evaluation:*   At this stage the individual makes mental application of
   the idea and weighs its merits for his own situation. He obtains more
   information about the idea and decides whether or not to try it.
4. *Trial:*   At this stage the individual actually applies the idea or
   practice—usually on a small scale. He is interested in how to apply
   the practice; in amounts, time and conditions for application.
5. *Adoption:*   This is the stage of acceptance leading to continued use.[1]

In the *awareness* stage, according to research reviewed by the
committee, mass communications—radio, television, newspapers,
and magazines—are the individual farmer's or homemaker's usual
sources of initial information about new technology.

[1] North Central Rural Sociology Committee, *How Farm People Accept New
Ideas,* Iowa Agricultural Extension Service Special Report No. 15, 1955, pp. 3-4.

In the *interest* stage, mass media still play an important function by providing timely and readily available additional information, though some individuals seek further knowledge from agencies like the Agricultural Extension Service, the Farmers Home Administration, and the Soil Conservation Service. Others rely more upon neighbors and friends who are considered to be well informed.

In the *evaluation* stage, the potential adopter imagines how the new practice may apply on his farm or in his own home.[2] If it is being considered by a commercial farm operator, he may appraise it economically in terms of potential gain, and make his decisions primarily on the basis of increasing his profit through increased efficiency in production.[3] However, even the operator of a highly successful commercial farm will generally evaluate the possible impact of the new practice on noneconomic aspects of his life. He will consider, for example, how it may affect his and his family's social relationships, goals, and resources. He will consult sources of information which he considers to be dependable; frequently he will have discussions with respected neighbors and friends who assist by evaluating the "legitimacy" of the practice. The committee noted that at this stage those who were classified as early adopters depend to a marked extent upon agricultural agencies for information and advice.

In the *trial* stage, the new practice is tried out, if possible, on a small scale. If it involves a new piece of equipment, arrangements may be made with the machinery dealer for a demonstration or for use on a trial basis. In the trial stage, according to the research evidence, agricultural agencies become important as well as neighbors and friends who have already adopted the practice. Salesmen are also important as sources of information where a commercial product is involved.[4]

In the *adoption* stage, the practice has been completely accepted and put into use. This completes the process. However, on a commercial farm continued scrutiny of the new practice is to be expected; the comparison of results between those who have adopted

[2] *Ibid.*

[3] See E. A. Wilkening, "The Process of Acceptance of Technological Inventions in Rural Society," in A. L. Bertrand, ed., *Rural Sociology*, McGraw-Hill, 1958, p. 391.

[4] *How Farm People Accept New Ideas, op. cit.*

the practice may lead to substitution of a still newer practice or reversion to the practice previously used.[5]

The stages outlined above seem very definite and the conclusions have been stated by the committee in positive terms, probably for the sake of simplicity. However, the reader should not be misled into thinking that all doubts and questions with respect to the process of adoption have been resolved. As Copp, Sill, and Brown have pointed out, the stages are to be regarded as a conceptual framework for organizing data rather than as a set of testable hypotheses.[6]

The length of time required for all five stages may be called the adoption period. Some types of practices take longer than others. The average length of the adoption period for 10 new farm and home practices studied by various investigators ranged from five years for hybrid seed corn in Iowa to six months for "miracle" fabrics by Ohio homemakers.[7]

It should be noted also that an average adoption period may differ greatly from one locality to another, and of course between countries, because of differences in culture or physical circumstances.

It is also true that not all people who might be regarded as potential adopters go through the same stages simultaneously or at the same rate. Some farmers never do adopt a specific farming practice[8] because it is not applicable to their farming operations or for a variety of other reasons, some of which are discussed later.

TYPES OF ADOPTERS

The first farmers to experiment with and adopt new practices are classified by the committee as *innovators*. These farmers are regarded locally as people who are always trying out new things, and were seldom named by others as sources of advice on farming.[9] In a recent Ohio study, Rogers classifies as innovators the first 2.5 percent to adopt a new idea, and finds that they differ from average

[5] *Ibid.*

[6] James H. Copp, M. L. Sill, and E. J. Brown, "The Function of Information Sources in the Farm Adoption Process," *Rural Sociology*, June, 1958, p. 147.

[7] See Everett M. Rogers, *The Adoption Period*, paper presented at the Rural Sociological Society Meeting, Ithaca, N.Y., August 27, 1959.

[8] *How Farm People Accept New Ideas, op. cit.*

[9] *Ibid.*

farmers in a number of important respects: they tend to be younger, more highly educated, more inclined to take risks, and so research-oriented that nearly all returned a mailed questionnaire. In addition, they operate more efficient, more specialized and larger farms, and are of higher social class.[10]

Farmers who are among the first to use, though not to try out, new practices are classified as *community adoption leaders* whom others in the locality regard as individuals with good judgment who adopt tried rather than untried ideas. They usually maintain direct contact with agricultural agencies. They may be farm organization leaders, usually have a relatively high level of education, and participate more than most farm people in formal organizations.[11]

Those classified as *local adoption leaders* are not necessarily early adopters, but they do adopt new practices sooner than the majority of farmers in the area. They are classified as leaders because they evidently have considerable prestige in the locality, and others look to them for information about new practices. They do not differ greatly from the majority of their neighbors in their personal and social characteristics and are not ordinarily thought of by neighbors and friends as leaders.[12]

The majority of the people in a locality who eventually do take up new practices are classified as *later adopters*. So far as their personal characteristics are concerned, they tend to have less education, to participate less than others in community affairs, and to be older than those who adopt ideas at an earlier stage.[13]

The nonadopters are those who do not accept the new idea. This category includes those for whom the practice is not applicable or who for one reason or another reject it.

FACTORS WHICH INFLUENCE ADOPTION

The many influences involved in the decision[14] to adopt or to reject a new practice include values, traditional practices and other

[10] Everett M. Rogers, *The Role of the Agricultural Innovator in Technological Change*, paper presented at the American Sociological Society Meeting, September 5, 1959; *Social Change in Rural Society*, Appleton-Century-Crofts, 1960, p. 412.

[11] *How Farm People Accept New Ideas, op. cit.*

[12] *Ibid.*

[13] *Ibid.*

[14] See Chapter 13 for a discussion of decision-making.

aspects of the existing culture, knowledge about the existence and nature of the new practice, personal and family goals, the influence of other family members, the influence of friends and respected neighbors, the prestige associated with adoption or rejection, and, in the case of commercial farm operators, the prospect of economic gain. A positive force is exercised by the persuasive efforts of business firms, farm organizations and educational agencies, and various branches of federal, state, and local governments. Also influential, though not readily perceived as such by individual farmers, are generalized attitudes toward change which are prevalent in the culture.

KNOWLEDGE

Regardless of other considerations, a new farm practice cannot be adopted until the farmer knows about it. Consequently, it is correct to regard dissemination of information as a key factor affecting adoption. The importance of knowledge is so great that a discussion of the channels through which agricultural information reaches farmers is presented later.

To an educated member of a capitalistic society, there might appear to be little reason why all farm operators should not immediately adopt all applicable improved practices of which they have knowledge.[15] It is a fact, however, that many farmers have little interest in increased productivity. This is particularly true of Asian peasants, but it is also true of many American subsistence and part-time farmers and others who value security more than risk-taking. There are, of course, many barriers to the acceptance of change besides knowledge. Some are economic, including such matters as the lack of adequate capital or credit. Some lie in the realm of social organization; for example, certain forms of tenancy offer relatively little incentive to the operator to increase production since he would not benefit by it. Still others are related to values and group norms.

THE STATE OF THE EXISTING CULTURE

Many practicable innovations are rejected because they do not fit into the existing culture considered as an integrated complex of

[15] Improved agricultural practices may be defined as those which increase productivity or reduce the cost of production.

interlocking behavior patterns and norms. For example, the airplane, which was proposed by Leonardo da Vinci, was not developed until modern times. Commercial farming cannot succeed except in a market economy; if large agricultural machinery were introduced rapidly in countries like India and Pakistan, it would result in widespread unemployment of displaced farm laborers.

The diffusion of new practices in agriculture depends also upon prevalent attitudes toward change. It has been said that Americans tend to value change for its own sake, but this is certainly not true generally throughout the world; and within the United States, as noted above, there are also variations in rate of adoption between areas, age groups, educational categories, localities, and families.

VALUES

In some social systems, prestige is gained by those who adopt new procedures and techniques readily, while in others considerably more value is placed upon the heritage of the past and individuals are encouraged not to deviate from accepted practices. The latter situation is most likely to be found in isolated, tradition-bound localities like a Middle East village.[16]

The relationship of values to change is of very great importance even within a society like the American which puts a premium on acceptance of change, as is illustrated by Hoffer's and Stangland's study of the failure of certain Michigan farmers to adopt specific improved corn-growing practices. The practices, which included (1) soil testing, (2) an increased amount of fertilizer at planting time, (3) minimum tillage, and (4) increased number of plants per acre, were known to all the farmers in the sample so that no question of communication of information was involved. The great variation in adoption—two-fifths applied increased fertilizer while only a fourth increased the density of plants—was evidently related to the values of the farmers. Values, of course, derive from the culture. Those who were classified as conservative, who placed a high value on security, were likely to adopt the practice slowly or not at all, while the group characterized as efficient, progressive, and high in

[16] See Afif I. Tannous, "Technical Exchange and Cultural Values: Case of the Middle East," *Rural Sociology*, March, 1956, pp. 76-79.

initiative were likely to adopt the practices.[17]

Ramsey, Polson, and Spencer found that New York dairy farmers who valued security were also somewhat less likely to adopt new practices than were risk-takers. This study also investigated the relationship of a number of other values to practice adoption, but found relatively little evidence that these values were greatly influential.[18]

Larson, Anderson, Smith, and Tannous have pointed out how local values have adversely affected rapid acceptance of improved agricultural technology in selected underdeveloped areas.[19]

The following quotation from an anthropological study made in an Indian village by McKim Marriott illustrates the wide ramifications of a seemingly simple change:

Let me list some of the objections which farmers in my village, and in other nearby villages, have raised against the improved wheat seed. It is true, they said, that if the Lord pleases, one will get a better weight of fat wheat from the field sown with Government's improved seed: the yield in weight is really very good. . . . The grain is indeed big—so big and tough that the women cannot grind it well in the old stone flour mills. Dough made from the new flour is difficult to knead and hard to bake into good bread. The new bread, which is all a poor farmer would have to eat, does not taste like the good old bread: it is flat and uninteresting (the explanation being in part, of course, that it does not contain that potpourri of barley, peas, gram and mustard seeds that "wheat" contained in the old days). Next, look at the cows and bullocks! They do not like to eat the straw of the new wheat; they will die of hunger if we grow it. The straw is worthless, too, for thatching roofs. It does not even make a good fire to warm our hands in winter.

An improved wheat seed thus does not appear to the Hindu farmer as a simple addition, or a simple replacement or improvement on one item of his technology. The new seed brings along with it a whole new plant; the many parts of the plant and their many uses lead to an unknown

[17] C. R. Hoffer and Dale Stangland, "Farmers' Attitudes and Values in Relation to Approved Practices in Corn Growing," *Rural Sociology,* June, 1958, pp. 112-120.

[18] C. E. Ramsey, R. A. Polson, and G. E. Spencer, "Values and the Adoption of Practices," *Rural Sociology,* March, 1959, p. 44. The authors considered that their methods of value measurement were inadequate even though they were developed with great care.

[19] O. F. Larson *et al.,* "Social Values and Technical Cooperation Programs," *Rural Sociology,* March, 1956, pp. 62-79.

series of threatening consequences. When techniques are so tightly inter-connected we must admit the wisdom of the Hindu farmer's conservatism. He rightly feels that even small alterations in his precarious, overdeveloped technology may lead to catastrophe. Somehow, the peasant's legitimate technical fears must be answered by the innovator.[20]

A similar reaction to hybrid corn by the Spanish Americans of New Mexico and by some farmers in the South has also been reported.[21]

One reason why American farmers have failed to accept efficient improved agricultural techniques, new machines, new breeds of live-stock, and new varieties of plants as widely as might have been expected is the fact that many are not primarily interested in farm-ing so as to maximize profit. This is particularly true of subsistence farmers, but it is also true of large numbers of part-time farmers who receive a substantial portion of their family income from off-farm sources. Alicja Iwanska, after a study of a part-time farming community in the state of Washington, advanced the following hypotheses regarding the low rate of adoption of improved agri-cultural practices advocated by the Agricultural Extension Service:

1. . . . Good Fortune farmers as well as their wives are greatly receptive to all new farm and homemaking techniques, as long as these do not conflict with their basic values and do not interfere with their cherished style of life. . . .
2. . . . the apparent resistance of some part-time farmers to new agricul-tural techniques comes often not from their resistance to new technology, but from their lack of interest in efficient farming.
3. . . . the apparent resistance of the farm housewives to some of the new homemaking techniques does not come from their resentment of new techniques in general but from their lack of interest in being efficient homemakers. . . .
4. . . . one of the reasons for the resistance of part-time farmers to some new agricultural techniques is the real or apparent threat which the promotion or application of these techniques presents to one of their chief values: the value of self-determination.
5. . . . new agricultural techniques diffuse easier among part-time farmers through the mass media of communication, chiefly magazines and

[20] McKim Marriott, "Technological Change in Overdeveloped Areas," in Lyle W. Shannon, ed., *Underdeveloped Areas,* Harper, 1957, p. 428.
[21] See Wilkening, in Bertrand, ed., *op. cit.,* chaps. 24, 25.

television broadcasts, than they do through such personal channels as lectures, demonstrations, visits of a county agent, the example of well-established farmers or influence of community leaders, and . . . this is due to:

    a. a characteristic tendency toward vicarious identification by Good Fortunites achieved mainly through the mass media with such abstract causes as progress, science and power;

    b. their fear of being controlled by people with whom they come into contact. . . .

6. . . . part-time farmers resent those new agricultural techniques which presuppose some sacrifices of time, money, or standard of living and do not yield immediate and tangible results. . . .

7. . . . those new agricultural and homemaking techniques which are relatively less useful but have a lot of prestige, are more easily accepted by part-time farmers and their wives than the more utilitarian and less prestigeful techniques. . . .[22]

Although Dr. Iwanska's insights about the influence of values are based upon the study of only one community of part-time farmers, it seems quite likely that further research may demonstrate much wider applicability for her hypotheses.

CHARACTERISTICS OF ADOPTERS

Research in the midwestern United States indicates that farmers in that region who are most likely to adopt the new practice tend to have somewhat different characteristics from nonadopters:[23]

1. They have more education than others.

2. Younger operators are more likely to be aware of and favorable toward new ideas but may not always be in a position to adopt them because of lack of capital, land, or freedom to make decisions.

3. They have a high level of participation in general farm organizations and farmer cooperatives.

4. They have children in 4-H Clubs or vocational agriculture.

[22] Alicja Iwanska, *Good Fortune: Second Chance Community*, Washington AES Bulletin 589, June, 1958.

[23] Rural Sociological Society, *Sociological Research on the Diffusion and Adoption of New Farm Practices: Report of the Subcommittee on the Diffusion and Adoption of Farm Practices*, Kentucky AES Report No. RS-2, June, 1952.

5. They have contact with or participate in agricultural extension programs.
6. They have contact with new ideas through bulletins, farm magazines, and newspapers.
7. They are risk-takers rather than security-seekers.
8. They derive satisfaction from individual achievements.
9. They practice democracy with respect to participation of family members in decision-making.

These characteristics would probably be applicable fairly generally to operators of commercial family-type farms in the U.S. Marsh and Coleman, for example, found similar characteristics among Kentucky adopters.[24] However, these characteristics would not necessarily be applicable to subsistence or part-time farmers.

Though some investigators have found that age is not related to the adoption of certain practices,[25] it is generally conceded that older farmers are less likely to be receptive to new techniques.[26] One reason why it is easier to get young people to accept change is the emphasis in most societies on youth as a learning period. Furthermore, many have not as yet established firmly their guiding values, ideas, and practices. This is particularly true, of course, in a society in transition where there are many conflicting norms. The ability of older persons to accept new ideas as theories may be very great, but implementing them is quite a different matter. For an older person, whether a new practice is agricultural or personal, it ordinarily has to compete with and displace an already existing pattern of some standing. Obviously there is a tendency for people to perpetuate practices which have been reasonably satisfactory. A person who moves frequently and who thus cuts off many of his group ties and interpersonal relationships would probably be more receptive to new ideas than one who is sedentary.

[24] C. Paul Marsh and A. Lee Coleman, "The Relation of Farmer Characteristics to the Adoption of Recommended Farm Practices," *Rural Sociology*, September-December, 1955, pp. 289-296.

[25] See E. A. Wilkening, *Acceptance of Improved Farm Practices in Three Coastal Plain Counties*, North Carolina AES Technical Bulletin 98, May, 1952, p. 50; Marsh and Coleman, *op. cit.*

[26] See Wilkening, in Bertrand, ed., *op. cit.*, p. 397; Marvin A. Anderson, *Informational Sources Important in the Acceptance and Use of Fertilizer in Iowa*, TVA, Division of Agricultural Relations (in cooperation with Iowa Agricultural Extension Service), Report No. P55-1, April, 1955.

LOCAL LEADERSHIP

The importance local leadership may have is illustrated by the following quotation from the report of the Midwest Rural Sociology Subcommittee: "In one community, none would agree to go along with a program to eradicate brucellosis in dairy herds until one man in the community was sold on the idea. Once sold, he influenced all farmers in the community to go along with it. In this situation, change was brought about by working through the leader of the group. In most communities, no single leader has such influence."[27]

SOCIAL ORGANIZATION

The nature of social organization in a locality, including the existence of neighborhoods, cliques, and other groups, seems to be of greater importance where the educational level is lower. This follows logically from the fact that educated people are able to obtain information from nonlocal sources, tend to be less subject to indigenous local norms which may represent barriers to new ideas, and presumably are also better able to evaluate information which comes to them through such sources.

The norms associated with social systems in some localities are favorable to adoption of new ideas, and in others not.[28]

An aspect of social organization which has a very important bearing on farm practice adoption is land tenure. A short-term tenant, for example, would obviously have no incentive to use soil conserving practices which might increase later production at the expense of present yields.[29]

ADOPTION RATES FOR DIFFERENT PRACTICES

Adoption rates for specific practices may differ greatly between major societies because of differences in culture. Profit-increasing

[27] *Sociological Research on the Diffusion and Adoption of New Farm Practices, op. cit.,* p. 7.

[28] See C. Paul Marsh and A. Lee Coleman, "Group Influences and Agricultural Innovations: Some Tentative Findings and Hypotheses," *American Journal of Sociology,* May, 1956, pp. 588-594.

[29] See Chapter 16 for a discussion of land tenure.

techniques that have great appeal for an American commercial farmer may have no attraction for a Pakistani cultivator who produces little for the market.

In addition, research indicates that there are differences in adoption rates for different farm practices. Rogers has pointed out that practices with the following characteristics tend to have slower rates of adoption:

1. Those which are expensive and whose probable returns are risky.
2. Those which are complex and must be adopted as a unit.
3. Those which are not easily observed.
4. Those which are not closely related to ideas already accepted.
5. Those which promise only minor benefits.
6. Those which require group action, such as REA power.[30]

CHANNELS AND SOURCES OF INFORMATION

Because information about prices and weather forecasts and technological knowledge of various kinds are indispensable to a commercial farmer, dependable and regular sources of such information have been developed. Not only do farmers actively seek data of this kind, but because of the benefits to business organizations and to the general society, active programs are established to communicate technological information to farmers. In a market economy like that of the United States, it is easy to identify these agencies and organizations. They include various branches of the U.S. Department of Agriculture, state departments of agriculture, the land-grant colleges and universities (particularly their agricultural extension services), and business firms. These organizations may be regarded as information-diffusing centers.

The efforts of vendors of technological knowledge appear to be based on the dual assumption that the goal of farmers everywhere is to increase production and that the main barrier to the achievement of this goal is lack of knowledge of the applicable techniques. The channels through which technological information travels from diffusion centers to farmers include radio, television, farm and general magazines, newspapers, circular letters, and personal contacts of various kinds.

[30] Rogers, *Social Change in Rural Society*, *op. cit.*, pp. 403-404.

Such diffusion centers are now to be found in most countries of the free world, including the nations of western Europe and many of the underdeveloped countries of Asia, Africa, and South America. The programs of technical assistance in agriculture which have been established to assist underdeveloped countries to increase agricultural production rely to a considerable extent upon the dissemination of information through organizations similar to the American agricultural extension services.

There is no doubt that communication is fundamental to diffusion of knowledge, and that knowledge, as we have seen, is one of the important factors in the adoption of a new idea. However, the sources of information about new technology tend to be different at different stages in the adoption process.[31] Studies have demonstrated also that some sources and channels are more effective than others in reaching farmers.

A number of studies have been made in various parts of the United States by rural sociologists and agricultural economists to identify the principal sources of information about new practices which are acknowledged by farmers. In evaluating such information, for the most part obtained through personal interviews with farm operators, it should be borne in mind that the responses of individual farmers are not always entirely valid with respect to data of this kind. In the first place, they are probably unable readily to recall the exact sources of specific information, because they are not sensitized to the importance of identifying sources. Furthermore, the prevalent image of the American farmer as a self-reliant decision-maker may predispose a respondent to believe that he has not been influenced by other people or organizations in his decision to adopt a new practice. In addition, information about new technology may come from more than one source and through several channels. Even granting these limitations, however, there is undoubtedly considerable validity to the information farmers provide, particularly where more than one study yields similar findings.[32]

[31] See E. A. Wilkening, "Role of Communicating Agents in Technological Change in Agriculture," *Social Forces*, May, 1956, pp. 361-367.

[32] Some people are very suspicious of information obtained by asking people what they want and what they do. Crossmon, for example, alleges that motivation-research psychologists have largely discarded this approach because they found the answers false (V. D. Crossmon, "Discussion: New Knowledge of

Mass Media

The majority of American farmers own TV sets, nearly all of them have radios, and a large proportion read daily and/or weekly newspapers. This is, of course, well known to governmental, educational, and business organizations which seek to facilitate the diffusion of new technological information. Consequently, the mass media are utilized to a considerable extent for this purpose. Major TV and radio network programs are not usually oriented specifically toward the farmer, but local radio programs are utilized, as are weekly newspapers and local dailies, by agricultural agents and home agents as well as by business firms. The major effort, however, is placed in the major farm magazines.

There is a sound basis for this concentration of effort. The Interstate Managerial Survey in the Midwest has shown that farm magazines were placed first by farm respondents as their source of information about new technology.[33] Magazines were a leading initial source for Washington farmers,[34] and Wilkening also indi-

Decision-Making Processes," *Journal of Farm Economics*, December, 1958, pp. 1404-1406). Rogers and Beal have tried projective techniques with a sample of Iowa farmers, and feel that such techniques offer advantages (E. M. Rogers and George M. Beal, *Reference Group Influences in the Adoption of Agricultural Technology*, Iowa State College, Department of Economics and Sociology, 1958). Murray A. Straus has also proposed the use of indirect methods (*Direct, Indirect and Disguised Measurement in Rural Sociology*, Washington AES Technical Bulletin 26, August, 1955).

However, the psychologist Gordon W. Allport, after reviewing psychological studies which compared the validity of information obtained through projective techniques with that obtained from direct questions and observations, cautions that projective methods should never be used in the study of motivation without allowing for the use of direct methods also. Projective techniques, he feels, are of particular value in obtaining information from neurotic or psychotic individuals but may cull no information from normal individuals about matters on which they could readily give information by direct methods (Gordon W. Allport, "The Trend in Motivational Theory," in C. E. Moustakas, ed., *The Self*, Harper, 1956, pp. 25-43).

[33] Glenn Johnson, "New Knowledge of Decision-Making Processes," *Journal of Farm Economics*, December, 1958, p. 1399.

[34] Walter L. Slocum, Owen L. Brough, Jr., and Murray A. Straus, *Extension Contacts, Selected Characteristics, Practices and Attitudes of Washington Farm Families*, Washington AES Bulletin 584, April, 1958, p. 16.

cates that farmers place major reliance upon farm magazines for information about new farm practices.[35]

TECHNICAL PUBLICATIONS

Agricultural experiment stations, extension services, farm organizations, and various agencies of the U.S. Department of Agriculture issue technical publications which contain information about new practices, chemicals, breeds, and varieties. The Inter-state Managerial Survey found that 6.4 percent of its sample used experiment station publications for information about new technology, while only .5 percent used publications of farm organizations.[36] In the Washington study, 5.3 percent reported that their initial information about the most recent farming practice adopted came from a bulletin or a book; only about half as many (2.7 percent) relied on this source for detailed reports.[37]

FIELD MEN OF PUBLIC AGENCIES

The agricultural extension services provide farm families with technical information about various aspects of agriculture and home-making. Local sources supply a substantial part of the support for these agencies, which thus play an important role in the dissemination of information about new practices. Various investigations have shown, however, that not all farm families make use of the facilities of the agricultural extension services.

In a study of the extension contacts of a statewide probability sample of commercial farmers in Washington, it was found that 37.6 percent of the farmers had the equivalent of a farm or home visit every second month or more frequently. On the other hand, 11.3 percent reported no contact with the agricultural extension service whatever.[38]

The study showed that 53 percent of the farmers obtained some information from the county agricultural agent, but when it came to information about new practices, only 6.1 percent listed the

[35] E. A. Wilkening, in Bertrand, ed., *op. cit.*, p. 26.
[36] Johnson, *op. cit.*, p. 1398.
[37] Slocum, Brough, and Straus, *op. cit.*, p. 18.
[38] *Ibid.*, p. 3.

county agent as the initial source and 6.9 percent as the detailed source of the most recent farming practice adopted. The writers state that the data suggest that "many farm operators regard the extension service not so much as the source of new ideas as a source of technical information bearing upon a specific problem."[39]

Other agricultural agencies are also acknowledged as sources of new information. Wilkening reports that farmers in North Carolina cited the Soil Conservation Service and the Production Marketing Administration of the U.S. Department of Agriculture as sources of specific practices.[40] In the state of Washington, the Soil Conservation Service was listed as the initial source of information about the most recent practice adopted by 7.6 percent and as the detailed source by 10.5 percent.[41]

BUSINESS FIRMS

Advertising is one of the principal sources of information about new technology which involves a salable product. Business firms use many types of appeals, and also employ salesmen who provide technical details and, in many cases, persuade the farmer to "sign on the dotted line." Ryan and Gross, in their classic study, have clearly demonstrated the important role of salesmen in the diffusion of information about hybrid corn.[42] Slocum, Brough, and Straus found that dealers were the leading source of detailed information about the most recent farming practices adopted by the farmers in their sample.[43] Midwestern farmers also reported dealers, salesmen, and buyers to be a leading source of information about new technology.[44]

LOCAL OPINION LEADERS

There is some question about the conditions under which local opinion leaders are most effective as sources of new agricultural

[39] *Ibid.,* p. 17.
[40] Wilkening, in Bertrand, ed., *op. cit.,* p. 381.
[41] Slocum, Brough, and Straus, *op. cit.,* p. 18.
[42] Bryce Ryan and Neil Gross, *Acceptance and Diffusion of Hybrid Corn Seed in Two Iowa Communities,* Iowa AES Research Bulletin 372, 1950.
[43] Slocum, Brough, and Straus, *op. cit.,* p. 18.
[44] Johnson, *op. cit.,* p. 1198.

information. The midwestern rural sociology committee, as noted above, indicated that local opinion leaders were very important. In a society with high educational attainments, there may be many opinion leaders in a given area. Wilkening is of the opinion that farmers who have a wide range of influence are more likely to obtain information from outside sources and to be innovation leaders in the area.[45] Lionberger found evidence in Missouri of reliance on local opinion leaders, who, according to his report, tended to have larger farms, higher incomes, and greater prestige than the average farmer.[46] Rogers and Beal found in a central Iowa rural community that personal influences were more important at certain stages in the adoption process than in others—specifically, later adopters reported that personal influence was more important for them, while the innovators and early adopters depended more upon personal sources of information.[47]

Paul F. Lazarsfeld and associates have suggested on the basis of a study of factors involved in political decision-making that opinion leaders mediate between mass media and the people so that political opinion change based upon propaganda is frequently a two-step process.[48]

There is need for caution in generalizing about the influence of opinion leaders. Empey and Slocum made a before-and-after analysis in a farmer-hunter conflict to test whether local opinion leaders were influential in changing the attitudes of individual farmers on this subject. They found no evidence that opinion leaders, self-appointed or otherwise, influenced the attitudes or relevant decisions of most farmers.[49]

[45] Wilkening, in Bertrand, ed., *op. cit.*, p. 376.

[46] Herbert F. Lionberger, "Some Characteristics of Farm Operators Sought as Sources of Farm Information in a Missouri Community," *Rural Sociology*, December, 1953, pp. 327-338.

[47] E. M. Rogers and George M. Beal, "The Importance of Personal Influence in the Adoption of Technological Changes," *Social Forces*, May, 1958, pp. 333-335.

[48] See Paul F. Lazarsfeld, Bernard Berelson, and Hazel Gaudet, *People's Choice: How the Voter Makes Up His Mind in a Presidential Campaign*, Duell, Sloan and Pearce, 1944.

[49] Lamar T. Empey and Walter L. Slocum, "Stability of Farmers' Attitudes in a Conflict Situation Involving Farmer-Hunter Relations," *Rural Sociology*, September-December, 1955, pp. 42-48.

NEIGHBORS AND FRIENDS

Studies in various parts of the U.S. indicate that many farmers regard neighbors and friends as important sources of information. A North Carolina study by Wilkening showed that farmers first approached their neighbors for details on improved practices,[50] and an extension service study in Vermont found neighbors and friends frequently credited as influential sources of information about new farm practices.[51] Slocum, Brough, and Straus found that neighbors and friends were most frequently listed by Washington commercial farmers as the initial sources of information about the most recent farming practice adopted.[52]

Loomis and Beegle have indicated a belief that cliques and friendship groups are of great importance as communication channels.[53] Barnett and Mayo, on the basis of research in North Carolina, have suggested that farm neighborhood cliques or neighbor groups can be utilized for extension work.[54] Studies by Lionberger in Missouri indicate, however, that informal groups can sometimes hinder the transmission of information about agricultural practices.[55]

Wilkening has pointed out that neighbors and clique groups are not necessarily the best channels for communication of technological information. As he correctly observes, many local residents do not have adequate information about technological changes, and furthermore that their transmission of such information as they do possess is likely to be incomplete and colored by subjective evaluations based upon personal experiences.[56]

[50] Wilkening, *Acceptance of Improved Farm Practices, op. cit.*
[51] U.S. Department of Agriculture, part I of *The Extension Service in Vermont, Farmers and the Extension Service,* July, 1947.
[52] Slocum, Brough, and Straus, *op. cit.,* p. 18.
[53] C. P. Loomis and J. A. Beegle, *Rural Social Systems,* Prentice-Hall, 1950, pp. 133-171.
[54] W. E. Barnett and Selz C. Mayo, *Neighbor Groups,* North Carolina AES, Progress Report No. 14, June, 1952.
[55] Herbert F. Lionberger, "The Relation of Informal Social Groups to the Diffusion of Farm Information in a Northeast Missouri Farm Community," *Rural Sociology, September,* 1954, pp. 233-243.
[56] Wilkening, in Bertrand, ed., *op. cit.,* p. 375.

FAMILY AND PERSONAL EXPERIENCE

The literature does not indicate that family members are regarded as important sources of information about improved technology. On the other hand, they are frequently influential in the decision to adopt or to reject new farm or home practices, and are doubtless the primary sources of information for most farmers about existing farming methods. Farm operators often regard past personal experience as a source of information about existing production methods, as Johnson reports on the findings of the Interstate Managerial Survey.[57] Wilkening found that two-fifths of a sample of Wisconsin farm owners regarded their fathers as a major source of their information about farming.[58]

The importance of perception and evaluation of personal experience and family customs and values to the study of the diffusion of new technology should be apparent. As in other aspects of life, new culture elements are interpreted in terms of their impact upon existing patterns of culture.

Diffusion of information necessarily precedes adoption, but information is not necessarily automatically followed by use. Adoption of a particular practice depends upon the decision made by a person or a group having authority to adopt it. For a family farm in the U.S., this decision is generally made by the farm operator with or without the assistance of other members of his family. Major decisions affecting a corporation farm would, of course, be made by the board of directors.

A special problem, from the standpoint of agricultural extension workers and agricultural technicians of various types, is how practices which have been developed primarily with the full-time commercial farmer in mind can be adapted to and incorporated in part-time farmers' enterprises. A related problem is the difficulty of communicating with part-time farmers, who are extremely hard to reach during the time that they are employed at their off-farm activities. Furthermore, the demands of their farm operations may be such that in many cases they have little or no free time after

[57] Johnson, *op. cit.*, pp. 1395-1396.
[58] E. A. Wilkening, *Adoption of Improved Farm Practices as Related to Family Factors*, Wisconsin AES Research Bulletin 183, December, 1953.

the journey home from work. Thus, it seems important to study not only their needs for agricultural and homemaking information but also to study their habits of work and play so as to facilitate communication.

DIFFUSION OF IMPROVED AGRICULTURAL TECHNOLOGY IN UNDERDEVELOPED AREAS

The pressure of population on the food supply in underdeveloped areas has led to efforts to increase agricultural production. Technical assistance programs of the United Nations and the United States and certain other countries have emphasized improved agricultural technology. Some progress seems to have been made in India, Pakistan, and elsewhere. However, it seems doubtful if the advances achieved have enabled such areas to provide for the increased population due to successful diffusion or death-control techniques like sanitation and improved medical care.

There are many barriers to the adoption of improved agricultural technology in such countries, the most important being cultural rather than physical. Traditional values, systems of farm organization, and marketing patterns are difficult to change.

A program of planned change might have a greater probability of success if preceded by careful studies of the adoption process in the culture under consideration. The general framework discussed in this chapter may prove useful, but allowance must be made for detecting the influence of unique values and patterns of social organization.[59]

QUESTIONS FOR FURTHER STUDY AND DISCUSSION

1. Discuss the problems involved in disseminating improved technology to farmers with a county agricultural agent and report to the class.
2. Why are farm programs seldom shown on TV?
3. Obtain one or more technical publication from your state agricultural experiment station. Read the publication and give your evaluation of its probable effectiveness as a source of information for farmers.

[59] See S. A. Rahim, *Diffusion and Adoption of Agricultural Practices: A Study in a Village in East Pakistan*, Pakistan Academy for Village Development, Technical Publication 7, 1961.

4. Comment on the hypothesis that opinion leaders are indispensable for the successful diffusion of new farm practices.
5. What is the function of personal experience in connection with diffusion of agricultural technology?
6. Why are Indian peasants more likely to resist technological changes than American commercial farmers?

SELECTED REFERENCES

Bertrand, A. L., ed., *Rural Sociology*, McGraw-Hill, 1958, chaps. 24, 25.

Bohlen, J. M., and G. M. Beal, *The Diffusion Process*, Iowa Agricultural Special Report No. 18, 1957.

Rogers, E. M., *Social Change in Rural Society*, Appleton-Century-Crofts, 1960, chap. 14.

Shannon, Lyle, ed., *Underdeveloped Areas*, New York, Harper, 1957, chaps. IX, XII.

III

SOCIAL PROCESSES:
DYNAMIC ASPECTS OF LIFE

The dynamic aspects of human relationships are of great importance.
Sociologists generally regard social interaction, defined as
communication between two or more people which involves mutual
stimulation and response, as the basic social process. Some types
of interaction may take only an instant; others may be of longer
duration. Cooperation, competition, and conflict are well-known forms
of interaction. Socialization and social control involve interaction;
few decisions are made without communication with others significant
to the decision-maker.

Social interaction occurs within or with reference to social systems.
It is influenced by culture and by the personal capabilities, motives,
and wishes of the persons involved.

11

Socialization and Social Control
in an Agricultural Environment

A new baby is completely helpless. As it grows it develops self-consciousness and becomes a person through interaction with its mother and father and other human beings; it is through its contacts with others that it learns the rules of society.

SOCIALIZATION

The process through which culture is transmitted to the developing individual and through which he becomes a full-fledged member of the social systems that form his society is known as *socialization*. A major part of this process consists of learning norms which govern roles. We may define a social role as a set of expectations regarding the behavior of a person who occupies a particular status or position in a group or other social system.

The principal agency of communication involved in the transmission of culture is language, both written and oral. As Gesell has pointed out, however, the capacity to absorb social training is dependent upon inherited capabilities.[1]

Socialization involves internalization of social norms, roles, and other aspects of culture, which occurs mainly through interaction with other persons—farmers' sons and daughters receive their social training from their parents and other human beings rather than from farm animals or machinery. At the same time, it cannot be denied

[1] Arnold Gesell, "Growth Potentials of the Human Infant," in A. M. Lee, ed., *Readings in Sociology*, Barnes and Noble, 1951, p. 65.

211

that certain aspects of culture and the roles which they learn to perform on the farm will reflect their rural environment.

A comprehensive study of the process of socialization would involve an investigation of the psychology of learning. This is, of course, important, but the division of labor between academic disciplines restricts the sociologist principally to those aspects of socialization which are influenced by and expressed in interpersonal relationships. In this book, interest is focused on the rural environment. We will consider the question: what difference does it make in the socialization of a child whether he is reared on a farm, in a village, or in a metropolis?

It is obvious, even in contemporary America, that some differences in environmental stimuli are involved; a generation or two ago the differences were very pronounced. They still are in many parts of the world, especially in areas which have experienced little industrial development. We need to ask whether different processes of socialization are involved in reacting to differences in environmental stimuli.

For any given person, society and culture both exist at the time of his birth. If he is born into a family that lives in an agricultural environment, he is, of course, affected by the attitudes and customs which have been adopted by his family in connection with their adjustment to agriculture.

Baldwin and his colleagues studied farm children in Iowa schools during the period 1923-1927, and investigated some aspects of rural socialization.[2] They found that the attitudes of parents were important in the socialization of the children. Many of the parents with whom they came in contact, especially those in the more isolated areas, were inclined to be extremely conservative with respect to accepting new ideas from outside the locality; the more isolated the area, the investigators concluded, the more likely farm children were to conform to the established norms of family and locality. This generalization is doubtless valid. However, there are today few really isolated farming areas in the U.S.; it is questionable, therefore, whether there is any substantial difference between farm and nonfarm people in receptivity to new ideas, and conse-

[2] B. T. Baldwin, Eva A. Fillmore, and Lora Hadley, *Farm Children*, Appleton-Century, 1930.

quently whether traditional rural conservatism plays much of a part in the socialization of farmers' children except in backward areas.

The 1934 report of the White House Conference on Child Health and Protection discusses certain aspects of rural socialization.[3] The authors of this report, which was written under the chairmanship of E. W. Burgess, indicated a belief that the farm child had fewer contacts with other children, more home duties, and more contact with his parents. They also indicated that a somewhat lower percentage of farm children than urban children had achieved good personality adjustment as reflected by a scale.

Evaluating the evidence available in 1948 concerning farm socialization of children, Landis listed as advantages (1) the development of mature realism through participation in farm work, (2) limited social participation outside the home which provides more time for interaction among members of the family, (3) lack of nervous tension due to the balancing of scholarly activities with physical work, (4) the development of self-discipline fostered by close contact with the inexorable processes of nature, and (5) the development of self-reliance and imagination due to a relative absence of manufactured items and commercialized recreation.

Discussing the disadvantages of rural socialization, Landis pointed out that a large percentage of farm children become urban dwellers, and raised the question of whether rural socialization provides the proper type of experience for urban life. He alleged that many farm children do not have sufficient social experience to prepare them for urban life. The evidence on which he based his comments, however, was drawn chiefly from the decade of the 1930s, and many changes have occurred in farm life since that time. Landis also observed that farm children may develop rigid personalities because of the inflexibility of the norms governing personal behavior in a rural community.[4] He did not present any empirical evidence for this, but his observation seems reasonable if applied to an isolated rural community of a generation or two ago. It is very doubt-

[3] White House Conference on Child Health and Protection, *The Adolescent in the Family*, Appleton-Century, 1934, pp. 8-29, 158-178.
[4] Paul H. Landis, *Rural Life in Process*, 2nd ed., McGraw-Hill, 1948, pp. 138-146.

ful whether it has wide applicability in commercial farming areas of the United States today.

Landis correctly pointed out that there is greater dependence upon the immediate locality among farmers than among city dwellers. He also suggested that since successful farming is dependent on soils, topography, rainfall, and other aspects of climate, the personality of a farmer within a specific culture may be influenced to some extent by these natural forces in themselves, and also by the uncertainty of weather and the slow pace of the natural processes involved in farming.[5]

With respect to the influence of the specific agricultural operations prevalent in the U.S., the variation is so great that it is hardly possible to construct any general typology of rural socialization. For example, some wheat farmers keep no animals whatever, whereas dairy farmers and ranchers are deeply involved in the natural rhythms and biological processes of animal life.[6] It seems reasonable to suppose that the socialization of a farm child is influenced to some extent by the pattern of work which his parents have developed in their adjustment to their farming operations. But as noted earlier, it is his contacts with people, particularly those in his primary groups such as his family, his school, and his play group, rather than his contacts with animals or machinery that are principally responsible for the development of his personality.

Within any major culture area such as the United States there are societal norms and values which substantially permeate the entire culture. In addition to this, there are local and regional culture patterns, and there may be particular culture patterns associated with membership in particular families or other important reference groups—ethnic, religious, racial. In the broad sense, then, the distinctive differences between rural and urban socialization will be minimized to the extent that general norms and stimuli surpass the local and group stimuli in importance. There is considerable evidence that these differences, once extremely important in the U.S., are rapidly disappearing.

Individual as well as group factors are important in social development even within a monolithic culture with clear-cut norms

[5] *Ibid.*, pp. 66, 68-71.
[6] See Chapter 7.

and rigid social control. Human beings are able to think abstractly, to make choices, and, within culturally established limits, to direct their own activities in terms of their anticipation of future events. People are able to evaluate their own actions and reactions to some extent and can develop a sense of responsibility for the outcomes of their behavior. People are adaptive; their conduct is conditioned but not entirely governed by culture. The human individual is not an automaton who is molded exactly by his culture but is himself a dynamic force with the ability to judge, to make decisions, and to act with some degree of independence. In consequence, people are never completely socialized, and further, culture is continually changing, since it is a product of behavior and human interaction as well as one of the determinants of action.

THE RISE OF THE SELF

Socialization cannot begin until the person becomes self-conscious, although some individual learning may occur before that time. It is said that the human infant does not have a self, meaning that he does not think of himself as separate from his environment and that he has at the outset no consciousness of himself as an object.

What is the self and how does it arise? Since the self is social-psychological in character, it cannot be perceived directly. It must be inferred from observation of behavior and through questioning. Modern social-psychological theory following Cooley, Mead, and others regards the self as that which is designated as *I, me,* or *myself.*[7] The self is not a simple concept; it has many facets because of the many points of view from which it can be regarded. The importance of the self sociologically resides in its importance for relationships between persons. The existence of the self confers upon the person the ability to view himself as separate from his environment. The fact that he is able to perceive that others react to him and his actions has enormous consequences for social interaction.

Although there are a few authentic cases of human beings reaching biological maturity without interaction with other persons, these

[7] See George Herbert Mead, *Mind, Self and Society,* University of Chicago Press, 1934; Charles H. Cooley, *Human Nature and the Social Order,* Scribner, 1902.

ferals were not human in a social sense. Social scientists generally agree that the self arises through interaction with other persons, and thus is itself a social product as well as a dynamic agent in subsequent social interaction.

There is no reason to suppose that the process through which the self arises is any different for children reared in rural areas than for those reared in cities. In both cases, personal relationships with other human beings are involved even though the cultural content, such as specific behavior patterns and values, may sometimes differ.

An understanding of the social implications of the self seems essential to an understanding of social interaction, social roles, and social systems. Consequently, it is worth while at this point to review briefly some current sociological theories of the self.

Charles Horton Cooley coined the phrase "the looking-glass self" which suggests that ideas of self develop through the individual's perception of the attitudes of others with respect to himself. Said Cooley:

> In a very large and interesting class of cases the social reference takes the form of a somewhat definite imagination of how one's self . . . appears in a particular mind, and the kind of self-feeling one has is determined by the attitude toward this attributed to that other mind. A social self of this sort might be called the reflected or looking-glass self:
>
> > "Each to each a looking-glass
> > Reflects the other that doth pass."
>
> As we see our face, figure and dress in the glass, and are interested in them because they are ours, and pleased or otherwise with them according as they do or do not answer to what we should like them to be; so in imagination we perceive in another's mind some thought of our appearance, manners, aims, deeds, character, friends, and so on, and are variously affected by it.
>
> A self-idea of this sort seems to have three principal elements: the imagination of our appearance to the other person; the imagination of his judgment of that appearance, and some sort of self-feeling, such as pride or mortification. The comparison with a looking-glass hardly suggests the second element, the imagined judgment, which is quite essential. The thing that moves us to pride or shame is not the mere mechanical reflection of ourselves, but an imputed sentiment, the imagined effect of this reflection upon another's mind. This is evident from the fact that the character and weight of that other, in whose mind we see ourselves, makes all the

difference with our feeling. We are ashamed to seem evasive in the presence of a straightforward man, cowardly in the presence of a brave one, gross in the eyes of a refined one, and so on. We always imagine, and in imagining share, the judgments of the other mind. A man will boast to one person of an action—say some sharp transaction in trade—which he would be ashamed to own to another.[8]

Kimball Young has said, "Self arises when the individual takes the view and action toward his own act and thoughts that he learns or infers that others take toward them."[9] Elsewhere, Young has presented a more detailed analysis of the rise of the self, which he credits largely to the influence of G. H. Mead, that emphasizes the development of social roles, a useful approach for sociological purposes.[10]

As an individual develops the ability to view himself as an object and learns to regard himself as he imagines others regard him, he is said to "take the role of the other." This role-taking ability greatly influences interpersonal relationships. Consider, for example, the reaction of a farmer who extends his hand in friendly greeting to another only to find that the intended recipient of the greeting is hostile. The friendly gesture disappears immediately as the initiator receives the signal of the hostile other. The immediate reaction is likely to be confusion followed by hostility on the part of the friendly greeter.

FUNCTION OF ROLES AND STATUSES IN SOCIALIZATION

As the self develops, the farm-reared person becomes a self-conscious member of various farm groups and other social systems. He is able to take the roles of others and thus to see himself as he imagines others see him. He also learns to perform various roles which are required by his membership in various social systems.

Role-taking and *role-playing* are entirely different. The first involves imagining the attitudes of others toward oneself, whereas the second involves the actual performance of functions associated with a given status.

[8] Cooley, *op. cit.*, pp. 151-153.
[9] Kimball Young, *Sociology*, American Book, 1940, p. 378.
[10] Kimball Young, *Personality and Problems of Adjustment*, Crofts, 1940, pp. 68-180.

The development of the ability to perform roles in accordance with the expectations of one's society is crucial to the functioning of social systems. Linton has described a social role as the expected pattern of behavior which is associated with a certain status in a social system. All of the members of a social system understand very well what is expected in a person who has a particular status. Thus, within a land-grant university, a set of expectations exist with respect to the type of behavior appropriate to agricultural students. There is another set of expectations relating to the behavior of those who have the status of professors of agriculture, still another for administrators, and so on.[11] Bates has proposed that the term *position* be utilized and that the concept *role* be reserved for distinguishable parts of the position. In his words, ". . . the position of father-husband . . . contains the roles of provider, disciplinarian, teacher or socializer. . . ."[12]

Merton has suggested that each social status is associated with a number of roles in what he has called a *role set*.[13] Although role expectations are shared to a considerable extent by all members of a role set, there are many situations, particularly in a highly mobile urbanized society, when the perceptions which occupants of a role have of the duties of the role do not correspond to those held by others in the role set. Thus agricultural extension agents do not necessarily perceive their roles in the same way as farmers perceive them; farm laborers may not view their roles as their employers do. These discrepancies in role perceptions cause many misunderstandings in interpersonal relationships.

MULTIPLE ROLES AND SOCIALIZATION

A member of any complex society performs not one but many roles, each associated with his participation, actual or imagined, in various social systems. For example, a farm man may be a husband and father in his immediate family group, a son in his family of origin, an elder in the church, a member of the Rotary Club, a

[11] See Ralph Linton, *The Study of Man*, Appleton-Century, 1936, chap. 8; R. L. Sutherland, J. L. Woodward, and M. A. Maxwell, *Introductory Sociology*, 4th ed., Lippincott, 1952, chap. 8.

[12] Frederick L. Bates, "A Conceptual Analysis of Group Structure," *Social Forces*, December, 1957, p. 103.

[13] R. K. Merton, "The Role Set: Problems in Sociological Theory," *British Journal of Sociology*, June, 1957, pp. 106-120.

dairyman in his occupational role, and so on. The process of learning, interpreting, evaluating, and performing various roles in accordance with group norms constitutes a crucial aspect of the process of socialization of the individual.

Most American farmers belong to many groups or social systems; others belong only to a few. Nearly all, however, are members of some groups, and even those who live in isolation from others act with reference to what they believe others think of them.

In addition to the specific roles which a farm-reared person may be assigned or may achieve in specific social groups, there are more or less generalized role expectations associated with sex, age, skin color, ethnic background, and membership in social classes or castes.

Experience gained in the performance of certain roles unquestionably influences conduct in others. Thus, the religious role of a farmer who is lay leader in a rural religious system may be expected to influence to some extent his business relationships with others. This does not mean that the performance of various roles is always consistent—it is not. Especially in groups organized on the basis of transitory and relatively impersonal contacts, role expectations and performances may be quite at variance from those the individual is expected to perform in other social systems. The process of integrating several divergent roles into a more or less harmonious generalized image of the self presents an unusually troublesome problem for some people, and may well play a large part in the prevalence of mental illness in the modern world.

The integration of roles apparently is not so difficult in an isolated primary group society such as the American rural neighborhood of a generation or two ago or an agricultural village in Pakistan. Inayat Ullah has said of the latter: "The first important fact about the village life is that it is not an aggregate of individuals. In fact, the real individual in the sense of Western urban society does not exist in the village. He is an inalienable part of multiple groups which completely overshadow his individuality. He is not master of his own will and architect of his own fate. The various decisions in different fields of life are made by groups for him and he rarely feels the need to challenge them."[14]

All members of such local social systems have an opportunity to

[14] Inayat Ullah, "Democracy in Rural Communities in Pakistan," *Sociologus* (Berlin), IX, No. 1 (1959), 36-47.

observe each other over a relatively long period of time in the performance of several different roles. This facilitates the development of a generalized image by significant others and by the individual himself.

In contemporary American rural society, it is not always clear to the occupant of a particular status exactly how he is expected to perform the associated role. On farms this is particularly true of adolescents because in one situation he may be considered an adult, and in others he may be treated as a child and given little if any encouragement to make his own decisions or to be responsible for the consequences of his actions. Another area in American culture which involves considerable role conflict confronts young women as they consider the roles of homemaker and mother in relation to the role of a productive member of the labor force. In this connection, it is noteworthy that an increasing percentage of married farm women (approximately 26 percent of farm homemakers) are now employed as gainful workers outside the home.

The problem of role integration in the personality system of a member of contemporary rural or urban society is further complicated by the fact that not only has any given person many roles at any given moment, but most of these change with the passage of time. For a farmer they change to some extent in accordance with the progression of the individual through his life cycle. They change as he migrates and becomes associated with new groups, as new individuals come into contact with him even though he does not move, if he moves from one type of farming to another, and as he develops new interests and makes new friendships.

THE EFFECT OF THE KEY ROLE ON SOCIALIZATION

Fichter has pointed out that each person has a key status associated with the major group or social category in which he plays his key role.[15] For most American males the key role is unquestionably related to his occupational status, which is the dominant interest and which greatly affects the performance of other roles. The key role for a farmer, then, is usually the role he performs in agricultural

---

[15] Joseph Fichter, *Sociology*, University of Chicago Press, 1957, pp. 210-211.

production. For the married American woman the key role tends to be that of mother and homemaker, and for an American adolescent, even one from a farm, that of student.

The key role tends to become an organizing principle; because of its greater importance, it materially influences the performance of other roles. Subsidiary roles are performed in such a way that the attitudes of significant others do not reflect discredit upon the individual as he performs his key role. The importance of the key role is acknowledged not only by individuals but also by formal organizations and agencies. For example, the 1960 faculty manual of the Washington State University contains the following words: "A faculty member may not undertake outside employment or service with or without compensation if in the opinion of the president it is inconsistent with the interests of the state university."[16] This is a clear recognition by the university that the key role of its employees is as faculty members. There are, of course, many subsidiary roles which an individual faculty member may accept, such as membership in community service organizations and, within prescribed limits, outside employment in his professional field. He can accept certain public service assignments from the federal and state governments. On the other hand, a professor would not be expected to become a member of any organization engaged in illegal activities, and outside employment in a low-status occupational role might be frowned upon.

SOCIALIZATION THROUGH PLAYING AT ROLES

The developing child, farm or nonfarm, is not actually able to perform various adult roles because of lack of experience, physical capacity, and general maturity; nevertheless, he does imagine himself in such roles. In other words, he plays *at* the roles. The little boy plays at being a cowboy, a farm operator, a pilot of a crop-dusting helicopter, or a spaceman. The little girl plays at being a mother, a secretary, or a hostess. A person cannot fully comprehend through this imaginative process all of the consequences which are involved with actual performance of the role, of course, but many

[16] *Faculty Manual,* Washington State University, 1960, p. 37.

aspects can be imagined, particularly if there is opportunity to observe others who are actually performing the role in real life or in a movie or a TV play. And there is the tendency, particularly in reference to glamorous occupations, to imagine chiefly the desirable rather than the undesirable consequences involved in a particular role.

This process of playing at roles appears to constitute an essential element in decision-making.[17] An essential element of playing at roles is evaluation of the imagined reactions of significant others. At this point one takes the role of the others, so to speak, and this has considerable effect upon decisions made.

REFERENCE GROUPS AS AGENCIES OF SOCIALIZATION

Sherif and Sherif have defined reference groups as "those groups to which the individual relates himself as a part or to which he aspires to relate himself psychologically."[18] The essential part of this definition is the psychological identification of the individual with the group. Reference groups include those associated with the performance of the key and other major roles. Viewed in this sense, not every group would be regarded as a reference group for every individual. The major reference groups for an American farmer include his family, the local school, the role set associated with his farming activities, and similar social systems.

It seems clear that social systems which may be classified as reference groups are effective agencies of socialization. Where there is psychological identification with a social system, the individual unquestionably has a greater tendency to learn the content of the role and to perform it more effectively and in accordance with the expectations of the social system. From a theoretical standpoint, it is well accepted that membership in particular groups which have more or less unique values and behavior patterns is likely to influence subsequent behavior of members materially. Empirical studies of the influence of specific reference groups as agencies of socialization are not, however, numerous.

[17] See Chapter 14.
[18] Muzafer Sherif and Caroline Sherif, *Groups in Harmony and Tension,* Harper, 1953, p. 161.

SOCIAL CONTROL IN RURAL COMMUNITIES

Social control is the process by which the actions of individuals are brought into conformity with the regulations and enacted laws and the mores and folkways of a social system.[19] It is closely related to the process of socialization. Since it deals with restraints, it may be thought of as emphasizing the negative rather than the positive aspects of culture.

One of the major sociological problems of modern times is the loss of intimate and continuous contact by many persons with their significant reference groups and a consequent breakdown of primary group contacts. This seems to be a corollary of urbanization.

We should recognize, of course, that many beneficial results have come from urbanization. It has released great creative forces; for example, most modern technological developments are urban in origin. It has freed the individual from the tyranny of inbred values and close social surveillance; it has brought increased leisure. It has promoted tolerance, but it has also created many problems of social control.

The cultural plurality of America, which is due in large part to the diverse ethnic origins of its people, has also created problems. There is fairly general agreement on many norms, but differences between various subcultural groups are sufficient to raise serious questions in the minds of particular individuals who come in contact with members of other subcultures. The great majority of Americans understand that many of the standards of behavior they follow are based upon relative rather than absolute principles of right and wrong. This, of course, was not the case in the isolated rural community of a generation or more ago, and agricultural populations in countries with little industrial development such as Pakistan evidently still tend to be guided by absolute and presumably infallible rules.[20]

The mobility of the American population, farm people included, has greatly increased the contacts of farmers with persons who have

[19] See J. L. Gillin and J. P. Gillin, *Cultural Sociology*, Macmillan, 1948, chap. 28; Paul H. Landis, *Social Control: Social Organization and Disorganization in Process*, rev. ed., Lippincott, 1957.

[20] See Inayat Ullah, *op. cit.*

different standards. It has also made it possible, because of the increase in impersonal types of relationships, for many adolescent individuals to perform some of their roles without supervision by parents or other possible censors.

All children test family norms from time to time to see how far they can violate the norms without punishment; they also seek to minimize the penalties. Adults also are inclined to test group and societal norms, an example being the common habit of drivers of exceeding the speed limit slightly.

The loss of continuous contact with significant reference groups like the family and church has permitted action without close surveillance. In some rural areas in the U.S. people may even act without being accountable except to impersonal agencies of social control for the consequences of their actions. This increases the possibility of unrestrained action not in accord with the rules and regulations presumably governing the social system, and though many offenders are caught, many are not.

RURAL DEVIATION

There is some evidence that farm people are less likely than city dwellers to deviate from group norms or to become law violators. Sorokin, Zimmerman, and Galpin cite statistics from a number of western countries which indicate that there was substantially less criminality in rural than in urban areas prior to 1930. The data also indicate a tendency for rural crimes to involve offenses against persons rather than property. In addition, urban criminals were more likely to be repeaters.[21] Unfortunately, law-enforcement agencies apparently keep few records according to residence and occupation, and there have been no recent comprehensive studies of rural crime, so that it is not possible to verify these conclusions for more recent periods.

There is widespread belief, however, that there still is proportionately much less delinquency and crime in rural than in urban areas. This belief may be well founded so far as the traditional isolated rural community is concerned. In countries like the United

[21] P. A. Sorokin, C. C. Zimmerman, and C. J. Galpin, *A Systematic Source Book in Rural Sociology*, University of Minnesota Press, 1931, vol. II, chap. XIII.

States where rural-urban differences in ways of living are decreasing, there is reason to expect the rates of crime and delinquency to converge as well. A recent study in six areas of the state of Washington provides some support for this expectation. Traditional differences showing less delinquent-type behavior among farm adolescents were present, but they were slight rather than marked.[22]

Less spectacular forms of deviation than crime are also of concern. These deviations include a wide range of behavior which is defined by group norms as undesirable. Impoliteness, betrayal of secrets, overt rejection of the central values of a group, and violation of mores are all examples of deviations which might result in the application of social pressure to bring about conformity.

Types of Social Pressures

All social systems have rewards and penalties of one type or another which are applied to a nonconforming member to bring his activities into compliance with the norms, to prohibit him from engaging in activities which are contrary to the norms, or to remove him from the group.

Legal Sanctions

A criminal or delinquent is defined as an individual who has violated one or more of the enacted rules of conduct imposed by society. Various legal sanctions have been authorized for various offenses, and these are imposed through law enforcement agencies which basically rely upon force.

The types of legal sanctions differ greatly from society to society and from one period to another within a society. In western civilization punishment was once very drastic, involving various forms of physical torture and capital punishment for a great number of offenses. At the present time, the trend is toward attempted rehabilitation of the criminal, a change based on a different understanding of the nature of social control from that which formed the basis for the severe punishments once meted out and on a growing acceptance of the view that the nonconforming individual is not com-

[22] Walter L. Slocum and Carol L. Stone, *Delinquent-Type Behavior of Farm and Nonfarm Teenagers,* unpublished paper, Washington State University, Department of Rural Sociology, March, 1961.

pletely socialized to the norms of the larger society. This leads to
the position that with sympathetic understanding and a new chance
many can be rehabilitated and thus can become useful and conforming members of society. It must be acknowledged, however,
that this view is not universally approved; some people still believe
that rigorous imprisonment and severe punishment are the best
methods of maintaining control because of the presumed deterrent
effect upon potential wrongdoers.

The use of force for restraining nonconforming members of a
social system is ordinarily regarded as a last resort and is in fact
generally applied only to a small minority of individuals except
during revolution or war. The great bulk of people everywhere
internalize the standards (mores, folkways, and enacted legislation)
which form the ideological basis for conduct and in general conform sufficiently well so as not to require overt force to comply.

All levels of government in the United States participate to some
extent in regulatory activities, although the laws are made principally by state and federal governments; counties and municipalities have only limited law-making powers. At the local level, law
enforcement is in the hands of an official usually known as the
sheriff. Most states have a police force which usually is concerned
primarily with enforcement of traffic laws. The federal government
maintains the Federal Bureau of Investigation, the Secret Service,
and other agencies which have police powers in respect to violation
of federal laws. As a matter of last resort, the armed forces are
available for the suppression of domestic disturbances; they were
used to occupy the South following the Civil War and to maintain
order during the outbreak of racial violence in Little Rock, Arkansas,
in the fall of 1957.

The laws which are enforced by American police agencies are
not formulated by the edict of some central authoritarian government, as is the case in some countries, but are enacted by the elected
representatives of the people. Perhaps because they are subject to
legislative change, many Americans tend to obey fully only laws
with which they are in sympathy and either overtly or covertly
evade compliance with others if the prospect of being apprehended
seems remote. This is a tradition of long standing in America and
has been commented on unfavorably by some foreign observers. In

general, however, open violation of significant laws is restricted to a small minority of the population. In absolute terms, of course, delinquent and criminal behavior is substantial, and there is little prospect that law enforcement will become unimportant.

The present situation in this respect may be contrasted with the situation which existed earlier when most of the citizens of the U.S. resided either on farms or in rather small villages or towns. At that time, most of the task of maintaining compliance with the far fewer laws which then existed fell upon the family and the local community. To some extent, of course, local and informal controls are still evident. Comparison of problems of social control in a metropolis and in rural areas indicates that great differences still exist. However, the increase in secondary group associations in rural life, the greatly expanded spatial mobility of rural people, and the corollary decline of the importance of the primary group as an instrument of social control make it clear that increasing attention must be devoted to more formal methods which apply to citizens generally regardless of residence.

Landis feels that social control is still maintained largely by informal means in rural areas. In his judgment, local government or local manifestations of government deal more with services than with discipline.[23] But a larger view of the matter suggests that even in the service functions, such as the recording of legal instruments, the provision of farm benefits, health services, and the collection of taxes, there are substantial elements of social control. Formal inspections are made to check compliance with various federal farm programs and farmers' income tax returns are scrutinized by officials.

Most farmers, however, at least while they are on their farms, encounter actual law-enforcement agencies very rarely, and when they do these are principally the agencies of the local government represented by the prosecuting attorney and the county sheriff.

A study by Nye suggests that only a small portion of teen-agers who commit delinquent or criminal acts are actually apprehended by law-enforcement agencies. He found proportionately more delinquent behavior among urban boys than among rural boys in the area studied.[24]

[23] Landis, *Rural Life in Process, op. cit.*, p. 359.
[24] F. Ivan Nye, *Family Relationships and Delinquent Behavior*, Wiley, 1958.

It is not possible in any society based upon the principles of democracy and equality to maintain a large enough law-enforcement staff to make people conform through fear of apprehension to all of the laws which society has established. However, there is no doubt that this fear is a factor in maintaining conformity with law.

Religious Sanctions

Moral standards taught by organized religion have great power. Promised rewards in heaven for the faithful and punishment in hell for sinners are especially effective in rural areas where religious conservatism is great. In a dynamic society characterized by social and cultural changes, religious sanctions tend to be less effective.[25]

In the United States and other predominantly Christian countries the Christian faith is the fountainhead and main source of ideas of morality. Although sanctions are infrequently invoked, temporal punishment of a sinner may be undertaken by the church. He may be excommunicated, expelled from the church, or otherwise penalized.

In other parts of the world, Islam, Buddhism, Hinduism, and other religions perform similar functions of social control.

Family Pressures

One method of obtaining compliance with family standards is the technique of ordering and forbidding, frequently enforced through corporal punishment for disobedience, found in the authoritarian type of family. As noted elsewhere, the authoritarian family appears to be giving way in the U.S., even in rural areas, to a democratic type which seeks to obtain compliance by indirect methods. This does not mean that the latter uses no sanctions and no punishments, but such punishments as are brought down more often involve withdrawal of privileges and appeals to reason and to family pride than imposition of corporal punishment. Punishment in such families is usually neither arbitrary nor excessively severe.

To a considerable extent the compliance of a young person with rules and regulations established by his family, by other social systems, or by the state rests upon the emotional bond between the individual and his reference groups. In the case of the family, this

[25] See Gillin and Gillin, *op. cit.*, pp. 705, 708.

bond is affection. Because of affection for a loved parent, a young person is more likely to be a conforming than a nonconforming person.

Discussing the functions of parents in relation to social control, Nye has identified three aspects of the relationship which appear to be of considerable significance: first, the parent's influence in forming the conscience of the child, which essentially involves providing concepts of right and wrong: second, providing an example to the child of a conforming adult; and third, the social pressure involved in the child's reluctance to discredit the parent for whom he has affection.[26] These forces reduce the possibility of deviant behavior and tend to induce conformity. The fear of creating an unfavorable image of the self or of the family among others one respects is unquestionably a very powerful instrument for maintaining social discipline.

Sanctions by Other Primary Groups

In agricultural villages or neighborhoods in a static society, primary group norms are very influential.[27] The standards that govern behavior in such social systems tend to be regarded as absolute instead of relative. Infractions of the norms may be met by ridicule and other painful types of social pressures. The entire group may act in concert against an offender. For example, according to Loomis, the Amish adolescent who attends a movie or succumbs to some other "worldly" pleasure may be disciplined by "shunning,"[28] which involves complete loss of social contact with other members. The power of group sentiment on an individual has been described by Landis as follows: "Fear of gossip, a desire for praise, and, above all, avoidance of censure come to motivate him. To one who is highly sensitive to group opinion nothing is more painful than the lash of ridicule; nothing has a deeper sting than unfavorable group judgment. 'What will the neighbors think?' always looms large in his consciousness."[29]

[26] Nye, *op. cit.*

[27] See W. I. Thomas and F. Znaniecki, *The Polish Peasant in Europe and America,* Chapman and Grimes, 1918-1920, vols. 1, 2, 5.

[28] See C. P. Loomis and J. A. Beegle, *Rural Social Systems,* Prentice-Hall, 1950, p. 12.

[29] Landis, *Rural Life in Process, op. cit.,* p. 294.

QUESTIONS FOR FURTHER STUDY AND DISCUSSION

1. Describe the acquisition of a specific social role.
2. What differences are there between urban and rural socialization processes in America?
3. Discuss the concept of the "looking-glass self."
4. What role conflicts are likely to be involved in the life of a part-time farmer?
5. Summarize the important findings of the study made in Iowa by Baldwin, Fillmore, and Hadley entitled *Farm Children*. Indicate which if any of the findings of this study are applicable at the present time in the United States.
6. What are some of the advantages and some of the disadvantages of limited social participation during the formative years?
7. In your opinion, is a changing environment or a stable one more conducive to developing a sense of security and assurance in a child? Give reasons for your answer.
8. Which environment, rural or urban, seems to prepare children better for living in a changing world?
9. Each member of the class will prepare a written report on the subject of social control in a rural locality. The report will be in two parts: Part I will deal with the theory of social control; Part II will present an analysis of the operation of informal social controls in a rural family and community. After presentation in class the reports may be collected by the instructor.

SELECTED REFERENCES

Baldwin, B. T., Eva A. Fillmore, and Lora Hadley, *Farm Children*, Appleton-Century, 1930.

Cooley, Charles H., *Human Nature and Social Organization*, Scribner, 1902.

Dewey, Richard, and W. J. Humber, *The Development of Human Behavior*, Macmillan, 1951.

Gillin, John Lewis, and John Philip Gillin, *Cultural Sociology*, Macmillan, 1948, chap. 28.

Landis, Paul H., *Rural Life in Process*, 2nd ed., McGraw-Hill, 1948.

Landis, Paul H., *Social Control: Social Organization and Disorganization in Process*, rev. ed., Lippincott, 1957.

Mead, George Herbert, *Mind, Self and Society,* University of Chicago Press, 1934.

Sutherland, R. L., J. L. Woodward, and M. A. Maxwell, *Introductory Sociology,* 4th ed., Lippincott, 1952, chap. 7, pp. 129-135.

Young, Kimball, *Personality and Problems of Adjustment,* Crofts, 1940, chap. IX, "The Rise of the Self in Interaction."

12

Interaction Processes Among Rural People

Interaction occurs when two or more persons establish social contact and communicate with each other. Social contacts may involve direct interpersonal relationships with other farmers or with nonfarm people. These contacts may lead to or be an expression of cooperation, friendship, or compromise; on the other hand, they may involve competition, conflict, or other forms of opposition. Social contacts may be primary (face-to-face) or secondary (indirect). During the course of social interaction, communication of information and opinions occurs. The principal means of communication is, of course, language.

The nature of the communication which is established subsequent to social contact determines how interaction should be classified. Thus, friendly communication between two farmers would be classified as *associative*, and unfriendly communication as dissociative. Most social interaction involving rural people occurs within established social systems and is guided by the cultural norms associated with these systems.

From a sociological point of view, study of the processes of interaction is of fundamental importance in any serious analysis of rural life. The reasons are as follows: social systems arise from and are sustained by continuing patterns of interaction; the culture associated with a social system is also a product of interaction; furthermore, while any specific or individual act involving relationships between two or more people may be relatively insignificant in personality development and socialization, it is through interaction that the self arises. Consequently, interaction is essential for the socialization or social training of every individual.

Any specific social contact is, of course, fleeting and dynamic in character; it lasts only an instant in many cases. Since this is true, it is extremely difficult to investigate the processes of interaction directly. Consequently, the few existing studies of interactive processes have dealt with the products of interaction, and the nature of the processes have been inferred from these end products.

The forms of interaction have been classified in minute detail by some writers. In the present discussion, attention will be devoted principally to a discussion of the two major types of interaction: (1) association, including cooperation, accommodation, and assimilation; (2) dissociation, including competition, contravention, and conflict.

DISSOCIATIVE INTERACTION

Much interaction between farmers and farm groups is characterized by competition, contravention, and conflict, which are the principal forms of dissociation.[1]

Daily and weekly newspapers in the U.S. carry relatively little information about contravention or covert forms of antagonism, but a great deal of information is presented on overt conflict and certain forms of competition.

It is sometimes difficult to distinguish clearly between competition and conflict. Gillin and Gillin, after considering various attempts to make the distinction, concluded that competition involves the efforts of rival individuals or groups to obtain advantages for themselves through the use of nonviolent means, whereas in conflict the individuals or groups employ violence or the threat of violence against each other.[2]

Park stated that conflict is always conscious and deeply emotional.[3] Hayes offered the view that the major aim of persons who are in conflict is "to impede, prevent, or destroy the act of another."[4] For present purposes, we will define conflict as struggles between

[1] Leopold von Wiese and Howard Becker, *Systematic Sociology*, Wiley, 1932.
[2] John L. Gillin and John P. Gillin, *Cultural Sociology*, Macmillan, 1948, p. 590-91.
[3] Robert E. Park and E. W. Burgess, *Introduction to the Science of Sociology*, rev. ed., 1924, University of Chicago Press, p. 574.
[4] E. C. Hayes, "Some Social Relations Restated," *American Journal of Sociology*, November, 1925, p. 337.

farmers and other persons or groups which are direct and violent and which involve an effort to discredit or destroy the opponent. Competition and conflict can occur between two farmers, between a farmer and a group, or between groups.

Contravention is interaction involving concealed antagonism. It is frequently classified as a form of conflict, but may be distinguished from conflict by its covert rather than overt nature. It is characterized by doubt concerning another person coupled with a feeling of aversion or dislike for the person or his proposals.[5]

COMPETITION

Competition may be either direct or indirect, but is frequently impersonal in character. By definition, it is not violent. The areas of competition involving farm people include economic competition, competition for favors of the opposite sex, competition in games, and competition for prestige.

Competitive interaction is continuous in the sense that the successful person or group cannot rest on his laurels. A scholar must keep on producing scholarly work; an athlete must keep on winning contests if he is to remain the champion; a businessman must keep on selling his products at a profit if he is to stay in business. A farmer must also be alert if he is to stay on top. With relaxation of effort and vigilance, the crown passes and even the old master must retire from the field.

Competition may occur in a rural locality between groups of the same type or even between groups of different types. For example, a church may compete with another church for members and constituents, and all churches compete with attractions provided by certain other organizations like motion picture theaters and television networks.

A farmer's son may compete with other young men of the area for the attention of the beautiful daughter of another farmer. On the other hand, he may be attracted by a nonfarm girl. The suitors may be unknown to each other. Furthermore, since the decision to select one mate rather than another rests with the girl in American rural society, conflict between suitors seldom ensues.

[5] See Wiese and Becker, *op. cit.*, chap. 19; Gillin and Gillin, *op. cit.*, chap. 25.

Within any social system, competitors who are successful according to the values of the system achieve high status, as, for example, will an economically successful farmer among other commercial farmers. It is essential, however, for the struggle to remain impersonal if it is to be classified as competition. In the economic field, business organizations compete for customers without specifically orienting their campaigns in such a way as to discredit their competitors. In fact, in the United States it is considered bad ethics to compete by deprecating the products of the competitor or by making disparaging remarks about his business practices or his personal life.

Economic competition is a characteristic of commercial agriculture. All farmers who produce for the market compete against all other farmers who produce the same type of product. Competing farmers may nevertheless be close friends, and they may exchange farming information. If there is a reasonably stable market, those who are able to compete efficiently survive and prosper. Those who are not able to do so may be forced into bankruptcy even though prices may be relatively favorable for an efficient producer.

The uncertainties of the market and certain federal statutes have created conditions which encourage a certain amount of group effort in economic competition. Farm cooperatives are formed and maintained because they assist the farmer in economic competition.[6]

Farmers who are not engaged in commercial production of crops and livestock but who utilize their land merely as a source of family subsistence are not engaged in economic competition. Intermediate between the full-time commercial farmer and the subsistence farmer in the U.S. there is an important middle group: part-time farmers. In some states they comprise 50 percent or more of the farm operators. These farmers sell some agricultural products, but also rely to a major extent upon income from nonfarm employment. So far as economic competition with other farmers is concerned, they may be regarded as competitors only to the extent that they dispose of their products in the market.

The farmer who is able to reduce his production costs through the application of more efficient methods of production increases his margin of profit and forges ahead of other farmers in economic competition.

[6] See Chapter 20.

Competition for ownership and control of land, another aspect of economic competition, is found to a major extent in all countries and does not appear to be limited to countries having commercial agriculture.[7]

In the United States a basic premise of most farm programs enacted by the federal government has been support for the family-sized farm. At the same time, however, with the exception of federally financed reclamation projects, there are few limitations on the size of land holdings. Thus, the more successful farmers are able to enlarge their holdings. This frequently makes it possible for them to compete even more favorably than previously because of the economies associated with large-scale operations. In spite of the efforts made through the Homestead Act of 1862 and other land settlement laws to distribute the land widely, there is a considerable trend toward concentration of desirable land holdings in the hands of a relatively small number of farmers. In 1949, 3 percent of owners held 41 percent of all farm land in the U.S. held by individuals.[8]

The farmer is affected by the competitive activities of rival trade centers and competing business firms which seek his dollar. Business competition in the rural U.S. is largely confined to persuasion through advertising and price competition. The rivalry between trade centers has resulted in the growth of some trade centers and businesses and the decline and disappearance of others.[9]

Much of the economic competition found in American agriculture involves separate individuals or families rather than large groups. We have already mentioned farm cooperatives as an exception to this. In addition, there are some communal societies, such as the Hutterites, the Amish, and the Amana Society, which compete on a group basis. In these cases, the salable products of the farm enterprise are pooled and sold, and the income from the sales accrues not

[7] Nelson holds that competition for land did not exist during the period of feudalism (see Lowry Nelson, Rural Sociology, 2nd ed., American Book, 1955, p. 152). This does not seem plausible since competition undoubtedly did exist among members of the privileged class. It may be correct to say that free competition for land did not exist.

[8] B. T. Inman and William F. H. Fippin, Farm Land Ownership in the United States, U.S. Department of Agriculture, Bureau of Agricultural Economics, Miscellaneous Publication 699, 1949.

[9] See T. Lynn Smith, The Sociology of Rural Life, 3rd ed., Harper, 1953, pp. 504-506.

to specific individuals but to the group. Groups such as these, which minimize the consumption of modern consumer goods like expensive clothing, automobiles, radios, and television, have been able to accumulate a considerable amount of capital. They are therefore able to compete successfully with individual farmers for acquisition of additional land, which has met with disapproval where it has occurred. In South Dakota, where there are quite a number of Hutterites, the disapproval of nonmembers in the area led to action by the South Dakota State Legislature prohibiting further acquisition of land by the Hutterite colonies. The incident illustrates the extent to which successful economic competition by a minority group is likely to be countered if possible. In this case the competitors sought to change the rules because they considered the competition to be unfair.

CONTRAVENTION

Little empirical information exists about contravention; in fact, since it is covert by definition, it is difficult to detect except through expression of attitudes. Farm people would naturally be reticent about expressing uncomplimentary attitudes toward others to research workers. Among their own circle of intimate friends, less reserve may be expected.

With respect to groups, programs or communities, contravention may be studied more easily. Strained relationships between town dwellers and farmers in the trade area of the town, although customarily referred to as town-country conflict, should usually be classified as contravention. Actual conflict is seldom involved.

C. J. Galpin, writing about town-country relationships in Walworth County, Wisconsin, in 1915, said that "puzzle, perplexity and embarrassment obscure the whole relationship and situation; and the universal process of legalized insulation of village and city away from the farm . . . is constantly shadowed by this overhanging cloud of doubt."[10]

A nationwide study in 1927 by Brunner, Hughes, and Patten included questions on the perceived causes of friction between farm-

---

[10] C. J. Galpin, *The Social Anatomy of An Agricultural Community*, Wisconsin AES Research Bulletin 34, May, 1915.

ers and their trade centers.[11] Taylor also discussed the problem in 1932, pointing out that many opportunities for misunderstanding existed at that time.[12]

The situation has apparently improved. Kolb recently reported better relationships and greater cooperation between farmers and villagers in the Middle West.[13] Bertrand and associates offer the view that only "vestiges of antagonism" remain.[14] The present writer has found little evidence of bad feelings between farmers and townspeople in the state of Washington.

Relationships between farmers and farm laborers may be characterized by mutual distrust and distaste. Haveman has reported the existence of tensions between farmer and farm worker in northern Holland;[15] no doubt this is true wherever such relationships exist. Occasionally the animosity becomes overt and takes the form of labor conflict.

CONFLICT

Competition and contravention sometimes change to open conflict between specific groups or persons.

Kimball Young has identified a number of different types of conflict, including racial, religious, sexual, age, class, political, and community.[16] T. L. Smith devotes major attention to town-country conflict, class conflict, and conflict between families and clans.[17] Nelson discusses principally conflicts involving property, wages, and prices.[18]

In the early days of settlement on the American frontier, there was overt conflict between cattlemen and sheepmen over the issue of land use. The land was owned by the public, and in many cases

[11] Edmund deS. Brunner, G. S. Hughes and Marjorie Patten, *American Agricultural Villages,* Doubleday, Doran, 1927.

[12] C. C. Taylor, *Rural Sociology,* Harper, 1933, pp. 612-616.

[13] See J. H. Kolb, *Emerging Rural Communities,* University of Wisconsin Press, 1959, pp. 109-110.

[14] See A. L. Bertrand, ed., *Rural Sociology,* McGraw-Hill, 1958, p. 318.

[15] J. Haveman, "Social Tensions Between Farmer and Farm Laborer in Northern Holland," *American Journal of Sociology,* November, 1954, pp. 246-254.

[16] Kimball Young, *Introductory Sociology,* American Book, 1934, p. 419.

[17] Smith, *op. cit.* pp. 506-521.

[18] Nelson, *op. cit.,* pp. 159-165.

possession was based upon force. Another major conflict on the frontier was between cattlemen who had grown accustomed to free use of the land and farmers who erected fences and plowed up the range.[19]

During the depression of the 1930s, there was some conflict between groups of farmers and others over marketing farm products. Some who attempted to deliver fluid milk to areas in the face of opposition by organized groups were attacked and their products dumped on the roadside.[20]

Smith has alleged that intergroup conflict in the rural community tends to be organized along family lines. He has cited as extreme examples of such conflicts the blood feuds found among Appalachian mountaineers.[21]

Agricultural conflict has appeared in strikes of farm laborers in California and Florida. Other acts of conflict have been recorded in connection with the efforts of various organizations to improve the economic status of agriculturists through group action, examples being the activities of the Sharecroppers Union of Alabama and the Southern Tenant Farmers Union.[22] The Farmers Holiday Association in the early 1930s, according to Taylor, gave rise to one of the most violent uprisings of farmers since Shay's Rebellion during colonial times.[23] The objective of this organization was to prevent mortgage foreclosures through group action. Members would attend sheriff's sales and intimidate any outsider who might intend to bid on the property through threat of force. The property would then be purchased for a fractional part of its value and returned to the original owner without any further compensation to the creditors.[24]

On the whole, however, there has apparently been relatively little group conflict in rural areas of the United States. In contrast, available information on relationships between agricultural people in India and Pakistan indicates that factional conflicts are anything

[19] *Ibid.*

[20] See Arthur Schlesinger, Jr., *The Crisis of the Old Order,* Houghton Mifflin, 1957, p. 267.

[21] Smith, *op. cit.,* p. 520.

[22] *Ibid.,* p. 519.

[23] See Carl C. Taylor *et al, Rural Life in the United States,* Knopf, 1949, p. 517.

[24] See Nelson, *op. cit.,* p. 163.

but rare. In some villages, intergroup hostilities apparently dominate social life.[25]

Conflicts may arise between individual farmers. A farmer may fail to keep his livestock confined to his own land and adopt a belligerent attitude when accosted. Conflict has developed from what might seem to outsiders to be trivial causes; in many cases, actual or presumed affronts have undoubtedly led to conflict. In areas where irrigation is practiced, there have been numerous conflicts about the use of water, as in a 1938 case cited by Nelson where a man killed his brother-in-law and the sheriff in a village in Utah.[26]

Sources of individual conflict are frequently emotional. Everybody has feelings of hostility when his wishes are thwarted. It is not unusual for people who cooperate overtly to nourish some inner feelings of antagonism at the same time. This ambivalence is perfectly normal, and is not ordinarily manifested in conflict unless there is some breach by one person or another of the norms which regulate social interaction. Interaction is, in fact, seldom entirely associative or dissociative. A specific individual interacting with others may be cooperating for the time being in order to compete or be in conflict with someone else, and may reverse these roles at some later time.

Conflict as an aspect of social relationships in rural areas of the U.S. has not been studied intensively by rural sociologists. The oversight is not entirely accidental; the fact seems to be that in comparison with other agricultural societies there is relatively little conflict among American farmers or farm groups.[27] The principal energies of American farmers seem to be channeled into cooperative and competitive activities.

The study of conflict is important from a sociological point of view to gain understanding of the uniformities and variations which exist in social life.

In the resolution of conflict, particularly intergroup, a sociologist can play an important role by identifying the causes of the conflict, and, through analysis of the social system or systems involved, indicating the points where corrective action may be applied. Citizens

[25] W. L. Slocum, Jamila Akhtar, and Abrar Fatima Sahi, *Village Life in Lahore District,* Lahore, Social Science Research Center, Panjab University Press, October, 1959.

[26] Nelson, *op. cit.,* p. 161.

[27] See Bertrand, ed., *op. cit.,* pp. 317-319.

and social engineers can put this knowledge to practical use, for in community development an important goal is to reduce tensions, minimize conflict, and encourage cooperative effort toward common goals.

ASSOCIATIVE INTERACTION

ACCOMMODATION

Conflict starts when opposed persons or groups seek to establish domination over each other. As the interaction progresses, this may, in fact, occur, in which case one or the other will be recognized as superior, or the opposition may end in a draw. The process by which the adjustment is worked out is known as *accommodation*. Some sociologists view it as the key process in social organization.[28] It enables persons or groups who do not agree to function as members of the same social system,[29] a solution sometimes called *antagonistic cooperation*.

Sutherland, Woodward, and Maxwell call attention to the compromises worked out in the American Constitution which made it possible for people with divergent interests to work together for common goals.[30] Another example would be the accommodation between North and South after the Civil War. In more recent times one might point to the course of events in France since the close of World War II, where an uneasy political situation in which governments rapidly followed each other was terminated by the establishment of the Fifth Republic under De Gaulle. Caste in India and Pakistan is, of course, a prime example. The system seeks to achieve stability in occupational distribution through application of the principle of heredity; insofar as it is accepted, it enables low-caste persons, such as sweepers, to rationalize their poor situation as a misfortune of birth.[31] Negro-white relationships are frequently characterized by accommodation, as are contracts between organized labor and management where neither side gets all it wants but a

---

[28] See R. L. Sutherland, J. L. Woodward, and M. A. Maxwell, *Introductory Sociology*, 4th ed., Lippincott, 1952, p. 222; Smith, *op. cit.*, p. 543.
[29] Sutherland *et al.*, *op. cit.*, p. 222.
[30] *Ibid.*, p. 223.
[31] See Chapter 17 for a discussion of caste.

truce is worked out since both must work together if business is to go on.

In all of these cases, of course, considerable social distance remains between the formerly conflicting individuals and social systems. In *assimilation,* another form of interaction to be discussed below, the social distance between groups tends to disappear.

Superordination and Subordination

A form of accommodation which is of tremendous importance is known as superordination and subordination, which involves the distribution and use of authority. In any social system certain people occupy dominant roles while others are submissive and perform subordinate roles. This state of affairs may be relatively permanent. In some cases, however, vertical organization may be in constant flux with different persons occupying the dominant role at different times.

Let us consider some aspects of this relationship in different types of social systems.

IN THE FAMILY. In a society having authoritarian family patterns like that in nineteenth-century rural America, the culture supports the type of accommodative interaction in which the husband-father is dominant (sometimes domineering) and the wife-mother and the children submit, within cultural limits, to his authority. There have been cases where the male head of the family has enforced unreasonable demands by physical force, and in such families the threat of such force is always present. Sometimes the cultural pattern is so well established that it would be unthinkable to resist the directives of the family head.

This is, of course, a much different social atmosphere than that found in the contemporary democratic farm family which is bound together by love and affection, where cooperation is voluntary and where a major value is enhancement of the happiness of members. This is not to say that conflict never arises in the latter type of family nor that accommodation does not occur, but superordination and subordination is not the dominant theme.

POLITICAL DOMINANCE AND SUBORDINATION. In Nazi Germany, Fascist Italy, the USSR, Communist China, and other totalitarian states, the individual is entirely subordinate to the state. The values declared by the leaders are considered superior, and those of the individual, if they differ, are suppressed.

The means by which Hitler, Stalin, and Mussolini established dominance are well known: they employed terroristic methods. The accommodation of their subjects to their rule was motivated by the desire to survive, for nonconformity meant liquidation.

After all political struggles some form of accommodation is worked out and patterns of domination and subordination are established. The essential difference between totalitarian and other states lies in the degree of independence permitted the citizens. In a democracy this may be very great.

DOMINANCE AND SUBORDINATION IN THE WORLD OF WORK. There is a wide range in the accommodations which characterize different forms of social systems in the world of work. These range from master-slave relationships of the southern plantation before the Civil War to those between president and the vice-president of a major farm corporation.

Slavery was once a fairly prevalent form of agricultural work relationship in most parts of the world. It was practiced by the Romans, by Mogul emperors of India, and by southern plantation owners in the U.S. Domination of the slave is initially established by force and the accommodation he makes is maintained through force or the threat of force. This relationship is harsh and onerous. T. Lynn Smith has called attention to three distinctive characteristics of slavery, pointing out that (1) the slave is legally owned by his master, (2) the slave has the lowest possible social rank, and (3) the slave works under compulsion.[32]

Fortunately, systems of slavery where persons are owned by other persons have virtually disappeared from the earth. This is not to say, however, that some employers do not use cruel methods of keeping their workers on the job. The division of labor and the conditions of work in Communist China sound very much like slavery under a different name.

Even in the most enlightened corporations some lead and others follow. It is as characteristic of the agricultural corporation or co-operative, as it is of governmental bureaucracy that the principal

[32] Smith, *op. cit.*, p. 543.

lines of interest and attention point upward rather than downward. This means that the aspiring young employee studies the man and the job above him and gives immediate attention to the suggestions of his boss, while at the same time he may be indifferent to the requests of his own subordinates.

ASSIMILATION

One type of adjustment between competing or conflicting ethnic or racial stocks is *assimilation*. About this process, Park and Burgess have said, "Assimilation is a process of interpenetration and fusion in which persons and groups acquire the memories, sentiments and attitudes of other persons or groups, and, by sharing their experience and history, are incorporated with them in a common cultural life."[33]

The outstanding example of assimilation in human history is found on the North American continent, where in the short span of two or three generations many people from widely divergent cultures with different languages and value systems have been assimilated to the point where the descendants of the white immigrants speak a common language, intermarry, and otherwise interact freely and share a common culture.[34] This may be contrasted with the accommodation existing in other parts of the world where minority groups within a common political state nevertheless maintain their own languages and separate values and a rigid system of social stratification which represents a formalized type of accommodation of long duration. It should be pointed out that American Negroes have not been *assimilated*, although they are *acculturated* in the sense that they share most of the values, norms, and customs of the dominant race.

Among whites, subtle ethnic differences and ethnocentrism still exist to some extent. As noted in Chapter 5, the Pennsylvania Dutch, the Louisiana French, and the Spanish Americans of the Southwest have resisted assimilation. This is also true of certain ethnoreligious groups like the Amish, the Hutterites, and the Amana. Most American Indian tribes have not been fully assimilated.

Because of its importance in resolving potential group conflict, we

[33] Park and Burgess, *op. cit.*, p. 785.
[34] See Chapter 5 for a discussion of immigration, acculturation, and cultural integration of non-English-speaking ethnic stocks.

will attempt to identify the factors which have facilitated or impeded assimilation in the United States.

Warner and Srole have suggested that skin color, language, and religious affiliation to a major extent determine the social rank given an ethnic stock. The resulting degree of subordination in turn is believed to determine to a large extent the strength of the social systems which ethnic stocks establish. Stocks that establish strong social systems will have a long period of assimilation, and vice versa. According to Warner and Srole, light-skinned English-speaking Protestant immigrants will be assimilated most readily in the shortest time. Next come non-English-speaking fair-skinned Protestants, then fair-skinned English-speaking Catholics, followed by non-English-speaking fair-skinned Catholics. At the lower end of their scale are the dark-skinned non-Christian, non-English-speaking East Indians, Chinese, and Japanese. Warner and Srole feel that these dark-skinned ethnic stocks and the American Negro may be doomed to inferior racial status for an indefinite period unless marked changes occur in American methods of evaluating social rank;[35] if this is true, it will lead to continued ethnic or racial identification.

Discussing the forces which have led to the assimilation and acculturation of the ethnic stocks that have contributed population to the United States, Warner and Srole point out that in general ethnic groups in America differ in fundamental ways from ethnic minorities in Europe. In Europe the minority group in a particular area may have been there longer than the dominant group. In America, because of its relative youth, a certain amount of tolerance for immigrants is to be expected, because even the native-born population can trace its ancestry to some foreign immigrant.[36]

The ideology of the U.S. and its form of political, social, and economic organization tend to facilitate assimilation and acculturation. Except for some areas of the South, almost all adults are able to vote. The number and variety of employment opportunities have led members of recently arrived ethnic stocks to take jobs and thus to mingle more or less freely with the dominant English-speaking majority. Although a considerable amount of education is now

[35] W. L. Warner and Leo Srole, *The Social Systems of American Ethnic Groups,* Yale University Press, 1945.
[36] *Ibid.*

necessary for employment in most occupations, this was not the case at the time when the greatest migration into industrial areas occurred. Many non-English-speaking immigrants, in fact, were recruited for work in the steel mills, coal mines, and other industries which sought unskilled workmen who were strong and vigorous.

Universal free education in the English language in both reading and oral skill has been a fundamental tool in the assimilation of immigrant stocks. For immigrant children, contact with other children at school has led to acceptance of social roles in youth groups. Many immigrant children, desiring to identify themselves as acceptable members of the dominant English-speaking majority, have rejected the image of themselves as foreigners and have consequently become ashamed of the customs and values of their parental ethnic groups.

The prevalent nuclear family system which is ideologically based on the concept of romantic love and free personal choice of one's mate has also operated in a powerful way to break up ethnic groups. It is true that in the first and second generations there may be a considerable amount of endogamy; but a substantial amount of intermarriage between ethnic stocks does occur. Though there is some intermarriage between Protestants and Catholics, a recent census survey on religious affiliation revealed that 93.6 percent of Protestant, Catholic, and Jewish married couples had mates in the same major religious group.[37] A few intermarriages between colored races and whites do occur, but strong social taboos exist with respect to such marriages.

Warner and Srole, commenting on the affect of memberships in cliques and other associations, indicate that the child or adult who is readily accepted into an American clique or association is thereby encouraged to adopt the American way of life.[38] In this connection it may be noted that most ethnic settlements in rural areas in the northern part of the U.S. were settled in such a way that immigrants were forced to intermingle with people of other ethnic stocks. In rural Wisconsin, leadership in community and political affairs was apparently taken by the Yankees.[39]

[37] U.S. Bureau of the Census, *Religion Reported by the Civilian Population of the United States: March 1957,* Series P.20, No. 79, February, 1958.

[38] Warner and Srole, *op. cit.*

[39] W. L. Slocum, *Ethnic Stocks as Culture Types in Rural Wisconsin,* unpublished Ph.D. thesis, University of Wisconsin, 1940.

Desirable as the goal of assimilation may appear to Americans, it doubtless will be a long time before Muslim, Sikh and Hindu are assimilated and have a common language and a fully shared set of social values; in fact, this may never happen. Caste, too, may long remain a factor blocking assimilation in India and Pakistan. Because of the importance of language psychologically and as a bearer of culture, it does not seem likely that true assimilation can be achieved without a common mother tongue, although the Swiss have demonstrated that many values and political institutions can be shared by people with different languages.

One may therefore legitimately ask whether it is possible to achieve assimiliation through coercion. We have already seen that it is possible to resolve conflict and achieve order through the process of accommodation. Force may be employed to secure and enforce such an accommodation.

In answer it can be said with reasonable certainty that recorded history does not present any outstanding examples of assimilation achieved through force. The Japanese tried to "Japanize" the Koreans, whose country they held for 40 years, by stern edicts enforced by severe punishment; the Koreans were forbidden to use any language other than Japanese even in their homes. The attempt was not successful. The USSR has attempted to assimilate various ethnic groups. The success of her efforts is not known, but the chances are high that assimilation has not occurred. We know that several languages are still spoken and occasionally we hear rumblings of discontent among the Georgians, the Kurds, or other ethnic minorities. But it may be possible to re-educate and acculturate minority groups and thus bring about assimilation by applying modern psychological and sociological principles; if they are backed by force and continued over a long period of time.

Cooperation as a Form of Association

Cooperation can be defined as a form of interaction consisting of joint efforts toward the achievement of a common goal. Rural Americans live in a culture that appears to place a higher value on competitive individual effort than on cooperation. Nevertheless, there is a tremendous amount of cooperative interaction among farm people. It is hardly possible to conceive of any substantial amount of integration or harmony in a social system without joint or cooperative effort toward common goals. Yet cooperative effort between two individuals is seldom if ever equal, since they will unquestionably attach different values to the end sought and will assess the situation differently because of different backgrounds and capabilities. Nevertheless, we should be aware that cooperative effort exists even in a competitive agricultural economy. It is a cement which binds the economy together and is responsible for much constructive activity.

Informal Cooperation

Informal cooperation occurs wherever people interact on an intimate basis in any type of primary group. It is present when farm parents work together toward a common goal, when farm children help with family ventures, when a farmer extends assistance to a neighbor who is in need, and when there is an agreement between farmers to trade work or machinery.

Within early American rural society informal cooperation was traditional, especially on the frontier where many problems were solved through mutual aid in the form of husking bees, barn raisings, and sharing of work. Kinship ties are frequently important in connection with the establishment and maintenance of patterns of mutual aid.

Informal cooperation is characteristic of primary group relationships, and thus will be found in the family, the kinship association, the country neighborhood and the play group. T. Lynn Smith refers to informal cooperation in primary groups as *symbiosis* or *commensalism*,[40] terms borrowed from plant ecology that refer to the situation where interdependent plants exist together in a close physical relationship.

Formal Cooperation

Cooperative interaction within formalized social systems tends to be formal in character. That is, persons who have common goals tend to set up formal organizations such as labor unions, purchasing or marketing cooperatives, mutual life insurance associations, and similar social groups to achieve the desired ends through cooperative efforts.

There has been considerable formal cooperation within American

[40] Smith, *op. cit.*, p. 523.

agriculture, some of it stimulated by the government through either preferential legislation or direct action by some governmental agency.[41]

The Impact of Cooperation upon Community Life

Informal cooperation, as noted above, has been traditional in rural America and is still of considerable importance in areas where family-type farms predominate; the tendency unquestionably helped create favorable conditions for the establishment of formal cooperatives. Although formal cooperatives in agriculture have their origin and their main justification in business relationships, interpersonal intercourse among members frequently involves social interaction of a noneconomic character.

Cooperation as a pattern has a beneficial effect on community life. Hoffer studied a Michigan community which had successful cooperative ventures over a period of approximately 45 years, and concluded:

> It appears that the community under consideration has acquired the pattern of cooperation in its culture. The idea of cooperation, separate and apart from any specific instance of cooperative activity, has permeated the community. Like a chemical solvent, cooperation extends from one activity to another, because the attitudes of the people are favorable to this method of meeting their common needs. . . . Each successful venture in cooperative activity in one phase of community life makes easier and more probable its development in other phases.[42]

Commenting upon the substitution of formal cooperation for informal mutual aid, Hoffer said:

> Mutual aid, considered as a process of extending assistance whenever needed without thought of compensation on the part of the person extending it, does not serve the needs of modern communities with complex social relationships. Cooperation, however, is a process which can be adapted to modern communities. It makes possible a systematic means of meeting the common needs of individuals in complex situations.[43]

[41] See Chapter 20 for a discussion of cooperatives in American agriculture from the standpoint of social systems.

[42] C. R. Hoffer, "Cooperation as a Culture Pattern within a Community," *Rural Sociology,* June, 1938, pp. 157-158.

[43] *Ibid.*

People in many rural communities have undertaken cooperative efforts to solve community problems.[44]

QUESTIONS FOR FURTHER STUDY AND DISCUSSION

1. What evidence can you find concerning the present condition of town-country relationships in your state? In your home locality? How would you classify these situations?
2. Do you agree that accommodation is a key *social* process? Why or why not?
3. Describe the distribution of authority in a family with which you are familiar. Comment on the accommodation of family members to this pattern.
4. Compare and contrast cooperation and competition.
5. Give examples of formal and informal cooperation in your home locality.

SELECTED REFERENCES

Bertrand, A. L., ed., *Rural Sociology*, McGraw-Hill, 1958, chaps, 20, 21.
Nelson, Lowry, *Rural Sociology*, 2nd ed., American Book, 1955.
Smith, T. Lynn, *The Sociology of Rural Life*, 3rd ed., Harper, 1953, chaps. 21, 22, 23.
Sutherland, R. L., J. L. Woodward, and M. A. Maxwell, *Introductory Sociology*, 4th ed., Lippincott, 1952, chaps. 11, 12.

[44] See Chapter 25.

13

Decision-Making Processes

The decisions of farmers are influenced by the opinions of significant persons with whom they interact, by the norms and values of their reference groups, by knowledge, and by the general culture.[1] Responsibility for some or all of their managerial decisions may be shared with wives or business partners. Tenants and owners jointly arrive at many decisions concerning land use, and the federal government places limitations on certain land uses and encourages others. Decisions of formal organizations are reached through group processes.[2] Business organizations seek consciously to influence farmers to buy their products or services; agricultural extension services try to persuade farmers to adopt new varieties and breeds of livestock as well as improved farming practices.

Farm people are not self-sufficient; they depend heavily upon others. Even such personal decisions as the choice of a mate and the selection of an occupation involve interaction with others. The image of the American farmer as an isolated self-reliant decision-maker requires correction in view of the facts of associated life.

Literally thousands of decisions must be made by any farmer during the course of his lifetime, some of which, naturally, are more important than others. Those involved in the management of a farm seem sufficiently comparable to classify together in a few major categories. The categories would be related to the interests of the person or group making the classification.

The choice of one's life work is sufficiently important in the lives of individual farmers to warrant separate treatment. In this chapter we will discuss the social and cultural factors involved in the selec-

[1] See Chapter 11 for a discussion of reference groups and Chapter 9 for a discussion of factors involved in decisions to adopt new practices.

[2] See Chapter 25 for a discussion of group action.

tion of farming as an occupation. Attention will also be directed toward some of the factors involved in the area of farm and home management.

FARM AND HOME MANAGEMENT DECISION-MAKING

DEMOCRACY IN FARM AND HOME DECISION-MAKING

The American farmer is traditionally pictured as a rather authoritarian figure who made the basic social and economic decisions concerning both farm and family all by himself. The accuracy of this image today is dubious. It may be true that the European peasant or even the early American farmer was the principal figure in all farm and home decisions, but his freedom in making decisions was never absolute; personal and cultural influences were undoubtedly involved. This seems to be true today in underdeveloped areas of the world like those found in India and Pakistan, even though the authority of the male head is undoubtedly much greater there than it has ever been in most American families.[3]

Few empirical studies have been made to ascertain the extent to which male heads of farm families are actually the principal decision-makers, but it is reasonably certain that in some cases, even a generation ago, the wife was more influential than the husband and joint decisions were fairly common. Today, the concept of democratic family management has attained great prevalence on farms.[4] There is an expectation of shared responsibility in the important decisions which affect the welfare of the family, though one spouse generally assumes the leadership role in relation to decisions falling in his or her respective area of major responsibility—the home and child-rearing for the wife and operation of the farm for the husband.

A study of 426 Pennsylvania farm families in 1950-1951 revealed a considerable number of joint purchase decisions, the majority, as in the case of Washington farm families cited below, occurring in purchases for the home.

[3] See S. C. Dube, *Indian Village*, Routledge & Kegan Paul, 1955, chap. 7.

[4] Recent data from nearly 2000 high-school seniors in the State of Washington indicates that the authoritarian family is extremely rare among both farm and non-farm segments of the population of that state (see, W. L. Slocum, *Occupational and Educational Plans of High School Seniors from Farm and Non-Farm Homes*, Washington AES Bulletin 564, February, 1956; see also chapter 14).

... joint decision by the husband and wife occurred more often regarding the purchase of home furnishings and equipment (73 per cent) than of the other kinds of goods studied. Other commodity purchases frequently planned together by husband and wife were the family car (53 per cent); children's play equipment (49 per cent); and reading material (44 per cent). Three-fourths of the wives made independent decisions about buying groceries but only half did the actual buying, 91 per cent decided about buying their own clothing, and 43 per cent made decisions about buying children's clothing. Two-thirds or more of the farm husbands decided by themselves about purchasing livestock, farm repairs, farm equipment, seed, feed, fertilizer, car repairs, and truck gas and oil.[5]

In a later study of attitudes toward joint decisions, husbands and wives in 252 Pennsylvania farm families unanimously agreed that decisions should involve both spouses; 90 percent of the wives and 75 percent of the husbands condemned the practice of one or the other making *all* of the important decisions, but about 40 percent thought that some independent decisions should be permitted. However, 20 percent admitted that, in practice, both husbands and wives customarily made independent decisions about certain types of purchases. Few had involved their children in family financial decisions.[6]

Wilkening classified a sample of Wisconsin farm families with respect to the degree of joint involvement of husband and wife in major decisions on planting crops, buying machinery, making changes in the farm, purchasing appliances for the house, and making changes in the home. Scoring of the responses showed the following distribution:

Degree of Joint Involvement	Percent
Very high	13.9
High	29.2
Medium	19.8
Low	14.8
Very low	22.3

SOURCE: E. A. Wilkening, "Joint-Decision-Making in Farm Families," *American Sociological Review*, April, 1958, pp. 187-198.

[5] Ruth R. Honey, Virginia Britton, and Alida S. Hotchkiss, *Decision-Making in the Use of Family Financial Resources in a Rural Pennsylvania Community*, Pennsylvania AES Bulletin 643, March, 1959, pp. 8-9.

[6] *Ibid.*, pp. 9, 38.

A recent statewide probability sample of commercial farmers under age 45 in Washington showed that in the great bulk of the families discussions between husbands and wives normally preceded decisions.[7] This was more pronounced for decisions affecting the home than for farming decisions.

TABLE 10.   Democracy in Farm and Home Decisions
on Washington Commercial Farms

Decision	Percent of Husbands Reporting	
	Discussion with Wife	Joint Decision
What crops to plant, when, where	70	27
Changes in farm	78	45
Buying machinery	84	47
Buying appliances for home	99	65
Changes in home	98	65

SOURCE: W. L. Slocum, *Decision-Making by Washington Farm Families,* unpublished paper, State College of Washington, Department of Rural Sociology, 1956. A statewide probability sample of 292 farmers under age 45.

Joint decisions were much less common than discussions preceding decision. However, a considerable amount of shared responsibility was reported. Joint decisions were more prevalent on home than on farm matters. As might be expected, the responses indicated that where joint decisions were not practiced, the husband normally made farm decisions while the wife normally took the responsibility for the home.

These data show clearly that there was a high degree of shared responsibility in the farm families studied, and the extent of reciprocal influence is probably understated. A married couple who have lived together for a considerable amount of time normally develop a facility for taking each other's role, and each spouse is thereby able to anticipate reaction. Thus, much of the accommodation to the attitudes of the other proceeds without actual dis-

[7] W. L. Slocum, *Decision-Making by Washington Farm Families,* unpublished paper, State College of Washington, Department of Rural Sociology, 1956.

cussion involving conscious weighing of all the elements in a particular decision.

On the basis of information from his sample of Wisconsin farm families, Wilkening has hypothesized that the extent of shared responsibility depends upon the perception by the spouses of decisions "as having joint consequences for both farm and home."[8] This hypothesis appears tenable primarily for a democratic family. As we have already noted, such families are not rare in this country. The hypothesis also assumes that the husband is farm-oriented and the wife is home- and family-oriented. Within the role expectations on an American family farm operated on a commercial basis, this may be a valid assumption.

ATTITUDES TOWARD DECISION-MAKING

In the Washington study referred to above, the farm operators were asked to express their attitudes toward decision-making. The responses indicate that only a small number of this sample of commercial farm operators (3 percent) considered farm management decisions to be very difficult. A still smaller percentage indicated a strong dislike for making decisions (1.3 percent), although an additional 12 percent expressed some dislike for the process. The responses indicate that a majority (55 percent) experienced only slight difficulty in making decisions, and a somewhat larger proportion (58 percent) rather enjoyed doing so. The last group had a higher level of contact with the extension service than others.[9]

HOW DECISIONS ARE MADE

It seems reasonable to believe that the decision to select one or another of perceived alternative courses of action is made on the basis of some test of the probable consequences of each alternative. Research on adoption of new agricultural practices by George Beal and his associates shows that adoption of a new farm prac-

[8] E. A. Wilkening, "Joint Decision-Making in Farm Families," *American Sociological Review*, April, 1958, p. 191.

[9] W. L. Slocum, Owen L. Brough, Jr., and Murray A. Straus, *Extension Contacts, Selected Characteristics, Practices, and Attitudes of Washington Farm Families*, Washington AES Bulletin 584, April, 1958, pp. 23-4.

tice is based principally on personal satisfaction with a trial.[10] Often, however, it is not possible to make even a small trial, in which case the decision must be based upon an evaluation of the possible consequences of each alternative. This mental exploration may be thorough or casual; it may glamorize certain aspects of one alternative, or it may be rational to a considerable degree.

RATIONAL DECISIONS

Agricultural economists have traditionally assumed a rather high degree of rationality in economic decision-making by farmers. The concept of the economic man is not entirely a thing of the past, although some economists acknowledge that people are affected by noneconomic influences. Crossmon, for example, recently quoted, with approval, a passage from a current best-seller which portrays people as anything but logical and rational.[11]

Dean, Aurbach, and Marsh recently studied some aspects of this problem. They devised a rationality index based upon nine questions which were considered by a board of judges in the Department of Rural Sociology at North Carolina State College to reflect rational decision-making in maximizing economic returns in farming. The rationality index showed a wide range of variation:

Rationality Score of Farmers	Percent
09-15	12.4
16-19	33.7
20-23	33.2
24-27	20.7
	100.0

The authors also found support for their hypotheses that farmers with higher rationality scores had (1) greater contact with the extension service, (2) a greater degree of mechanization, (3) larger farms, (4) younger ages and more control over farm operations as

[10] See E. M. Rogers and George M. Beal, "The Importance of Personal Influence in the Adoption of Technological Changes," *Social Forces*, May, 1958, p. 331.

[11] See B. D. Crossmon, "Discussion: New Knowledge of Decision-Making Processes," *Journal of Farm Economics*, December, 1958, pp. 1405-1406.

reflected by tenure status, (5) greater participation in formal organizations, (6) more formal education, and (7) a greater likelihood of accepting approved farm practices.[12]

Wilkening and Johnson concluded from a study of 184 farm
owners in Rock County, Wisconsin, that the prospect of making
money was an important factor in deciding whether certain types
of farm changes would be made. However, they also concluded
that noneconomic considerations were more important for a number
of farmers and for others were consistently most important.[13]

Attempts have been made to introduce more rationality into farm
management decisions. College courses are being given on the subject, and some agricultural extension services and private firms are
providing farm management advisory services. In addition, the
state agricultural extension services under the leadership of the
Federal Agricultural Extension Service have recently introduced a
fairly large-scale program known variously as farm and home planning, farm and home development, and the farm and home unit
approach, which consists basically of the application of rational
methods of thought to farm and home problems.[14] In some states,
a farm agent and a home agent sit down with the farm operator
and homemaker and help them take an objective inventory of the
capabilities and limitations of the farm and the human and economic
resources of the family. Consideration is then given to how the
farm can best be managed in order to meet the goals which the
family decides are most important.[15]

Millions of dollars of federal funds have been channeled into
this program. Participation by farm families has not been very
great in most states, and the unit costs are high because continuing

[12] Alfred Dean, Herbert A. Aurbach, and C. Paul Marsh, "Some Factors Related to Rationality in Decision Making Among Farm Operators," *Rural Sociology,* June, 1958, pp. 121-135.

[13] E. A. Wilkening and Donald Johnson, *A Case Study in Decision Making
Among a Farm Owner Sample in Wisconsin,* paper presented at Rural Sociological Society Meeting, August, 1958, p. 14.

[14] See Iowa Agricultural Extension Service, *Farm and Home Development,*
September, 1955.

[15] This approach is similar in some respects to the supervisory methods used
by the Farmers Home Administration and its predecessor the Farm Security
Administration. The extension agents, however, have no authority over the
farm family while the FHA supervisors do have because FHA loans are involved.

personal attention is required if the advice is to be effective. Results of a field experiment in Washington showed clearly that sample families who participated in farm and home development in that state made greater economic progress during the five year period of the study than a matched control group of nonparticipating families. Participants did not increase their levels of living proportionately but instead increased their capital investments which indicates that they may make still greater economic progress in the future. There was a marked change in patterns of farm management decision-making of participants but not of control group families; the shift was away from sharing of responsibility by husband and wife and toward decisions by the husband. Analysis of questionnaires completed by virtually all of the professional staff of the Washington Agricultural Extension Service indicates that experience with the farm and home unit approach changed the views and/or methods of a substantial majority.[16]

OCCUPATIONAL DECISION-MAKING BY FARM BOYS AND GIRLS

Analysis of the subject of occupational planning or decision-making involves several related social science disciplines: vocational psychology, labor economics, and occupational sociology. We shall deal here principally with the sociological aspects of the decision-making process without in any way attempting to minimize the contributions of either psychology or economics.

From a practical standpoint, the subject is of importance to farm boys and girls and their parents because the opportunities for acquiring a commercial farm are now relatively limited. This means that the great majority of farm youths must seek nonfarm employment.

Types of Occupations Chosen by Farm Youth

What sorts of occupations do young farm people choose? The answer seems to be: all sorts. Information obtained in connection

[16] Walter L. Slocum and Owen L. Brough, Jr., *Family and Farm Changes Associated with Farm and Home Planning in Washington*, A Report to the W. K. Kellogg Foundation, Washington State University, August 30, 1961, pp. 51-55. (Hectograph). Similar studies were made in North Carolina, Iowa, New York, and Wisconsin but results were not available at press time.

with a statewide study in Washington indicates that farm boys and girls who were seniors in public high schools in the spring of 1954 aspired preponderantly, as did their nonfarm contemporaries, to enter professional and technical occupations rather than manual or service types of work.[17]

WHO CHOOSES FARMING?

Some people have viewed with considerable concern the movement of competent and well-educated farm youth to nonfarm employment. In 1920 E. A. Ross asked if it was milk or cream that was leaving rural areas to go to the cities. His belief was that the most capable persons were leaving, resulting in "folk depletion" in the country.[18]

Since the time that Ross first made this statement, a number of studies have attempted to validate, verify, or disprove his observations. Gee and his associates in Virginia concluded that their findings supported Ross's point of view.[19] Dorothy S. Thomas, on the other hand, failed to find a clear-cut picture, saying, "Migration selects the better elements, the worse elements, both the better and the worse, and also . . . it is unselective."[20] Murray Straus concluded that there was little or no difference between Washington farmers' sons who expressed a preference for farming and those who choose nonfarm occupations. Said he, "Over-all, it can be said that the findings of this study show that there is little or no difference between the physical and intellectual ability of farmers' sons in the State of Washington who desire to farm and farmers' sons who express a preference for nonfarm occupations. . . . It can be concluded that the occupational selection process . . . is such that

[17] Slocum, *Occupational and Educational Plans of High School Seniors, op. cit.*, p. 25.

[18] E. A. Ross, *The Principles of Sociology*, Century, 1920, p. 24; and *New Age Sociology*, Appleton-Century, 1940, pp. 55-56.

[19] Wilson Gee and Dewees Runk, "Qualitative Selection and Migration," *American Journal of Sociology*, September, 1931, pp. 254-266; Wilson Gee and J. J. Corson, *Rural Depopulation in Certain Tidewater and Piedmont Areas of Virginia*, University of Virginia Institute for Research in the Social Sciences, Monograph 3, 1929, p. 102.

[20] Dorothy S. Thomas, "Selective Migration," *Milbank Memorial Fund Quarterly*, XVI 1938, pp. 403-407.

Washington's agriculture receives at least a proportional share of the physically, intellectually and socially well endowed."[21]

How Are Occupational Choices Made?

There is no reason to suppose that the decision-making processes of farm-reared youth are any different from those of urban or village young people. Studies made at the State College of Washington and elsewhere indicate that substantially the same types of influences are involved regardless of residence or the occupational classification of the male parent.[22]

Both farm and nonfarm adolescents are called upon to make decisions and long-term commitments at a time when they have a minimum of the type of experience and information needed for sound decisions on what occupation is most suitable for their aptitudes and capacities. If there is any difference in the needs of farm versus nonfarm young people in respect to vocational counseling, it would seem that the needs of farm youth are greater because of their somewhat smaller experience worlds.

The actual selection of one's life work in most cases involves not one but a series of decisions made over a period of time. Some of these decisions may greatly limit the range of future decisions. For example, the farm boy who decides to major in poultry science will find it difficult to effect a change of course and enter agricultural economics if he waits until his senior year in college. To do so would require a substantial amount of additional training time. In this connection, it may be noted that many educational planning decisions turn out to be occupational decisions. Much of modern education, even at the university level, involves preparation for employment in specific types of work.

Each occupational decision involves consideration of the requirements and rewards of the role, which includes evaluation of the actual or presumed approval of significant others. This process,

[21] Murray A. Straus, "Personal Characteristics and Functional Needs in the Choice of Farming as an Occupation," *Rural Sociology,* September-December, 1956, pp. 257-266.

[22] See W. L. Slocum, "Some Sociological Aspects of Occupational Choice," *American Journal of Economics and Sociology,* January, 1959, pp. 139-147, (this paper has been drawn upon for much of the material on occupational decision-making).

which can be designated as "playing at" an occupational role, appears to be central to the selection of one role from the alternatives considered by the decision-maker at any particular time. Alternative roles are frequently perceived, though information on them may well be incomplete, and the choice made is not necessarily fully rational, if by this term we mean that the consequences are fully considered before a decision is made.

If this is a correct analysis of the decision-making process, it follows that assistance can be given to young people by helping them visualize more clearly the disadvantages as well as the rewards and benefits of the various occupational roles they are considering. To some extent this can be done through the communication of personal experiences by people in the particular occupational field. Some of it can be done through tours or job descriptions that cover the requirements of particular fields and particular roles within the fields. There is, however, no real substitute for actual practical experience in dramatizing for an individual the satisfactions and disadvantages of an occupational role. Consequently, to the greatest extent possible, young people should be helped to obtain employment as a means of testing their abilities against the requirements of different types of work. This is difficult if not impossible in the case of certain highly specialized technical and professional occupations, but there are a great many occupations where it is entirely feasible. There can be little if any question about its desirability.

WHAT INFLUENCES ARE INVOLVED IN OCCUPATIONAL DECISION-MAKING?

The short answer to this question is that many influences ordinarily are involved at any given time in a decision by any particular individual. The common scientific practice of abstracting specific aspects of a process for study, however, can lead researchers to overlook the complex interdependence of multiple influences and to conclude that one or two aspects are all important. To some extent this has already happened. Most of the studies on occupational choice to date have been conducted either by psychologists who tend to accent individual differences in aptitudes and interests or by economists who tend to emphasize employment requirements, opportunities, and prospects. These emphases have led to the development of specific instruments for use by counselors such as interests and aptitude tests. Relatively few studies have been made of the influence of reference groups or the function of imagining or playing at occupational roles in the decision process.

In giving consideration to the important influences on occupational planning, it is not adequate to dismiss the subject by saying that there are many influences. It seems desirable to comment on four major constellations.

Personal Variables

The significance of many personal variables is obvious without detailed comment. For example, the importance of attained age requires no documentation; the person who has reached late adolescence is usually ready to consider the choice of his life's work in a realistic manner, whereas children are not.

Physical characteristics such as size and strength are important only for specific occupational roles which require these characteristics. More physical strength is required in hoe or plow culture than in mechanized scientific farming. Good health, on the other hand, appears to be a prerequisite for most full-time occupational roles. The sex of the individual is important because in most societies there are clearly defined occupational sex roles. Furthermore, the occupational planning of young women is usually influenced by the desire for marriage and performance of the roles of wife, mother, and homemaker.

Psychologists have verified the existence of individual differences in aptitudes and interests—not every person has the same interests and certainly not all have equal aptitudes. At the same time, psychologists have also demonstrated that most people have the potentiality for success in more than one occupational role.[23] This is a very important idea for vocational counseling, a substantial part of which, as it is presently conceived, consists of helping the client to identify and understand his interests and aptitudes as they apply to more than one potential job.

[23] See Donald E. Super, "A Theory of Vocational Development," *American Psychologist*, May, 1953, pp. 185-191.

General Cultural Factors

Occupational decision-making takes place within a cultural context. A person's plans may be influenced by such general cultural factors as societal values, the state of technological development, and the relative prosperity of the economy as translated into employment opportunities.

An example of the significance of societal values is the fact that free choice of an occupation theoretically exists in contemporary America but not in all societies. It is an attribute of the culture system. An American farm boy is not expected to continue to live on the farm and make farming his life's work unless he wishes to do so. Rather, he is expected to select his own work from all the occupational roles which are open to a man. He is also expected to be accountable for the consequences of his choice. Farm girls like their nonfarm contemporaries also have considerable freedom of occupational choice, though of course the occupations available to them tend to be restricted to those roles which within American culture are regarded as women's work.[24]

There are negative as well as positive factors of an impersonal character which influence occupational choice. Certain barriers exist to entrance into certain occupations. Traditionally, in India and Pakistan, caste was a barrier. Apprenticeship is required in certain crafts, specific formal education is needed for professional occupations, and admittance into a labor union is a prerequisite for acquisition of a specific job for certain factory operatives. A few occupations may in effect be hereditary even in the United States. This is more often true of commercial farming than of most other occupations in contemporary America. In fact, it is sometimes said that the best way for a young man to get into farming today is to inherit a good farm or to marry a girl who will inherit one.[25]

With respect to employment prospects in specific occupations, a considerable amount of information has been compiled by various organizations, individuals, and agencies.[26] The most authoritative

[24] W. L. Slocum and L. T. Empey, *Occupational Planning by Young Women*, Washington AES Bulletin, 568, August, 1956, pp. 25-26.

[25] See E. M. Rogers, *Social Change in Rural Society*, Appleton-Century-Crofts, 1960, p. 118.

[26] See Gertrude Forrester, *Occupational Pamphlets—An Annotated Bibliography*, Wilson, 1948.

work for the U.S. is the *Occupational Outlook Handbook* prepared
by the Bureau of Labor Statistics of the United States Department
of Labor for the Veterans Administration, which is revised periodically. This book is found in most college libraries and guidance
centers. In utilizing the information it contains, however, it should
be noted that while the information was undoubtedly accurate as
of the time of preparation, it is very difficult to make an accurate
forecast of specific employment prospects in any occupation over
a long period. As an example, in 1949, just prior to the outbreak
of the Korean conflict, the Bureau of Labor Statistics, doubtless
recalling the situation in the early 1930s, predicted an oversupply
of engineers. The prediction could not have been more wrong:
there was a shortage of engineers throughout the 1950s.

The Influence of Perceived Interpersonal Relationships

Studies at the State College of Washington indicate that young
men and women generally recognize that their relationships with
other people have played an important part in helping them make
their occupational plans. Three out of four high-school seniors acknowledged that some person had influenced their planning in a
helpful way; on another question a third reported negative influences. Parents were found to head the list of those exercising a helpful influence. Teachers were in second place, close friends of the
students' own ages were in third place, and vocational counselors
were placed fourth.[27]

Miller and Form have suggested that older persons like parents
serve as primary work models with whom the child identifies
himself by role-taking.[28] This is undoubtedly a correct interpretation. The research findings cited above indicate, however, that the
potential influence of people with whom adolescents are in contact
is much more comprehensive. These persons may be of assistance
to an adolescent in helping him, through advice as well as by example, to clarify his perception of the requirements and disadvantages of various occupational roles.

[27] Slocum, *Occupational and Educational Plans of High School Seniors,*
op cit., pp. 21-22.
[28] Delbert Miller and William Form, *Industrial Sociology,* Harper, 1951,
p. 522.

The Influence of Values and Behavior Patterns of Reference Groups

As noted elsewhere, it is generally acknowledged by sociologists that the values of reference groups, those groups with which the individual is associated or desires to associate himself, have a significant influence on the socialization of the individual.[29] Their values come to be internalized and in this way influence his actions. Decision-makers are generally not consciously aware of such influences, even though they may be transmitted through personal contacts; they operate subtly and usually cannot readily be perceived. Specific evidence relative to the operation of the values of specific reference groups on occupational choice is not plentiful. However, in the high-school study previously cited, statistical analysis of associations between variables disclosed that seniors whose fathers held high-status occupational roles were significantly more likely to decide to enter college than those whose fathers occupied lower-status roles.[30]

In the same study it was found that particular school systems and families with particular types of management patterns had exercised measurable influences upon occupation-related decision-making. Hollingshead has reported that the ideas which adolescents have about desirable jobs "reflect significantly their family's position in the class structure."[31]

STAGES OF OCCUPATIONAL CHOICE

As indicated earlier, occupational choice may be regarded as a developmental process consisting ordinarily of a series of decisions rather than a single decison. The intellectual parent of this idea is the general concept of life stages familiar in the field of education and the companion concept that the individual matures as he passes through these stages. Occupational decisions made at any given age are not necessarily final, although some of them, in fact, may greatly limit or otherwise influence the nature of subsequent decisions. But even so, there are many entirely feasible changes

---

[29] See Chapter 11.

[30] Slocum, *Occupational and Educational Plans of High School Seniors, op. cit.*, p. 6.

[31] A. B. Hollingshead, *Elmtown's Youth*, Wiley, 1949, p. 287.

in specific occupational roles before a person reaches maturity and even after entrance into the labor force. It is obvious, of course, that young people can change their occupational objectives before they enter the world of work. Jaffe and Carleton, in their study of occupation mobility in the United States,[32] found that *only about one-fifth* of American men remain even in the same major occupation group during their entire working lives. Most, of course, begin near the bottom of the occupational ladder and gradually work their way upward as attractive employment opportunities present themselves. It is quite unlikely that this high rate of occupational mobility is applicable to farmers, but Straus and Parrish found that many settlers in the Columbia Basin had urban job experience (42 percent).[33]

Ginzberg and his associates, on the basis of some exploratory studies, postulated three periods with rather specific age boundaries.[34] These are the fantasy period, extending from age 6 to about age 11; the tentative period, from 12 to 17; and the realistic period, which starts at 18 and includes early adulthood. Within the realistic period, he has identified three *stages* which have been found useful in the analysis of information obtained from farm and nonfarm adolescents in the state of Washington.[35] These are (1) the exploration stage, (2) the crystallization stage, and (3) the stage of occupational specification. A third of the Washington high-school seniors were classified as exploratory because they reported that they were still considering two or more occupations. Two-thirds, however, expressed a definite preference for a single occupation. More than half of the latter had already narrowed their choice to a specific job within the occupation.[36] This does not mean, of course, that even those who were classified as the most advanced

[32] A. J. Jaffe and R. O. Carleton, *Occupational Mobility in the United States, 1930-1960*, Kings Crown Press, 1954, p. 56.

[33] M. A. Straus and B. D. Parrish, *The Columbia Basin Settler*, Washington AES Bulletin 566, May, 1956.

[34] Eli Ginzberg *et al.*, *Occupational Choice*, Columbia University Press, 1951, chap. 9.

[35] Herman M. Case and W. L. Slocum, "Factors Associated with Three Postulated Stages of Occupational Choice Behavior of College Students," *Research Studies of the State College of Washington*, September, 1953, pp. 242-246.

[36] Slocum, *Occupational and Educational Plans of High School Seniors, op. cit.*, pp. 26-29.

would necessarily enter the occupation of their present preference. Entry is not merely a matter of choice; a job must exist and an employer must hire the candidate.

Statistical analysis of the Washington high-school data indicates that those who had progressed furthest through these stages had the following characteristics. They were more likely to have had a conference about their life's work with a teacher, counselor, or principal in their high school. They had somewhat better grades. Their fathers were more often employed in middle status than in high- or low-status occupational roles. They expressed a desire to do work which involved relationships with people rather than to work with things or ideas. They were more likely to have reported personal influences as important in their occupational planning. They had more often done some actual work in the field of their present preference. Girls were somewhat more likely than boys to have reached the stage of specificity. Those who were planning to attend college the year following graduation from high school tended to be somewhat further advanced than others.[37]

Farm youth tended to be more advanced than those who did not live on farms. This was evidently due to occupational rather than residential factors; there were no statistically significant differences between residential categories when arranged in accordance with the concept of the rural-urban continuum.[38]

Other factors were examined and found not to be associated with the progression through the stages of choice at statistically significant levels among Washington high-school students. These included income of parents, number of full- and part-time jobs held, rating by the student of the degree of democracy practiced in his home, membership in a normal versus a broken family, and degree of participation in extracurricular activities in the high school.[39]

SUMMARY OF THE PROCESS OF OCCUPATIONAL CHOICE

It appears then that the essential elements of occupational decision-making include the following:

[37] *Ibid.*
[38] *Ibid.*
[39] *Ibid.*

1. Occupational choice decisions which are made before entrance into a job are accomplished through "playing at" occupational roles. It seems quite likely that this is also the way in which a member of the labor force decides to take another job open to him.

2. Occupational choice decisions are not necessarily made rationally. This does not mean, however, that more rationality in such decisions would not be desirable.

3. Occupational choice decisions are influenced by multiple factors operating concurrently. Those which appear to carry significant weight include (a) personal variables such as age, physical characteristics, aptitudes, interests, and personal experiences; (b) cultural factors such as societal norms and values, job requirements, and general employment opportunities; (c) perceived interpersonal relationships and (d) reference group values.

ASSISTANCE BY PARENTS WITH OCCUPATIONAL CHOICE

Youth look to many persons for assistance with occupational planning. Consequently, parents, teachers, and others who have significant relationships with young people have more than a casual responsibility in providing assistance in the choice of an occupation.

The fact that parents are listed most frequently as the persons who had the greatest influence indicates that it is not proper in many cases for them to discharge their responsibility by simply referring their adolescent offspring to professional counselors.

In a study at the college level, students were asked, "In your opinion should parents help to decide what kind of occupation their children should prepare for?" Forty-four percent answered in the negative and 81 percent of those who answered affirmatively specified that the participation of the parent should be restricted to information and advice. Relatively few parents (only 4 percent of those of the high-school seniors) were reported to have actually chosen an occupation for their children; most adolescents seem not to want this type of assistance. It is likely, however, that many young people would appreciate a greater amount of interest and assistance than they now receive. There appears to be a tendency on the part of many parents to take a strictly hands off attitude.

In response to a question, "To what extent have your parents attempted to influence your occupational plans?" which was included in the high-school study, 28 percent checked the response, "They have not attempted to influence me in any way."[40]

QUESTIONS FOR DISCUSSION AND FURTHER STUDY

1. Analyze the cultural and social influences in a major decision which you have made.
2. Describe the decision-making process involved in the purchase of a new car by a family well known to you; the purchase of a new tractor; the purchase of a new automatic clothes washer-dryer.
3. To what extent are farming decisions arrived at by democratic processes in commercial farm families? Evaluate the advantages and disadvantages of group decisions in farm management.
4. Discuss the process of playing at roles in occupational decision-making. Illustrate your answer by case histories if possible.

SELECTED REFERENCES

Dean, Alfred, Herbert A. Aurbach, and C. Paul Marsh, "Some Factors Related to Rationality in Decision Making Among Farm Operators," *Rural Sociology*, June, 1958.

Dube, S. C., *Indian Village*, Routledge & Kegan Paul, 1955.

Ginzberg, Eli, *et al.*, *Occupational Choice*, Columbia University Press, 1951.

Hollingshead, A. B., *Elmtown's Youth*, Wiley, 1949.

Honey, Ruth R., Virginia Britton, and Alida S. Hotchkiss, *Decision-Making in the Use of Family Financial Resources in a Rural Pennsylvania Community*, Pennsylvania AES Bulletin 643, March, 1959.

Rogers, Everett M., and George M. Beal, "The Importance of Personal Influence in the Adoption of Technological Changes," *Social Forces*, May, 1958.

Slocum, W. L., "Some Sociological Aspects of Occupational Choice," *American Journal of Economics and Sociology*, January, 1959.

Wilkening, E. A., "Joint Decision-Making in Farm Families," *American Sociological Review*, April, 1958.

[40] *Ibid*, p. 22.

IV

SOCIAL SYSTEMS: NETWORKS OF RELATIONSHIP

Farm people are members of and participants in a great number of social systems. These include farm families, cliques and other informal groups, voluntary formal organizations like farm cooperatives, and local systems associated with various social institutions including churches, schools, and government.

Membership and participation in social systems provide farm people with values, behavior norms and status-roles. Consequently, it is necessary for us to study the structure and functioning of the major relevant social systems if we wish to understand farm life.

14

Farm Families

The basic unit of all societies is the family, whether we speak of a village of 20 people or the entire population of the modern world.

What is a family? A family is a group of individuals who are closely related by blood or marriage and who live together. Almost all human beings are born into families, spend their formative years as members of families, and when they are mature, marry and establish families of their own. Since family membership is almost universal, almost every human has a background of concrete experience which can be used to evaluate and interpret information about family life.

The term *family* is sometimes used to denote other groups than father, mother, and their children, which is perfectly proper if the meaning is clear. The *household*, as distinguished from the family, refers to all the persons who occupy a dwelling unit whether related or not. A household may include more than one family. However, some households do not contain a family since the unit of a household head living alone or with unrelated persons is classified as a household but not as a family.

Why study farm families? The answer to this question is that they are the most important groups in rural America. Most American farms are operated by families. Usually the family lives on its farm and its members provide most of the human labor required by the enterprise.

In 1960 there were more than 45,000,000 families in the United

States. Of these, 27,620,000 were classified as urban, 13,642,000 as rural nonfarm, and 3,800,000 as rural farm.[1] This was a decline of 1,620,000 rural farm familes from 1950, partly due to a change in the definition of the farm population used by the Census Bureau.[2]

THE COMPOSITION OF FARM FAMILIES AND HOUSEHOLDS

Rural families and households differ greatly in composition (Table 11). Strictly speaking, it is not correct to talk of *the* rural family or *the* rural household.

TABLE 11. Composition of Rural Farm Households, March, 1960

Households	Percent
Head only	7.1
Head with relatives	92.9
Husband-wife households	85.0
Other households with male head	3.5
Households with female head	4.4
All households	100.0
Number of households	4,076,000

SOURCE: U.S. Bureau of the Census, *Household and Family Characteristics: March 1960*, Series P-20, No. 106, January 9, 1961.

The sociological significance of variations in family composition is that interaction patterns and individual and family interests are influenced by the ages, sex, and numbers of family members. The extent of variation in the composition of farm families and households is a matter of great importance to agricultural extension workers and others who seek to educate or otherwise influence farm families. Failure to evaluate properly the interests of families may easily result in improper program design and subsequent failure.

[1] U.S. Bureau of the Census, *Household and Family Characteristics: March 1960*, Series P-20, No. 106, January 9, 1961.

[2] See Chapter 2.

TYPES OF FAMILIES

While it is unquestionably true that family membership is virtually universal, there is a great variation in the forms of families that are found in different cultures.[3]

The typical family in American society consists of husband, wife, and their children. This may be called an elementary or nuclear family. Usually grandparents do not live in the same dwelling with the child-rearing family. Providing a home for grandparents was common at an earlier period in American history, and it still occurs more frequently among farm than nonfarm families. The change is probably due in part to the development of governmental programs which provide some economic security for the aged.

The American family is monogamous, which means one wife for one husband at a particular time. Polygamy was prevalent among the Mormons when they first settled in the West.[4]

In the Indian subcontinent, the joint family is common in agricultural villages. According to Dube, an ideal joint family would include husband and wife, brothers and their wives, sons and their wives, paternal parents and grandparents, unmarried sisters, daughters, and grandchildren. Families with five generations under the same roof are rare. More common is the joint family which consists of parents and married sons and their wives and children or of brothers and their wives and children. Nuclear families are also common, frequently established because of conflict between the wife and members of the husband's family, particularly the mother-in-law.[5]

FUNCTIONS OF FAMILIES

Families perform many useful functions for their members and for society as a whole. Among the more important are the following:

1. They provide the socially approved basis for the satisfaction of sexual needs and hence insure the propagation of the species.

---

[3] Ralph Linton, *The Study of Man,* Appleton-Century, 1936, chap. X.
[4] See Kimball Young, *Isn't One Wife Enough?* Holt, 1954.
[5] S. C. Dube, *Indian Village,* Routledge & Kegan Paul, 1955, pp. 133-134.

2. They provide a basis for the satisfaction of emotional and affectional needs.

3. Through precept and example on the part of adult members, families transmit habits, attitudes, values, and other aspects of the cultural heritage. In sociological terminology, they socialize their children.

4. They provide sustenance and care for dependent members.

5. They provide social rank for members in the community.

6. They maintain social control.

There is no doubt that the farm family performs the same basic functions as the urban family. However, there may be some difference in the performance of the functions due to the unique nature of agriculture as an occupation, which may be engaged in jointly by all able-bodied members of the family group.

Although all of the functions listed above are important, the three of greatest interest from a sociological point of view are socialization, provision of social rank for members, and social control.

Sociologists, social psychologists, psychiatrists, and others agree that the social training received by a child as a member of his family is of great importance in the development of his personality; furthermore, the family continues to be an important reference group and hence influences conduct even after an individual leaves it physically.[6] It is certainly true that a child learns how to talk, how to walk, how to clothe and feed himself and how to care for his bodily needs before he has much contact with persons outside his family.

A child's contacts with his parents and other members of his family normally continue over a longer period of time than contacts with other groups or individuals. Nevertheless, the range of variation in family values, habits, and interaction patterns is so wide and the amount of interaction with individuals outside the family is so great that it is virtually impossible to isolate the causal factors involved in the development of particular patterns of personality.

No true experimental studies have been made to learn whether a particular type of family culture invariably produces individuals with a particular personality configuration. It is not likely that

[6] See Chapter 11 for definition of reference group.

experiments of this type will be conducted in the future because of the difficulties inherent in long-term experiments involving human subjects. Evidence available from anthropological studies of families in different cultures is not conclusive, because the influence of family patterns cannot be readily isolated from the influences of other groups or other aspects of the culture. In the absence of definitive evidence about the influence of family patterns upon personality, the most that can be done is to formulate hypotheses on the basis of fragmentary information from case histories, statistical enumerations, and sample surveys.

With respect to social rank, it has long been observed that family considerations are of great significance in small communities. The social rank of the head of the family tends to be used to establish that of other members of the family.[7]

The function of families in establishing and maintaining social control is recognized to some extent by nearly everyone.[8] It is not generally realized, however, that the many differences in family values and culture patterns which exist in America contribute to divergent reactions to general norms. Plurality rather than uniformity in family norms appears to be typical except perhaps in "cultural islands" such as the Hutterites'.

FORMATION AND DISSOLUTION OF FAMILIES

The informal norms and laws which govern the formation and dissolution of families vary greatly from one society to another. In rural India and Pakistan, for example, nearly all marriages are arranged by parents. The sexes are segregated. Neither bride nor groom has any voice in the matter. Among Muslims in Pakistan, the ideal marriage is between cousins. Girls are frequently married by age 15. After the wedding, it is customary for the couple to live with the parents of the groom.

Among Muslims a marriage may be dissolved if the husband says three times, "I divorce you." This privilege is not extended to the wife. However, divorce is not common because of strong social pressure against it.[9]

---

[7] See Chapter 17 for a discussion of social stratification.

[8] See Chapter 11 for a discussion of social control.

[9] W. L. Slocum, Jamila Aktar and Abrar Fatima, *Village Life in Lahore District,* Lahore, Social Sciences Research Center, Panjab University Press, 1959.

In the rural United States, on the other hand, the ideal marriage is a romantic or love marriage. Boys and girls are not segregated and dating may begin in the early teens. After courtship, the boy is supposed to propose marriage, and the couple then become engaged. The marriage is generally followed by a honeymoon trip. The couple usually lives in a separate dwelling rather than with the parents of either party. Divorce can be obtained only for cause, and can be granted only by a court. There is a widespread belief that divorce is less common among rural than urban families in the U.S.[10] Landis opined that the greater stability of the rural family is due in large measure to its sociocultural characteristics. Specifically, he listed more dependents, the prevailing authority pattern, the fact that the rural home has many functions to perform, and a common interest in home functions.[11]

Age at marriage has traditionally been lowest among rural farm groups. Writing in 1948, Landis called earlier rural marriage an established fact.[12]

Rural girls tend to marry somewhat earlier than urban girls, but in 1950 rural nonfarm girls were most likely to marry young. At that time, among girls of 17 the percentages married were: rural-farm 12.5, rural nonfarm 16.9, and urban 10.3. Farm boys tend to marry much later than boys in other residential categories. In 1950 in the 20-24 age group, 36.9 percent of the rural farm boys, 45.4 percent of the rural nonfarm boys, and 64 percent of the urban boys were married. In the state of Washington, the reversal of the traditional position of age at marriage was even more pronounced.[13]

The lateness in the age of marriage for farm males is due to the interaction of many factors. One of the most important is probably the difficulty a young man now has in becoming established in farming in contrast to the relative ease of obtaining nonfarm employment which pays sufficiently well to provide for the support

[10] A. L. Bertrand, ed., *Rural Sociology*, McGraw-Hill, 1958, p. 218. See also Chapter 2 of this book.

[11] Paul H. Landis, *Rural Life in Process*, 2nd ed., McGraw-Hill, 1948, chap. 21.

[12] *Ibid.*, p. 46.

[13] W. L. Slocum and Carol L. Stone, *The Farm People of Washington at Mid-Century*, Washington AES Bulletin 557, February, 1955, pp. 22-24.

of a beginning family. Along with this latter factor is doubtless the fact that more urban and rural nonfarm than farm wives are also members of the gainful labor force.

Men ordinarily marry somewhat later than women. This is true of all residential categories, and it is true in India and Pakistan as well as in the U.S. No doubt this is related to the earlier physical maturation of human females.

PATTERNS OF INTRAFAMILY INTERACTION

The principal roles in a nuclear family are husband-father, wife-mother, and child. In a joint family there are, of course, additional roles.

The patterns of relationship among family members are not identical from one family to another. On the other hand, these relationships are not unique but are governed in major outlines by cultural norms. In a stable society with little mobility, especially when the joint family is prevalent, these norms are likely to be well defined. In the U.S., on the other hand, there is likely to be considerable uncertainty about intrafamily relationships. Partners are likely to have come from families with somewhat different norms.

The traditional patterns of intrafamily relationships on American farms are similar to those found by Brown in Beech Creek, a Kentucky Mountain locality:

HUSBAND-WIFE RELATIONSHIP

According to the ideal patterns on Beech Creek a husband should be the head of the household; he was expected to be dominant. . . . the husband as farmer was expected to be the director of the farm work and to take the lead in doing this work. This dominance was not confined to economic relationships but was extended, in theory at any rate, to all relationships with his wife. The husband was expected to speak for the family in public; the family was identified by his name; when people outside the family wished to negotiate with the family, for example, to borrow a tool, it was to the husband that they must go.

But this dominance by the husband was by no means as great as it once had been. The limits within which he exercised his authority were much narrower than they used to be. . . .

Husband and wife were expected to be completely loyal to each other and to stand by each other through every fortune or misfortune. This, with their loyalty to the welfare of their children, was expected to be the strongest loyalty in their lives, and any loyalty to others outside this relationship (such as to the parents of either husband or wife) was definitely secondary.

Parent-Child Relationship

Within the . . . family, parents were in a superordinate position and children were in a subordinate position. Parents were expected to direct their children; children were expected to obey their parents. Parental controls were established over a long period of time so that they were, for the most part, not repressive from a child's standpoint, but were expected and natural, backed by the beliefs of the children as much as those of the parents. In addition to this internal reinforcement of parents' authority, there were external reinforcements too. Such physical punishment, for example, as whipping and spanking were looked on as parents' rights and were freely used by Beech people, especially among younger children. Possession of authority meant responsibility and obligations, and parents were held responsible by Beech society for their children. Failure of the children to meet the expected standards brought disapproval upon the parents.

It is worth noting at this point that the authority of parents was closely guarded. With the possible exception of the school teachers and the older children, no one other than the parents had the right to punish children physically. . . .

Parents were expected to consider the child's best interests as well as their own; they were not free to promote their own self-interest at the expense of a child's development and rights. One man, for instance, was criticized by Beech Creek people because he collected a son's wages from his employer. . . . parents were very unselfish so far as their children were concerned; some people deprived themselves of necessities so that their children might have advantages.

Parents were expected to be affectionate and kind toward their children, and vice versa; for the most part, parents and children conformed to this pattern. Their affection was not often expressed openly and publicly, but the affection was evidenced in many ways. . . .

. . . it was the mother who was the center of the family's affection. She was always at home to go to, to come back to. It was to her that children, boys and girls alike, confided their troubles and secrets. In later as in earlier years the surest source of sympathy and understanding was apt to be the mother.

The father, on the other hand, never had such close affectionate relationships with the young child as the mother. Though he was usually not away from home at work to such an extent as the urban middle-class father, his work was outside and away from the house. . . .

Perhaps the best way of stating the difference in attitudes toward fathers and toward mothers is to say that the dominant feeling for mothers was love, for fathers respect. Boys and their fathers were not likely to be "pals", for there was a certain constraint in boys' behavior around fathers that impeded the development of such friendship. . . .

RELATIONSHIPS AMONG SIBLINGS

Brothers were treated as equals. They worked together under their parents', especially their father's, supervision. They saw much more of each other, as a rule, than of other boys, and in the years of work and play together usually developed a solidarity and loyalty which lasted all their lives. In the same way, sisters, possibly even more than boys, developed in their long period of close association very strong friendships. Sisters in a family were equals; there was, for example, no institutional preference for the youngest or the oldest daughter.

The brother-sister relationship was close too. Brothers and sisters were expected to be affectionate, kind, and loyal. There often was . . . much the reaction a boy had to his mother in his attitudes toward his sister; and the girl looked on her brother much as she looked on her father.

With the arrival of a new baby the youngest child lost his position as the center of the family's affection. This undoubtedly is a potential point of strain among siblings but difficulties arising from this situation were mitigated by the fact that usually a child occupied the affectional spotlight for only a short time. . . .

In the large families characteristic of Beech Creek another interesting relationship among siblings was found. In many cases, an older sister took charge of the younger children, and as a consequence a younger child sometimes developed feelings toward his older sister much like those toward his mother, and the older sister, in turn, sometimes developed maternal feelings toward the younger brother or sister. . . .

To an observer from an urban society outside the mountains, the self-sufficiency of the Beech family in both economic and social relationships was very striking. Already it has been stated that the greater part of a Beech Creek family's time was spent performing the activities necessary to earn a living and maintain the family economy, and that each family constituted a separate unit, the members of which did their work together and how little time different members of a family spent in other groups. There were few extra-familial organizations in the neighborhood, and informal recreational groups outside the family did not exist to the extent common among urban people. Except for school and play with close kin or near neighbors, most children on Beech Creek had as playmates only their brothers and sisters. It is not surprising under these circumstances that siblings developed very close friendships, and that brothers and sisters seemed to "think more" of each other than is general in the urban situation.[14]

The rural family is frequently considered to be more authoritarian than the urban family. A few studies of small samples have tended to confirm that the democratic philosophy of family management is more characteristic in urban than in rural life in some areas of the country. Stott concluded on the basis of a study conducted in Nebraska that "farm parents are inclined to favor the greatest degree of parental control, while city parents seem to favor granting the most freedom to their adolescent children."[15] Duvall and Motz studied 400 midwestern girls aged 14-24 and suggested that home training of rural girls was much more strict and firm than that of urban girls.[16] In his studies in Oregon and Michigan, Nye concluded that, in general, teen-ager-parent relations in junior high-school years were more harmonious in town and city than on farms.[17] In addition, the White House Conference report on adolescents indicated that the authoritarian pattern of the farm home was centered about work relationships and hence often caused difficulties between parents and adolescents.[18]

There is evidence, however, that this difference is disappearing. A study conducted by Landis and Stone in the state of Washington, based on information supplied by 4400 high-school students who were seniors in 1947, revealed little evidence of "a greater carry-

[14] James S. Brown, *The Farm Family in a Kentucky Mountain Neighborhood,* Kentucky AES Bulletin 587, 1952, pp. 32-39.

[15] L. H. Stott, "Parental Attitudes of Farm, Town and City Parents in Relation to Certain Personality Adjustments in Their Children, *Journal of Social Psychology,* May, 1940, pp. 325-339.

[16] Evelyn Millis Duvall and Anabelle Bender Motz, "Are Country Girls So Different?" *Rural Sociology,* September, 1945, pp. 263-274.

[17] Ivan Nye, "Adolescent-Parent Adjustment—Rurality as a Variable," *Rural Sociology,* December, 1950, pp. 334-339; and "Adolescent-Parent Adjustment —Social-Economic Level as a Variable," *American Sociological Review,* June, 1951, pp. 341-349.

[18] White House Conference on Child Health and Protection, *The Adolescent and the Family,* Appleton-Century, 1934, pp. 156-157.

over of authoritarian patterns in farm than in city families."[19] These findings were supported by a study of students at Washington State University which showed no evidence of greater democracy in the families of students from cities than in the families of students from farms.[20]

In the modern democratic family, husband-wife relationships tend to be equalitarian; important decisions are often shared. At the same time, there is likely to be a division of responsibility, with the wife making decisions affecting child care and home management and the husband farm management decisions.[21] Parent-child relationships are permissive. Children are encouraged to accept responsibility for decisions of increasing importance as they grow older. Thus, when the time comes for them to leave home they are at least theoretically better prepared to make their own choices.

THE FAMILY CYCLE

Students of the family have long recognized that the needs, desires, and interaction patterns of families are dependent to a considerable degree upon the size and stage of development of the family. Most families pass through a characteristic cycle.

A generalized pattern showing the cycle of American families which have not been broken by separation, divorce, or death has been constructed from census data by Glick, who has identified the stages of (1) marriage, (2) child-bearing, (3) children leaving home; and (4) dissolution of the family. The significant events which form the division points between these stages are:

1. The marriage which establishes the family
2. The birth of the first child
3. The birth of the last child
4. The marriage of the first child
5. The marriage of the last child

[19] Paul H. Landis and Carol L. Stone, *The Relationship of Parental Authority Patterns to Teen-Age Adjustment,* Washington AES Bulletin 538, September, 1952, p. 28.

[20] W. L. Slocum, *Parental Authority Patterns and Adjustment at College,* paper presented at the American Sociological Society Meeting, August, 1953.

[21] See Chapter 13 for a discussion of decision-making.

6. Death of one of the original pair, which dissolves the family[22]

The general pattern is, of course, similar for farm, village, and urban families, although farm families may be less subject to dissolution by separation or divorce before the cycle is completed.

Glick's system of classification needs supplementing for sociological research purposes because it fails to identify significant stages within the child-rearing period, a break-down desirable for analysis of family interaction patterns. The presence of children of different ages in the family has a great deal of influence on the types of activities in which the family engages as a group. A review of previous studies reveals that while this principle has been acknowledged by various investigators, there is considerable variation in the stages identified within the child-rearing period, which comparison shows to be largely due to lack of agreement on what ages of children are to be used as the division points between the different stages.[23] To some extent this may be attributed to the requirements and limitations of particular research studies.

For purposes of the present discussion, the life cycle of the American farm family may be divided into the following five stages: (1) the prechild stage; (2) the younger-child stage (all children under high-school age); (3) the younger-and-older-child stage; (4)

[22] Paul H. Glick, "The Family Cycle," *American Sociological Review*, April, 1947, pp. 164-174.

[23] The justification given by W. A. Anderson for establishing the upper level of the young child period at age ten is that "most organization opportunities are available to youth when they are ten or more years old; that is, in the teen ages" (*Rural Social Participation and the Family Life Cycle, Part I: Formal Participation*, Cornell University AES Memoir 314, January, 1953). As a matter of fact, however, it would be difficult to demonstrate that a sharp break actually does exist between age 9 and age 10 with respect to this matter or related items of behavior. C. P. Loomis has established a division point between stages when the oldest child is 14; he does not, however, acknowledge the existence of a stage involving both younger and older children, nor does he give any justification for choosing age 14. Blackwell, who generally follows Loomis's system of classification, found it necessary to establish subgroups. E. L. Kirkpatrick and associates established a break at the high-school level but separated the younger child group into preschool and grade school periods. Kirkpatrick, however, does not acknowledge any overlapping between categories. In terms of contemporary American patterns of behavior, it would appear appropriate to establish the upper limit of the younger child period at a time when the oldest child enters high school and the lower limit of the older child period at the time when the youngest child enters high school.

the older-child stage (all children of high-school age or older); (5) the all adult stage.

THE PRECHILD STAGE. The family is established by marriage. Some couples never have children, and in that case do not enter stages 2, 3, and 4 as identified in this discussion. For most families, the prechild period is relatively short, perhaps not more than a year or two. Fragmentary evidence indicates that farm families do not differ materially from other families with respect to the length of this period, although there may be a tendency for farm and other rural couples to start having children slightly sooner than do nonfarm and urban residents.[24]

During the early months of married life a series of adjustments or accommodations occur between husband and wife. This is a time when many basic attitudes and behavior patterns with respect to the home and family and relationships in general are established. The adjustments are not always easy, and some aspects are more difficult than others. It seems reasonable to suppose that the success of the family depends heavily on the establishment during the early weeks and months of marriage of a framework for resolving differences of opinion and reaching mutually acceptable decisions. Where the couple is unable to create a basis for mutually satisfactory relationships, the marriage is doomed to failure even though not broken by separation or divorce.

There is no reason to believe that the emotional adjustment required of farm couples is basically different from that of other residential and occupational groups. However, more problems of adjustment in work relationships will normally be involved in the farm family because it tends to be a work group as well as a social group.

THE YOUNGER-CHILD STAGE. Children spend practically all of their their time at home during the early years of this stage. Consequently, the mother will normally devote a large part of her working day to caring for them and supervising their activities, which

[24] Harold T. Christensen, "Rural-Urban Differences in the Spacing of the First Birth from Marriage: A Repeat Study," *Rural Sociology*, March, 1953, p. 60; see also E. L. Kirkpatrick, Rosalind Tough, and May L. Cowles, *The Life Cycle of the Farm Family*, Wisconsin AES Research Bulletin 121, 1934, p. 2.

will limit the time and energy that she will have for activities outside the home. Because small children are seldom left alone on an isolated farm, the family will tend to engage in activities as a family group or employ a baby-sitter when husband and wife go to social affairs as a pair; or one parent may stay with the children while the other participates in group relationships outside the home.

When the child is 5 or 6 years old, it enters school. This experience has a great deal of significance not only for the child but also for the parents and other members of the family, because the child's interests and wants are conditioned by contacts with teachers and with other children.

THE YOUNGER-OLDER-CHILD STAGE. By the time it reaches this stage, the family will have established many rules governing the conduct of the children. At the same time, however, new situations will constantly arise as children grow older. The oldest child continues to serve as a pilot for the parents, who learn through experience with him how to meet the problems encountered at each new stage in the development of their other children. Even though the problems may vary slightly for the younger offspring, they are likely to be easier for the parents to handle.

THE OLDER-CHILD STAGE. During this stage, when the family has only teen-age children, the emphasis is usually upon activities and values which are of concern to adolescents. The youngsters mature in the biological sense near the beginning of adolescence, but their social development and training is far from complete. Many perplexing problems are likely to be encountered both in the home and outside as a result of contacts which the children establish. It is during this period that interest in members of the opposite sex develops and the children normally participate in social relationships as individuals. Their basic reference group continues to be the family, as is recognized by common usage of tags like "the Smith girl" or "the Jones boy."

THE ALL-ADULT STAGE. A family enters this stage when all of its members are grown. Normally all of the children will leave the parental home to live elsewhere when they become adults. The family thus reverts to the original pair, who usually continue to live together until the union is dissolved by the death of one of the partners. The man more often dies first, leaving the woman to face several years as a widow.

Comparison of Patterns in Various Stages

Verified and generalized information concerning the activity and interaction patterns of farm families in the several stages enumerated above is not available. Only a few studies of the family cycle have been made, and the emphasis in most of these has been upon consumption patterns and economic considerations rather than upon attitudes, values, and patterns of interaction. W. A. Anderson, in a recent study of 343 families in Ontario County, New York, found that families in the younger-child stage held more memberships in organizations than did families in other stages of the cycle.[25] These families also had the highest average formal participation scores. However, Anderson also found that families in this stage participated as a group in a smaller number of activities than families in later stages of the cycle. Kirkpatrick, Tough, and Cowles found that in 1929-1930 time spent in attending moving pictures was greatest for Wisconsin families with older children and for all-adult families.[26] At the same time, these investigators noted that these older families spent less time in meetings and belonged to fewer organizations than families with only younger children. Loomis summarized his findings as follows: "In the first stage where there are no children to bind the parents to the home, outside activity is great. With the addition of children, this activity away from home decreases both because the children are a burden and because they make the home life more intensive. When the parents are old, they are either too infirm to take up outside activity again or they satisfy themselves with contacts with their children's families. . . ."[27]

These studies do not provide definite information except for specific localities, but they do indicate some of the types of data which can be obtained by studies of the effect of the family cycle on family interaction patterns.

[25] Anderson, *op. cit.*, and *Rural Social Participation and the Family Life Cycle, Part II: Informal Participation*, Cornell University, AES Memoir 318, January, 1953.

[26] Kirkpatrick, Tough, and Cowles, *op. cit.*

[27] C. P. Loomis, *The Growth of the Farm Family in Relation to Its Activities*, North Carolina AES Bulletin 298, June, 1934, p. 60.

RURAL-URBAN DIFFERENCES IN FAMILY LIFE

The available evidence indicates that there is great variation in patterns of both rural and urban family life in contemporary America. There may be as much variation among farm families as there is among village, town, and city families, but many writers consider that the typical rural farm family has a set of distinctive social characteristics which identify it as different from the typical urban family.

Urban families, it is believed, tend to be held together by affectional bonds, with emphasis on individual rather than group values and activities. At the other extreme, the traditional rural farm family is conceived to be held together to a considerable extent by common participation in the farm enterprise and by emphasis upon family solidarity, kinship ties, and participation as a family group in the affairs of neighborhood and community.

The dominant contemporary values established by advertising, universal education, modern transportation, and communication facilities of various types are urban values. That this is true is easily demonstrated by the evidence the United States Census Bureau has collected concerning the extent to which farm homes have been equipped with such facilities as electricity, water systems, refrigeration, radio, and television. Farm families with sufficient means have modernized their homes with conveniences to the point where many of them are now fully equal to city homes.

It cannot be denied, however, that there are some differences between farm and nonfarm families with respect to conditions of life and patterns of activity. Many of these differences have been decreasing for at least half a century and some have practically disappeared, especially in highly commercialized farming regions and areas where off-farm employment is common; some of the differences and similarities follow.

Size of Family

Farm families have been called the seedbed of the nation's population because, in the past, farm families have been much larger than urban families.[28] Farm families are still larger. In 1950, the average

[28] P. A. Sorokin, C. C. Zimmerman, and C. J. Galpin, A Systematic Source Book in Rural Sociology, University of Minnesota Press, vol. II, 1931, chap. X.

number of persons in urban families was 3.3, in rural nonfarm families 3.5, and in farm families 4.0. In some areas of the country, however, the gap was smaller; the average size of the urban family in the state of Washington, for example, was 3.23 compared to 3.73 for farm families.[29]

Family Relationships

Kolb and Brunner have said that since agriculture is operated on the family plan, close working relationships within the family unit are essential.[30] It is true that most contemporary American farms are

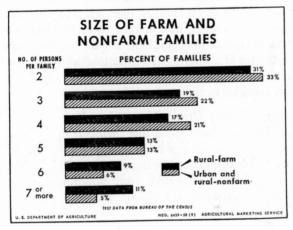

FIG. 17.

operated by family groups with relatively little outside labor, but this is not universal. There are a considerable number of American farms at the present time which are operated on a commercialized basis where relatively little family labor is used and the enterprise is organized according to industrial management principles. Sometimes the family does not live on the farm. Examples are the huge orchards in the fruit-producing areas of the country, the large

[29] U.S. Bureau of the Census, *Characteristics of the Population: United States Summary,* vol. II, part 1, *U.S. Census of the Population: 1950,* 1953.

[30] John H. Kolb and Edmund deS. Brunner, *A Study of Rural Society,* 4th ed., Houghton Mifflin, 1952, p. 142.

vegetable farms in Florida, California, and elsewhere, and many types of irrigation enterprises.

Statistics on education show that most farm families now send their children to school. The 1950 census indicated that 78 percent of farm children of high-school age (14 to 18) were actually in school on the census date. In most areas, a high-school education is now taken for granted for farm children of both sexes. It may be inferred from this that the farm family is no longer able to regard its children as a free labor source. By the time the children have finished high school they are almost ready to leave the home farm to marry or to undertake economic activities of their own elsewhere.

With respect to nonfarm families, one cannot say that close family relationships do not exist; as a matter of fact, because of greater leisure time in nonfarm occupations, it may be that there is more time for activities of a family nature, particularly when the children are small. In this respect, the farm family may actually be inferior rather than superior to the nonfarm family.

Membership in Family Groups

Kolb and Brunner have noted that membership in family groups is a distinctive characteristic of rural society, particularly of the farm population.[31] This distinction continues to be valid. In March, 1960, 93.2 per cent of farm households were families compared to 90.4 percent of rural nonfarm households and 82.6 percent of urban households.[32]

QUESTIONS FOR FURTHER STUDY AND DISCUSSION

1. What are the principal sociological implications for farm families of the fact that most American farms are "family farms"?
2. Are there any major differences in the United States between farm and nonfarm child-rearing practices? If so, what are the differences?
3. Discuss the principal stages in the family cycle, illustrating the characteristic problems of each stage by reference to a family with which you are familiar.
4. What significance has the concept of the family cycle for the sociological study of families? For the study of relationships between families?

[31] *Ibid.,* p. 144.
[32] *Household and Family Characteristics, op. cit.*

5. What are the fundamental functions of the family? Discuss the relationship between family groups and other agencies such as the school in connection with social training.

6. Discuss the concepts of the joint family and the nuclear family indicating historical and current distribution. Compare or contrast with Oriental cultures.

SELECTED REFERENCES

Bertrand, A. L., ed., *Rural Sociology*, McGraw-Hill, 1959.

Burgess, E. W., and Paul Wallin, *Engagement and Marriage*, Lippincott, 1953.

Dube, S. C., *Indian Village*, Routledge & Kegan Paul, 1956.

Kolb, John H., and Edmund deS. Brunner, *A Study of Rural Society*, 4th ed., Houghton Mifflin, 1952, chap. 11.

Landis, Paul H., *Rural Life in Process*, 2nd ed., McGraw-Hill, 1948, chap. 21, "The Farm Family in a Changing Culture."

Loomis, C. P., and J. A. Beegle, *Rural Sociology*, Prentice-Hall, 1957.

15

Family Farms and Other Systems of Farm Organization

Work relationships in agriculture may be organized in a number of different ways, but two are basic patterns: management decisions may be separated from physical labor, as is characteristic of slavery, feudalism, the plantation system, and corporation farms; or, in the system known as the family farm, the functions of management and labor may be combined in the same person. A moment's reflection will make it clear that these arrangements can be looked on as social systems. The organization of work on any farm involves performance of specific roles for which definite expectations, duties, obligations, and privileges become established through interaction. On the family farm, these work relationships are, of course, part of the complex fabric of family life, but they may be studied separately as a distinctive aspect of family relationships.

Except in the Cotton Belt, the dominant form of farm organization in the U.S. has always been the family farm. Other important types of organization systems include subsistence farms, plantations, corporation farms, contract farming arrangements, and large privately owned farms operated by managers who supervise the activities of hired laborers. In addition, there are a few communal farms operated by colonies of ethnoreligious groups. In Communist countries various types of collective farms are to be found; such are the large-scale state farms of Communist Russia and the communes recently organized by the Communist régime in China.

Closely related to the organization of labor on a commercial farm are specialized agricultural services provided on a customary or contract basis by individual specialists or firms to a large number of farm operators.

Farms in the U.S. increased from 1,449,000 in 1850 to 6,448,000 in 1920, as European immigrants and other settlers surged westward across the continent. The number has been declining since 1920 except for a temporary upsurge during the 1930s when many unemployed urban workers returned to the land. In 1939, there were 4,782,000 farms, of which 3,100,000 were classified as commercial. Noncommercial farms included 175,000 subsistence farms and 1,507,000 part-time and residential farms. McElveen has classified commercial farms into large-scale farms and family farms, and has further subdivided family farms into family-scale and small-scale farms. The 998,000 small-scale farms identified for 1954 were ". . . too small in volume of business to employ productively a full-time able-bodied operator."[1] This distinction is doubtless valid for economic purposes, and there may also be differences of sociological importance.

Between 1954 and 1959, the number of farms declined by 23 percent to 3,703,000, the smallest number for the continental U.S. since 1870. Most of the decrease occurred among smaller farms; more than 70 percent was experienced by the 16 southern states. The Census Bureau has developed an economic classification of farms (Table 12). The 1959 revision of categories[2] was responsible for part (21.5 percent) of the 1954-1959 decline.

FAMILY FARMS

It is not possible to define the family-size farm in terms of physical numbers of acres or even in terms of the capitalized value of land and equipment. As Nelson has correctly pointed out, it is difficult to give a precise definition.[3] It is defined roughly as a farm which can be managed and operated by one family with major reliance on its own financial and labor resources.

The family farm as a work unit may be characterized sociologically as a system of roles in which leadership position is occupied by the

[1] J. V. McElveen, *Family Farms in a Changing Economy,* U.S. Department of Agriculture, Agricultural Research Service, Agricultural Information Bulletin 171, March, 1957, pp. 8, 50.

[2] U.S. Bureau of the Census, *1959 Census of Agriculture—Preliminary,* Series AC59-1, January, 1961.

[3] Lowry Nelson, *Rural Sociology,* 2nd ed., American Book, 1955, p. 265.

TABLE 12.   U.S. Farms by Economic Class, 1959
(Total for the 48 States)

Commercial farms	2,412,160
Class I (sales of $40,000 or more)	102,143
Class II (sales of $20,000–$39,999)	209,974
Class III (sales of $10,000–$19,999)	481,884
Class IV (sales of $5,000–$9,999)	652,938
Class V (sales of $2,500–$4,999)	616,839
Class VI (sales of $50–$2,499)	348,382
Other farms	1,289,166
Part-time (operator under 65 years of age, and working off farm 100 or more days or with income from other sources greater than farm products sold, and sales of farm products $50–$2,499)	882,371
Part-retirement (operator 65 years old or over and sales $50–$2,499)	403,696
Abnormal	3,099

SOURCE: U.S. Bureau of the Census, *1959 Census of Agriculture—Preliminary*, Series AC59-1, January, 1961.

farm operator, who is usually the male head of the family. Most farm management decisions fall within his area of responsibility, although as noted earlier there is some tendency for wives to share important management decisions. In the traditional farm family, the operator allocated daily tasks to his children, usually at the breakfast table. He instructed them in the technical aspects of their work, provided leadership for work done in groups,[4] supervised the operation of various farm tasks, reprimanded or otherwise punished them when he considered that their work was improperly done, and managed the reward system for proper performance of the various roles involved in the operation of the farm.

The wife on a traditional family farm performed the roles of mother and homemaker, taking responsibility for the work of maintaining the house, feeding and clothing the family, and supervising the household tasks. She also frequently had the duty of keeping a

[4] See C. P. Loomis and J. A. Beegle, *Rural Social Systems*, Prentice-Hall, 1950, pp. 43-44.

home garden and preserving and processing home-produced food. In pioneer times the homemaker had the tasks of spinning, weaving, and making cloth into garments. On some farms, particularly those of immigrants, the farmer's wife and her adolescent daughters were also expected to help with field work and other hard physical labor. This, however, is generally not defined at present as a proper activity for women; their work activities are usually confined to the house, gardening, the care of poultry, and perhaps minor farm chores.[5]

To the extent that the family actually help make management decisions and work at operating the family-sized farm, it is justifiable to regard farming as a way of life as well as an occupation. We must keep in mind, however, that there is now considerable variation in the extent to which family members other than the farm operator actually participate to any important degree in the agricultural enterprise. On more prosperous farms it is probably rather rare for the homemaker actually to do field work or help care for major livestock except in cases of emergency.

In pioneer days the school term covered only the winter months in most agricultural areas. The extent to which farm youth devote their time to elementary and secondary education in most areas of the United States today, however, means that their participation in actual farming operations is much reduced from what it was even a generation ago. The time has passed when farm work took precedence over educational activities and farmers were allowed to keep their children out of school during spring work and the fall harvest season.

The organization of effort on a farm depends upon many physical and cultural factors, and varies as well from one part of the United States to another. For example, in the wheat regions one family may operate hundreds or even thousands of acres; wheat farms are highly mechanized with relatively little hand labor and in many cases practically no livestock. This permits many wheat farmers to live in town rather than on the actual farm.[6]

[5] See Chapter 2.

[6] See Belcher, "The Nonresident Farmer in the New Rural Society," *Rural Sociology*, June, 1954, p. 134. C. C. Taylor and his associates have presented a considerable amount of information relative to the farming systems associated with the dominant type of agriculture in major type of farming areas in the

The farm operator has the primary responsibility for field work and the care of animals, and since family members usually do not constitute a dependable major source of human labor, the farm operator himself is the major source of labor on a large but unknown proportion of American family farms. Prior to the present highly mechanized era it would not have been possible to operate a commercial farm with such a small labor force.

The Ideology of the Family Farm

The family farm is widely regarded as one of the most cherished ideals of American culture. As noted in Chapter 6, the policy which governed the settlement of much of the United States was designed to establish family-size holdings. The Pre-emption Act and the Homestead Acts gave preference to families on relatively small farms rather than to wealthy individuals with important political connections, a pattern followed in the plantation area of the South and in many countries of Latin America. Furthermore, contemporary farm programs, including crop controls and price supports, are ordinarily justified to the voters in terms of their presumed importance in preserving the family farm as a bulwark of American democracy.

Many historians have discussed the salient functions performed by family farms in the development of American democracy. Brewster[7] has offered the opinion that certain values associated with the family farm greatly facilitated the transition from feudalism as a form of farm organization and political structure to an agrarian-oriented democracy on the North American continent. Under feudal conditions management was reserved for persons of high rank, and serfs and other common laborers were considered as servile and degraded. Work was not one of the customary values.

The settlers in the northern colonies were mostly Protestants who subscribed to the Protestant tradition of hard work as a basis for salvation.[8] The combination of this Calvinistic emphasis on work

---

United States. This discussion appears in Part IV, "Rural Regions," of Carl C. Taylor et al., Rural Life in the United States, Knopf, 1949.

[7] John M. Brewster, "Technological Advance and the Future of the Family Farm," Journal of Farm Economics, December, 1958, pp. 1596-1609.

[8] Max Weber, The Protestant Ethic and the Spirit of Capitalism, Allen and Unwin, 1930.

with relatively small farms on which both management and labor functions were performed by the owner-operator was essentially a new social development. Brewster has attributed to this newly acquired managerial role "the high sense of personal dignity and independence which their feudal heritage had confined to the few who lived without work." He has expressed the opinion that the development of this sentiment on the part of farm operators rendered unthinkable any social order other than democracy.[9] There may be doubt as to whether Brewster is correct in linking a political leadership role with the growth of the family farm in America, but the combination of management and labor functions under the conditions then existing in America did provide a broad base for the acceptance of an ideology of equality in social, economic, and political affairs.

It is certainly true that the institutionalization of democratic procedures such as the New England town meeting gave an important impetus to citizen participation in the affairs of local, state, and national government as the settlement of the continent spread. Apart from the South, the dominant political and social systems closely resembled those developed in the northern colonies.

According to Motheral, three important American traditions have been associated with the family farm: (1) the tradition that man-land relationships are of unusual importance, (2) the tradition of democracy, and (3) the tradition of efficiency which requires every self-respecting citizen to make the most of his resources and avoid waste.[10]

There has been a tendency in some quarters to idealize the family farm, especially the owner-operated farm; it has been referred to as a character-building institution worthy of preservation at almost any cost. Loomis and Beegle cite a poll which indicated that 71 percent of the rural sociologists and 41 percent of the agricultural economists who answered believed that the goal of American agriculture should be a small family-sized farm operated by an owner even though income might be low.[11]

In their summary of the proceedings of the 1946 conference on the

[9] Brewster, *op. cit.*, pp. 1599-1600.
[10] J. R. Motheral, "The Family Farm and the Three Traditions," *Journal of Farm Economics*, November, 1951, pp. 514-530.
[11] Loomis and Beegle, *op. cit.*, p. 339.

family farm in the United States land policy, Ackerman and Harris have taken a less sentimental view.

. . . the predominance of family farms has had a retarding influence in the attainment of a satisfactory educational program in many communities. Children are a part of the labor force on family farms, and funds for educational purposes are frequently less because of the demand for capital with which to make progress up the agricultural ladder. In many rural communities family farms have also had a deleterious effect upon recreational activities; leisure time is either seriously limited or is restricted to certain periods of the year when farming activities slacken.

The family farm is generally looked upon as providing its own old age security, and it is expected that family farmers can tighten up their belts in times of adversity. This attitude has delayed the general extension of social security to farm families. The very fact that the farm operator may complete a full family cycle on the farm offers serious difficulties. Life-and death-processes mean that farms must be transferred at least once each generation. Frequently, inheritance causes the disruption of the farm as a going concern. The farm is often too large for the family when the children are small and too small when the children are large. Low intensity of use during old age is frequent.[12]

Without minimizing in any way the importance of the self-sufficing family farm in the development of American agriculture and democratic values, the present writer feels that insistence on its preservation in an unchanged archaic form is inconsistent with other dominant American values. It is difficult to justify, for example, the survival of any form of economic organization if it does not provide sufficient income to permit attainment of current living standards. Actually, there seems to be little public support for subsistence farms. In the depths of the 1930 depression there was a considerable amount of discussion favoring the development of a back-to-the-land movement with a revival of subsistence farming as a solution for industrial unemployment. The movement attracted relatively few followers and prompted little action, although during part of the depression period there was a substantial urban-to-farm migration consisting primarily of persons who had recently moved to cities and returned to their home farms and communities when they lost their jobs.

[12] Joseph Ackerman and Marshall Harris, eds., *Family Farm Policy*, University of Chicago Press, 1946, p. 17.

Although substandard farms are still found, there is considerable evidence that many contemporary family farms are adapting to changing conditions successfully. McElveen has estimated that family-sized farms accounted for 69 percent of the products of commercial farms in 1954 as compared to 66 percent in 1944.[13] Brewster says that available evidence indicates that the economies of large-scale operations under the most complete mechanization now conceivable do not threaten the future of the family farm, but rather that mechanization has simply made it possible for a family farm to grow larger.[14] Sinclair has criticized Brewster's idea that a farm can grow indefinitely and still be a family farm; he has predicted that operations on the large commercial farm of the future will closely resemble those of a large industrial plant rather than a family farm by current standards.[15]

COMMERCIAL FAMILY FARMS

These are farms which produce agricultural commodities for the market. The income from sales may be used for family living purposes and for enlarging the scope of the farming enterprise. Ideally such farms are operated on business principles: records are kept, costs are analyzed, and ways are sought to improve efficiency for the purpose of increasing income. Many farms classified by the census as commercial are not really operated on business principles. Quite a large number without nonfarm income appear to have inadequate income from farming to provide what would be considered a decent living by current American standards. In 1959, for example, there were 348,000 small-scale farms which sold products valued at less than $2500.

PART-TIME FAMILY FARMS

An important variant of the family farm in terms of numbers, although perhaps not in terms of agricultural production, is the farm which is operated on a part-time basis by a farmer who also

[13] McElveen, *op. cit.*, p. 54.
[14] Brewster, *op. cit.*, pp. 1606-1607.
[15] Sol Sinclair, "Discussion: Technological Advance and the Future of the Family Farm," *Journal of Farm Economics*, December, 1958, p. 1611.

has off-farm income. In some sections of the U.S. more than half of the operators now work off the farm 100 days or more per year.[16] In 1959 there were 1,286,000 part-time farms, including 404,000 with operators 65 years of age or over.

Areas of heavy concentration of part-time farming are found in all parts of the country, with the heaviest concentration in the Pacific Northwest, the intermountain states, the South, the lake states, the Appalachian-Allegheny area, and the Gulf Coast (Fig. 18). Most of the farms are owned by the operator; many are quite small.

The structure of the social system on a part-time family farm may differ to a considerable extent from that described above for the full-time family farm. There may be conflicting roles of considerable importance involving the loyalties of the operator and other members of his family. The nature of the resolution of any such conflicts depends upon the importance of the various roles. Some part-time farmers are primarily dependent on agriculture, and undertake their off-farm work simply to enable them to meet family living needs, accumulate sufficient capital to finance desired farming operations, or pay off debts.

Many part-time farm operators undoubtedly view their nonfarm occupational role as primary and the farm as secondary. Farming operations would then be relegated to an incidental place. The operator may, in fact, support the farm rather than vice versa. Farm residence may be justified on the grounds that living in the country is more desirable from the standpoint of family living, especially for rearing children in a "wholesome rural atmosphere" as contrasted with the alternative of life in a city or town. In other cases, part-time farmers may own and reside on a farm because they feel it provides a haven in times of economic distress or a basis for independence from the domination of industrial bosses or labor unions.[17]

In spite of the importance of this type of farming from a sociological point of view, the characteristics and social participation patterns of part-time farmers have been studied relatively little. It is a chal-

[16] Many prosperous farmers have substantial nonfarm economic interests. In 1950, 45 percent of the most prosperous farmers (those with sales of farm products of $10,000 or more) were only partly dependent on agriculture.

[17] Alicja Iwanska, *Good Fortune: Second Chance Community*, Washington AES Bulletin 589, June, 1958, p. 18.

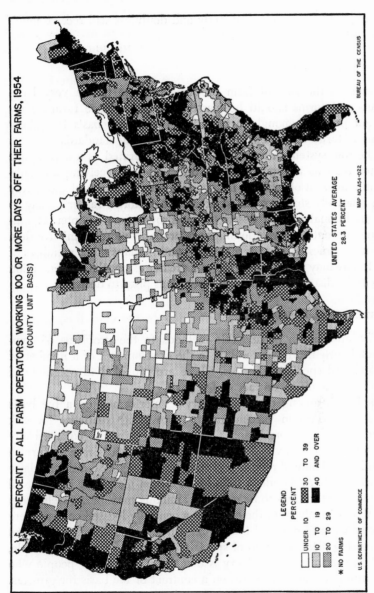

Fig. 18. Distribution of Part-Time Farming by County, 1954.

lenging field for sociological study and doubtless will receive much more attention in the future.[18]

Subsistence Farms

Data on the sale of farm products indicate that a very large number of farms should be classified as subsistence farms. They do not produce enough to provide an adequate basis for family living in terms of contemporary American living standards.

The role system of a family on a farm operated as a subsistence rather than as a commercial venture and not receiving any substantial amount of off-farm income from any members of the family is a relatively simple social structure. It conforms rather closely to the traditional pattern described by Brown (see Chapter 14), although parent-child relationships are probably more permissive than in earlier times. Husbands and wives and perhaps other members of the family may also be involved to a greater extent than a generation ago in the discussion of farming operations prior to decisions.

Agricultural Specialists

The application of scientific methods to the problems of commercial agriculture has resulted in the development of a number of agricultural specialty services. These are provided to operators of family farms on a contract or fee basis.

Included, among others, are services performed on a fee basis by veterinarians in vaccinating and providing treatment for sick animals. Farm record-keeping services are provided commercially for some farmers by centrally located data processors who furnish monthly and annual reports and analyses. On highly developed dairy farms producing Grade A milk for an urban market, it is not at all unusual for the cows to be milked by milking machines which pump the fluid directly from the cow into a centrally located cooler where it remains until pumped into a tank truck to be hauled to a central processing plant. In areas of specialty crops, like hops, for example, certain specialized machinery is owned by only a few people who perform particular processes on a contract or fee basis for growers.

[18] Walter L. Slocum, ed., *The Research Clinic on Part-Time Farming*, papers presented at the Rural Sociology Society Meetings, August 25, 1958.

The services are usually performed on the farm and in many cases replace activities previously performed by the farm operator, his hired hands, or unpaid family help. Consequently, agricultural specialists may properly be regarded as an essential part of modern commercial agriculture on family farms.

Some farmers contract with farm management firms for complete farm management services. Others obtain specialized advice as desired. In some farming areas, such as the Palouse wheat country of southeastern Washington, weeds are controlled to a large extent by crop-dusting firms which apply chemicals from planes. The same procedure is used in various regions for the application of insecticides and pesticides.

In general such services can be provided at lower unit cost more rapidly or more efficiently by the specialists than by the farmer himself.

CONTRACT FARMING OR VERTICAL INTEGRATION

Vertical integration can be defined as the coordination by contract of decision-making in two or more stages of agricultural production, processing, and/or marketing by two or more firms, one of which is a farm.[19] This type of farm organization differs from nonintegrated agriculture chiefly because in the latter each individual farmer makes his own production and marketing decisions, takes whatever risk is involved, and reaps the profit, if any. Normally, family farms do no processing.

Vertical integration has recently become very widespread in the broiler industry. In 1958, 88 percent of the broilers grown in North Carolina were produced on a contract basis.[20] By 1960, according to the U.S. Department of Agriculture, 90 percent of all broilers "were produced under contract or some other type of integrated basis."[21] Vertical integration in the broiler industry was stimulated by supermarkets, which sought specific quantities of uniform quality

[19] See W. P. Mortensen, "Possible Future Trends of Vertical Integration in Agriculture," *Journal of Farm Economics*, December, 1958, p. 1860; J. A. Seagraves and C. E. Bishop, "Impacts of Vertical Integration on Output Price and Industry Structure," *Journal of Farm Economics*, December, 1958, p. 1814.

[20] Seagraves and Bishop, *op. cit.*, p. 1815.

[21] See USDA, *Power to Produce: Yearbook of Agriculture 1960*, 1160.

at the lowest possible price.[22] The contracting parties may include a food chain, a processor, a feed dealer, and individual growers. So far as the farmers are concerned, the feed dealer occupies the dominant role. He buys the chicks, provides credit, sells feed to the farmer, and markets the broilers. The processor, feed dealer, or other contractor assumes all or a substantial portion of the price risk involved in this production. Consequently, the operator may obtain a lower return than he might otherwise get, but he may be willing to do so because of the provision of credit, an assured market, and a definite price for a given quantity.

There is evidence that vertical integration, at least as practiced in the broiler industry, does not necessarily lead to stable prices and assured markets. Production expanded from 1,000,000,000 pounds in 1945 to 4,700,000,000 pounds in 1957.[23] In the summer of 1959 supplies exceeded demand, and broilers were available in the supermarkets at the lowest prices since 1940. In addition, eggs were available for 19¢ a dozen, the lowest since the depression days of the 1930s. Poultry producers sought assistance from the federal government in stabilizing the economic conditions in the industry.[24]

Producers of sugar beets and certain types of vegetables like asparagus, green peas, and tomatoes have long produced on a contract basis for processing plants which generally have offered a predetermined price at the time the contract was signed. A large proportion of turkeys are produced under contract.[25]

The question has been raised as to whether vertical integration will spread to other types of agriculture, including feeding of hogs, lambs, and beef cattle.[26] Mortenson is of the opinion that integration in these types of enterprises will not be spectacular. He feels that automation of field work and chores is replacing farm labor and forcing farmers into larger-scale farm operations rather than toward contract farming or vertical integration.[27]

A study reported in 1959 of some of the sociological implications

[22] Seagraves and Bishop, *op. cit.*, pp. 1817-1818.
[23] Mortensen, *op. cit.*, p. 1862.
[24] *Newsweek*, international ed., June 15, 1959, p. 16.
[25] Mortensen, *op. cit.*, p. 1861.
[26] See John Harms, "Washington Today," *County Agent*, March, 1958, p. 8.
[27] Mortensen, *op. cit.*, pp. 1863-65.

of contract farming in a rural Ohio county revealed that most growers were satisfied with their contractual arrangements. Those who accepted contracts tended to value independence less than economic security. The investigators concluded that contract farming had not been practiced long enough to have any major social consequences. However, they predicted that the long-term outcome would include more rapid adoption of efficient methods of production and changes in grower-dealer relationships which may further reduce the independence of growers.[28]

A 1959 study by Louis A. Ploch in Maine indicated that most of the broiler growers were "relatively satisfied" although there appeared to have been some dissatisfaction with the necessity of sharing income with processors. Almost half of the growers regarded their occupational role as similar to that of an employee. Analysis of their characteristics revealed that they were younger and better educated than the average Maine farmer. They also had higher levels of living. A substantial proportion had evidently been recruited by the contractors from nonfarm sources; 52 percent had been employed as blue-collar workers before they began to raise broilers.[29]

It remains to be seen whether the reduction of individualism which accompanies contract farming will prove to be a desirable feature relative to such aspects of farm family life as the preservation of democratic values, the maintenance of satisfactory family life in terms of contemporary American standards, and its effect on participation of the farmer and his family in informal and formal activities. In general, if the effect of the contract is to reduce the economic status and the social rank of farm operators the results may be regarded as undesirable. If on the contrary integration increases economic status and improves social rank for farmers, it will be a stabilizing and constructive force.

The Farmers Union has taken a strong stand against vertical integration unless it is controlled by and in the interests of farmers; operations controlled by feed dealers or others are considered by the

[28] R. L. Pitzer et al., A Sociological Investigation of Contract Farming, paper presented at the Rural Sociological Society Meeting, August 27, 1959.

[29] Louis A. Ploch, Social and Family Characteristics of Maine Contract Broiler Growers, Maine AES Bulletin 596, August, 1960.

Union as a means of enlarging the profit of the middleman at the expense of farmers.[30]

LARGE FARMS

Many farms operated by families are substantial in size. Brewster implies that there may be no absolute upper limit,[31] but it seems reasonable to‧ assign a boundary at the point beyond which the labor of the individual farm family is clearly inadequate and is replaced by a regular hired labor force supplemented at various seasons of the year by additional seasonal workers. In 1959 there were 136,000 farms of 1000 acres or more in the 48 states compared to 63,000 in 1925. In 1959 there were 1200 farm units with annual sales of a half-million dollars or more.[32] Smith has expressed the opinion that the definitions used in the census conceal and badly understate the actual extent of large holdings in the United States, particularly in the Cotton Belt.[33] With the great decline in the number of sharecroppers, this criticism may be less valid than previously.

Large-scale farms are of several types, among them the plantation, the corporation farm, and the farm cooperative. All are characterized by contractual relationships between owners, managers, and workers as distinguished from the noncontractual type of work relationships found on a family farm.

Although the number of large-scale farms is relatively small when considered as a proportion of all farms in the United States, the acreage they control is large and productivity is generally high. The extent to which land ownership is concentrated is indicated by a nationwide survey which disclosed that 41 percent of the total farm acreage in the U.S. was held by 4 percent of the private owners. The 134,000 farms (4.3 percent of all commercial farms) classified by McElveen as large-scale farms accounted for 31 percent of agricultural products sold in 1954.[34]

[30] National Farmers' Union, *This We Believe*, Denver, Program Bulletin 1, undated.

[31] Brewster, *op. cit.*

[32] *1959 Census of Agriculture, op. cit.*

[33] T. Lynn Smith, *The Sociology of Rural Life*, 3rd ed., Harper, 1953, p. 307.

[34] B. T. Inman and W. H. Fippin, *Farm Land Ownership in the United States*, USDA, Bureau of Agricultural Economics, 1949, pp. 50, 54; McElveen, *op. cit.*, p. 53.

Evidence collected by the Census Bureau shows clearly that the trend toward larger holdings is continuing. The average size of farm has grown greatly since 1920, with an especially large increase in the number of farms with more than 1000 acres. The average number of acres per farm for the United States as a whole increased from 148 in 1920 to 215 in 1950 and 302 in 1959. According to Belcher, this expansion is due to the tendency toward industrialization of agricultural operations. He has predicted increasing control of agricultural operations by individuals who do not reside on farms.[35]

Large holdings have been severely criticized by some rural sociologists because of their actual or presumed detrimental effect upon family life and community organization. Smith has gone so far as to allege that large-scale farming operations inevitably lead to the establishment of a small high-ranking elite class of owners and the subsequent impoverishment of agricultural workers. He cites as evidence for his conclusion the situation existing among workers on large-scale farming systems among the Romans, in East Germany, in Latin America, in Cuba, in South America, and especially in the American South.[36]

Goldschmidt studied two California localities, one with large-scale farms and the other with small family farms, and has presented evidence that the large-scale operations resulted in a much less desirable social situation than found in the locality with the small farms. Acreage and population were nearly equal in the two areas. The essential differences were as follows: the area with large farms had no bank compared to 2 in the small-farm area; 1 newspaper compared with 2; 60 business establishments compared with 156; 1 grammar school and no high school compared with 4 grammar schools and 1 high school; 2 service and commercial clubs compared with 5; no fraternal and women's clubs compared with 7; no veterans' associations compared with 2; 6 churches, 3 inadequately housed, compared with 14, mostly in good condition; poor housing crowded onto small lots compared with adequate though modest housing; fairly serious juvenile delinquency and limited recreational opportunities compared with little juvenile delinquency and adequate

[35] Belcher, *op. cit.*
[36] Smith, *op. cit.*, p. 298.

recreational facilities.[37] These findings are of course not conclusive; it is not possible to generalize from two cases.

Historical evidence, together with contemporary data from California and the rural South, suggests that workers on large-scale agricultural estates have frequently been less fortunate than independent small operators. Whether a large agricultural operation must inevitably produce such results seems open to question, however. The same charges have been made about large-scale industrial organizations in the past, and industrial experience in the last half-century in the United States and elsewhere has demonstrated that the welfare of factory workers can be materially improved even though industrial corporations continue to grow larger. Collective bargaining and government economic security programs for the protection of those who might otherwise be exploited have been important. Even more important has been the general expansion of the market for industrial products and services, which has created employment opportunities for the rapidly expanding labor force. These developments have apparently solved the difficulty of providing employed nonfarm workers with adequate income for the maintenance of their families in accordance with the American standard of living. Who can say that similar developments will not benefit agriculture? Average farm family income is now much lower than the average income of urban families.

The crucial problem is to develop the occupational role of farming in such a way that it permits the incumbent to receive financial and other rewards which are commensurate with those he can receive in other occupations. Theoretically there is no obstacle which prevents a large farm from providing rewards that will enable workers to maintain a decent family life as judged by the practices and standards of the larger society.

THE SOUTHERN PLANTATION

The historical origins of the southern plantation have been described previously.[38] This form of farm organization has played a dominant part in commercial agriculture in the South since colonial

[37] Carey McWilliams, *Small Farm and Big Farm*, Public Affairs Committee, Pamphlet 100, 1955 (based on a study by Walter R. Goldschmidt).

[38] See Chapter 6.

times. A study of the plantation system made by Woofter and associates and published in 1936 indicates that at that time the original plantations established early in the settlement of the South had persisted to a marked extent; apparently few were broken up after the Civil War.[39] The current situation is difficult to ascertain because of the inadequacy of census statistics: Smith, who has been a lifelong student of rural life in the South, is of the opinion that most plantations have persisted. He points out that the areas of plantation farming are substantially those which were dominated by plantations 150 years earlier.[40]

The system of labor organization on the traditional cotton plantation included the following roles: the owner who established major policies and made basic decisions on the overall operations of the enterprise (some plantations have incorporated, although corporation ownership of land in the South is relatively low);[41] a bookkeeper, a farm manager, an overseer of farm laborers, and an overseer of croppers; and, of course, wage hands and croppers. On a large plantation there would also be assistant overseers or riders to supervise from 20 to 30 wage hands or croppers.[42] Business relationships involving the operation of the plantation such as purchasing, marketing, and credit would normally be carried on by the owner or manager. A plantation may also employ artisans such as blacksmiths, mechanics, tractor operators, truck drivers, and other agricultural specialists. As Smith has pointed out, the organization of work on a plantation involves domination by owners and supervisors with subordination of those at the bottom who take orders and carry them out as directed by overseers who in turn work under managers for the owner.[43]

During the period of slavery when the southern plantations were established and took shape as a form of farm organization, the domination of the master was reinforced by the fact that his slaves were actually property. They could be bought, sold, and punished at will. After slavery was abolished, an economic bond was main-

[39] T. J. Woofter, Jr. *et al.*, *Landlord and Tenant on the Cotton Plantation*, WPA Research Monograph V, Washington, 1936.
[40] Smith, *op. cit.*, p. 318.
[41] Nelson, *op. cit.*, p. 268.
[42] Woofter, *op. cit.*
[43] Smith, *op. cit.*, pp. 311, 318.

tained between the owner and his wage hands and sharecroppers on many plantations. Sharecroppers were paid only once a year at the time of marketing the crop. They obtained the necessities of life on credit from a plantation store operated by the owner. The cropper was usually in debt, which greatly restricted mobility.

The recent introduction of large-scale machinery on southern plantations has greatly diminished the need for a large unskilled labor force. Consequently, there has been a heavy migration of surplus agricultural workers and their families from the South to other areas and other types of employment, especially since World War II. In particular, a tremendous number of southern rural Negroes have migrated to cities. Due to these developments, the social organization of the plantation is undergoing major changes.[44]

CORPORATION FARMS

Many large farms which started as family-sized enterprises have been incorporated. Comprehensive statistics on farm incorporation are not readily available, but it is interesting to note that during the period 1910-1951 farm incorporations in California are reported to have varied between 1,745 and 11,412 per year.[45] A study by Krausz of 13 Illinois farm corporations established since 1950 showed that although three-fourths restricted shares to family members, nearly all had professional managers.[46]

Incorporated agricultural enterprises have an organizational structure similar to that of many other corporations. Shares are sold and profits, if any, are distributed in accordance with the value of the shares held. Relationships between stockholders and management may be highly impersonal in nonfamily corporations. The board of directors of the corporation establishes general policies which are carried out by a hired manager.

The labor force on corporation farms includes regular hired laborers who are generally employed the year round and who provide a

[44] See Nelson L. LeRay, G. L. Wilber and Grady B. Crowe, *Plantation Organization and the Resident Labor Force, Delta Area, Mississippi*, Mississippi AES Bulletin 606, October, 1960.

[45] W. H. Yaw, "Discussion: Corporate Organization of Family Farms," *Journal of Farm Economics*, December, 1958, pp. 1633-1635.

[46] N. G. P. Krausz, "Corporate Organization of Family Farms," *Journal of Farm Economics*, December, 1958, p. 1632.

continuing cadre to perform certain specific functions. Seasonal laborers may be taken on during peak periods, in many cases obtained through negotiation with crew leaders who establish contractual relationships with the management on the farm on one hand and the laborers on the other. The crew leader may have the responsibility of supervising the workers and collecting and distributing pay for work accomplished to the workers.

The relationships between management and labor are not unlike those existing in certain types of industries, although they are characterized by a higher degree of seasonality than is normal in most industries except those associated with the processing of agricultural products.

COOPERATIVE FARMS

Cooperative ownership and management of farm enterprises has had relatively little success in America. During the first half of the nineteenth century there were a few cooperative farm enterprises, but these were short-lived. During the drought-depression years of the 1930s, some farm cooperatives were established under the sponsorship of the Resettlement Administration and its successor, the Farm Security Administration (now named the Farmers Home Administration). These enterprises have also largely disappeared.

COMMUNAL FARMERS

Certain ethnic and religious groups like the Hutterites and the Dukhobors have established communal farm enterprises in the United States and Canada. According to Riley, there were 91 Hutterite colonies in North America in 1950 with a total population of 8500.[47]

The Hutterites have adopted a distinctive costume and style of life. The men wear full beards and clothes made of black denim; The women wear full dark skirts and head scarves. To a considerable extent each colony is self-sufficing.

Hutterites live as a communal group without private ownership of

[47] Marvin P. Riley, "Communal Farmers, The Hutterite Brethren," *South Dakota Farm and Home Research*, (South Dakota State College), November, 1956, p. 5.

productive property—the land and the implements used in production belong to the community. They practice nonresistance, avoid contact with outside groups insofar as possible, and do not tolerate what they consider to be worldly pleasures.

According to a study by Deets,[48] very clearly structured role expectations exist between the sexes and the generations, and nonconformity is met with social sanctions. For example, an individual, usually a young person, who succumbs to the attractions of the outside world is likely to find himself socially ostracized and completely shut off from contact with his loved ones. This "shunning" is also practiced by other communal groups similar to the Hutterites in order to maintain control over deviant members.

The description of the organization of work by Riley and Priestly emphasizes leadership roles:

The older, more responsible men of the colony serve as department heads in charge of the various farm enterprises, such as crops, cattle, and poultry. Work is organized so each department head is responsible to the colony business manager. The colony labor supply is divided among the various departments. Each department head may have working under him an assistant and one or more helpers, depending on the size of the enterprise. This arrangement allows flexibility in the use of manpower. When the work requirements of the departments change during the year, men can be shifted to where the demand is greatest.

Although election to the position of department head is usually annual, a capable man may be reelected time and again. After years of experience in an enterprise visiting with feed company salesmen, and reading articles in farm journals, most department heads become "specialists" in their field.[49]

The denial to members of these colonies of the worldly possessions —fine clothes, automobiles, television, and so forth—which are enjoyed by members of the general American society coupled with the efficiency of farming operations has made it possible for the Hutterites to accumulate substantial capital. Because of this, some local and state groups have acted to restrict the expansion of their

[48] Lee E. Deets, *The Hutterites: A Study in Social Cohesion*, Gettysburg, Times and News Publishing, 1939.

[49] M. P. Riley and David T. Priestley, "Agriculture on South Dakota's Communal Farms," *South Dakota Farm and Home Research*, February, 1959, p. 14.

holdings, notably the South Dakota State Legislature, which passed a measure in 1955 severely limiting their acquisition of additional land.[50] In Canada, the expansion has been restricted south of a line 50 miles north of Edmonton under the Alberta Communal Properties Act of 1947.[51]

An Iowa communal settlement known as the Amana Society has abandoned communal practices and adopted many of the folkways of the surrounding Corn Belt people. The Society is now a multimillion-dollar corporation which manufactures freezers and other products.[52]

QUESTIONS FOR FURTHER STUDY AND DISCUSSION

1. Suggest concrete criteria for differentiating a family-sized farm from a large farm. If possible, illustrate your discussion by reference to examples with which you are familiar.
2. What is your view of the potential importance of the survival of the family farm as a bulwark of American democracy? Explain your answer.
3. Since large-scale organizations have been successful in American industry and undesirable consequences of industrialization have been mitigated, is there any real reason for opposition to the application of tested industrial principles to agriculture?
4. What are the disadvantages and advantages of a cooperative farm? What are the prospects of successful cooperative farming in the United States?
5. Comment on the idea that the family farm is a superlative place for the development of desirable traits of character. Do you agree that a farm home is superior to a village or city home?

SELECTED REFERENCES

Ackerman, Joseph, and Marshall Harris, eds., *Family Farm Policy,* University of Chicago Press, 1950.

Bertrand, A. L., ed., *Rural Sociology,* McGraw-Hill, 1958.

Iwanska, Alicja, *Good Fortune: Second Chance Community,* Washington AES Bulletin 589, June, 1958.

[50] See Chapter 15, South Dakota Session Laws of 1955.
[51] *Calgary Herald,* September 21, 1957.
[52] See Robert L. Schiffer, "Capitalist Revolution in Iowa," *Reporter,* January 5, 1961.

Kolb, John H., and Edmund deS. Brunner, *A Study of Rural Society*, 4th ed., Houghton-Mifflin, 1952.

McElveen, Jackson V., "Family Farms in a Changing Economy," USDA, Agricultural Research Service, Agricultural Information Bulletin 171, 1957.

Nelson, Lowry, *Rural Sociology*, 2nd ed., American Book, 1955.

Smith, T. Lynn, *The Sociology of Rural Life*, 3rd ed., Harper, New York, 1953.

16

Land Tenure Systems

Land tenure systems consist of customary and legal arrangements which regulate interaction between people in relation to agricultural land. Considered in the abstract, tenure systems may be regarded as an aspect of culture, since the forms of tenure define the rights and duties of owners and tenants and sometimes of others in respect to land. At the same time the specific tenure arrangements which govern the relationships between people concerning a given farm, plantation or agricultural village may be thought of as a concrete social system. The important point here is the fact that tenure not only regulates relationships to land but governs specified relationships between people. As noted elsewhere, the tenure status of a farmer may have definite bearing on his social rank.[1]

Farm property is frequently associated with a high degree of emotion. Nelson has observed that land is something sacred to the "farmer-peasant,"[2] and family farm ownership by operators has been one of the major objectives of American agricultural policies. However, this sentimental attachment to a particular tract of land is not characteristic of highly commercialized agriculture.

Tenure statuses have meaning primarily in relationships governed by the control of agricultural land. Agricultural economists have suggested that property in land can be viewed as a bundle of rights,[3] certain of which are reserved by the state and the remainder divided according to law and custom between owner and operator if the two are not the same. Thus, an owner may collect rent and in return surrender some of the control over the use of his land for a specified

[1] See Chapter 17.
[2] Lowry Nelson, *Rural Sociology*, 2nd ed., American Book, 1955, p. 241.
[3] R. R. Renne, *Land Economics*, Harper, 1947.

315

period. If the land is mortgaged, the mortgagee also owns certain of the residual rights to the land which he may exercise in the event that the payments agreed on are not made on schedule. In the United States, these relationships are primarily contractual in nature.

NONCONTRACTUAL SYSTEMS OF LAND TENURE

American land tenure systems evolved from European systems which, at least in medieval times, were fundamentally noncontractual in nature. Although there were differences from area to area, of course, a typical early pattern involved royalty, nobility, and lesser gentry under whom were slaves who could be bought and sold and serfs who were bound to the soil but had certain rights. These arrangements were traditional and customary and not subject to periodic renegotiation by the parties involved. In fact, the conditions of life and patterns of permissible behavior of serfs and slaves were very limited.[4]

Peters has described medieval land tenure in the following words: "We find in western Europe in the early Middle Ages that practically all land was owned by the nobility and the church and that the peasants worked on the farms of these owners. These peasants were generally unfree, attached to the land on which they lived and worked. This bondage was varied; one could find pure serfdom, and one could find all variations of semifreedom. The different types of bondage carried with them various types of compulsory payments, deliveries in kind, and services to the owner or master."[5]

Other types of noncontractual land tenure systems include the southern slave plantations of pre-Civil War times and the haciendas and large estates granted by the Spanish and Mexican governments in what is now the southwestern U.S.[6]

On the contemporary scene certain aspects of the land tenure systems of Pakistan may be classified as noncontractual. Some villages, for example, do not recognize individual ownership; the land

[4] Paul Vinogradoff, *The Growth of the Manor,* Macmillan, 1905, p. 307.

[5] A. H. Peters, "Land Tenure in the Netherlands," in Joseph Ackerman and Marshall Harris, eds., *Family Farm Policy,* University of Chicago Press, 1946, p. 213.

[6] C. P. Loomis and J. A. Beegle, *Rural Social Systems,* Prentice-Hall, 1950, pp. 312-314.

is held and managed in common and rights are regulated by inherited shares similar to the shares in a corporation. Again, villagers may own and operate individual tracts and be bound together in the sense that they will all aid one of their number who falls into arrears in his payment of taxes to the government. In addition to these types of tenure, a tenant who occupies and operates a tract of land for a definite period of time, which may vary from locality to locality in length, acquires permanent rights to the operation of the land and cannot be evicted by the owner.[7]

On reviewing the historical evidence up to 1930, Sorokin, Zimmerman, and Galpin concluded that there are long-time cycles in land tenure characterized by small-scale peasant land holdings at one extreme and large-scale concentrations operated by farm laborers or tenants at the other. Evidence was cited to indicate that such cycles have occurred in China, ancient Greece, the Roman Empire, and medieval Europe.[8] These so-called cycles can hardly be regarded as an inevitable pattern which can be used as the basis for predicting the course of events in any particular society. Furthermore, it should be borne in mind that the specific character of the relationships among participants may differ in various tenure systems. Ownership, for example, does not have the same meaning in a tenure system where farm land can be bought and sold freely (ownership in fee simple) as in systems where an owner may enjoy a life estate but cannot irrevocably sell the land to anyone outside the family. In Communist countries private ownership of land is not permitted; all the land belongs to the state. Even in capitalist nations the state holds title to land used for public forests, military reservations, historic monuments, roads, streets, experimental farms, and the like. All governments reserve the right of eminent domain, by which private lands can be acquired for public purposes through prescribed procedures. In the U.S., court action is required for compulsory public acquisition of private land, and the value of the land is fixed by the court and payment made from public funds.

[7] Government of Pakistan, *Report of the Land Reforms Commission for West Pakistan*, Lahore, January, 1959.

[8] P. A. Sorokin, C. C. Zimmerman, and C. J. Galpin, *A Systematic Source Book in Rural Sociology*, Univ. of Minnesota Press, 1930, I, 370 ff.

LAND TENURE PATTERNS IN THE UNITED STATES

Historic Goals

If there has been any governmental land tenure policy in the U.S., it has been to encourage operator ownership of family-sized farms. Much of the country aside from the original 13 colonies and the South was settled under legislation designed to promote attainment of this ideal. The Pre-emption Act of 1841 guaranteed the prior right to purchase land up to 160 acres to a settler who was living on it when it came on the market. The Homestead Act of 1862 extended the policy further by providing for a grant of 160 acres free of charge to an individual who had lived upon it for five years. In the semiarid West the acreage was subsequently increased to 320 acres in recognition of the fact that larger holdings are necessary to provide a family's economic support under such conditions.

The southeastern states have always been dominated by large-scale plantations which monopolized most of the productive land, but there have also been large numbers of small farms occupied by poor white owner families.[9] In the Southwest land grants were made by the king of Spain to favored nobles, thus establishing the basis for large holdings.[10]

More recent agricultural policies of the federal government have also been designed to support ownership of family-operated farms. These include such matters as federal support for farm-to-market roads, federal aid for the teaching of vocational agriculture in rural high schools, and provision of credit at favorable rates for the purchase and operation of family-sized farms. Rural electrification, soil conservation programs, and agricultural extension services may also be cited. In addition, programs of price supports and acreage control have been justified largely on the basis that these programs will assist owners who operate their own family-sized farms, even though a disproportionate share of the benefits of some federal farm programs apparently have been collected by efficient operators of large commercial farms.

[9] T. Lynn Smith, *The Sociology of Rural Life*, 3rd. ed., Harper, 1953, chap. 12.

[10] Loomis and Beegle, *op. cit.*, p. 314.

These programs have helped materially. A recent Department of Agriculture study called attention to the current situation in the folowing words: "At mid-century, the people of the United States are closer to their farm-tenure goal of owner-operated family farms than ever before."[11]

TENURE STATUSES AND ROLES

There are several types of tenure statuses in the United States which are of significance from a sociological point of view. These include:

Landlords
Farm operators
    Owners
        Debt-free
        Mortgaged
    Part owners
        Debt-free
        Mortgaged
    Farm managers
    Tenants
        Cash tenants
        Share-cash tenants
        Share tenants
        Livestock-share tenants
        Crop-share tenants
Farm laborers
    Sharecroppers
    Wage hands
        Year-round
        Seasonal
            Local
            Migratory
    Unpaid family laborers[12]

[11] Frank H. Maier, Sheridan T. Maitland, and Gladys K. Bowles, *The Tenure Status of Farmworkers in the United States,* U.S. Department of Agriculture, Technical Bulletin 1217, July, 1960, p. 1.

[12] Smith, *op. cit.,* p. 287; U.S. Bureau of the Census, *Agriculture, 1954, A Graphic Summary,* vol. III, Special Reports, part 4, of *U.S. Census of Agriculture 1954,* 1956.

In addition to the above categories, it would be possible and meaningful to classify tenants according to length of lease. Another classification which might be quite revealing would be kinship of owners and tenants. Miller has suggested that "integrated farmers" are really a new farm tenure class or subclass.[13]

It may be worth while at this point to discuss some of the rights, duties, and obligations of persons who perform the roles associated with the tenure statuses enumerated above.

Landlords

A private landlord is a person who owns a farm but does not live on it or operate it. Some landlords are corporations. Many absentee landlords own farm land for investment purposes; farm land is frequently considered to be a good long-term investment. The landlord may attempt to obtain a tenant who will farm his land so as to maintain rather than destroy fertility, but this is by no means a universal effort. Some are interested merely in the maximum yearly return. In the event that the land is rented for cash, practically no supervision is involved. If, however, the farm is rented on a crop-share basis, either the landlord or his agent will try to be present at harvest time to insure a proper division of the produce. Landlords generally participate to a greater extent when livestock is raised on shares. Absentee landlords generally have few if any important community or neighborhood relationships, and do not participate in local social systems except through payment of taxes on real estate, farm equipment, and improvements. Since a single landlord may own many tracts of land, it is not possible to learn the number of landlords from census sources.

Full-Owner Operators

A full-owner operator does not rent any land from others. He may own his land free of debt or may have a mortgage on it. He has complete control of his farm, subject only to governmental regulations which are imposed on all farmers of the same type. If he owns the land in fee simple, he can sell the farm, lease all or part of it, or mortgage it as he pleases. In most cases he owns the mineral rights, so that he would profit by any oil or gas found. He may not have

[13] Walter G. Miller, "Farm Tenure Perspective of Vertical Integration," *Journal of Farm Economics*, May, 1960, p. 311.

full control over his operations if he has heavy debt, or the burden of debt may keep his level of living low. Full owners may have farms of any size. Owners of large commercial farms tend to have higher incomes and social ranks than owners of small farms.

Part-Owner Operators

A part-owner operator is a person who owns some farm land but also operates additional rented land. Many part owners are financially quite successful, and in fact may have greater net worth and larger operations than many full owners. Part owners like full owners may operate farms of any size. Large part owners may have higher incomes and social ranks than smaller full owners.

Farm Managers

A farm manager is a person who operates farms for others and is paid a wage or salary. The category does not include caretakers or manual laborers. A professional farm manager is usually a graduate of an agricultural college. He undertakes the management of a farm for an owner who may or may not live on the place. Ordinarily he does not invest any capital or take any risk but works for a specified wage or salary plus housing and other specified perquisites, in some cases including a percentage of the net or gross income of the farm. A manager supervises the day-to-day farming operations of a hired labor force, makes plans for farm operations, and conducts business relationships as specified in his contract. He does little if any manual labor himself. Since he ordinarily lives on the farm or in its vicinity, he may participate in local social systems to the extent he deems desirable.

Tenants

Tenancy is an important tenure category in the U.S. From an economic point of view, a significant feature is the fact that it may permit a person to operate a farm even though he has limited capital. There are major differences among different categories of tenants in regard to the extent of control over farming operations. As will be noted later, some types of tenancy carry higher local prestige than others.

CASH TENANTS. In some parts of this country it is customary for tenants to pay a specified rental in cash. Ordinarily this is payable in advance and is computed on the basis of a specified amount per acre. Under this type of arrangement, the tenant takes all the risks associated with the operation of the farm and the landlord none. This type of tenure arrangement is usually found in areas with low risk of crop failure and relatively stable income. A typical cash lessee owns his own machinery and livestock. He may not live on the farm since farm land is sometimes rented without buildings. A cash tenant has more freedom in farm operations than share tenants. Cash tenancy is a high-status occupation in most farming localities.

SHARE TENANTS. As noted above, there are several categories of share tenants. The crop-share tenant ordinarily owns his own machinery and livestock, and the livestock-share tenant usually owns his own machinery and part of the livestock.

Crop-share tenancy is normally found in areas of substantial risk. The prevalent leasing arrangements provide for the landlord to receive a portion of the crop ranging from one-third to one-half depending on whether the landlord furnishes anything besides the land. A share-cash tenant may produce crops and livestock on a share basis and pay cash for pasture, hay land, and buildings.

If the share tenant furnishes seed, machinery, and fertilizer, he is ordinarily allowed considerable freedom in tillage and harvesting methods. If his lease is only for a year, he is, of course, subject to eviction, which may occur if he does not pay attention to the owner's wishes. However, it is rare for landlords to attempt to interfere with the personal lives of share tenants. The lease is primarily a contractual business relationship, and termination or continuation depends upon the mutual satisfaction of the contracting parties from a business standpoint. In the northern states share tenants may have high rank, but in the South, they nearly always rank below owners.[14]

A long-term tenant may be encouraged by the landlord in clauses in the lease to make improvements and use soil-conserving practices which will yield returns over a period of years. In relatively prosperous farming areas, share tenants are frequently sons or other

[14] E. A. Schuler, *Social Status and Farm Tenure—Attitudes and Social Conditions of Corn Belt and Cotton Belt Farmers,* USDA, Social Research Report No. 4, 1938.

relatives of the landlord. In such cases, the operator may have a greater interest because of his expectations of inheriting the farm.

Farm Laborers

Tenure classifications prepared by agricultural economists do not ordinarily include any farm laborers except croppers. From a sociological point of view, however, there is ample justification for including all categories of farm workers. Their roles in relation to land and to persons in other tenure statuses are prescribed by local custom.

CROPPERS. Croppers are found in large numbers only on plantations in the South. A cropper is a person who receives a share of the crop but provides no work equipment, seeds, or fertilizer. These are furnished by the landlord who generally supervises the sharecroppers closely either directly or through a farm manager. The land on which sharecroppers work is usually part of a larger enterprise operated by a landlord as a single unit. This is not reported by the census, which counts each unit operated by a cropper as a farm. A large proportion of croppers are Negroes. Most of them are descendants of slaves who were plantation laborers prior to the Civil War. Croppers have low social rank.

Smith has classified croppers as farm laborers, pointing out that the only difference between wage laborers and croppers is that the wages of the latter are paid by a share of the crop, usually one-half.[15] The cropper has few resources. He is paid after the annual crop is harvested and sold, and consequently is ordinarily obliged to rely upon credit for food and clothing. These are provided by the landlord in most cases. Historically croppers have usually been in debt to their landlords since they have a tendency to buy more than the crop will pay for. It is difficult for a cropper who is in debt to move to another farm, and in fact, he has relatively little opportunity to improve his lot unless he leaves agriculture and moves to some city. With the recent trend toward diversification and mechanization of southern agriculture, large numbers of croppers have migrated to cities where they have become factory or unskilled workers. Some have simply joined the ranks of the urban unemployed who rely on public assistance for income.

[15] Smith, *op. cit.*, p. 284.

YEAR-ROUND FARM LABORERS. The year-round hired farm laborer (commonly called the hired man) was once a familiar figure on American farms. The traditional model of upward mobility in agriculture known as the agricultural ladder called for progression from the status of hired man to tenant and eventually to owner.

The hired man on a family-sized farm works under the daily supervision of the farm operator. He does what he is told. Nevertheless, he is expected to have some knowledge about farming, including proper care and operation of farm machinery and care of various farm animals. Some are now specialists. The hired man is ordinarily paid a monthly cash wage, the level of which is determined by custom or by bargaining. In addition, he is generally provided with food and housing. He buys his own clothing. If single, he frequently occupies a room in the farmer's house and eats with the family. If married, he may live in a separate house provided by his employer.

His social rank in the locality depends to a large extent upon his family connections. If he is the son of a local farmer, his rank will derive from and be in accordance with that of his family. If he is not from a local family and particularly if he is thought to be a "career hired man," his social rank will be relatively low.

SEASONAL LOCAL FARM LABORERS. Local nonfarm people are frequently hired as seasonal laborers in periods of peak needs, particularly during the harvesting of vegetables, fruits, and nuts. These people are employed for cash wages—by the hour, by the day, or per unit of work. Generally, they provide their own food and housing and commute daily in their own cars to the place of work. Since the work is temporary, it does not have any great bearing on the question of social rank, but it is doubtless true that most local nonfarm people who regularly engage in seasonal agricultural work come from relatively low-status families.

MIGRATORY SEASONAL FARM LABORERS. As noted earlier, there are perhaps a million migratory agricultural workers in the United States.[16] Some are single; others are married and take their families with them from job to job. Perhaps half are U.S. citizens, and the remainder principally Mexicans.

[16] See Chapter 4.

The relationship of migratory agricultural workers to land is based on a short-term labor contract. Such workers are usually paid on a piece-work basis.

The President's Commission on Migratory Labor has said migrants are expected to be available when needed and to be gone when not needed.[17] Many of the Mexican nationals are called "wetbacks" because they enter the United States illegally by swimming the Rio Grade River, usually under cover of darkness. These persons are subject to arrest and deportation. Because of their lack of legal status, they are at a disadvantage in obtaining satisfactory housing and terms of employment.

The bulk of migratory labor needs, as noted previously, exist on large-scale agricultural enterprises. Employers are not interested in workers as individuals and do not ordinarily establish personal contact with them, but instead deal with labor contractors who supervise and pay each of the workers. According to the President's Commission, a contractor or crew leader may exact a heavy financial toll for his services as an employment intermediary.[18]

Because they are constantly on the move, migratory agricultural workers are unable to develop stable social relationships outside their family groups. They are seldom if ever accepted as members of the established social systems in the localities where they work. They belong to no stable organizations. No community accepts responsibility for them. While they are employed as migratory laborers, their children receive little schooling because they have no established residence and hence do not contribute directly to the support of schools. Some of their children also work for pay in agriculture. The President's Commission reported the Bureau of the Census estimate that in August, 1950, 190,000 children 10 through 13 years of age and 205,000 aged 14 and 15 were working for pay in agriculture.[19]

UNPAID FAMILY LABORERS On most family farms, the main labor force is the operator. However, he is assisted by unpaid family members who perform various operations as a matter of duty. The

[17] President's Commission on Migratory Labor, *Migratory Labor in American Agriculture,* 1951, p. 16.
[18] President's Commission on Migratory Labor, *op. cit.,* pp. 18, 91.
[19] *Ibid.,* p. 161.

work roles of unpaid family members are discussed in some detail in the section dealing with the family farm as a social system.[20]

TENURE TRENDS

LANDLORDS

As noted above, systematic data concerning the trend in number of landlords is not available. This is unfortunate, since many landlords exercise considerable control over farming operations on their holdings. In the Southeast, plantation owners and managers determine farm policies to a much greater extent than the croppers who are counted by the census as operators.

In 1959, there were 2,116,026 full owners, 809,600 part owners, 20,503 managers, and 757,513 tenants (including 121,053 sharecroppers).[21]

FARM OPERATORS

The trend in tenure of farm operators for the whole country and major census regions has shown an increase in ownership. The decrease in the number of farms since 1935 has been accompanied by marked decreases in the number of tenants and croppers. The number of part owners increased from 1940 to 1954. There was a slight decline in 1959. Regional comparisons show that tenure changes have generally taken the same direction since the 1930s, although marked differences still exist between regions in the proportions in various tenure categories.

The trend between 1880 and 1954 in the number of farms operated by tenants in the U.S. by major census regions is shown in Table 13. In 1954, there were 1,700,000 fewer tenants than in 1935. Those who owned none of the land they operated were a smaller proportion of all farm operators in 1959 (20.5 percent) than at any previous date in the history of the U.S. This means, of course, that the proportion of operators who owned all or part of the land they operated stood at an all-time high.

[20] See Chapter 15.

[21] U.S. Bureau of the Census, 1959 *Census of Agriculture—Preliminary*, Series AC59-1, January, 1961.

TABLE 13. Percent of All Farms Operated by Tenants for the
United States and Regions, 1880-1954

Year	United States	Northeast	North Central	South	West
1954	24.0	6.0	23.3	29.4	12.1
1950	26.8	6.8	24.2	34.1	12.9
1945	31.7	8.6	29.1	40.4	14.5
1940	38.7	12.6	35.4	48.2	21.3
1935	42.1	13.8	36.3	53.5	23.8
1930	42.4	12.5	34.1	55.5	20.9
1925	38.6	13.0	32.0	51.1	18.7
1920	38.1	17.2	31.1	49.6	17.7
1910	37.0	18.2	28.9	49.6	14.0
1900	35.3	20.8	27.9	47.0	16.6
1890	28.4	18.4	23.4	38.5	12.1
1880	25.6	16.0	20.5	36.2	14.0

SOURCE: Mary M. B. Harmon, *A Statistical Summary of Land Tenure, 1954,*
Agricultural Research Service, USDA, 1958, p. 6.

Even so, tenancy remained an important tenure category since
they operated a fourth of the farms and a fourth of the crop land.[22]

FARM LABORERS

The number of farm laborers has decreased considerably during
the past 30 years. The average number of farm workers in 1929 was
10,450,000 compared to 5,723,000 in 1960.[23] The productivity of
labor has increased, largely due to mechanization, as the number
of hours worked has declined. Thus, one farm worker now provides
agricultural products for 23 other persons.

The great changes in the requirements for farm labor which have
been brought about by the increasing mechanization of American
farms during the last half-century have sharply altered the picture
with respect to use of and opportunities for farm laborers. Perhaps
the largest numerical changes in the farm labor force have occurred
in the category of unpaid workers. Information collected by the

[22] *Ibid.,* p. 140.
[23] U.S. Bureau of Labor Statistics, *Employment and Earnings,* February, 1961.

census does not adequately reflect these changes. Prior to the expansion of free public education, particularly at the high-school level, farm boys and some farm girls constituted a major portion of the labor force on family-sized farms. At present, as we have said, few farmers can count their school-age children as a source of dependable day-to-day help on a year-around basis, and by the time most children have completed high school, they are ready to leave the home farm.

The number of croppers has been reduced drastically since 1929. At that time there were 776,000 cropper units compared to 273,000 in 1954 and 121,000 in 1959.[24] These decreases reflect changes in farm organization requiring less labor and increasing mechanization of southern farms.[25]

There are still a large number of migratory agricultural workers, perhaps more than a million. However, farm labor opportunities were once much greater. Prior to the development of the combined harvester-thresher, now nearly universal in the wheat areas, migratory workers followed the wheat harvest from Texas north into Canada. Some operators of combine harvesters still do the same, but the tendency now is for individual farm operators to own their own machinery.

REGIONAL PATTERNS

Tenancy as a form of farm tenure is concentrated mainly in the Cotton Belt, the Corn Belt, and the Great Plains (Fig. 19). With local exceptions, less than 20 percent of the farms in other areas were operated by tenants.

There are pronounced regional differences in types of tenants. Croppers are concentrated in the Southeast, cash tenants and share tenants are widely distributed, and share-cash tenants are found principally in the Midwest.

---

[24] *1959 Census of Agriculture, op. cit.,* p. 35.
[25] J. V. McElveen, *Family Farms in a Changing Economy,* USDA, Agricultural Research Service, Agricultural Information Bulletin 171, March, 1959, p. 35.

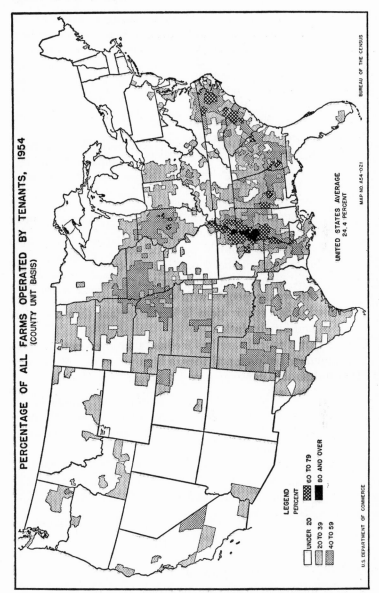

PERCENTAGE OF ALL FARMS OPERATED BY TENANTS, 1954
(COUNTY UNIT BASIS)

LEGEND
PERCENT

UNDER 20
20 TO 39
40 TO 59
60 TO 79
80 AND OVER

UNITED STATES AVERAGE
24.4 PERCENT

U.S. DEPARTMENT OF COMMERCE

BUREAU OF THE CENSUS

MAP NO. A54-021

FIG. 19.

TENURE PATTERNS AND COMMUNITY LIFE

Rural sociologists have sought to learn the implications of various types of land tenure upon community life. Interest was greatest during the depression of the 1930s when the proportion of farms operated by tenants was at its peak.

As we have noted, the long-prevailing tendency in North America has been to regard owner operation of a family-sized farm as the most desirable tenure status. This aspect of the culture has doubtless prevented some students of land tenure from taking an objective view of tenancy. However, studies in various parts of the U.S. have shown that the participation of tenants in community affairs tends to be more restricted than that of owners. Church membership is lower among tenants, as is membership in farm organizations. Owners are more likely to be active in local government.[26] The lower level of social participation may be due in part to insecurity of occupancy and consequent high mobility. However, many tenants are young people with small children who may feel that participation in organizations is less important than attention to farm work and family duties.

It is clear that if tenants are less inclined than owners to participate in community building activities, a high proportion of tenancy will have undesirable consequences for community life. Kolb and and Brunner have advanced the opinion that the social effects of high tenancy are usually unhappy.[27]

Within the context of American culture, the research evidence indicates that the tenure pattern most conducive to a vigorous and wholesome community life is found where there is security of tenure on the part of the majority of the farm operators in the locality. Greater stability is, of course, found among owners and tenants with long-term leases.

A tenant with a short-term lease, who is subject to eviction on short notice, is not likely to be greatly concerned with the development and maintenance of schools, churches, roads, and other community facilities; nor are absentee landlords. As Landis has pointed

[26] See Ackerman and Harris, eds., *op. cit.*, p. 421.
[27] John H. Kolb and Edmund deS. Brunner, *A Study of Rural Society*, 4th ed., Houghton-Mifflin, 1952, p. 90.

out, it is difficult to convince the absentee landlord that better community facilities for other people are sufficiently important to him to offset the cost of higher taxes.[28] As noted, the percentage of church membership as well as the frequency of church attendance is much higher among owners than among tenants, and there is evidence that owners contribute more generously to the support of church activities.[29]

Short-term tenancy clearly has an undesirable effect on the conservation of agricultural fertility and on the support of facilities for community living. These consequences are not necessarily attributes of tenancy as such, but rather reflect the low economic status and social rank of farm tenants which provides them with relatively little incentive to become community-building persons. The same observation may be made with respect to farm laborers.

Efforts have been made by some of the land-grant colleges to develop leases which would place a premium on residential stability by emphasizing long-term commitments and payment for improvements made by tenants.

A committee of the 1946 Conference on Family Farm Policy offered several recomendations designed to improve security and stability of occupancy for tenants:

1. Clearly drawn lease forms, developed with the benefit of suggestions from farmers (owners and tenants) and economists, as well as lawyers, should be used in making leasing agreements.
2. Agricultural extension services should continue to foster community, county, and other landlord-tenant conferences.
3. Standardization of lease forms would be helpful in improving tenure conditions. Within a state, all agencies, both governmental and private, concerned with farm leasing agreements should cooperate in the formulation and use of standard lease forms.
4. Experience of landlords who have had notable success in helping their tenants to be "graduated" into successful owners should be given more widespread attention.
5. The lease should provide for notice to be given so that at least six months would intervene before a tenant would expect to move to another farm. After a year or two of successful lease relations, the

[28] Paul H. Landis, *Rural Life in Process*, 2nd ed., McGraw-Hill, 1948, p. 427.
[29] See Schuler, *op. cit.*; President's Committee on Farm Tenancy, *Farm Tenancy*, U.S. National Resources Committee, February, 1937.

tenant and landlord might agree upon every other year as the one in which such notices might be given, and if the landowner, because of sale of the property, should need to give the new owner possession, adequate compensation for shortened notice should be made to the tenant.

6. On government lands, especially on reclamation projects, further experimentation is needed with respect to use of long-term leases, including a lease for the life of the lessee.[30]

SOME FEATURES OF LAND TENURE SYSTEMS IN OTHER COUNTRIES

It is not feasible to attempt to cover the details of land tenure systems in all parts of the world. However, some of the outstanding features of land tenure arrangements in selected countries are worth noting.

GREAT BRITAIN[31]

Under a common system found in Great Britain in 1946, landlords owned the land and fixed equipment, including buildings, and tenants paid cash rent and owned their own machinery and livestock. In contrast to the prevalent short-term lease found in the U.S., leases provided security of tenure and compensation for disturbance if the lease was terminated capriciously by the landlord. The power of the landlord to influence farm operations was extremely limited. Since 1906, tenants have had the right to decide what system of farming is to be used, although they are required to follow good soil conservation practices. Duckham reported in 1946 that this landlord-tenant system had greater political support in Britain than the owner-occupied farm.[32]

THE NETHERLANDS[33]

Owner operation and tenant operation were the principal types of land tenure found in the Netherlands in 1946 according to Peters.

[30] Ackerman and Harris, eds., op. cit., p. 441.
[31] Edgar Thomas, "Tenure of Agricultural Land in Britain," in Ackerman and Harris, eds., op. cit., pp. 164-170.
[32] A. N. Duckham, in a comment on Thomas, op. cit., pp. 170-171.
[33] A. H. Peters, op. cit., pp. 209-218.

However, he reported a form of permanent tenancy under which the farmer owns the house and buildings and has a right to use the land without consulting the owner. These rights are permanent and can be transferred to others. The owners receive a fixed annual rental and certain other fees.

Prior to 1937, most tenants operated their farms under leases made by free bargaining between landlord and tenants. Because of the heavy demand for land, landowners were able to dictate the terms of leases. However, the Tenancy Act of 1937 ended the favored position of the landlord, giving tenants nearly as much security as owner operators.

DENMARK[34]

Land tenure in Denmark, according to Sorenson, is characterized by owner operation of family-sized farms. In 1946, approximately 94 percent of Danish farmers were owner operators. His evaluation of this tenure system follows:

The experiences regarding land tenure in Denmark during the last one hundred years have proved that occupying ownership is superior to tenancy. First of all, it is in conformity with the sentiments of the Danish farmer, who wants to be free to manage his farm as he pleases. It is a fact that owners and their families are more progressive than tenants, since they know that they will get the full benefit of their extra endeavors. Ownership, or freehold tenure, gives more stability in agriculture as the owner prepares to stay on his farm for a lifetime. During periods of crises he will tighten his belt and work harder, while a tenant is more likely to give up during difficult times.

Ownership is also more favorable to cooperation than tenancy, because the owner prepares to stay on his farm for a long time; and he is willing to take shares in cooperative organizations, while a tenant will hesitate to do so because he may be moved to another farm or another district. . . .[35]

WEST PAKISTAN

West Pakistan has a complicated land tenure system which is not readily comparable to that of any contemporary western nation.

[34] Soren Sorenson, "The Family Farmer in Denmark," in Ackerman and Harris, eds., *op. cit.*, pp. 243-247.
[35] *Ibid.*, p. 247.

Prior to the land reforms of 1959, much of the better land was owned by wealthy landlords; about 6000 landlords owned more than 7,500,-000 acres in properties of more than 500 acres each. Some of these large owners were descendents of famous warriors or other notable figures. Ownership rights varied from full proprietorship to the right to collect land revenues, rents, or fees. The Land Reforms Commission observed with reference to persons who had a hereditary right to land revenue (*jagirdirs*):

The governments preceding the British Rule found it convenient to secure the sword of the brave and the prayer of the pious man, to pacify the deposed chiefs and to reward powerful servants by assigning to them the Ruler's share of the produce of land in particular villages or tracts . . . after the Mutiny of 1857 when the British Government thought it particularly prudent to reward loyalties, a number of jagirdirs were able successfully to establish proprietary claims to vast tracts of lands with which they were connected only as revenue farmers.[36]

The land reforms of 1959 limited ownership to 500 acres of irrigated land or 1000 acres of unirrigated land and abolished *jagirdirs*.

In addition to individual ownership, as noted above, there are two main types of communal ownership. Prior to the land reforms, over half the land was operated by tenants who had no permanent rights in land. This type of tenant was called a tenant-at-will because he could be evicted at the will of the landlord. There was also a form called occupancy tenancy which was relatively permanent. Occupancy tenants enjoyed most of the privileges of owners.

The 1959 land reforms insured substantial security for tenants. Among other things it provided that:

No tenant should be ejected unless it is established in a revenue court that he has:
(a) failed to pay rent; or
(b) used the land in a manner which renders it unfit for the purposes for which he held it; or
(c) failed to cultivate the land without sufficient reason; or
(d) sublet his tenancy. . . .[37]

[36] *Report of the Land Reforms Commission, op. cit.*
[37] *Ibid.*

The foregoing examples will serve to emphasize that not only are tenure systems extremely varied but that tenure arrangements are subject to change. The systems found in a particular area at a given time are established and maintained by law and custom.

QUESTIONS FOR FURTHER STUDY AND DISCUSSION

1. Discuss the origins and social significance of the regional differences in tenure patterns.
2. What are the disadvantages from a sociological point of view of being a migratory farm laborer?
3. Are there definite regional differences in the social rank of the farm owner if size of farm is held constant? Explain why or why not.
4. Write a job description which would apply to a person occupying the status of farm tenant in a locality with which you are acquainted. Contrast this with the farm owner insofar as its sociological implications are concerned. Under what circumstances might the absence of farm tenants be detrimental to a community?

SELECTED REFERENCES

Ackerman, J. A., and Marshall Harris, eds., *Family Farm Policy,* University of Chicago Press, 1946.

Kolb, John H., and Edmund deS. Brunner, *A Study of Rural Society,* 4th ed., Houghton-Mifflin, 1952.

Loomis, C. P., and J. A. Beegle, *Rural Social Systems,* Prentice-Hall, 1950.

McElveen, J. V., *Family Farms in a Changing Economy,* U.S. Department of Agriculture, Agricultural Research Service, Agricultural Information Bulletin 171, March, 1959.

Maier, Frank H., Sheridan T. Maitland, and Gladys K. Bowles, *The Tenure Status of Farmworkers in the United States,* USDA, Technical Bulletin 1217, July, 1960.

Sorokin, P. A., C. C. Zimmerman, and C. J. Galpin, *A Systematic Source Book in Rural Sociology,* University of Minnesota Press, 1930, vol. I.

U.S. Bureau of the Census, *Agriculture 1954, A Graphic Summary,* vol. III, Special Reports, part 4, of *U.S. Census of Agriculture: 1954,* 1956.

17

Rural Systems of Social Stratification

Some farmers in any locality are considered by their neighbors to have more prestige than others. Their prestige may be based upon personal achievement or inherited wealth, or a combination of factors. Whatever the basis, there seems to be some form of social inequality in every human society and lesser social system, including those which claim to have abolished all distinctions among members. Social stratification is a general term which covers all types of social inequality—caste, class, and other systems of assigning social rank.

Societies differ greatly with respect to the forms and bases of social stratification. The particular forms found in a specific agricultural locality are colored by the ideology and other traditions of the general society. They are also influenced by the specific traditions of people in the locality and, in the United States, by personal achievements.

The American farmer's attitudes toward social inequalities are likely to be affected by the political ideology, which tends to minimize political differences. The signers of the Declaration of Independence were opposed to the types of political inequalities that existed in England at the time, as is reflected in the statement that all men are created equal. Full political equality was not granted by the first seven articles of the U.S. Constitution, but Article I of the Constitution prohibited titles of nobility. The Thirteenth Amendment abolished slavery, and the Nineteenth gave women the right to vote. More recently, the 1954 antisegregation decision of the U.S. Supreme Court seeks to abolish educational inequalities based on race.

However, the political ideology of democracy has not wiped out economic and social inequalities, which are still to be found throughout the U.S., including rural localities. These differences are recognized by farmers and influence interpersonal relationships among farm people.

In view of the equalitarian and democratic philosophy of this country, it may seem paradoxical that social stratification has been one of the most popular subjects for sociological studies. Numbers of empirical investigations have been made to discover and describe types of social stratification existing in specific social systems and to analyze their signigficance for various forms of social and economic interaction. Many different approaches have been utilized in these investigations, among them (1) opinions of local judges or raters,[1] (2) sociometric techniques for mapping the actual patterns of interaction among specific people,[2] and (3) indicators such as material possessions, income, and occupation.[3]

Other sociologists have developed scales for use in attempting to measure what has been called social distance between ethnic and racial groups.[4]

There has been no comprehensive nationwide study of rural social stratification in the United States, but there have been enough careful investigations in specific localities to make it clear that there is tremendous variation in the forms and significance of social stratification. These range from virtually none in a part-time farm-

[1] See Harold F. Kaufman, *Prestige Classes in a New York Rural Community*, Cornell University AES Memoir 260, 1944; James West, *Plainville, USA*, Columbia University Press, 1945.

[2] See Charles P. Loomis, *Studies of Rural Social Organization*, Michigan State College Book Store, 1945; Loomis and J. A. Beegle, *Rural Social Systems*, Prentice-Hall, 1950, chaps. X, XI.

[3] See W. H. Sewell, *The Construction and Standardization of a Scale for the Measurement of the Socio-Economic Status of Oklahoma Farm Families*, Oklahoma AES Technical Bulletin 9, April, 1940; and "A Short Form of the Farm Family Socio-Economic Status Scale," *Rural Sociology*, June, 1943, pp. 161-170; J. C. Belcher and E. F. Sharp, *A Short Scale for Measuring Farm Family Level of Living: A Modification of Sewell's Socio-Economic Scale*, Oklahoma AES Bulletin T-46, September, 1952.

[4] See Emory Bogardus, "A Social Distance Scale," *Sociology and Social Research*, January-February, 1933, pp. 265-271; "Social Distance and Its Practical Implications," *op. cit.*, June, 1938, pp. 462-476; and "Scales in Social Research," *op. cit.*, September-October, 1939, pp. 69-75.

ing area in western Washington as reported by Iwanska,[5] to the tremendous differences found on a southern plantation, in an eastern locality containing the country estates of millionaires, or on a corporation farm in California. In addition to differences in rank based upon wealth, family background, and personal achievement, the social position of a farm family may also be influenced by religion, ethnic background, or racial origin.

While many social distinctions are readily evident to the casual observer, others are extremely subtle and known only to the insider.

The principal forms of stratification found in rural populations throughout the world are castes, classes, and of course individual social rank.

CASTE

Caste is a hereditary system of social stratification which is restricted at present mainly to the subcontinent of India and Pakistan. One born into a caste in Hindu society does not leave it except through change of religion or excommunication.[6] The European feudal system involving lords, serfs, and slaves was a caste system since a person's social position was then determined almost exclusively by birth. Others have been reported in Polynesia, Peru, and Egypt.[7]

CHARACTERISTICS OF CASTE

Kingsley Davis has summarized the salient characteristics of Indian castes as follows:

(1) Membership is hereditary, and is fixed for life.
(2) Choice of the marriage partner is endogamous.
(3) Contact with other castes is further limited by restrictions on touching, associating with, dining with, or eating food cooked by outsiders.
(4) Consciousness of caste membership is emphasized by the caste

[5] Alicja Iwanska, *Good Fortune: Second Chance Community*, Washington AES Bulletin 589, June, 1958.

[6] S. C. Dube, *Indian Village*, Routledge & Kegan Paul, 1955.

[7] Marvin Harris, "Caste, Class, and Minority," *Social Forces*, March, 1959, pp. 248-254.

name, by the individual's identification with his caste in the eyes
of the community, by his conformity to the peculiar customs of his
caste, and by his subjection to government by his caste.

(5) The caste is united by a common traditional occupation, although
it may be united also by the belief in a common tribal or racial
origin, by adherence to a common religious sect, or by some other
common peculiarity.

(6) The relative prestige of the different castes in any locality is well
established and jealousy guarded.[8]

It is evident from this list that membership in a caste has tremendous consequences for the life chances and day-by-day patterns
of social interaction of members. Caste is strongest among the
Hindus, which is understandable since it is supported by the Hindu
doctrine of *Karma*. This concept holds that after death a person's
soul is either reborn or is sent to heaven or hell. For one who is
reborn, his past life determines whether the birth is into a higher
or a lower caste or perhaps into some other form of animal life.[8]

Theoretically castes are not recognized in Islam, but there is evidently a considerable amount of caste custom among the Muslims
in Pakistan. Davis reported that 81 percent of the Muslims in the
United Provinces in 1931 were members of 14 castes.[10] Qureshi
classified the population of six Punjab villages into 25 castes.[11] A
study of six different villages in the Lahore District of West Pakistan in 1956 also revealed that nearly all of the villagers except
Christians reported a caste affiliation.[12]

Davis has indicated that caste principles are even found to some
extent among Christians in India and Pakistan. He points out,
however, that since a large percentage of the converts were drawn
from the lowest castes, there is considerable opposition among
Christians to the caste system. These people in most cases probably
become Christians partly to attempt to improve their social and

[8] Kingsley Davis, *The Population of India and Pakistan*, Princeton University
Press, 1951, p. 162.

[9] Dube, *op. cit.*, pp. 90-91.

[10] Davis, *op. cit.*, p. 164.

[11] J. M. Qureshi, *Economic Survey of Eight Typical Villages in Thal*, Punjab
(Pakistan) Board of Economic Inquiry, 1955, p. 6.

[12] W. L. Slocum, Jamila Aktar, and Abrar Fatima Sahi, *Village Life in
Lahore District*, Lahore, Social Science Research Center, Panjab University
Press, 1959.

economic position which they were unable to do within the caste system.

Among the Hindus, the Brahmins are the highest caste. Brahmins serve as priests for several of the other castes and are consulted concerning the best dates for starting various agricultural operations, weddings, and other social ceremonies.

The interdependent character of relationships between various Hindu castes is indicated by the following description from Dube:

> In Shamirpet there are five families of potters, with fourteen people actually working at the wheel. Each family is attached to some agriculturists in the village, and it periodically supplies them with a certain number of earthen pots for domestic use. Every two or three years they also supply the agriculturists with large baked earthen bins for storing grain. For this they do not expect cash price. At the time of harvesting the potter visits the fields of the family to which he is attached, and is given his share of the new crop. . . . If he can arrive at an agreement with the other occupational castes, such as the barber, the washerman and the weaver, he will offer them his services in return for their occupational services to his family. The details are fixed by the parties concerned, and often considerable haggling and making of charges and counter-charges against one another go on. Notwithstanding this, the system works quite satisfactorily. . . .[13]

The operational unit in the caste is the local group. At the village level the number of families from a particular caste varies. Since some castes repersent occupational specialties, the fact that villages generally do not have a full set of castes makes it necessary for people in one village to depend upon the services of specialists in other villages. The practice of intermarriage within the caste makes it necessary for mates to be obtained from other villages if suitable matches cannot be arranged within one's own village.[14]

THE PERSISTENCE OF CASTE

Although there has been some effort by the present government of India to abolish caste distinctions, particularly by attacking the doctrine of untouchability, it is still a very pervasive system which has behind it the force of centuries of tradition.

[13] Dube, *op. cit.*, p. 63.
[14] Davis, *op. cit.*, p. 175.

Although it is perhaps less important than previously in the cities, it is apparently still strong in the agricultural villages. Since more than three-fourths of the people of India and Pakistan live in agricultural villages, caste is important in regulating the lives of perhaps as many as 300,000,000 rural people.

Caste is supported also by interrelated aspects of the culture, including the arranged marriage, which still persists in India even though the legal ban on intermarriage between castes was removed by the November, 1948, Indian Constitution. Very few young people are allowed to choose their own mates either in India or in Pakistan at present. It is hardly conceivable that intercaste marriages could be prevented if free choice of one's mate were customary.

The fact that the great majority of Indian and Pakistani agricultural villagers are illiterate also contributes to the persistence of caste distinctions. Western-type education, on the other hand, tends to break down caste lines. It is meant for all the people and is scientific and technical in nature rather than mystical or religious like the traditional education of the priestly Brahmin class.

There are some indications that education has become a channel of upward social mobility, although it still does not permit an individual to change his caste. Many Muslims apparently changed their castes at the time of the partition of India and Pakistan. Davis feels that the forces which oppose caste are more definite and numerous than the forces which favor it, but he also points out that caste has the very great advantage of being established. He believes that there will be caste influences in Indian life for centuries to come, though he has ventured the opinion that caste may eventually disappear in Pakistan.[15]

There is evidence from recent studies which indicates that some contemporary castes in India are attempting, through social action, to improve their social standing. Srinivas reports that the Kammalans (smiths) have disputed the ranking given to them in relation to the Brahmin.[16] Cohn writes of an effort by a tenant caste, the Camars, to throw off the subordinate position which they have

[15] *Ibid.*, p. 176.
[16] M. N. Srinivas, "The Social System of a Mysore Village," in McKim Marriott, ed., *Village India*, American Anthropological Association Memoir 83, June, 1955.

traditionally held under the Thakurs, their landlords.[17]

In theory the Hindu caste system is a graded hierarchy of strata in which each makes a fuctional contribution to the social system and derives its rank from the presumed value of the contribution. But some castes are too exalted and others too lowly to benefit from the services of other castes—the barber castes among the Hindus, for instance, will not serve the untouchables, nor will the Brahmins.

The caste system is theoretically incompatible with change. It requires a static social order with a uniform growth rate in each caste for perfect functioning. Actually, the system is not perfect, of course, and some modifications apparently have taken place with more in prospect.

SOCIAL CLASS

Social classes may be defined as groups of people who have like occupations, economic status, prestige, and style of life and who recognize that they have a community of interests with others similarly situated. Consciousness of belonging to a class is an essential part of this definition. Members of a class group do not, of course, utilize technical sociological terminology; they may speak of "society" or their "set" or "club."

In countries like England and the nations of western Europe where well-established traditional social classes exist, the requirements for membership, at least in the upper classes, are definite and well known to all. An essential theoretical difference between caste and class is that classes are not endogamous and thus are not marriage-regulating groups. In practice, however, there is a tendency, particularly for the upper classes, to restrict marriage to other members of the same class. Members of lower classes who have acquired attributes such as wealth, position, and style of life which are similar to those which are customary in the upper class may also be accepted.

A social class may be regarded as a system of relationships among people. The boundaries of a class may be nearly as rigid as those of a caste (as in the case of New York "society"), or membership may

[17] Bernard S. Cohn, "The Changing Station of a Depressed Caste," in McKim Marriott, ed., *op. cit.*

be open to all or nearly all on the basis of achievement. If classes are viewed as social systems, more than mere consciousness of belonging to some diffused category seems essential. Interaction among members is also required to generate genuine class feelings. In a large and complex modern society, this means that class affiliations are primarily of significance in a definite geographic locality. Furthermore, because of the tremendous differences in wealth and cultural backgrounds of people in various regions, members of the upper class in one locality may not qualify elsewhere. For example, the members of the upper class (if such exists) in a small city in South Dakota would not be accepted in New York "society," which is a definite social class with a distincitive style of life, carefully maintained boundaries, and all the other attributes prescribed for a social class by authorities on the subject.

Some nationwide sampling surveys have revealed that many people are willing to classify themselves as members of broad classes such as upper, middle, lower, or working. However, these categories are so general and the actual reference groups or classifications involved are so ambiguous that they have little sociological meaning, though they may have some validity as a rough means of determining an individual's economic rank.

While there may be distinct social classes within the definition presented above in some agricultural localities, there appear to be no clearly defined classes in American agriculture that are valid from one part of the country to another or even within broad regions. It is clear that farm owners as such do not constitute a social class; neither do farm tenants, farm croppers, or wage hands. Even the category of large owners does not constitute a class in the true sense of the term.

PERSONAL SOCIAL RANK AS A STRATIFICATION PRINCIPLE

It seems futile to try to fit the social stratification system of American farmers into the strait jacket of traditional concepts of caste or class which have been borrowed from other societies. Nevertheless, great inequalities in social rank are found within many local social systems in agricultural localities. In some cases these differences may be of a classlike or even castelike character. And nearly always, regardless of the existence of such groups, there are substantial differences in the social ranking of specific individuals or families.

Social rank may be conceived as an abstract classification which applies generally in a society. For example, in the nationwide ranking of occupations, the concept has some value as a means of gauging roughly the change in rank of an upward- or downward-mobile individual. If we look at the matter more closely, however, the concept of social rank really has significance only within a concrete social system with specific roles and direct interaction among members.

Within a concrete social system, people of superior rank are able to control or otherwise influence their associates; the behavior of the subordinate who approaches a socially powerful person is obviously conditioned by such considerations. For example, a farm laborer will speak in different terms to another farm laborer on his own level than to the foreman or farm operator. The great interest which people show in the wealth and other indicators of rank of an outsider indicates their desire to make an estimate of where the stranger would fit into the ranking order of their own social systems.

A person who is not a member of or in contact with one's own concrete social systems does not constitute for him a significant person and consequently rank is of no concern. Thus, public figures like Queen Elizabeth, Nelson Rockefeller, or Elvis Presley are as remote from and insignificant for most American farmers as comparable persons of prestige who are now dead, like Julius Caesar or Louis XIV.

Differences in rank are based upon many factors, several of which may operate for a given person, and some of which may be more important at times than others.[18] These factors include skin color, ethnic background, income or other evidence of wealth, tenure status, size of holdings, length of residence, family connections, style of life, education, and such personal attributes as reputation, attitudes, and perceived ability. In some cases, contrary to the

[18] See O. D. Duncan and Jay W. Artis, *Social Stratification in a Pennsylvania Rural Community*, Pennsylvania AES Bulletin 543, October, 1951.

situation in the traditional agricultural community, it may be the nonfarm rather than the farm occupational role which is most important.

The social rank of the head of the family generally determines that of other members of the family until such time as they leave the family home and establish themselves as independent adults. Even then family connections are by no means unimportant.

ECONOMIC STATUS

In a society like the American where great emphasis is placed upon financial success, it is inevitable that economic status should be an important factor in determining a farmer's social rank. Several indicators of economic standing are available, including size of holdings, evidence of consumption, and gross income. The last, of course, may be difficult to obtain readily from a particular farmer in a specific locality. The Census of Agriculture has collected some information on gross income which is probably approximately correct in most cases.

The owner or operator of a large plantation, ranch, or farm ordinarily does not engage in manual labor and may not even directly supervise those who do have farming operations on his holdings.

Here and there, particularly along the eastern seaboard, are found the country estates of wealthy men who did not derive their fortunes from agriculture. Some of these people engage in agricultural operations (keeping blooded livestock is a favorite enterprise) and charge off their losses on their federal income tax returns. Other rich gentleman farmers make little if any attempt to farm their acreages but regard them as country retreats. For the most part, these owners are economically far above even the most wealthy of the farmers who actually operate lands commercially. They normally have their social contacts with other urbanites on their own economic and social levels. Some belong to the upper classes whose names are listed in the social registers of the principal eastern cities. These socialites, of course, do not enter easily into social relationships with commercial farmers in the locality.

Although the census statistics make it difficult to identify large-scale plantation operations in the South, Woofter indicated in 1936 that there had been little change from the 33,900 reported by the census in 1910.[19] Smith implies that this is still true.[20]

The owner or operator of a large-scale agricultural enterprise would naturally have higher social rank than those working under his direction. Because of his economic, political, and social power, he would also be expected to have higher social rank than the owner of a nearby small holding. Size of holding may be indicated to some extent by acreage, but value or some measure of farm productivity is probably a better measure; 1000 acres of fertile irrigated land involves a much larger economic operation than 1000 acres of range land.

Information obtained by the U.S. Census Bureau in connection with the census of agriculture reveals that there were 102,000 farms in 1959 with gross farm sales of more than $40,000 during the preceding year. Although 102,000 may seem like a large number, it is a relatively small percentage of the total of 2,412,000 commercial farms.[21]

Many of the part-time and residential farms listed in the referenced tabulation are probably occupied by individuals with substantial economic means. Some of these no doubt have higher economic status and social rank than many Class I full-time commercial farmers.

STYLE OF LIFE

There has been some emphasis in contemporary American society on conspicuous consumption as a means of influencing others to believe that the consumer has high economic and social rank. This is probably more true of urban dwellers than of farmers, for whom emphasis traditionally has been upon saving for the purpose of enlarging holdings and operations rather than upon purchasing luxury goods and services.

On the other hand, many farmers have overextended themselves

[19] T. J. Woofter, Jr. *et. al.*, *Landlord and Tenant on the Cotton Plantation*, WPA Research Monograph V, Washington, 1936.

[20] T. Lynn Smith, *The Sociology of Rural Life*, 3rd ed., Harper, 1953, pp. 304-313.

[21] See Chapter 15 for an economic classification of farms in 1959.

to pay for new machinery, buildings, and other farm improvements which could scarcely be justified solely on rational economic grounds. Farm people once lagged far behind urban dwellers in possession of various home facilities and conveniences, but the gap has narrowed markedly in recent years.

There is little doubt that the style of life of a farmer and his family does contribute to the evaluation of his social rank by people in his locality. The nature of the evaluation, however, depends to a major extent upon the values found in the locality.

RACE AND SKIN COLOR

There are few American Negroes on farms outside the South, where there are, of course, a great many. In some areas there are two sets of social systems, white and colored, with social gradations within each. There may be some overlapping as to social rank, but in general the highest-ranking rural Negroes are little above the lowest-ranking white farmers.[22] As noted previously, most of the Japanese farmers are to be found along the Pacific Coast. While they are considered to be very successful truck farmers, they do not in general possess high social rank.

The swarthy rural Mexicans and Spanish Americans in the Southwest, including California, are generally either migratory farm workers or impoverished small farmers. As such they do not make much money, and the combination of their low economic status, skin color, and ethnic origins combine to give them rather low social rank.

ETHNIC ORIGINS

As noted in the discussion of national origins among American farmers, there are major differences in the social ranks accorded to various ethnic stocks.[23] It has also been observed that recent immigrants from a foreign country tend to have lower social rank-

[22] W. E. Moore and R. M. Williams, "Stratification in the Ante-Bellum South," *American Sociological Review*, VII (1942), 343-351; W. L. Warner, "American Class and Caste," *American Journal of Sociology*, September, 1936, pp. 234-237.

[23] See Chapter 5.

ings than those who have been in the country for substantial periods.[24]

Ethnic differences are likely to be of particular importance in a specific agricultural locality. Membership in the locally dominant ethnic group may contribute materially to the high social rank of an individual who also possesses other prestige-inducing characteristics.

PERSONAL REPUTATION

The social rank of an individual in American culture ideally depends primarily upon personal ability and achievement. In practice many other factors are also involved. It is nevertheless true that personal ability and known achievements contribute materially to one's reputation, which in turn is undoubtedly an important factor in determining one's social rank within a locality-based social system. If inquiries are made about the prestige of a particular family who is well known to a respondent, he will ordinarily not hesitate to indicate the prestige ranking of that family. Other raters may not agree fully, of course, but studies of social prestige based upon the opinions of local people have indicated a reasonable degree of accord.

It should be borne in mind, however, that personal qualities which are important in terms of social rank within one social system may not be important in another. Thus, a religion-oriented communal society like that of the Mennonites may prize characteristics much different from those which would be likely to bring high social rank to a commercial corn-hog farmer in Iowa.

Kaufman obtained prestige rankings for 1235 people in a rural New York locality from 14 local raters. He reports that most of these judges were of middle or high rank themselves.[25] Kaufman's approach seems highly useful as a means for identifying the social rank of farm people in a particular locality; it cuts through all subsidiary factors and gets to the heart of the matter, and obtains in a single operation the summary judgment of raters concerning the

[24] W. L. Warner and Leo S. Srole, *The Social Systems of American Ethnic Groups,* Yale University Press, 1945.
[25] Kaufman, *op. cit.*

social rank of the person or family. Care must of course be taken to locate qualified raters.

On the basis of his study, Kaufman classified his subjects into 11 prestige categories or classes (Table 14).

TABLE 14.   Prestige Classes in a Rural New York Community

Prestige Classes	Number of Persons	Percent
1	25	2.0
1.5	51	4.1
2	44	3.6
2.5	68	5.5
3	199	16.1
3.5	324	26.4
4	289	23.4
4.5	108	8.7
5	87	7.0
5.5	30	2.4
6	10	0.8
Total	1235	100.0

SOURCE: Harold F. Kaufman, *Prestige Classes in a New York Rural Community,* Cornell University AES Memoir 260, March, 1944, p. 7.

While these classes may seem too minute, they serve a useful purpose because they emphasize that social rank in a rural locality is a matter of degree. Although the tabulation does not show it, not all of the 14 raters agreed on the individuals who should have any specific rank. Such ratings are also subject to alteration. It is important to bear these points in mind when considering the significance of social rank in an American farming community.

OCCUPATION

When compared to other occupations, farming does not carry high social rank. North and Hatt found that farm ownership and operation stood at 39 out of 90 occupations rated in a nationwide sample.[26] In a Kansas study farm owner operators were ranked 50th, tenants 72nd, and farm laborers 86th among 100 occupations rated by high-school and college students.[27] There are also differences within the occupational subclassifications in agriculture. In other parts of the world, the term *peasant* carries a connotation of low rank.

There is a hierarchy of occupations within any society or smaller social system which may differ greatly from one to another major society. In Hindu India, for example, the highest caste is that of the priestly Brahmin, and the lowest that of the sweepers or other untouchables who handle filth. Within American society, if we can accept the information from sampling surveys presented above as valid, the highest rank goes to positions of political and economic power with the professions, technical work, skilled crafts, and manual labor following in order.

Within agriculture there are at present many occupational special-ists, among them dairymen, wheat ranchers, fruit growers, and live-stock ranchers. In addition, there are associated specialties such as entomology, horticulture, dairy herd testing, and veterinary medi-cine. However, these tend to be associated with particular types of agriculture and are not universal. The closest we can come to a universal classification of the rank of basic agricultural occupa-tions at present is probably tenure status.[28] In the U.S., owners generally have higher rank than tenants, although this is not always true. There are several classifications of tenants; the tenant who owns his own machinery and has ample credit would obviously have higher rank than one who owns nothing but a mule. At the bottom are farm laborers, of which there are several types including sharecroppers, year-round or regular workers who have permanent or semipermanent employment on specific farms, and seasonal laborers, both local and migratory. In addition there are, of course, unpaid family laborers, but these seldom have social rank apart from that of the family. Because of the central importance of land

[26] Cecil C. North and Paul K. Hatt, "Jobs and Occupations: A Popular Evaluation," in Logan Wilson and William L. Kolb, eds., *Sociological Analysis*, Harcourt Brace, 1949, pp. 464 ff.

[27] Mapheus Smith, "An Empirical Scale of Prestige Status of Occupations," *American Sociological Review*, April, 1943, pp. 185-192.

[28] See Chapter 16.

tenure to an understanding of the relationships of people to each other and to agricultural land, the subject of land tenure has been discussed at length in Chapter 16.

THE MEANING OF SOCIAL RANK IN A RURAL LOCALITY

Any rural locality may contain a number of social systems.[29] The members will have specific ranks within each system to which they belong. In addition, a person or a family may have a generalized rank, a sort of composite of all his separate ranks, which will be recognized by most people within the range of his acquaintanceship. The generalized rank, however, may be assigned on the basis of a single factor such as occupation, wealth, or skin color. Thus a migratory farm laborer, because of his occupational status, will automatically have very low rank. Normally he will be excluded from all the social systems in an agricultural locality except those involved specifically in the agricultural operations he performs. His children will not be allowed to attend school, and he probably will not be welcome in the church attended by the farm owners. He certainly will not be invited to join any prestige-bound local organizations like Kiwanis or the Rotary Club, nor will he be invited to the homes of his employers. The leading town banker, on the other hand, because of his generalized high social standing will be welcome in most organizations and homes, except, of course, those where a different social philosophy or significantly lower social rank would make his presence unsettling. These will normally be well-known and studiously avoided on both sides.

There is some evidence that people with higher social ranks are more active and take leadership more often in rural organizations than others.[30] However, it does not necesarily follow that formal office holders are always the highest-ranking persons in a social system; they may prefer to be the "power behind the throne" and to manipulate affairs without appearing to do so. Loomis and Beegle

[29] See Chapter 19.
[30] W. A. Anderson, *The Membership of Farmers in New York Organizations,* Cornell University AES Bulletin 695, April, 1938; D. E. Lindstrom, *Forces Affecting Participation of Farm People in Farm Organizations,* Illinois AES Bulletin 423, May, 1936; E. L. Kirkpatrick, *et al., Rural Organizations in the Farm Family,* Wisconsin AES Research Bulletin 96, November, 1929.

present an interesting case study which illustrates this point.[31] In every locality there seem to be some individuals who are looked on as opinion leaders. Usually their approval must be obtained before a program of community action can be successfully carried out. Obviously these legitimizers or opinion leaders hold high social rank within the locality.

SOCIAL MOBILITY

The existence of social stratification in human societies and lesser social systems cannot be questioned. The social rank of an individual within a given system or locality may have a tremendous bearing on the opportunities and patterns of social interaction open to him. Where the stratification is characterized by caste, there is relatively little opportunity for major changes in social rank. On the other extreme, in an open-class society such as exists in the U.S. where social rank depends to a considerable extent upon achievement rather than inherited characteristics, individuals can change their social standing by their own efforts.

In the United States the major channels for upward mobility have come to be occupation and education. These are closely related since specific educational preparation is now required for entry into and subsequent progress in a large number of occupational fields. Education also serves as a means for determining who may advance and who may not, so that it may form the basis of stratification as well as a channel for upward mobility. So far as agriculture is concerned, education probably has less influence than in many other occupational areas, but it is becoming more important. The application of scientific principles to agriculture has made it essential for the progressive farmer in a market economy to have sufficient educational background to keep abreast of rapid technological developments. In addition, gaining an education with emphasis upon agricultural economics and some branch of technical agriculture will prepare a poor farmer's son to become a farm manager, a much higher-ranking position than that of farm laborer to which he might aspire without this training.

Regarding social mobility in America, Lipset denies Vance

[31] C. P. Loomis and J. A. Beegle, *Rural Sociology*, Prentice-Hall, 1947, pp. 195-201.

Packard's allegation in *The Status Seekers* that there has been a decline in social mobility or that the plight of the lowest ranks is worse than it has ever been. A review of the reports of early European travelers in America, says Lipset, indicates that Americans have always been rank-conscious, and he suggests that this may be due in part to the fact that there are no titles of nobility or other generally accepted symbols of social rank.[32]

THE AGRICULTURAL LADDER

The type of vertical mobility of the generation following initial settlement of the midwestern United States has been referred to as moving up the agricultural ladder.[33] In the ideal case, a farm boy who aspired to become an owner began his apprenticeship in agriculture as an unpaid farm laborer on the home farm. At 19 or 20 he obtained a job on a neighboring farm where he worked for cash wages. Since board and lodging was provided, he was able to save most of his wages, with which he purchased a team of horses and some equipment. This enabled him to rent a piece of land which he operated himself. If he was frugal his earnings eventually permitted him to accumulate a down payment and buy a farm of his own, the balance being secured by a mortgage.

A study by Spillman of 2112 owners in Illinois, Iowa, Kansas, Nebraska, and Minnesota reported in 1919 showed that only one-fifth of all the owners in the sample had passed through all four stages of the agricultural ladder. Thirteen percent omitted the tenant stage, 32 percent moved directly from the home farm to the status of tenant, and 34 percent had taken over the operation of the home farm without experience as paid farm laborers or tenants.[34]

Tenure status tends to improve with age. Information from the agricultural census indicates that a substantial portion of white American farmers had attained the status of owner operator by the time they had reached 65 years of age. In 1910, 90 percent of the white farm operators 65 and over in the United States were farm owners. In 1940 the comparable figure was about 87 percent. In

[32] Seymour M. Lipset, "Vance Packard Discovers America," *Reporter*, July 9, 1959, pp. 31-33.

[33] W. J. Spillman, "The Agricultural Ladder," *American Economic Review Supplement*, IX (1919), 170-179.

[34] *Ibid.*

the South, this group at both dates included more than 80 percent
of the white farmers in the region. The situation of southern Negroes
was substantially different; less than 50 percent of those age 65
or over had attained ownership status at either of the two dates.
Smith suggests that the difference is due to the close association of
Negroes with the plantation system coupled with limited training
in the habits, skills, and techniques which are essential for success
in commercial agriculture.[35]

There is ample evidence that the agricultural ladder as a method
of gaining ownership is no longer open to many people. Commercial
agriculture in the U.S. has become very competitive and the amount
of capital required has become great. It is now virtually impossible
for a young man without financial backing or technical agricultural
education to rise unaided from the lowly position of an agricultural
laborer to be the owner operator of a successful commercial farming enterprise. Rogers and Beal allege that about three-fourths of
Iowa farmers "receive their farms by direct lineal descent."[36] This
should not be interpreted to mean that there is no upward mobility
in American agriculture. In addition to inheritance, farms may be
bought with savings from nonfarm employment, and there are a
large number of smaller holdings which can be acquired through
purchase. Many of these are operated on a part-time basis by individuals who hold nonfarm employment.

Nelson is of the opinion, however, that the future mobility from
tenant to owner status in American agriculture is likely to be limited
because of the difficulty of obtaining adequate financing. He suggests that inheritance will be a much more important element in
the future than it has been in the past.[37]

VERTICAL MOBILITY OF RURAL-URBAN MIGRANTS

As noted in the section on migration, there has been and continues to be heavy migration of people out of agriculture into non-

[35] Smith, op. cit., pp. 582-583.

[36] E. M. Rogers and G. M. Beal, Reference Group Influences in the Adoption
of Agricultural Technology, Iowa State College, Department of Economics and
Sociology, 1958, p. 53.

[37] Lowry Nelson, Rural Sociology, 2nd ed., American Book, 1955, pp. 234,
236.

farm employment, most of them no doubt motivated in part by the desire to attain a higher occupational status, more income, and a higher social rank. Some, of course, have achieved high rank; many outstanding public figures in American life boast of a farm background.

The question may be raised as to whether the occupations which farm-reared individuals obtain when they leave the farm are higher in the occupational status hierarchy than farm ownership. The answer is obviously negative. The great majority are young people who generally start at the bottom in any particular occupational sequence. Furthermore, the level at which a new member of the labor force enters an occupation is largely determined by the amount and nature of his education; college graduates, particularly those trained in technological specialties like engineering or technical agriculture, can obviously obtain better-paying employment than high-school graduates with no specialized training. The fact is that many migrants from farms to cities, especially those from the southeastern U.S., are at a relative disadvantage with respect to educational opportunities. This means that when they obtain nonfarm employment it will not be very high up in the occupational status scale.

Research evidence from a number of sources indicates that farm-reared men generally have less occupational success in urban areas than those who are reared in nonfarm homes. Support for this observation comes from Germany in 1895, Sweden in 1954, Kentucky in 1945, California in 1955, and for the United States as a whole in 1956.[38]

PROSPECTS FOR OCCUPATIONAL MOBILITY

A study by Jaffe and Carleton indicates that outside of agriculture most American men do not stay in the same job throughout their occupational career. The work they are doing at the end of their careers may be very different from that in which they began. As they move from occupation to occupation, most have succeeded in climbing at least a few rungs of the occupational ladder, and

[38] See A. O. Haller, "Research Problems on the Occupational Achievement Levels of Farm Reared People," *Rural Sociology*, December, 1958, pp. 355-362.

many ultimately reach jobs considerably higher than those in which they began. The study shows that the majority of men during the past generation have improved both their economic and status levels with advancing age.[39]

As this information pertains to a period of considerable economic and social expansion in the U.S., we must recognize that there has been a general upward bias. The economy has increased tremendously—millions of new jobs have been created; manual labor has to a very appreciable extent been superseded by machine processes both on farms and in factories, and the financial rewards of the workers have been greatly augmented. There has been and is a tremendous demand in industry for additional professional and technological specialties, most of which carry much greater prestige and higher pay than the occupations associated with simpler technology. This is also true in agriculture, particularly in highly commercialized types of farming.

There seems to be little indication at the moment of any substantial future reduction in occupational mobility except perhaps in agriculture, where, as we have said, the traditional channels of upward mobility are restricted. The possibility of accumulating adequate capital to purchase and equip a large enough farm to be a going concern in the economic sense is now beyond the reach of one who starts as a farm laborer and who has no prospect of financial assistance from relatives or friends. However, the investment of nonfarm capital in agriculture and the growing importance of agricultural education indicates that alternative channels of mobility are now available.

The movement of young men and women out of agriculture into nonfarm jobs is likely to continue for a substantial period, and some of these will rise. Nelson has estimated that less than half of the young men who reach maturity on farms will be needed as replacements for farm operators.[40] Furthermore, nonfarm occupations continue to present employment opportunities.

There is likely to be some change in the social rank of any particular migrant if one compares his position in the original and the

[39] A. J. Jaffe and R. O. Carleton, *Occupational Mobility in the United States, 1930-1960*, Kings Crown Press, 1954.

[40] Nelson, *op. cit.*, p. 231.

new social systems. Whether the movement has been up or down will of course depend on the individual case; it is not possible to determine such matters conclusively by reference to a single indicator of social rank such as occupation. As the old saying goes, one may be a big frog in a small puddle, but find himself a small one in a good-sized lake.

The concentration of better farm lands in the hands of a hereditary farming class might have many undesirable implications. At present, however, there are sufficient alternative channels to farm ownership so that this prospect does not appear to constitute any major threat in the United States as a whole.

QUESTIONS FOR FURTHER STUDY AND DISCUSSION

1. Why do agricultural occupations have low rank in the U.S. in view of the tremendous productivity of American commercial farms?
2. Discuss the occupation of farm laborer from the standpoint of social stratification.
3. Why is skin color an element in the determination of social rank? Would you classify American Negroes as a caste? Why or why not?
4. Each member of the class will prepare a written report on the subject of social stratification with special reference to rural America. The report is to have two parts: Part I will deal with stratification theories and will be based on your reading of the text plus one or more references; Part II will present an analysis of social stratification in your home locality (neighborhood or community). Reports will be presented in class and may be collected by the instructor.
5. What changes do you expect in rural stratification in the next 25 years?

SELECTED REFERENCES

Davis, Kingsley, *The Population of India and Pakistan,* Princeton University Press, 1951.

Dube, S. C., *Indian Village,* Routledge & Kegan Paul, 1955.

Kaufman, Harold F., *Prestige Classes in a New York Rural Community,* Cornell University AES Memoir 260, March, 1944.

Loomis, C. P., and J. A. Beegle, *Rural Social Systems,* Prentice-Hall, 1950.

Loomis, C. P., and J. A. Beegle, *Rural Sociology,* Prentice-Hall, 1957.

Nelson, Lowry, *Rural Sociology,* 2nd ed., American Book, 1955.

Smith, T. Lynn, *The Sociology of Rural Life,* 3rd ed., Harper, 1953.

18

Informal Primary Groups

The significant types of informal primary groups in which contemporary farm people participate are friendship groups, kinship groups, work-related groups, and factions. An informal primary group can be defined as a group other than a family involving two or more persons which is characterized by face-to-face relationships and some continuity but is without elected officers or a formal written constitution and bylaws.

There is little doubt that informal primary groups are of fundamental importance in all contemporary societies in the socialization process, in providing emotional security to members, and in furnishing communication channels. Even in formal agencies and organizations, they are sometimes more influential in making policy and dispensing favors than the formal bureaucratic channels depicted by organization charts. Furthermore, the number of informal primary groups is undoubtedly much greater in any society than the number of formal agencies and organizations.

Because they have no formal organizational structure, informal primary groups are not always easy to identify. Some, like criminal groups, are actually secret and nearly impossible to detect, much less to study. Some may be of long duration while others may exist only for short periods. Informal groups may vary in size, but range from a definite lower limit of 2 to a flexible upper limit of 15 to 30. Most are quite small.

All informal primary groups arise out of direct face-to-face interaction within a specific locale. Most are probably maintained through face-to-face relationships, although letters and telephone conversations can undoubtedly be used for communication.

While the volume is probably less than a generation ago, a new type of informal association with neighbors that preserves many of the same characteristics has come into being. This is the informal gathering that occurs before and after the meetings of voluntary formal organizations.[1]

Informal primary groups may be important as reference groups; that is, those of considerable duration may develop traditions and common values which subsequently influence the members not only in their relationships with others within the group but also in associations outside it.[2]

KINSHIP SYSTEMS AMONG FARMERS

The bonds of kinship, whether through birth or marriage, are still powerful in contemporary rural America, though they may be less strong than in earlier days. The customs and values stressed may differ somewhat from one kinship group to another.

In American genealogy, the male rather than the female line of descent has usually been emphasized, a patriarchal pattern that is part of the cultural heritage. It is related to the custom that requires the wife to take the husband's surname and to the custom of property inheritance through the male line. However, the fact that a wife takes her husband's surname does not mean that she thereby renounces her own kinship ties or that these are subsequently of less importance to her.

In early rural America, kinship ties were very important. Kolb and Brunner indicate that neighborhood settlements of kinfolk were common on the frontier. People frequently migrated in company with relatives, and letters and visits to the old home served to maintain contacts with kin left behind.[3]

Dependence on kinfolk for economic assistance and emotional

---

[1] See Alicja Iwanska, *Good Fortune: Second Chance Community*, Washington AES Bulletin 589, June, 1958, p. 24.

[2] See R. K. Merton and A. S. Kitt, "Contributions to the Theory of Reference Group Behavior," in R. K. Merton, ed., *Continuities in Social Research*, Free Press, 1950; S. M. Eisenstadt, "Reference Group Behavior and Social Integration," *American Sociological Review*, April, 1954, pp. 175-185.

[3] John H. Kolb and Edmund deS. Brunner, *A Study of Rural Society*, 4th ed., Houghton Mifflin, 1952, p. 141.

security is by no means a thing of the past. Kinship ties are still numerous and important to rural people, though the degree will differ between localities.

There has been no comprehensive nationwide investigation of the prevalence or significance of kinship ties among either rural or urban Americans. The subject has been included, however, as an incidental part of a substantial number of studies by rural sociologists. The findings of some of these studies are presented briefly here as the best available basis for appraising the importance of kinship ties.

During the early 1940s, the Bureau of Agricultural Economics of the United States Department of Agriculture made several studies of contemporary rural communities in which this subject was included. Five are cited here.

EL CERRITO, NEW MEXICO, A SPANISH-AMERICAN COMMUNITY

Olen Leonard lived five months and Charles Loomis three months in the village of El Cerrito. Both of them spoke Spanish fluently, and consequently were able to communicate readily with the residents.

On the basis of their study, they concluded that kinship was the chief factor affecting the frequency of social interaction in the village.[4] This observation is illustrated by a sociogram from their report which shows the pattern of visiting between relatives (Fig. 20).

THE OLD ORDER AMISH OF LANCASTER COUNTY, PENNSYLVANIA

Walter Kollmorgen and his sister lived in this Amish community for four months. Both spoke German and evidently achieved a high degree of rapport with the Amish, for Carl C. Taylor states that they "probably came as near to developing the status of participant observers as is possible without being members of the Amish Church."

[4] Olen Leonard and C. P. Loomis, *Culture of a Contemporary Rural Community: El Cerrito, New Mexico*, U.S. Department of Agriculture, Bureau of Agricultural Economics, Rural Life Studies: No. 1, November, 1941, Washington, D. C.

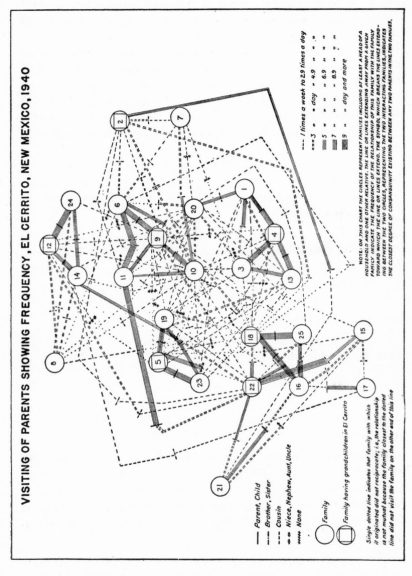

VISITING OF PARENTS SHOWING FREQUENCY, EL CERRITO, NEW MEXICO, 1940

——— Parent, Child
–·–·– Brother, Sister
–··–··– Cousin
-+--+ Niece, Nephew, Aunt, Uncle
+++++ None

◯ Family
⊡ Family having grandchildren in El Cerrito

Single dotted line indicates that family with which
it originated did not reciprocate; i.e., the relationship
is not mutual because the family closest to the dotted
line did not visit the family on the other end of this line

NOTE: ON THIS CHART THE CIRCLES REPRESENT FAMILIES INCLUDING AT LEAST A HEAD OF A
HOUSEHOLD AND ONE OTHER RELATIVE. THE LINE OR LINES EXTENDING AWAY FROM A GIVEN
FAMILY INDICATE THE FREQUENCY OF THE RELATIONSHIP OF THIS FAMILY WITH THE FAMILY
TOWARD WHICH THE LINE OR LINES EXTEND. THE SYMBOL WHICH BREAKS THE LINES EXTEND-
ING BETWEEN THE TWO CIRCLES, REPRESENTING THE TWO INTERACTING FAMILIES, INDICATES
THE CLOSEST DEGREE OF CONSANGUINITY EXISTING BETWEEN ANY TWO PARENTS IN THE TWO FAMILIES.

––– 1 times a week to 2.9 times a day
=== 3 "   "   " day " 4.9   "   "   "   "
≡≡≡ 5 "   "   "   "   " 6.9   "   "   "   "
≣≣≣ 7 "   "   "   "   " 8.9   "   "   "   "
▐▐▐ 9 "   "   "   "   " day and more

FIG. 20.

On the basis of personal observation, Kollmorgen had the following to say with respect to the significance of kinship in this community: "All the Amish have a wide Freundschaft—many relatives—and it is taken for granted that at least the near kinfolks must be visited as often as possible. Parents and grandparents made it a point to visit all children and grandchildren at least several times a year. As only every second Sunday is really available for family visits and as children and grandchildren are usually numerous, most of these people are behind in what they consider an ideal visiting schedule."[5]

IRWIN, IOWA

Carl C. Taylor was born and reared on a farm near the community and lived there until 1931, and Edward O. Moe lived as a participant observer in the Irwin community for four months. On the basis of this knowledge of the community, the authors wrote that kinship was the most important factor in determining visiting relationships.[6]

SOUTH HOLLAND, ILLINOIS

South Holland is described as an old, cohesive community, dominated largely by ethnic and religious factors. Dodson obtained his information by means of personal interviews, attendance at public meetings, discussions with teachers and officials, and life histories. He found kinship relationships to be extremely important. In fact, he wrote that more than half of the population belonged to four extended family groups: "Most of the families in the village have so many relatives to visit that they haven't the time or the desire to visit their nearest neighbors."[7]

[5] Walter M. Kollmorgen, *Culture of a Contemporary Rural Community: The Older Order Amish of Lancaster County, Pennsylvania*, USDA, Bureau of Agricultural Economics, Rural Life Studies No. 4, September, 1942, pp. 1, 57.

[6] Edward O. Moe and Carl C. Taylor, *Culture of a Contemporary Rural Community: Irwin, Iowa*, USDA, Bureau of Agricultural Economics, Rural Life Studies No. 5, 1942.

[7] L. S. Dodson, *Social Relationships and Institutions in an Established Rurban Community: South Holland, Illinois*, USDA, Social Research Report No. XVI, February, 1939, p. 14.

HAMILTON COUNTY, IOWA

More recent information for Hamilton County, Iowa, was obtained from a study by Jehlik and Wakeley of a sample of 273 families in the Webster City trade area community in 1944. The authors concluded that kinship groups were probably more important than is often recognized. They commented that not infrequently acceptance or rejection of an organizational activity by key families was responsible for the difference between strength and weakness of that particular organized effort.[8]

OTHER STUDIES

Other investigations have reported similar findings. In a study of a stable residential area in the Missouri Ozarks, Almack and Hepple found kinship bonds especially important when relatives lived close enough together to maintain daily contacts.[9] In three rural New York areas, W. A. Anderson found that kinfolks comprised nearly half of the families with which informal activities were carried on.[10] In highly urbanized Connecticut, Riecken and Whetten found kinship more important among the foreign-born than among "old Yankee stock."[11] Stone and Slocum found kinship ties of major significance to older residents of Thurston County, Washington, even though few lived in the homes of their children.[12] Hanna found that 78 percent of farm families interviewed in a Kentucky locality visited relatives more frequently than they did friends.[13] Kinship relationships are also of paramount importance among agriculturists

[8] Paul J. Jehlik and Ray E. Wakeley, *Rural Organization in Process: A Case Study of Hamilton County, Iowa*, Iowa AES Research Bulletin 365, September, 1949, p. 166.

[9] Ronald B. Almack and Lawrence M. Hepple, *Rural Social Organization in Dent County, Missouri*, Missouri AES Research Bulletin 458, August, 1950, p. 36.

[10] W. A. Anderson, *Some Factors Associated with Family Informal Participation*, Cornell University AES Bulletin 36, March, 1953, pp. 7, 8.

[11] Henry W. Riecken and Nathan L. Whetten, *Rural Social Organization in Litchfield County, Connecticut*, Storrs AES Bulletin 261, May, 1948, p. 120.

[12] Carol L. Stone and W. L. Slocum, *A Look at Thurston County's Older People*, Washington AES Bulletin 573, May, 1957.

[13] E. B. Hanna, *The Integration of Locality Groups in an Eastern Kentucky County*, Kentucky AES Bulletin 640, February, 1956, p. 48.

in other parts of the world. In Pakistan, where 85 percent of the population lives in agricultural villages, the extended family is of basic importance. In fact, cousin marriages are the ideal sought by the Muslim majority.[14] Dube also found kinship relations of major significance in his study of an Indian village.[15]

FRIENDSHIPS AND CLIQUES

Friendships are based on common interests and values, and develop among other ways at work and around recreational activities. The smallest and probably the most common friendship group is, of course, a dyad. Friendship groups may, however, include more than two people, in which case they may be called cliques by nonmembers. Such groups have various names. Loomis and Beegle comment on this saying, "In some places one speaks of his 'crowd', in other places one may speak of one's 'set', 'neighbors', 'group', 'friends', and so forth."[16] The authors present material from empirical studies by Loomis, and use sociograms to illustrate cliques. Loomis and Beegle have severely criticized other rural sociologists for failing to emphasize the importance of small social systems, observing that neighborhoods or villages may contain a number of smaller informal social systems, including cliques and factions.[17]

Friendships may be quite transitory in duration or may last for a long time. Friendship groups are of many types—teen-age gangs, bridge clubs, poker groups, various mutual aid groups, hunting and fishing groups. Arensburg has given an interesting account of the role structure of a rural Irish clique,[18] but not many studies of such groups have been reported.

Friendship groups are valuable networks of communication and influence in rural society. Loomis and Beegle consider that the leaders in cliques and friendship groups are of great importance as

[14] W. L. Slocum, Jamila Akhtar, and Abrar Fatima Sahi, *Village Life in Lahore District*, Lahore, Social Sciences Research Center, Panjab University Press, 1959.

[15] S. C. Dube, *Indian Village*, Routledge & Kegan Paul, 1955, p. 135.

[16] C. P. Loomis and J. A. Beegle, *Rural Social Systems*, Prentice-Hall, 1950, p. 134.

[17] *Ibid.*, pp. 137-149, 156-171.

[18] Conrad Arensburg, *The Irish Countryman*, Macmillan, 1937.

information channels for the Agricultural Extension Service and other educational and action agencies.[19] This is probably correct, but it is not always easy to identify clearly who the influential clique leaders are, and it does not necessarily follow that they would be regarded as opinion leaders for all types of activities. Barnett and Mayo have suggested that farm neighborhood cliques, or neighbor groups as they call them, are important for extension work.[20]

FACTIONS

Factions are conflict groups. Where found in a rural setting, they may be characterized as "we" groups which derive their significance from their opposition to other "we" groups. They may survive for long periods with changing leaders and may oppose each other over different issues at different times.

Rural sociological studies in the U.S. seldom report factions, although evidence from novels and other sources about celebrated rural feuds indicates their existence. To some extent, this failure to study rural conflict groups may reflect a professional bias in favor of cooperative activities, but it more likely indicates the empirical situation. The energies of American farmers are focused on economic competition in an impersonal market rather than upon personal strife.

This evidently is not the case in all parts of the world. In India and Pakistan, for example, factions are apparently found frequently in agricultural villages. A Pakistani sociology student cited an authority who alleged that three-fourths of the villages in the Panjab were dominated by factions.[21]

Following is a report of factional and intervillage strife in some villages in West Pakistan:

Active factions were found in two of the six villages. In the village which had a large proportion of refugees, no active factions existed at

[19] Loomis and Beegle, *op. cit.*, p. 156.

[20] W. E. Barnett and Selz C. Mayo, *Neighbor Groups*, North Carolina AES Progress Report No. RS-14, June, 1952.

[21] Mohammed Iqbal, *Factionalism as a Hindrance to Cooperation . . .* , unpublished M.A. thesis, Lahore, University of the Panjab, Department of Sociology, 1959.

the time the field work was conducted. Conflict apparently had been confined to individuals or families.

Village B, which had a long record of hostile relations with neighbouring villages, had no factions. There were some reports of sex irregularities, abductions and cattle stealing. It appears, however, that external conflict operated to minimize internal strife which might have resulted from these events.

Village F had a long history of factional strife, first between two parties of Rajputs and second between Muslims and Christians. The conflict between the Rajput factions had existed for 30 years but was diminishing in intensity due to new leadership. Reconciliation was indicated by some cases of inter-marriage between the factions. The conflict between Muslims and Christians, also of long standing, was still virulent. Most of the Christians were agricultural labourers. During the pre-partition period, the British were reported to have interceded in favour of the Christians at the request of the Christian Bishop. After partition, the position of the Christian faction was said to have deteriorated and many had shifted to non-agricultural occupations. Some were employed outside the village.

Village G also had a long history of factions. In this village, the attempts of one sect to convert members of the other led to strife but eventually a substantial victory was achieved. A significant number of the members of one sect were converted and others left the village.

Villages Q and J did not have a recent history of factional strife. Conflict situations had been confined largely to individuals.

The functions of factional groups are primarily destructive although they do result in co-operation and social cohesion within the factions.[22]

Dhillon has said of Indian villages, "The factions are hostile and aggressive groups, which are constantly quarreling and as a result of which the village remains like a house divided against itself. . . ."[23]

WORK EXCHANGE

To the extent that agriculture is dominated by family enterprises which employ no outside labor, work relationships are, of course, entirely within the family. In contemporary commercial agriculture, at least in the U.S., this is seldom the case. Although relatively few

[22] Slocum, Akhtar, and Sahi, *op. cit.*, pp. 30-31.
[23] Harvant Singh Dhillon, *Leadership and Groups in a South Indian Village*, New Delhi Planning Commission Evaluation Organization, 1955, p. 30.

farm operators employ substantial numbers of hired workers, most establish business relationships with agricultural specialists—pest- or insect-control firms, fertilizing services, veterinarians, marketing agencies such as cooperatives, or in the case of contract agriculture, the feed dealer, the sugar beet factory, or the cannery.

While work exchange is diminishing in the U.S. because farmers are acquiring more adequate machinery, it is still quite important in many sections of the country. Some of the evidence on this follows.

In a recent study by personal interview with a statewide proba- bility sample of 314 Washington farm families, 60 percent of the operators indicated that they exchanged work with one or more other farmers. The distribution of responses showed, however, that relatively few farmers were involved in work exchange groups; in fact, less than 12.8 percent exchanged work with as many as four others.[24] Hanna found little labor exchange in Magoffin County, Kentucky, but cited instances of emergency assistance to neighbors.[25]

Alexander and Nelson in 1949 found many work-exchange groups in Goodhue County, Minnesota. They state that most of the "work- rings [vary] from three to six or seven farmers although sometimes a ring may have as many as a dozen members. . . . Examination of a number of rings showed the following factors to be involved: compatibility; convenience in terms of propinquity; marriage or blood relationship; proximity of smaller operators to a large one who owns machinery; and ownership by each member of the group of a different machine which all need at some time. Perhaps the most important of these factors is convenience, based on nearness."[26]

Almack and Hepple reported a considerable amount of exchange of work or machinery in Dent County, Missouri.[27]

It should not be concluded on the basis of the foregoing examples that work exchange is universal. As a matter of fact, it probably is

[24] Walter L. Slocum, Owen L. Brough, Jr., and Murray A. Straus, *Extension Contacts, Selected Characteristics, Practices and Attitudes of Washington Farm Families*, Washington AES Bulletin 584, October, 1958, p. 10.

[25] Hanna, *op. cit.*, p. 47.

[26] Frank D. Alexander and Lowry Nelson, *Rural Social Organization, Good- hue County*, Minnesota AES Bulletin 401, February, 1949, p. 59.

[27] Almack and Hepple, *op. cit.*, p. 20.

relatively infrequent among operators of large commercial farms and ranches. Such operations tend to be self-contained with respect to both labor and machinery, and rely little, if at all, upon the resources of other farmers or ranchers.

YOUTH GROUPS

Although relatively little systematic study has been given to informal youth groups in rural America, fragmentary information indicates that such associations are numerous, although perhaps not so prevalent as friendship groups in rural nonfarm and urban areas. In the early years of childhood, farm children associate with others of comparable age on interfamily visits and in play situations with youngsters who live reasonably nearby. Obviously children who are reared on dispersed farmsteads have less opportunity for this type of interaction than those in villages, towns, or cities.

As soon as the children are old enough to attend school, however, this deficiency is remedied to a very large extent, especially in consolidated schools. Associations with others of the same age in school is generally considered to be extremely important and to have a tremendous impact upon the conduct of the child in the school, on the playground, and at home, since children communicate with each other. It is believed that such interaction frequently forms the basis for challenges to family values and authority patterns.

In a recent study of the activities of teen-agers in the state of Washington, informal friendships with other youngsters were by far the most common form of association, formal or informal, identified by the respondents of every grade from 7 to 12.[28] Some of the work done by sociologists and others in urban areas illustrates the significance of association in "gangs," some of which may be thought of as formal rather than informal groups.

With later adolescence, informal associations with members of the opposite sex come to be relatively common through the American custom of dating. This pattern is prevalent in urban and rural areas both, and performs a useful function in assisting young people to ascertain the extent of their interest in each other as possible

[28] See W. L. Slocum and Carol L. Stone, *Activities and Interests of Teenagers,* reports on four school communities, Washington AES, 1958. (Mimeo)

marriage partners as well as providing socially approved hetero-sexual companionship with little or no idea of eventual matrimony.

QUESTIONS FOR FURTHER STUDY AND DISCUSSION

1. Make an inventory of all of the informal primary groups in your home locality. Classify these groups according to the major bond.
2. Describe relationships between your family and close relatives. Indicate the location of these relatives, the frequency of interfamily visits, and the nature of interaction.
3. Investigate the prevalence of work exchange among farmers in a rural locality. Note the type of work and number of farmers involved.
4. Ask about the existence of factions in a rural locality. If you discover any, find out as much as possible about the reasons for them and their influence on interaction patterns in the locality.

SELECTED REFERENCES

Arensburg, Conrad, *The Irish Countryman,* Macmillan, 1937.
Loomis, C. P., and J. A. Beegle, *Rural Social Systems,* Prentice-Hall, 1950.

19

Rural Communities

The dominance of the metropolis in western countries, the United States included, is well known. As our cities have grown, the pervasive influence of urban ways has changed the patterns of farm families and communities.

The onward sweep of urban ideas and standards of behavior has all but wiped out the small, isolated, self-contained rural community in the U.S. American folklore tends to idealize the presumed virtues of this relatively simple social system with its intimate and enduring patterns of social life, its puritanical mores, and its subsistence economy. Some even yearn nostalgically for its restoration, forgetting that it was not an unmixed blessing. As Howard Beers has reminded us, "It was a place of neighboring—but gossip could be petty and not always kindly. It was a place where many hearts were warm and some of the minds were narrow. It was a place of security, but the restraints of convention were often oppressive. It was a place where life was whole, to be sure, but sometimes life was also small."[1]

The small, relatively simple community has been superseded by a plurality of new social systems. The range of contacts of country people has expanded. They have greater mobility and broader interests, which leads them to make common cause with others besides those who live on adjacent farms. As in the city, specialization is the order of the day, and this has given rise to many specialized groups within local communities. Furthermore, most rural people, like their urban brethren, live segmented lives, giving al-

---

[1] Howard W. Beers, "American Communities," in *The Community School*, Chicago, National Society for the Study of Education, 1953, p. 17.

legiance in greater or lesser degree to each of the many social systems in which they participate. Contacts are frequently casual and impersonal. Outside the intimate circle of kinfolk and close friends, they have little chance to come to know one another as "whole persons" in the way that was common in the little community of yesteryear.

WHAT IS A COMMUNITY?

There are many definitions of the community in the sociological literature,[2] and no two are exactly alike. In addition, the concept is used in a variety of ways in everyday speech: we hear and read of the school community, the business community, the North Atlantic community, the town-country community. Some are large, others small.

The term has so many meanings that some sociologists have seriously advocated dropping it from sociological usage and replacing it with other concepts.[3] This does not seem to be a practicable solution—a concept with such wide usage can neither be dropped abruptly nor altered radically. Moreover, there seems to be a common core of meaning even though specific applications of the term may vary. It gives recognition to the existence of common interests among people who live in the same area.

Sociologically speaking, the concept has other important connotations, including the dimensions of time and space, the presence of networks of social interaction, and a psychological bond or sense of belonging. The problem of definition may be difficult largely because communities are actually of many different kinds, and because in modern urbanized America even a rural person may simultaneously be a member of more than one community. Thus, it seems appropriate to think of rural communities rather than of

[2] See R. M. MacIver, *Society: A Text Book of Sociology*, Farrar and Rinehart, 1937, pp. 8-9; Dwight Sanderson, *The Rural Community*, Ginn, 1932; C. J. Galpin, *The Social Anatomy of an Agricultural Community*, Wisconsin AES Research Bulletin 34, May, 1915.

[3] Frank D. Alexander, "The Problem of Locality-Group Classification," *Rural Sociology*, September 1952, p. 237; Selz Mayo and Robert McD. Bobbitt, *Rural Organization: A Restudy of Locality Groups in Wake County, North Carolina*, North Carolina AES Technical Bulletin 95, September, 1951.

the rural community which was typical of an earlier and simpler time.

Howard Beers has identified the following salient features of communities: "Our communities are locations in space; they have physical layouts and patterns of habitation discernible to the eye and noted as pleasing or not pleasing. They have roots in nature— environments of resources. They have traditions and history. They are theaters in which people play various roles. They have systems of business, politics, religion, and education. They have social networks of families, cliques, clubs, and classes. They have patterns of harmony and dissension. They have value systems—or patterns of feeling and conviction."[4]

The lack of emphasis in Beer's listing on identification of members with their communities is a striking omission; a sense of belonging seems essential in an integrated social system. However, the omission is consistent with much usage. The concept of community is frequently used in common parlance to refer to local areas rather than to an integrated social system within a definite locality. The term *community organization* is used for the processes through which people who live together in a locality are made aware of common interests and led to take social action for the solution of common problems. Thus, we should acknowledge that the term *community* may refer to latent social systems as well as to those which are manifestly social entities in the full sense.

COMMUNITY SUBCULTURE

Every local community has a history of development which is shared only by its members. There may be unique local values and other norms some of which may be regarded as distasteful or even immoral by outsiders. So distinctive are these culture patterns at times that certain communities may be described as having dominant traits of character; one may be thought of as liberal and another conservative, while a third may be characterized as having lax moral standards. Vogt and O'Dea have called attention to the contrast between the stress on community cooperation in one south-

[4] Beers, *op. cit.*, p. 20.

western community and the emphasis upon individual independence in another.[5]

The diversity of community subculture in America must be interpreted against the backdrop of common values shared by all members of the society. This has been called the American creed. It emphasizes equality of economic opportunity, fairness in legal treatment, political democracy, universal education through high school, religious freedom, respect for individual differences of opinion, and a puritanical cast in its codes of morality.[6]

The study of the subculture of a community is a matter of great practical interest to new residents, salesmen, and other individuals who have contact with its people. Knowledge of community values is also very important to the agricultural extension services and other agencies concerned with adult education, cultural change, or community development.[7]

LOCALITY-BASED COMMUNITIES

In this chapter we will focus our attention on three types of local communities in which rural people may participate: neighborhoods, villages, and town-country communities. All three have definite physical boundaries, although they may differ in other important ways.

The common locality dimension raises an important question: what is the influence of physical proximity on the interaction patterns of rural people?

This question, put in various ways, has received a great deal of attention from American rural sociologists; a considerable amount of the research conducted during the past 25 or 30 years has dealt with social organization in rural localities. However, there is still much disagreement about the prevalence and significance of locality groups.

Research data indicate that the answer to our question is not

[5] Evon Z. Vogt and Thomas F. O'Dea, "A Comparative Study of the Role of Values in Social Action in Two Southwestern Communities," *American Sociological Review*, December, 1955, p. 649.

[6] See Arnold Rose, *The Negro in America*, Harper, 1948, chap. 1; Beers, *op. cit.*, p. 27.

[7] See Chapter 25.

simple. It is probably correct to say that nearly all interaction, formal and informal, is affected to some extent by the physical proximity of those who are interacting, but it is also true that other factors, such as social distances or the nature of common interests and values, are more influential.

In contemporary rural America, physical proximity to other farmers or to towns is obviously much less important than it was during the horse and buggy days that preceded the development and widespread adoption of the automobile. Nearly every American farm family has at least one automobile or truck, and many have more than one. With modern transportation and communication facilities, the social contacts of the American farmer and members of his family are not restricted to those who live on nearby farms. Furthermore, interfarm and rural-urban migration has greatly affected families and communities.

Contemporary studies made in various parts of the United States indicate that there tends to be considerable interaction between people whose residences are physically close to each other. Neighbor groups (cliques) and open-country neighborhoods exist in many localities; furthermore, farm people frequently consider themselves to be members of a local community which includes their principal trade center.

OPEN-COUNTRY NEIGHBORHOODS

The open-country neighborhood is a relatively simple type of community. While they are not unique to the United States, they are not a universal phenomenon. Most agricultural people in other countries live in villages, although some dispersed farmsteads are found in many countries.[8] Empirical neighborhood studies on a worldwide basis are not available, but similar locality groups certainly occur to some extent wherever dispersed farmsteads form the pattern of settlement.

The forms of contemporary rural American neighborhoods vary greatly. The range extends from the well-structured, clearly articulated neighborhoods typical of pioneer areas in the North to the almost total lack of community consciousness within a local area

[8] See Chapter 6, "Patterns of Settlement."

in portions of the urban fringe. Even with such variation, however, the closely knit, traditional open-country neighborhood is an important concept. It is useful as a standard by which to evaluate the character of the relationships existing in any particular locality.

Contemporary rural sociologists generally agree that some neighborhoods are to be found in most sections of the country, but that neighborhoods were more prevalent and sociologically more important in early America than they are at the present time.

What is a neighhborhood?

A neighborhood can be defined as an interacting group of families and individuals residing in a particular locality, most of whom consider themselves to be members of a distinctive neighborhood group which comprises all or most of the families within a definite and contiguous geographic area. Although a neighborhood is likely to be characterized by neighborly relationships such as visiting between families and various forms of mutual aid, conflict may exist between members. In fact, there may be bitter feuds and disagreements between individual families or opposing groups or factions of families within the neighborhood as a whole.

More important than any other factor in the opinion of the present writer is the matter of social consciousness. An area should not be regarded sociologically as a neighborhood unless most of the people who live within its boundaries consider that they are members of a neighborhood, think of it as a cohesive social unit, and act accordingly. Even so, there are unquestionably many degrees of social cohesiveness depending upon the intensity and frequency of the interaction among the members and the number of neighborhood interests which serve to cement it together—church, school, Grange, and other organizations and agencies.

J. H. Kolb's studies of rural neighborhoods in Dane County, Wisconsin, are of great importance in the development of rural sociology. Repeated at 10-year intervals, they cover a time span of more than 30 years. The first study was published in 1921 by the Wisconsin Agricultural Experiment Station under the title *Rural Primary Groups*. Neighborhoods were delineated on the basis of neighborhood names supplied farm families on a card distributed and collected by elementary-school children. "The theory was that when a family recognized some grouping as its own, and was willing to confess this name as it would its own family name, there was evidence of group consciousness and unity."[9] This was the question:

By what name is the country neighborhood called in which you live?
We do not mean the name of the township nor the name of the nearby village or city, nor even necessarily, though it may be, the name of your district school, but we do mean the name of the country locality or neighborhood in which your home is located. Some such names in the country are Albion Prairie, Spring Valley, Pierceville, Springfield Corners, etc.[10]

After the 1950-1951 restudy, Kolb concluded that names were not so dependable as they had been 30 years earlier as a basis for identifying neighborhoods.[11]

The boundaries of the 1921 neighborhoods were tentatively identified by mapping the family responses. In addition, a responsible person in each neighborhood was interviewed to verify the boundaries and to gather information about neighborhood history and current conditions. Although there were some interstitial areas without neighborhood consciousness, most farm families in 1921 considered that they were members of definite neighborhoods with well-established names. Analysis of the nature of neighborhood contacts revealed that 85 percent of the contacts in order of frequency were religious, educational, social, or economic.[12]

Similar studies of open-country neighborhoods were made in the early 1920s in Otsego County, New York, by Sanderson and Thompson;[13] in Wake County, North Carolina, by Taylor and Zimmerman;[14] in Ravalli County, Montana, by Baumgartel;[15] and in Boone County, Missouri, by Morgan and Howells.[16] Neighborhoods were found to

[9] J. H. Kolb, *Rural Primary Groups,* Wisconsin AES Research Bulletin 51, December, 1921.

[10] *Ibid.*

[11] J. H. Kolb, *Emerging Rural Communities,* University of Wisconsin Press, 1959.

[12] *Ibid.,* pp. 30-31.

[13] Dwight Sanderson and Warren S. Thompson, *Social Areas of Otsego County,* Cornell University AES Research Bulletin 422, July, 1923.

[14] Carl C. Taylor and Carl C. Zimmerman, *Rural Organization,* North Carolina AES Bulletin 245, 1922.

[15] Walter H. Baumgartel, *A Social Study of Ravalli County, Montana,* Montana AES Bulletin 160, 1923.

[16] E. L. Morgan and Owen Howells, *Rural Population Groups,* Missouri AES Research Bulletin 74, 1925.

vary in both form and function in the different areas studied.

These investigators did not regard rural neighborhoods as fixed or permanent. In the words of Kolb, "Society is never a fixed or static thing and rural society is no exception. Even as one would describe and map these rural groups, changes appear and differing characteristics manifest themselves."[17]

Although these early studies emphasized locality bonds, recognition was soon given to the growing importance of special interests as a basis for the organization of rural life. In 1927, Kolb and Wileden wrote: "Fundamental changes are taking place in rural group relations, locality no longer holds country people to such restricted social or business contacts. . . . neighborhood groups are no longer the important organization units."[18]

While the Dane County record is doubtless unique in many respects, the findings of 30 years of change are of general interest. Kolb found a trend toward a decline in the number of neighborhoods, but he noted that some neighborhoods had persisted as relatively stable social entities throughout the period covered by his studies (compare Figs. 21a and 21b). The early importance of proximity of residence, nationality or kinship ties, and friendly "neighboring" gave way to deliberate choice, organized relationships, and special interests as the major forces maintaining neighborhoods. Kolb has pointed out that neighborhoods are to be regarded as "'part and parcel of a complex of intergroup relations'" rather than as self-contained and self-sufficient social systems.[19]

In the 1950-1951 restudy, attention was focused on the significance of neighborhoods for member families. This study revealed that neighborhood families had a greater number of personalized and localized contacts than nonmember families; however, members were unequally involved in neighborhood activities at different times even though they had been continuous residents. With respect to the cognitive meaning of neighborhood relationships to member families, Kolb found evidence which "suggested" that neighborhoods were important to their family members and that these influences

---

[17] Kolb, *Rural Primary Groups, op. cit.*, p. 31.

[18] J. H. Kolb and A. F. Wileden, *Special Interest Groups in Rural Society,* Wisconsin AES Research Bulletin 84, December, 1927, p. 1.

[19] Kolb, *Emerging Rural Communities, op. cit.*, pp. 42, 61.

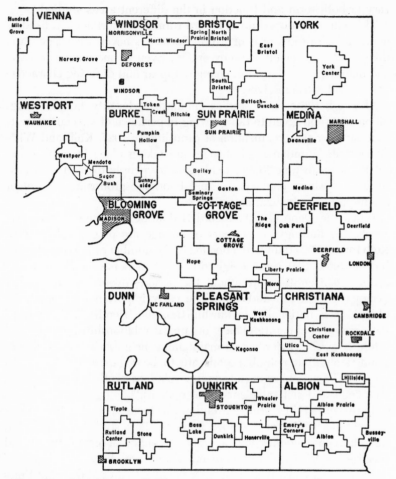

Fig. 21. Neighborhood Changes in Dane County, Wisconsin, East Division, 1920-1950.

A. Neighborhoods Active in 1920.

were expressed both in attitudes and in patterns of social participation.[20]

Recent studies in several widely separated sections of the U.S. raise doubts about the prevalence and social significance of the tra-

[20] *Ibid.*, pp. 72, 76-77, 79.

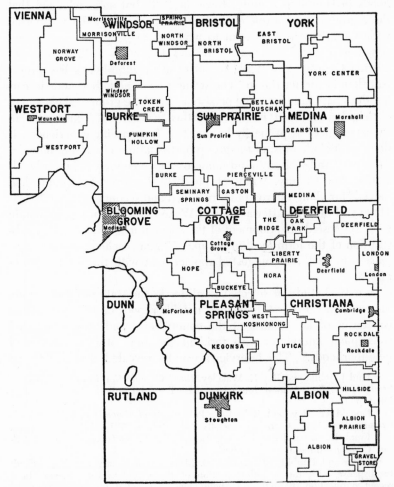

B. Neighborhoods Active in 1950. (J. H. Kolb, *Neighborhood-Family Relations in Rural Society,* Wisconsin AES Research Bulletin 201, 1957.)

ditional type of neighborhood in contemporary rural America. Jehlik and Losey concluded that neighborhoods had been substantially supplanted as "meaningful areas of social togetherness" in Henry County, Indiana.[21] Jehlik and Wakeley found 180 neighbor-

[21] Paul J. Jehlik and J. Edwin Losey, *Rural Social Organization in Henry County, Indiana,* Purdue University AES Bulletin 568, November, 1951, p. 57.

hoods in Hamilton County, Iowa, in 1949, but acknowledged that these groups "play a role of declining importance."[22] They reported wide variations in the extent to which farm people identify themselves with neighborhoods. Hay and Polson in a 1951 study of Oneida County, New York, found rural neighborhoods less prevalent than in former times: "The strong role of neighborhoods in earlier days has made for some persistence of these groups. Place names of neighborhoods survived; . . . but this awareness of 'common locality experiences' is primarily limited to a few specific experiences. It does not include most of the group participations of rural families."[23] Alexander and Nelson found numerous open-country neighborhoods in Goodhue County, Minnesota, in 1949; however, the county had moved "far along the road to formalized and secondary group life."[24] Mayo and Bobbitt, after a study of Wake County, North Carolina, in 1951, suggested abandonment of the concept *neighborhood* and substitution of the term *locality group*.[25] Hanna reached a similar conclusion in 1956 and suggested replacement with the term *community*.[26]

In a 1953 study of selected localities in the state of Washington, Slocum and Case first delineated neighborhoods on the basis of the concensus of lay experts at the county level and then conducted subsequent interviews with residents in some of these presumed neighborhoods.[27] The interviews usually revealed that substantial

[22] Paul J. Jehlik and Ray E. Wakeley, *Rural Organization in Process: A Case Study of Hamilton County, Iowa,* Iowa AES Research Bulletin 365, September, 1949, p. 126.

[23] Donald G. Hay and Robert A. Polson, *Rural Organizations in Oneida County, New York,* Cornell University AES Bulletin 871, May, 1951, p. 18.

[24] Frank D. Alexander and Lowry Nelson, *Rural Social Organization, Goodhue County,* Minnesota AES Bulletin 401, February, 1949, p. 85.

[25] Mayo and Bobbitt, *op. cit.,* p. 30. Mayo has evidently found it difficult to dispense with the *neighbor* portion of the *neighborhood* concept. In a recent publication, Barnett and Mayo have commented favorably about the utility of the *neighbor group* for extension work (William E. Barnett and Selz C. Mayo, *Neighbor Groups,* North Carolina AES Progress Report RS-14, June, 1952, p. 12).

[26] E. B. Hanna, *The Integration of Locality Groups in an Eastern Kentucky County,* Kentucky AES Bulletin 640, February, 1956, p. 53.

[27] Walter L. Slocum and Herman M. Case, "Are Neighborhoods Meaningful Social Groups Throughout Rural America?" *Rural Sociology,* March, 1953, pp. 52-59.

numbers of the residents of the localities in question did not consider that they were members of the predesignated neighborhoods (Fig. 22); with a few notable exceptions, residents did not have a clear-cut idea of the social-psychological meaning of the term. Neither did their relationships with nearby open-country families, again with some exceptions, indicate the existence of neighborhoods

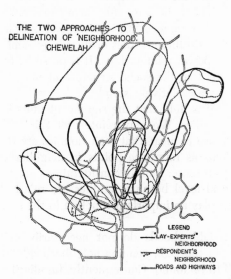

THE TWO APPROACHES TO
DELINEATION OF NEIGHBORHOOD:
CHEWELAH

LEGEND
——— LAY-EXPERTS'
NEIGHBORHOOD
⌐⌐⌐ RESPONDENT'S
NEIGHBORHOOD
——— ROADS AND HIGHWAYS

FIG. 22. (Walter L. Slocum and Herman M. Case, "Are Neighborhoods Meaningful Groups Throughout Rural America?" *Rural Sociology*, March, 1953.)

as generally defined in the texts by rural sociologists. Distinctive topographic features did not appear to have any influence on the existence of neighborhoods, nor was length of residence in the locality positively associated with recognition of neighborhood. However, the study did indicate that respondents had a personal feeling of *community* identification. A later study in the same county showed that 88 percent of a probability sample of farmers felt that they belonged to a neighborhood and 71 percent were able to name their neighborhood.[28] Perhaps, as Kolb has suggested, it is only respectable for country families to have neighbors.[29]

Kolb and other American rural sociologists who have studied neighborhoods have devoted much attention to classifying neighborhood activities, identifying the bonds which hold neighborhoods together, and delineating boundaries. One may search the literature in vain for any systematic description of a neighborhood as a system of social roles. This is because role theory was not used as a theoretical frame of reference for sociological research until quite recently. Neither do these studies ordinarily present any analysis of stratification or power relationships. It is possible, however, to infer from the reports that the social structure of most of the neighborhoods studied was relatively simple.

Most sociologists hold that the significant units in a rural neighborhood are families. We may reinterpret this within the current frame of reference to mean that their families are the groups which serve individuals as reference points in neighborhood interaction. This makes good sense. Family considerations are especially important at the local level because families are relatively stable social systems which play an important function in the socialization of the individual.

Although neighborhoods do not necessarily exist in all open-country areas of the U.S., genuine neighborhoods in the traditional sense are still to be found. Consequently, familiarity with neighborhood structure and functioning appears essential to an understanding of the development of American rural values, attitudes, and folkways. Furthermore, the concept of the neighborhood as a local community would be useful as a sociological tool for the study of rural social systems in any part of the world.

VILLAGE COMMUNITIES

There are two principal types of villages in agricultural areas: (1) the agricultural village and (2) the trade center. The distinction between the two is primarily that in an agricultural village, unlike

[28] Walter L. Slocum, "Community Development Needs Perceived by Stevens County Adults and Teenagers," in *Human Resources in Stevens County*, Washington State University unnumbered publication, September, 1959, p. 3.

[29] Kolb, *Emerging Rural Communities, op. cit.*, p. 76.

the trade center, most of the resident families are farmers, peasants, or farm laborers. Relationships between the trade center and farm families in its trade area will be considered in greater detail in connection with the discussion of rural trade-centered communities.

Agricultural Villages

As noted previously, agricultural villages are mainly occupied by farm people, although most other occupations are also to be found. In colonial times, settlements of cultivators established villages in the New England area, laying them out in the English pattern.

The New England village was a political democracy in the sense that all qualified electors had a voice in its affairs through the town meeting. Not every resident was an elector, however. Women were denied the vote at that time, and there were also age and property qualifications. The geographic boundaries were established by property holdings of residents.

The economy operated by a division of labor which included herdsmen who had charge of the livestock and poultry pastured on the common land, blacksmiths, weavers, and other artisans. These occupational specialties were required because the colonial village was largely self-sufficient.

The church was the dominant social institution, and in early colonial times those who differed in any respect from the official views were harshly dealt with. Religion was of paramount importance; it dominated the lives of the villagers. People were highly superstitious, and persons suspected of witchcraft were sometimes burnt at the stake.

Cruel punishments—whipping, torture of various forms, the stocks —were sometimes inflicted on those who violated laws. Perhaps even more efficient methods of social control existed in the form of gossip and social ostracism of offenders.

About 20 years ago Loomis and Leonard described life in a Spanish American agricultural village in New Mexico. At that time the village could be classified a self-contained community from a sociological point of view. The authors reported:

The sense of community is strong with these people. Individuals are identified as much by the community in which they live as by family name. To be born into a community is to inherit an identification with it that is never forgotten. The few families from El Cerrito who are living away always refer to the village as their home. The reputation of the home village fixes to a certain extent the general status of a resident. The esteem for an individual is measured largely by the general opinion of the village as a whole. Loyalties to the community and to its people amount almost to a passion. It is not uncommon to hear someone speak in derogatory terms of a neighboring community or its people, but seldom does he dare breathe criticism of his own community or of its residents.[30]

The patterns of interaction among residents of agricultural villages in the U.S. have not been studied to any appreciable extent, but it may be hypothesized that informality is the keynote, and that because of proximity the rate of interaction among residents is higher than among people in an open-country neighborhood.

Trade Centers as Social Systems

The trade center in the United States is connected through commercial trade activities with larger centers of population. Sometimes it is called a hamlet or village, but frequently, regardless of its size, it is called a town. The center serves the people who reside on farms in its trading area, providing markets for farm produce and offering goods and services. The importance of the latter can be understood better if one keeps in mind the fact that a very high percentage of the food, clothing, and other goods and services used by American families living on commercial farms is purchased rather than produced at home.

What we are concerned with at this point is the social organization of the village itself. In this connection, it may be noted that through the legal act of incorporation many village trade centers have set themselves apart to some extent from their country constituents with respect to local government.

Most trade centers undoubtedly also have within their boundaries many informal and formal social systems including cliques, neighborhoods, social clubs, economic systems such as factories and stores, and, of course, governmental relationships.

In very small villages, as in any other small social system, every

[30] C. P. Loomis and Olen Leonard, *Culture of a Contemporary Rural Community: El Cerrito, New Mexico*, U.S. Department of Agriculture, Bureau of Agricultural Economics, Rural Life Studies No. 1, November, 1941, p. 8.

person comes to play roles which are well known to others. With
increasing size and high mobility, intimate acquaintance of this type
becomes less frequent. Instead only the few people who occupy
leadership positions or who for some other reason are in the public
eye will perform roles which are known to all.

There have been few if any thorough sociological studies of
American trade centers as social systems. The residents of such villages and towns have occupied an intermediate position between
farm and city, both of which have been studied more fully. Most
of the available information deals with numbers, sizes, and functions, with some attention to occupations and special categories
such as age.[31]

Loomis and Beegle cite a study by Miller of the social system of
a hamlet or small village. This study revealed conflict between two
factions over the location of a school.[32]

There have been quite a number of village self-surveys in the U.S.
in connection with the current community development movement.[33]
Most of these, however, have little or no scientific value because they
lack an adequate theoretical frame of reference. In addition, novels
have been written about life in trade centers, among them Sinclair
Lewis' *Main Street* and Thornton Wilder's *Our Town.*

Town-Country Communities

The interdependence of the people who live in and adjacent to
American trade centers is well known. Recognition of the conver-
gence of common interests between town and country in 1915 led
Galpin to coin the term *rurban community.*[34]

The town-country trade-center community has been called *the*
rural community by distinguished American rural sociologists.[35]
This seems too narrow a use of the term. As noted earlier, open-
country neighborhoods and agricultural villages and towns may
also be regarded as types of rural communities.

[31] See John H. Kolb and Edmund deS. Brunner, A *Study of Rural Society,*
4th ed., Houghton Mifflin, 1952, chap. 13.

[32] C. P. Loomis and J. A. Beegle, *Rural Social Systems,* Prentice-Hall, 1950,
pp. 178-179.

[33] See Richard W. Poston, *Democracy is You,* Harper, 1953.

[34] Galpin, *op. cit.,* p. 32.

[35] See Sanderson, *op. cit.,* p. 481.

In simple, uncomplicated form, a composite town-country community may be defined as an area with a trade center where there is a network of relationships involving nearly all the common interests of the residents who recognize the community as a cohesive social unit to which they feel they belong. Such a community arises from the interaction of farm people living on dispersed holdings with each other and with the people in the trade center. Both economic and social relationships are involved. Since it is associated with dispersed farmsteads, it may be found in other countries; Kolb and Brunner mention studies of rural communities in England, New Zealand, pre-Communist China, Japan, Thailand, Korea, the Pacific islands, Argentina, and Brazil. They acknowledge, however, that differences exist between countries in the forms and activities involved.[36]

Many studies have been made to ascertain the functions, characteristics, and problems of American rural communities, and their findings make it clear that membership in one town-country community does not preclude membership in another which embraces a larger area. Furthermore, people within any specific town-country area may join with others in special-purpose community organizations such as a church or school.[37] A cumulative or composite sharing of interests in all aspects of life is seldom achieved. The people who reside in the trade and service area of a village center are rarely all community-conscious unless the feeling has been fostered by community development programs.

Because of the central importance of economic relationships in contemporary American life, it is plausible to identify community boundaries by mapping such relationships. This was the assumption upon which Galpin based his early Wisconsin community study: "It is difficult, if not impossible, to avoid the conclusion that the trade zone about one of these rather complete agricultural civic centers forms the boundary of an actual, if not legal, community within which the apparent entanglement of human life is resolved into a fairly unitary system of inter-relatedness. The fundamental community is a composite of many expanding and contracting feature

[36] Kolb and Brunner, *op. cit.*, pp. 212, 213, 222-223.
[37] Dr. Galpin used the term "feature communities" to cover this aspect of rural social organization (Galpin, *op. cit.*, p. 19).

communities possessing the characteristic pulsating instability of all real life."[38]

Fig. 23 represents the Elkhorn trade areas delineated by Galpin in 1923 and by Kolb and Day in 1948 by combining information about

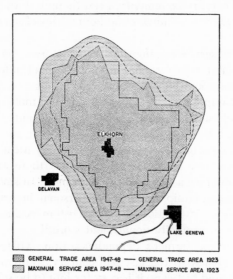

GENERAL TRADE AREA 1947-48 —— GENERAL TRADE AREA 1923
MAXIMUM SERVICE AREA 1947-48 —— MAXIMUM SERVICE AREA 1923

Fig. 23. A Trade-Centered Community: Elkhorn, Wisconsin, 1923 and 1947. (J. H. Kolb and L. J. Day, *Interdependence in Town and Country Relations in Rural Society*, Wisconsin AES Research Bulletin 172, December, 1950, p. 32.)

the spatial arrangement of various forms of interaction.[39] Patterns of participation in specific social, political, or economic relationships are clearly not adequate as a basis for identifying integrated com-

[38] Galpin, *op. cit.*, p. 18.

[39] Another approach which is frequently used in the family survey in which families are asked to reveal their community affiliations. Another is the neighborhood cluster method used by Ensminger. This method involves delineation of neighborhoods, usually through the use of lay leaders, after which neighborhood leaders are asked to verify the neighborhood boundaries and indicate the trade centers patronized by neighborhood members (Douglas Ensminger, "Rural Neighborhoods and Communities," in Carl C. Taylor *et al.*, *Rural Life in the United States*, Knopf, 1949, chap. 4).

munities; statistical combination of disparate patterns of interaction cannot be substituted for the psychological dimension expressed in a feeling of belonging and a sense of community responsibility. In fairness to Galpin, it should be noted that he did not claim that trade *makes* a town-country community, even though he did believe that the general trade zones indicate the boundaries of an existing community.[40]

The trade and service relationships between trade center agencies, organizations, and business establishments are of sufficient importance to warrant closer examination.

BUSINESS RELATIONSHIPS. Unquestionably the most important set of economic interactions involve selling farm products and buying commodities for family or farm. For the most part, each transaction involves interaction between one or more family members and one or more members of a business firm. Generally there will be little if any interaction between customers as customers. In small communities, business relationships tend to be personal in contrast to the impersonal type of interaction between customers and clerks commonly found in a large city department store.[41]

The extent of the farmer's dependence upon village merchants has decreased greatly in the last half-century. With the advent of improved roads and fast cars, it is easy for him to be selective in his business dealings; he can go to the city or to another small trade center if he wishes. Some small-town merchants have been able to meet the competition while others have not. In general, however, there has been a shift of emphasis. Many farmers who still buy work clothes, groceries, and small convenience items from nearby small trade centers patronize larger centers for expensive items like dress clothing, furniture, and automobiles.[42]

CREDIT RELATIONSHIPS. Credit is indispensable for a commercial farmer. Not only does he frequently need loans for the purchase of feed or seed, but he may want to borrow to buy machinery or land. He may also purchase various consumer goods on the installment

---

[40] See Kolb, *Emerging Rural Communities, op. cit.,* pp. 8-9.
[41] See J. H. Kolb and L. J. Day, *Interdependence in Town and Country Relations in Rural Society,* Wisconsin AES Research Bulletin 172, 1950.
[42] See Kolb and Brunner, *op. cit.,* chap. 13.

plan. With rare exceptions all of his credit sources are located in trade centers. His dealings with credit agencies, including private banks, farm credit organizations, retail firms, and private lenders, obviously involve interactions which fulfill the requirements of the concept of a social system. In some cases the relationships are informal; in others, he is required to join a loaning organization to get credit, pledging some property as security.

As in the case of buying and selling, there is some tendency for large credit needs to be met in larger centers. Many small-town banks disappeared during the depression of the 1930s. Even in some larger centers locally owned banks are being superseded by chain banks;[43] with such a change there is inevitably some alteration in the relationships between farmer and banker.

PROFESSIONAL SERVICES. The trend toward specialization has also affected relationships with doctors and dentists. The "old country doctor" who was a general practitioner is rapidly passing from the rural scene. In his place is a clinic staffed by two or more doctors and nurses. But it is likely that the clinic will be located in a larger center. In sparsely settled areas, the residents may band together in a hospital association and provide buildings and equipment for a clinic.[44]

EDUCATIONAL SERVICES. In many parts of the U.S. the one-room open-country rural school has disappeared completely, and in others school consolidation is still proceeding. In most cases such schools are located in centers of population and farm children commute daily in school buses. The public school is today probably the most important community social system in rural America.[45] Kolb has suggested that high-school attendance may be one of the better ways to locate town-country community boundaries.[46]

RELIGIOUS SERVICES. Like the one-room school, the country church is a thing of the past in many areas. Membership in village churches has brought farm people into closer contact with villagers.

---

[43] Note, for example, the large number of branches of the Bank of America and the Seattle First National Bank found in California and Washington respectively.
[44] There are several of these in rural areas of the state of Washington.
[45] See Chapter 20 for a more complete discussion of school and community.
[46] Kolb, *Emerging Rural Communities, op. cit.*, p. 9.

Of course, a single village church is rarely dominant; there will ordinarily be several in a village of any size.[47]

SOCIAL AND RECREATIONAL ACTIVITIES. Rural interest groups of various kinds may meet in the trade center. Some of these have only farm people as members, while others, such as service clubs, include both townspeople and farmers.

Trade centers contain many commercialized forms of recreation, among them moving picture theaters, dance halls, bowling alleys, pool halls, and ball parks. Small centers will not be so well supplied with such facilities as large centers, but those which exist are likely to be patronized by farm as well as nonfarm people. We should note that the widespread diffusion of television to farm homes has doubtless reduced the use of movie theaters and perhaps other forms of recreation also.

PROSPECTS FOR RURAL COMMUNITIES

Prediction is hazardous. Nevertheless, it seems reasonably safe to suggest that rural communities of the future will probably be even more complex than those of the present. There is little likelihood of a return to the simple small community of our ancestors' times. At the same time, it is not unlikely that greater community consciousness will be generated. Emphasis upon community responsibilities by church and school combined with further programs of community development may be expected.

QUESTIONS FOR FURTHER STUDY AND DISCUSSION

1. What are the distinctive features of traditional patterns of association in rural localities?
2. What is the trend in rural associational life so far as primary relationships are concerned? To what is this trend attributable?
3. a. Draw an outline map of a rural or urban locality with which you are acquainted, locating the following:
    (1) A home with which you are familiar.
    (2) The location of the important social and economic institutions with which this family has contact.

[47] See Chapter 23 for a fuller discussion.

    (3) Other families with which this family is on intimate terms.

    (4) Neighborhood boundary, if a neighborhood exists.

  b. If a neighborhood exists, what factors have created it? If not, what factors have prevented it?

4. How stable are the boundaries of American rural communities? Why do changes occur?

5. Comment on the following statement from Kolb and Brunner's *A Study of Rural Society, op. cit.,* p. 228: ". . . community organization in present-day North American rural life is almost entirely dependent upon the voluntary, deliberate effort of leaders and citizens."

SELECTED REFERENCES

Beers, Howard W., "American Communities," in *The Community School,* Chicago, National Society for the Study of Education, 1953.

Galpin, C. J., *The Social Anatomy of An Agricultural Community,* Wisconsin AES Research Bulletin 34, May, 1915.

Kolb, J. H., *Emerging Rural Communities,* University of Wisconsin Press, 1959.

Kolb, J. H., and Edmund deS. Brunner, *A Study of Rural Society,* Houghton Mifflin, 1948, chaps. 12, 13, 14.

Loomis, C. P., and J. A. Beegle, *Rural Social Systems,* Prentice-Hall, 1950, chap. 6.

Nelson, Lowry, *Rural Sociology,* 2nd ed., American Book, 1955, chap. 5.

Nelson, Lowry, Charles E. Ramsey, and Coolie Verner, *Community Structure and Change,* Macmillan, 1960.

Sanders, Irwin T., *The Community: An Introduction to a Social System,* Ronald, New York, 1958.

20

Voluntary Formal Organizations

The majority of American farmers and members of their families voluntarily participate in a great variety of formal organizations.

Formal organizations have elective officers, written constitutions, bylaws, membership requirements, and sometimes elaborate rituals. Ordinarily they are established primarily to promote some specialized common interest of the members, but once in operation, other considerations are likely to become involved. Subsidiary interests may develop, and a social program is likely to be designed to assist in maintaining interest and enlisting support for the activities which are of basic concern to the organization.

Such organizations are evidently quite rare in some parts of the world, like rural Pakistan,[1] but they are and have long been a prominent and much-studied aspect of the social landscape in rural America. The famous French writer Alexis de Tocqueville commented in 1835: "Americans of all ages, all conditions, and all dispositions constantly form associations. . . . They have associations of a thousand . . . kinds—religious, moral, serious, futile, general or restricted, enormous or diminutive."[2]

There are, as de Tocqueville said, a great number of formal organizations in rural areas. These include general farm organizations like the Grange, the Farm Bureau, and the Farmers' Union; agricultural cooperatives; fraternal organizations like the Masons and the Elks; service organizations like Kiwanis and the Rotary; the Parent-

[1] W. L. Slocum, Jamila Akhtar, and Abrar Fatima Sahi, *Village Life in Lahore District,* Lahore, Social Sciences Research Center, Panjab University Press, October, 1959.

[2] Alexis de Tocqueville, *Democracy in America* (1835), tr. Henry Reeves, Knopf, 1945, p. 242.

Teachers Association and other organizations affiliated with education; learning groups like 4-H Clubs, FFA, and home demonstration clubs, and many others.

Kolb and Brunner along with other sociologists have called attention to the increased emphasis on interest groups and a corresponding decrease in emphasis on locality groups in American rural society.[3] This significant trend is at least half a century old.[4]

Why do people join voluntary formal organizations?

Determination of motivations for behavior is a difficult matter; there are probably many reasons for joining such organizations, including the fact that they are available to join and provide an opportunity for interaction with like-minded others. Basically, however, people generally join formal organizations because they believe that in one way or another they can serve one or more of their own interests—a desire to help others, to obtain financial gains, to influence legislation, to have a good time. Many undoubtedly join because they believe they can attain ends through joint effort which they could not attain as individuals. If American society were organized along authoritarian lines rather than as a democracy, there might be less incentive for people to form interest groups.

In the present discussion, primary emphasis will be focused on general farmers' organizations, agricultural cooperatives, and commodity organizations. This should not be interpreted as indicating that farm operators do not belong to other interest groups, but rather that these are the groups which at present are devoted principally to strictly agricultural matters.

The extent to which farm people participate in formal voluntary organizations has not been investigated on a comprehensive nation-wide basis at a particular time. However, there have been a large number of studies in various parts of the country at different times. The evidence from these studies indicates that the degree of participation varies considerably from one locality to another. Buck and Mudge found that all but 6.2 percent of the heads of rural households in a central Pennsylvania rural community belonged to at

---

[3] John H. Kolb and Edmund deS. Brunner, *A Study of Rural Society*, 4th ed., Houghton Mifflin, 1952, p. 241.

[4] P. A. Sorokin, C. C. Zimmerman, and C. J. Galpin, *A Systematic Source Book in Rural Sociology*, University of Minnesota Press, 1930, I, 330-333.

least one organization.[5] W. A. Anderson reported that families in a
New York village averaged membership in 4.5 different formal organizations.[6] Slocum, Brough, and Straus, on the basis of a statewide
probability sample in Washington, reported that few commercial
farm operators (6.4 percent) or their wives (9.5 percent) were without organizational affiliations. This study also showed, however, that
relatively few belonged to large numbers of organizations. Only 9.6
percent of the operators and 4.9 percent of the homemakers belonged
to more than 5 organizations; the operators belonged to an average
of 3.1 and their wives to an average of 2.6.[7] On the other hand,
Beegle and Schroeder reported a low rate of participation in voluntary organizations in the urban fringe of North Lansing, Michigan.
Aproximately 31 percent belonged to no voluntary organizations and
another 25 percent reported that they belonged to only one.[8]

GENERAL FARMERS' ORGANIZATIONS

At the present time there are three general farmers' organizations
which operate on a nationwide scale in the United States: the
Grange, the American Farm Bureau, and the Farmers' Union. There
have been other general farm organizations in the past, but these
have now largely disappeared.[9]

THE GRANGE

The Patrons of Husbandry, commonly known as the Grange, was
organized in 1867. Its membership reached an early peak of nearly
three-quarters of a million members in 1874-1875 in 43 states and

[5] Roy C. Buck and B. P. Mudge, *Formal Participation Patterns in a Central
Pennsylvania Rural Community,* Pennsylvania AES Progress Report No. 129,
January, 1955, p. 3. (Mimeo)
[6] W. A. Anderson, *Formal and Informal Participation in a New York Village,*
Cornell University AES Bulletin 28, January, 1952, p. 2.
[7] W. L. Slocum, Owen L. Brough, Jr., and Murray A. Straus, *Extension
Contacts, Selected Characteristics, Practices and Attitudes of Washington Farm
Families,* Washington AES Bulletin 584, April, 1958, p. 12.
[8] J. A. Beegle and Widick Schroeder, *Social Organization and Land Use in
the North Lansing Fringe,* Michigan AES Bulletin 251, September, 1955.
[9] See C. C. Taylor, *The Farmers' Movement, 1620-1920,* American Book,
1953.

then declined somewhat;[10] since that time it has fluctuated. Membership in 1957 was 850,103.[11]

The Grange is a fraternal order which incorporates a substantial amount of ritual in some of its meetings. Both men and women may join, and although it is classified as a farm organization, the occupation of farming is not a prerequisite for membership. There seems to be no reliable information concerning the number of nonfarmer members.[12]

The Grange is a national body with state and local branches, the latter usually neighborhood organizations. Any three locals can unite to form what is called a Pomona Grange, which is usually countywide. The masters of the local Granges and their wives constitute the voting delegates to the state Grange which meets annually. The national Grange in turn consists of the masters of the state Granges and their wives. It also meets yearly.

All of the levels of the Grange award degrees to their members for proficiency in its ritual.

Although the Grange is basically a fraternal organization, its objectives are not restricted simply to fraternal fellowship and the promotion of agriculture from an economic standpoint, but include in addition the fostering of wholesome home and community life in rural areas.

The conditions of membership are of interest from a sociological point of view. Prospective members must be over 14 years of age. They are first screened by a membership committee and elected at a secret election. Before an initiate can become a full member, he is required to go through the ritual of the first four degrees.

The officers of each local Grange include master, lecturer, secretary, treasurer, chaplain, steward, lady assistant steward, Pomona, Ceres, Flora, and gatekeeper. Each of these unpaid officers has a definite role within the local Grange. Interaction between members is generally friendly and includes calling other members "brother" or "sister" as in many other fraternal organizations. Pomona, state, and national Granges have similar officers. The officers of the state

[10] Dwight Sanderson, *Rural Sociology and Rural Social Organization*, Wiley, 1942, p. 506.

[11] A. L. Bertrand, ed., *Rural Sociology*, McGraw-Hill, 1958, p. 367.

[12] Personal observation based on discussions with officials of the Washington State Grange.

and national Granges are paid salaries and provided with expense accounts for official travel.

Most of the meetings of the local Granges are secret, although some are open to the public. Meetings are opened and closed with a formal ritual, and the business meeting is conducted in accordance with parliamentary rules of order. There is an educational program under the direction of the lecturer which includes talks, discussions, and related matters together with musical numbers and other forms of entertainment such as amateur drama. Participation in the ritual is presumed to promote unity by furnishing members with common interests and experiences. The Grange local provides opportunities for open discussion by members of policy questions relating to agriculture and the rural home, as well as occasions for social recreation and for sharing of common interests on an informal basis.

In some sections of the country the Grange has sponsored associated economic organizations and activities operated on a cooperative basis, some of which have been quite successful. On the local level the Grange is an important neighborhood social system, and at the state and national level its function is principally as a spokesman for agricultural interests in connection with legislative proposals.

THE FARM BUREAU

The American Farm Bureau Federation arose largely through the stimulation of the agricultural extension services of the U.S. Department of Agriculture and the state colleges of agriculture. Its initial function was to provide support for the work of county agricultural and home demonstration agents. The first Farm Bureau association was formed in 1913 by residents of Boone County, New York.[13] Shortly thereafter, Illinois, Iowa, and West Virginia also established county organizations to support extension activities. The association grew rapidly after enactment of the Smith-Lever Act of 1914 which provided federal support for the agricultural extension program. Federations were organized in a number of states and a national federation of the state groups was established in 1919. In 1958 it claimed over 1,500,000 members in over 2600 county Farm Bureaus.[14]

[13] Sanderson, *op. cit.*, p. 516.

[14] American Farm Bureau Federation, *This Is the Farm Bureau*, Washington, D.C., 1958.

The Farm Bureau Federation has more memberships in Iowa, Illinois, Indiana, and New York than in most other states.

In some states the county Farm Bureau still maintains official relationships with the Agricultural Extension Service, but this is not true everywhere. The state and national organizations of the Farm Bureau do not, however, have any official relationship with the Agricultural Extension Service. These bodies were organized for the purpose of providing a formal channel for the expression of members' opinions on legislation affecting farmers.

The Farm Bureau, unlike the Grange, is not a secret fraternal organization. Membership is ordinarily open to any person who is interested in its objectives and is willing to pay dues. Men and women do not usually hold separate memberships, although in New York there is an affiliated Home Bureau which Sanderson labeled as "practically a separate organization"; he described the Farm Bureau as a loosely knit group which is somewhat like a commercial club or a chamber of commerce as contrasted with the closely knit Grange. The work of the organization, according to Sanderson, is done principally by officers with the rank and file members participating only occasionally.[15] Contacts between members evidently depend principally upon the common interests of individual members, and meetings are held relatively infrequently.

The Farm Bureau Federation gives considerable support to efforts to get members and other farmers to accept improved farming and homemaking practices. This, of course, is consistent with its historical role as a supporter of the Agricultural Extension Service, which is an adult education organization.

With respect to its objectives, Sanderson has stated, "The purposes and aims of the County Farm Bureau are broad and in many instances not too clearly defined."[16] From a sociological point of view, it may be characterized as a secondary group. Interaction tends to be on a relatively impersonal basis, and apparently there is weak identification of many members with the organization and its principal purposes. As Sanderson stated, it is kept active principally through the efforts of paid officers at the state and national level. In states where the Farm Bureau has a close tie-up with the Agricul-

[15] Sanderson, *op. cit.*, pp. 517, 518.
[16] *Ibid.*, p. 520.

tural Extension Service, the agents of the Service play a major function in maintaining active local organizations.

THE FARMERS' UNION

The Farmers' Educational and Cooperative Union is not comparable to a labor union. It is, however, a rather militant organization with a definite economic and social philosophy. Like the Grange, it is a secret organization, but it differs from the Grange in having relatively little ritual. It has both county and state units. Principal emphasis in the meetings of local Unions is upon economic problems, although there may also be social and recreational programs.

Membership is by families. In 1957 the Union had approximately 300,000 members,[17] with greatest strength in the Great Plains and other sections of the Midwest. It has a youth program with training camps and institutes.

The Farmers' Union has sponsored a number of cooperative economic enterprises, including the Farmers' Union Grain Terminal Association and the Farmers' Union Central Exchange, both at St. Paul, Minnesota. There are also other associated cooperative organizations in various states. The Union maintains a vigorous lobby in Washington, D. C.; its objectives include maintaining and protecting the family-type farm, promoting cooperative purchasing and marketing organizations, and promoting the economic welfare of farmers. It has taken a stand against vertical integration unless controlled by farmers.[18]

AGRICULTURAL COOPERATIVES

Agricultural cooperatives may be classified as social systems based on a type of formal cooperation.[19] They occupy an extremely important position in that part of the social structure of American agriculture which is concerned with economic competition. Almost without exception, farmer cooperatives have been established and

[17] National Farmers' Union, *The Farmers' Farm Organization,* Denver, September 1, 1957.

[18] See National Farmers' Union, *This We Believe,* Denver, Program Bulletin 1, undated, on which this discussion is based.

[19] See Chapter 12 for a discussion of cooperation as a social process.

are maintained for the principal purpose of enabling the members to compete more successfully with other segments of the economy. They may be regarded as a form of economic democracy.

BASIC CHARACTERISTICS OF AGRICULTURAL COOPERATIVES

The principles of organization generally regarded as ideal by leaders of the cooperative movement lay great stress upon democratic procedures. These principles were first set forth in Rochdale, England, in 1844 by a group of textile workers who established a consumers' cooperative. The major principles developed by this group are as follows:

1. Democracy in policy-making. This is achieved by allowing each member only one vote without reference to the number of shares of stock owned.

2. Low returns on capital invested. According to the ideology of the cooperative movement, the economic advantages gained through cooperation are really savings for its members. The cooperative does not attempt to make a profit; consequently, capital is paid for at a specific rate of interest. This is a marked difference from the corporation which returns a share of profits to stockholders in proportion to capital invested.

3. Returns are based on patronage. Consistent with the second principle, savings are returned to the members in proportion to the volume of business of the member. Of course, overhead costs such as rent, salary, and taxes, along with an allowance for contingencies and depreciation, must be set aside prior to the distribution of the savings if the enterprise is to prosper.

4. Few restrictions on membership. The cooperative philosophy of equality is quite similar to that expressed in the Declaration of Independence and the Constitution of the United States. Membership is generally open to all without restriction because of race, creed, or color.

HISTORY OF THE COOPERATIVE MOVEMENT IN THE UNITED STATES

Economic cooperatives are not prevalent in the United States except in the field of agriculture, where, however, they have a long history. Stitts gives a brief summary of their development:

The first [period] began around 1810, when cheese-making enterprises were cooperatively organized. It ended about 1870, with a record of accomplishment that included formation of mutual insurance and irrigation companies and supply purchasing cooperatives.

The second period began with the rise of the Grange, Patrons of Husbandry. Grange-sponsored cooperatives marketed farm products, bought supplies, and manufactured farm implements. They were short-lived for the most part, but a few continued well into the present century.

The third period started in the early nineties and continued about 30 years. It saw the perfection of techniques for operating the various types of local associations, and the development of federations, large-scale centralized associations, and cooperative selling on terminal markets.

It was this third period that merged and developed into the fourth period, beginning about 1920. Large-scale cooperative marketing of various commodities reached a high state of development. Committees, councils, and an annual institute were organized to seek out the essentials necessary for continued substantial progress. Numerous federal and state laws facilitating farmers' cooperative business activities were put upon the statute books.[20]

The fourth period, extending to the present, has been characterized by the continuation of activities of the type commenced earlier. National farmers' cooperative organizations were formed and the Farmer Cooperative Service was established in the U.S. Department of Agriculture. Other notable developments included the creation of banks for cooperatives, farm loan associations, soil conservation cooperatives, and rural electrification cooperatives. These last, sponsored by the Rural Electrification Administration, have been largely responsible for the amazing progress which has been made in bringing electricity to American farmers.

A review of the statistics of growth shows that cooperatives which handle the marketing of farm products are fewer in number than in the 1920s, although both the number of members and the volume of business have increased (Table 15). During the period covered by the statistics, cooperatives which handle farm supplies continued to increase. The gross value of supplies purchased cooperatively for

[20] Tom G. Stitts, Foreword, in R. H. Ellsworth, *The Story of Farmers' Cooperatives,* Farm Credit Administration, 1938, p. 1.

TABLE 15. Statistics of Growth of Farmers' Marketing and Supply Cooperatives in the United States, 1915-1959

Year	Marketing Cooperatives		Supply Cooperatives		Business Volume (in Thousands of Dollars)	
	Number	Membership	Number	Membership	Marketing	Supply
1915	2,988	591,683	111	59,503	624,161	11,678
1925-1926	9,586	2,453,000	1,217	247,000	2,265,000	135,000
1935-1936	8,388	2,710,000	2,112	950,000	1,586,000	254,000
1945-1946	7,378	3,150,000	2,772	1,860,000	5,147,000	923,000
1955-1956	6,268	4,222,000	3,373	2,970,000	9,505,945	2,970,880
1958-1959	6,042	3,860,950	3,387	3,643,525	11,379,606	3,549,922

SOURCE: A. L. Gessner, *1956-57 Statistics of Farmer Cooperatives*, USDA, Farmer Cooperative Service, General Report No. 93, 1961, Appendix, Tables 5, 6, 7 and pp. 5, 12, 21.

members of farm supply cooperatives in 1958-1959 included the following:

Building materials	$ 127,116,000
Containers and packaging supplies	56,669,000
Farm machinery and equipment	108,749,000
Feed	1,222,317,000
Fertilizer	518,000,000
Meats and groceries	62,841,000
Petroleum products	930,356,000
Seed	135,826,000
Farm chemicals	70,918,000
Other supplies	317,930,000
Total	$3,549,922,000

SOURCE: A. L. Gessner, *1956–57 Statistics of Farmer Cooperatives,* U.S. Department of Agriculture, Farmer Cooperative Service, General Report No. 93, 1961, p. 26.

The total volume of business handled by cooperatives of all types in 1958-1959 was $15,202,000,000.[21]

In addition to marketing and supply cooperatives, statistics are available concerning service cooperatives. There were 234 such cooperatives in 1956-1957 with a membership of 61,920.[22]

Many private businessmen have protested the activities of farmers' business cooperatives. Consequently, efforts have been made from time to time to persuade Congress to withdraw their federal income tax benefits. These are substantial since patronage refunds to members are not classified as profits for tax purposes. In addition, cooperatives have been fought in the courts by commercial interests. Recently the presumed exemption under the Capper-Volstead Act of farm cooperatives from the antitrust laws has been successfully challenged in the federal courts.[23]

Farmer cooperatives are found in all parts of the United States. However, there is a heavier volume of business in the more prosperous farming sections. In 1956-1957 nearly half (48.9 percent) of

[21] A. L. Gessner, *1956-57 Statistics of Farmer Cooperatives,* U.S. Department of Agriculture, Farmer Cooperative Service, General Report No. 93, 1961, p. 21.

[22] *Ibid.,* pp. 5, 12.

[23] *Spokane Spokesman-Review,* December 18, 1960.

the farm products marketed and more than half (53.5 percent) of the supplies purchased by cooperatives were accounted for by the north central states which include the Corn Belt, the spring wheat area, and the dairy section in the lake states.

TYPES OF COOPERATIVES

Cooperatives may be classified into three major types according to organizational structure.

1. Local cooperatives. These are not linked with similar cooperatives elsewhere, and as a consequence are relatively weak both economically and politically.
2. Federated cooperatives. In this type of structure a number of local associations band together in order to increase efficiency, improve the quality of service, and employ more capable management employees.
3. Centralized cooperatives. This type of organization is characterized by a widely scattered membership distributed over a substantial geographic area but having one board of directors; although there may be local field men in the case of a production association, locals do not exist.

Another system of classification is according to major function. There are marketing, purchasing, service, and production cooperatives (see Table 16).

MEMBERSHIP RELATIONSHIPS WITHIN COOPERATIVES

Some cooperative organizations are relatively simple in structure with small-scale operations. As noted above, federated and centralized cooperatives may be very large with operations extending over vast geographical areas. Examples of the latter would be the citrus fruit cooperatives of California and the Western Farmers Association which covers nearly the whole of western Washington.

The relationship between members and the management, including the board of directors, will differ greatly from one cooperative to another depending upon the scope of operations and the complexity of the organizational structure. Intimate personal relation-

TABLE 16.   Major Types, Number, and Memberships of Farmer
            Cooperatives

Type	Year or Date of Data	Associa- tions	Estimated Member- ships or Partici- pants
Marketing and farm supply:			
Marketing	1958-59	6,042	3,860,950
Farm supply	1958-59	3,387	3,643,525
Miscellaneous services	1958-59	229	54,075
Service:			
Federal land bank associations	1961	797	375,868
Production credit associations	1961	488	514,790
Banks for cooperatives	1960	13	3,812,252
Rural credit unions	1961	700	225,000
Rural electric cooperatives	1960	910	4,513,876
Rural Electrification Administra- tion telephone cooperatives	1960	211	440,653
Rural health cooperatives	1960	19	65,907
Farmers' mutual fire insurance companies	1959	1,650	3,000,000
Production:			
Mutual irrigation companies	1959	7,729	161,679
Dairy herd improvement associations	1961	1,395	42,558
Dairy-cattle artificial breeding associations	1960	47	636,500

SOURCE: A. L. Gessner, *Statistics of Farmer Cooperatives, 1958–59*, U.S.
Department of Agriculture, Farmer Cooperative Service, General Report No. 93,
1961, Appendix, Table 9.

ships are possible only in a local cooperative with a relatively
restricted territory. In the large-scale cooperative, salaried field men
may attempt to simulate this type of relationship by maintaining
close contact with members. In a production type of cooperative
which attempts to maintain some control over the quality of the
product which members produce, relationships between management and individual members may sometimes become strained; they

resemble the relationships found in industrial organizations operated on a profit-making basis. The cooperative's management, however, has at least the advantage that the members presumably subscribe to the cooperative ideology.

Beal, Fessler, and Wakeley studied the attitudes of Iowa cooperative members toward their organizations, and found that generally they reflect the degree of satisfaction with the policies and operations of the local which directly affect the member. They also found some differences between members and nonmembers.[24] In another study Beal found that participation scores of members of Iowa cooperatives differed according to such factors as socioeconomic status, general social participation, degree of understanding of cooperative principles, and degree of identification with the cooperative as a social system. Age, educational level, tenure status, and stage in the family cycle were not correlated with the scores.[25]

The economic functioning of particular cooperatives has been investigated, but so far as the writer has been able to ascertain, there have been no systematic sociological studies dealing with the patterns of relationships, the social structure, and the functioning of the values of particular cooperatives.

COMMODITY ORGANIZATIONS

Organizations of farmers engaged in the production of various commodities have become quite numerous, and are aggressive in the promotion of legislation desired by their membership. Among them are such powerful groups as the Cattlemen's Association, the Cotton Growers, the Wheat Growers, and the Wool Growers. Some commodity organizations maintain state headquarters with a paid secretariat and perhaps also offices in the nation's capital. Most have a slate of unpaid officers and a salaried secretary who carries on the routine of collecting dues, sending out notices of meetings, and keeping the members posted on public issues which concern them and on related activities.

[24] G. M. Beal, D. R. Fessler, and R. E. Wakeley, *Agricultural Cooperatives in Iowa*, Iowa AES Research Bulletin 379, 1951, pp. 179-180.

[25] G. M. Beal, *The Roots of Participation in Farmer Cooperatives*, Iowa State College Book Store, 1954, pp. 117-121.

Recently national commodity organizations have joined forces to form the National Association of Commodity Organizations.[26]

ORGANIZED YOUTH GROUPS

The principal agricultural organizations to which American rural young people belong are the 4-H Clubs for boys and girls sponsored by the agricultural extension services and the Future Farmers of America sponsored by high-school vocational agriculture teachers. These groups are quite similar. Both require a project such as raising a calf, both are primarily educational in intent, and both are sponsored by educational agencies. There are, of course, some differences; the bulk of 4-H Club members are below high-school age and 4-H Clubs make greater use of voluntary local adult leaders, whereas the FFA members receive personal guidance from vocational agriculture teachers. Mention should be made of the Future Homemakers of America Clubs for high-school girls sponsored by high-school home economics teachers. Farm youths also participate in youth organizations sponsored by schools and churches.

With relatively few exceptions, formal youth organizations have some adult leadership. Usually these adults are volunteers who serve in an advisory capacity, generally keeping in the background and giving encouragement and advice. Youth organizations have a shifting membership. Young people's interests change as they mature, and it is not easy for a particular group to satisfy them all. These youth organizations usually elect officers, who generally perform roles analogous to those in adult organizations.

WOMEN'S ORGANIZATIONS

The major women's educational organizations in rural areas are home demonstration clubs, or homemakers clubs as they are sometimes known, which are organized under the sponsorship of the agricultural extension services for the purposes of studying new homemaking practices and technology. These associations are open to women who live in villages, towns, and cities as well.

[26] *Agricultural Leaders' Digest*, November-December, 1957, p. 7.

A recent nationwide study made by the Federal Extension Service has provided sample information concerning the characteristics and activities of the 1,250,000 women enrolled in home demonstration clubs. One of the most interesting findings is that only a third of the families of the members received all of their income from agriculture; half of the members were nonfarm residents.[27] Since a large proportion of home economics extension work is carried on through these clubs, it is clear that educational services are being provided to a broad spectrum of the population. In some states, including Washington, some services are provided to women who live in metropolitan centers. Although the report does not present the farm-nonfarm membership ratio of individual clubs, many clubs probably contain women from both residential categories, which would tend to diminish differences in values and attitudes.

Another interesting finding was that young families with homemakers under 30 were not represented proportionately. Two out of five families had only adult members. About half of the members had accepted leadership responsibilities. This may be in part a reflection of the relatively high level of educational achievement: 59 percent had finished high school or more compared to 38 percent of all women in the U.S. in 1950.[28]

Many farm organizations have women's auxiliaries, such as the Associated Rural Women of the Farm Bureau and the Cow Belles associated with the Cattlemen's Association. These auxiliaries may or may not be primarily oriented toward the major purposes and objectives of their partner groups.

Nearly all rural churches have women's groups which are partly social and partly religious and charitable. In addition, some rural women are members of general women's clubs, recreational organizations, and such organizations as the American Association of University Women.

The organizational structure of most women's formal voluntary groups is similar to those of other interest groups, and their affairs are conducted in much the same manner.

[27] Jewell G. Fessenden, *Home Demonstration Members and Their Families*, USDA, Federal Extension Service, Circular 520, August, 1959, p. 1.
[28] *Ibid.*, pp. 1, 7, 15.

OTHER FORMAL ORGANIZATIONS

Farm people also participate in social clubs, general fraternal orders, and other types of organizations set up to promote or other-wise consider particular special interests.

GENERALIZED PATTERNS OF ORGANIZATION AND OPERATION

The exact form of organization, of course, varies somewhat from group to group, but local associations which are affiliated with a state or national body ordinarily have a fairly standard organiza-tional structure. The terms of office are ordinarily one year except for organizations with business functions such as cooperatives. The local chapters of interest groups, except those with economic func-tions such as cooperatives, do not usually have any paid staff. The elected officers are responsible for the conduct of the affairs of the organization during their terms of office, and members participate in the formation of policy in accordance with their interests and the nature of the organizations.

The variation in the types of organizational patterns is not great. Generally there is an elected slate of officers consisting of a presi-dent, vice-president, secretary, and treasurer. Sometimes there is an executive committee, usually consisting of the president and two or three other persons who are empowered to make decisions concern-ing the expenditure of organizational funds. In addition to these elected officers, there will ordinarily be a program committee, headed by a chairman, which has the responsibility for programs at the regular meetings of the group.

On the question of concentration of leadership, Richardson and Bauder reported that in a Kentucky community of 2000 people, 11 persons held 15 percent of all the offices in formal organizations.[29] Kaufman reported similar findings in other parts of Kentucky, but observed that in communities with high educational levels there

[29] Paul D. Richardson and Ward W. Bauder, *Participation in Organized Activities in a Kentucky Rural Community*, Kentucky AES Bulletin 598, June, 1953.

tends to be less concentration.[30] In such areas leadership may be expected to be fairly widely diffused, with the officer positions rotated among the members rather than being regarded as permanent. This is to be expected since the officers in most voluntary formal organizations at the local level receive no financial compensation whatever.

Though some of the formal organizations to which farm people belong are purely local in their origin, orientation, and program, many are affiliated with county, state, or federal associations which play an important function in starting local groups and in keeping them alive.

Most formal statewide organizations do maintain a paid secretariat. This may consist simply of one person with few if any assistants. In some cases, however, state offices have a substantial staff which performs various functions for members. If there is a national office there will almost invariably be paid personnel to carry on the activities associated with the affairs of the organization providing leadership training, promoting educational programs, working on legislation affecting the interests of members, and performing related types of activites.

The ordinary members of many formal organizations apparently are not very active in its affairs, leaving the direction of program largely to the elected officers. Beal has commented that this fact together with the failure of some adults to join any organizations at all has been regarded by many people as a threat to democracy.[31]

Most voluntary formal associations, including those which have no nonfarm members, meet in a village center or town; in the open country a one-room country school or a Grange Hall may provide a suitable meeting place. Many interest groups are relatively impermanent in character and do not possess the resources to justify the construction of meeting places. Consequently, they are dependent upon facilities which can be obtained free or at nominal expense. Some, such as 4-H Clubs, meet in the homes of leaders or members. Larger groups generally meet in some public building.

Informal contacts between farm people may occur in conjunction

[30] Harold F. Kaufman, *Participation in Organized Activities in Selected Kentucky Localities,* Kentucky AES Bulletin 528, February, 1949.

[31] Beal, *op. cit.,* p. 2.

with the scheduled meetings of formal organizations, as we have said. Alicja Iwanska reporting on Good Fortune a community of part-time farmers in the state of Washington, writes that there was relatively little informal interfamily visiting among part-time farm families in the area, but that there was a great deal of informal gathering both before and after the formal program of various organizations in the area.[32]

LIFE CYCLE OF VOLUNTARY FORMAL ORGANIZATIONS

On the basis of a study of the life histories of local voluntary organizations in five Wisconsin counties, Kolb and Wileden concluded that such interest groups follow cycles.[33] They identified four stages: stimulation, rise, carrying on, and decline. There is no doubt that such organizations do tend to follow this cycle.

Stimulation

The first step is an idea; two or more people talking together decide that group action should be taken for some specific purpose. The idea frequently has come from outside the locality, sometimes communicated by an active promoter. When a small core group has become sufficiently convinced that the support of a larger group of people is desirable, an active campaign is undertaken to enlist the interest of others.

Rise

In this stage meetings are held to discuss the problem or other interests. If many of those present feel that action is important, steps will be taken to organize a group. A constitution and bylaws will be drawn up, officers will be elected, dues will be collected, and a program of activities planned.

Kolb and Wileden note that even at this early stage an inner circle is established: "It is noticeable from the very start that practically every organization has its select group (officers, committee chairmen, and volunteer speakers from the floor) which

[32] See Alicja Iwanska, *Good Fortune: Second Chance Community*, Washington AES Bulletin 589, June, 1958, p. 24.
[33] The present discussion is based principally on J. H. Kolb and A. F. Wileden, *Special Interest Groups in Rural Society*, Wisconsin AES Research Bulletin 84, December, 1927.

virtually run the organization. The officers may change about, and new committees may be added, but this inner circle remains about the same."[34] It is their observation that a major problem from the start is how to create loyalty to the leaders and through them to the organization. During the formative period, important group norms are established, and the precedents set during this time tend to govern the subsequent activities of the group. Ordinarily they cannot be changed in any substantial respect without a major struggle which may completely change the purpose and even the membership of the organization.

Carrying On

After the promotional period is over and the novelty of the organization has disappeared comes the stage Kolb and Wileden have called "carrying on." During this stage factions within the group and conflicts with other organizations may develop. Some of the members may lose interest. There may be a challenge to the initial leadership. The leaders are confronted with a challenge: "The leaders must keep on the aggressive, planning new things, and finding new and ingenious ways of presenting old ideas and plans. If they do not, the membership will drop out, as they frequently do, because there is nothing to interest them any more. Rather dramatic things must sometimes be undertaken, campaigns and drives put on, and special events arranged."[35]

There is also the problem of assimilating and socializing new members who are unfamiliar with the original objectives of the organization and who have not experienced the triumphs and failures encountered by the founders. If a successful adaptation is worked out and if the basic membership is stable and remains interested or replacements are obtained, this period can be of considerable duration.

Although the Kolb-Wileden study does not cover this point, it seems clear from subsequent experience that interest groups which achieve a state or national organization are longer-lived than purely local groups. The reason for this lies at least partly in the fact that they employ paid functionaries who have a vested interest in

[34] *Ibid.*, p. 76.
[35] *Ibid.*, p. 77.

perpetuating the organization even after its major objective has been attained. A state or national headquarters which has a salaried staff finds it relatively easy to provide continuity for a program of activities, including specialized leadership training for officers of locals, program hints, and the like.

Decline

At some point in the life of a formal organization, forever, people tend to lose interest. It may be that the purpose for which it was formed is no longer relevant and a new objective has not appeared; so many other organizations and activities may have appeared that people no longer have time to attend the meetings; or the members may have become displeased with the leadership. Whatever the cause, when the period of decline begins it is difficult to arrest without drastic measures. If these are unsuccessful, "The organization just ceases to meet and to carry on its regular activities. In the minds of many of the people it is not dead for a long time, because they still have their constitution and records, and some money in the treasury . . . the organization simply is inactive."[36]

QUESTIONS FOR FURTHER STUDY AND DISCUSSION

1. Write a case history or life story of a voluntary formal organization which you know by first-hand contacts, such as a social club, a parent-teacher association, a cooperative marketing organization, a young people's society, or a fraternity or sorority. Give special attention to the following points:
   a. Circumstances explaining its origin
   b. How members are recruited
   c. What kind of leaders are chosen
   d. Plans for keeping members loyal
   e. Difficulties with other groups
   f. Conflicts within the group
   g. Readjustments made to overcome difficulties
   h. Evidence of permanence or decline
2. What are the principal interests about which voluntary formal organizations are formed?
3. What are the generalized characteristics of interest groups?

[36] *Ibid.*, p. 79.

4. Read the report and describe briefly the method used by Kolb and Wileden in their study of rural interest groups. Comment on the adequacy of their approach.
5. Do you feel that membership in interest groups can be regarded as an indication of social adjustment? Why or why not?
6. Bertrand and associates have discussed the Grange, the Farm Bureau, and the Farmers' Union under the heading "The Farmers' Movement" in their book *Rural Sociology*. Discuss the relationship of social movements in agriculture to voluntary formal organizations in general. Do you think there is a genuine farmers' movement in the U.S. at present?
7. Bertrand and associates suggest that special interest groups tend to sort people into social strata. Comment on this, giving evidence to support or reject it if possible.

SELECTED REFERENCES

Bauder, Ward W., "The Characteristics and Functions of Special Interest Groups," in A. L. Bertrand, ed., *Rural Sociology*, McGraw-Hill, 1958, chap. 22.

Kolb, John H., and Edmund deS. Brunner, "Rural Interest Groups and Classes," *A Study of Rural Society*, Houghton Mifflin, 1952.

Kolb, J. H., and A. F. Wileden, *Special Interest Groups in Rural Society*, Wisconsin AES Research Bulletin 84, December, 1927.

21

Rural Public Schools

The school systems which now serve American farm families did not spring into existence in their present forms, but are rather the result of long and gradual development. Many unique historical events as well as the general characteristics of American culture have influenced this development.

THE HISTORY OF SCHOOL DEVELOPMENT

In England and in the continental European countries from which the ancestors of most white Americans came, formal education was mainly reserved for the children of the wealthy upper classes; also, few if any rural schools existed. Thus, colonists did not bring with them a tradition of rural schools, and such schools as were established during colonial times were supported privately. In colonial America there were no county school authorities; neither was there any systematic educational theory, any conception of the significance of education as a responsibility of government, or any taxes for the support of schools. Formal schooling was restricted for the most part to the sons of gentlemen, many of whom were sent to Great Britain for their education. When the American Constitution was formulated, there was no demand for central control of educational activities. Consequently, education was one of the functions left to the states.

According to Cubberly, the right to an elementary school education at public expense became an issue around 1835.[1] The influx after 1830 of great numbers of immigrants from countries where the

[1] See Elwood P. Cubberly, *Rural Life and Education*, Houghton Mifflin, 1914. Information concerning the historical development of rural schools has been drawn chiefly from this source.

English language was not used provided a stimulus to the development of public schools. Education was correctly perceived as an important aid to the process of assimilation or "Americanization." By 1850 the principle had been established in the northern states that property taxation could be used for the support of elementary education, and by 1870 free public education at the elementary level was also available in the South.

These were the beginnings of free education for rural people. From the beginning of public support for rural schools, local school boards had an important voice in the management of rural schools.

These early rural schools were to a large extent one-room, one-teacher schools located in the open country. They served principally the children of farmers—at this period in American history the great bulk of the population lived on farms. These schools were not very good by modern standards. The teachers were poorly paid, the school term was three to five months in the winter, and the curriculum consisted of the three R's—reading, 'riting, and 'rithmetic. Graded courses of study and uniform textbooks were later developments, occurring principally after 1880.

The principle of free public education was eventually extended by public demand to the secondary school level, but this has been largely a development of the twentieth century.

FUNCTIONS OF SCHOOLS

Elementary and secondary schools are regarded by the American public mainly as agencies for the transmission of American culture. As such, they are primarily concerned with the diffusion of existing notions and values rather than with the development of new ideas, and thus are essentially conservative. At the same time, it is true that education is also considered to be a means of promoting technological advance. Especially since the launching of the Soviet earth satellites in the fall of 1957, achievements in science and engineering have been considered an important aspect of national defense and hence essential for survival. Even at the university level, however, innovations in the social, economic, and political areas are generally frowned upon unless relatively minor in character and fully in harmony with existing values and forms of social organization.

The schools are also considered to be agencies for occupational preparation, and as such provide channels for upward social and occupational mobility. Within contemporary America, both urban and rural, a high value is placed on successful completion of various stages of formal education as evidenced by the possession of diplomas and degrees. Specified courses are required for entry into occupations like teaching, and professions like medicine are accessible only through successful completion of a rigorous curriculum.

PUBLIC FINANCING OF SCHOOLS

In modern America any child, rural or urban, is entitled to receive a certain amount of education at public expense. Free education generally extends at least through elementary school on a mandatory basis and is available through the high-school level if desired. All of the states have compulsory education laws which require attendance in school until a stated minimum age, usually 16 to 18, if the person has not reached a specified level in school prior to that age.

Although there are some private rural schools, most of which are operated by church groups, rural education at both the elementary and secondary levels is basically a governmental function. Under the constitution of the United States, as noted above, responsibility for the development, support, and supervision of the public educational system is a function of the several state governments. Consequently, there is considerable variation from one state to another in the legal regulations governing curricula, financing, personnel policies, and other aspects of school administration. In many states the heaviest burden falls on the property owners in the locality in which the school is located. In others, state support is the major source of funds.

The federal government does grant some financial assistance on a fund-matching basis for various types of educational activities. Federal support is provided for vocational agriculture and home economics courses in high school, and for similar courses in distributive education. There is also a Federal school lunch program which is designed partly to help dispose of surplus agricultural products. There is a federal-state program of vocational rehabilitation for physically disabled persons. Control over the educational content and teaching methods involved in these programs has been left in the hands of state authorities.

Substantial programs of education and training were made available at federal expense to veterans of both world wars. Expenditures for the World War II program for able-bodied veterans during the fiscal year 1949 alone was more than $2,700,000,000. Large sums were also spent for vocational rehabilitation of disabled veterans. More than half of the 15,400,000 veterans of World War II received some training under the GI Bill.[2] Of particular interest to agriculture was the so-called institutional on-farm training which was designed to provide a combination of classroom instruction and supervised farming experience to farm veterans.[3] Even though funds for veterans' education came exclusively from federal appropriations, control over the program was considered to be a state responsibility.

There have been proposals for continuing federal aid for school construction and general aspects of the operation of school systems, but up to the time of the present writing these have not been successful. Opposition to federal aid to education is frequently justified on the grounds that such aid would carry with it the right to supervise the subject matter included in the school curriculum, which might provide an opportunity at some later date for a centralized government to establish effective control over education and thus abolish freedom of thought. There are, of course, other reasons for opposition, including the white southerners' fear that federal aid would hasten racial integration of the schools.

Those who argue for federal support of education justify their stand mainly on the basis that there is a national stake in providing equal educational opportunities. Educational facilities are very unequal because of the differences in resources among states and localities. Since a person who is reared, for example, on a farm in the rural South may eventually be a resident and worker in metropolitan New York, it is argued that part of the cost of providing him with an adequate education should be furnished by taxes from other states.

[2] Walter L. Slocum, "Veterans' Education—Investment or Handout?" *College and University Business*, August, 1952, p. 21.

[3] Walter L. Slocum, *Adjustment of Veteran Trainees to Farming and Rural Life*, Washington AES Bulletin 541, April, 1953.

RURAL ENROLLMENTS

Butterworth and Dawson have estimated that more than half of the elementary school children in 1947 were living in rural areas, while a little more than half of the rural children lived on farms.[4] In 1945-1946 nearly 72 percent of all public high schools were located in rural areas, although these schools only had 32 percent of the secondary-school enrollment and 37 percent of the instructional staff.[5]

Although full-time participation in occupational roles directly associated with farming is declining rather rapidly, the rural population of the United States is still very large, and is in fact increasing. Many of the elementary schools which farm children attend are located in hamlets, villages, towns, or even cities. Consequently, many farm children associate with children from nonfarm homes in the classroom and on the playground.

EDUCATIONAL ATTAINMENTS

The educational attainments of American farm adults are substantial and increasing. The number of persons receiving a high-school education has been steadily increasing for more than 20 years. The educational attainments of colored people are considerably below those of white people, reflecting the limited educational opportunities of the former, especially in the rural South.

In some sections of the United States there is now little difference between farm and nonfarm people with respect to the percentage of school-age children enrolled in school. The rural lag in education in the past was due to the inferior quality of instruction in one-room schools and the relative inaccessibility of high schools to farm youth coupled with some distrust of education. The rural-urban gap has been narrowed, however, and from all prospects will eventually be closed. The prosperous farmer of today is likely to be well informed and receptive to general as well as technical educa-

[4] Julian E. Butterworth and Howard A. Dawson, *The Modern Rural School*, McGraw-Hill, 1952, p. 138.
[5] *Ibid.*, pp. 156-157.

tion. Many farm operators and their wives are high-school graduates; a good number have completed college, and a few have advanced degrees.

ATTITUDES OF FARM PEOPLE TOWARD FORMAL EDUCATION

Sims indicates that the traditional attitude of early American Farmers toward formal education was one of indifference or even antagonism.[6] It was difficult for the "practical" farmer to understand what could be learned from books that would be useful in the operation of a farm. Prior to the development of scientific agriculture,[7] it was widely believed that a man who was ignorant of information from books could be as fully successful a farmer as a well-educated man, and perhaps more so. This attitude apparently still prevails among illiterate farmers in other countries, including Pakistan.[8]

In many sections of the United States today this traditional outlook on education has largely disappeared. The fear that schools might motivate young people to leave the farm was not unfounded, nor is it entirely a thing of the past; but many farm parents are anxious for their children to obtain as much education as possible so as to be able to compete on a more favorable basis for high socioeconomic status. There is also a growing recognition of the importance of formal education for those who expect to prosper under the competitive conditions of modern scientific agriculture.

ORGANIZATION OF LOCAL SCHOOL SYSTEMS

The members of local school boards are elected, and have an important voice in the management of the school. They approve budgets, employ teachers, and determine certain aspects of curriculum. This has been true from the beginning, and thus the school is in a very important sense a community agency rather than something imposed from above.

[6] N. L. Sims, *Elements of Rural Sociology*, 3rd ed., Crowell, 1940, p. 460.
[7] See Chapter 8.
[8] W. L. Slocum, Jamila Akhtar, and Abrar Fatima Sahi, *Village Life in Lahore District*, Lahore, Social Sciences Research Center, Panjab University Press, October, 1959.

Viewed as a social system, the school consists of a network of relationships between people who play roles as teachers, students, parents, taxpayers, community leaders, and school supervisory officials. From an educational standpoint, the most important groups in a school system are the learning groups or classes. There are other important student-teacher relationships, including individual contacts. Many extracurricular groups have been established by the schools when possible to occupy constructively the energies of the students outside their classrooms.

The membership requirements for students are simple. All normal children of the school district who have passed their sixth birthday and have not yet reached the age of 16 are required to attend public schools unless they are enrolled in an accredited private school. Since elementary schooling is ordinarily completed at 13 or 14, this means that high-school attendance is compulsory until the age of 16.

Each state has a department of public instruction. The chief school officer is ordinarily an elected official. He has a staff of appointed professional assistants who assist him in the formulation of policy and the administration of school laws and regulations. These administrative officials do not have legislative powers. The basic educational policies are laid down by the state legislature and approved by the governor, but the state department of public instruction does have considerable latitude in their interpretation and application. The borderline between law and administrative regulations is sometimes difficult to establish.

In most states, each county has a chief school officer who is usually elected by the people. He provides leadership and administrative supervision for the rural public schools within the county. There are usually a number of school districts in a county, each of which has an elected school board of from three to five members with a chairman. The board acts as an administrative body for the local school system. It delegates many of its administrative functions, except in the case of the one-room school, to an appointed superintendent who is charged with the responsibility for administering the school system in accordance with state laws and local policies. This official also has the responsibility of employing teachers, recommending promotions and adjustments in rank and salaries for the teachers, and constructing an annual budget.

SUBCULTURE OF SCHOOL SYSTEMS

The subculture of a school system is affected by the general culture of the society; there are certain societal standards or values which permeate the entire school system. At the same time there are local variations, and these frequently of considerable magnitude, because specific schools are social organizations which emphasize local participation and have a large degree of local control.

Every operating school system has an established official set of values and rules which are usually consistent with those of the general society but may vary from one school to another because of unique traditions or local circumstances. In addition, there will be unofficial values or standards among the students, for the most part the product of student relationships with each other and with the faculty. The social tradition of a student body is passed from older to younger schoolmates. If it conforms with the official values and rules and supports academic achievement as a means of gaining prestige within the school system and the student body, social control will not be a formidable task. Sometimes, however, the tradition of the student body emphasizes nonconformity, which gives rise to serious problems of maintaining discipline and transmitting the approved social heritage.

The values of the typical American school system are consistent with those of the society. An effort is made to find the better qualities rather than to emphasize the defects of children, and success rather than failure is expected in school as in later life. The high rate of promotions through the various grades has been criticized by many, and some schools are now beginning to adopt more demanding scholastic standards.

ELEMENTARY SCHOOLS

ONE-ROOM SCHOOLS

As noted above, the one-room, one-teacher rural school was essentially an American development. With its local board of directors who determine many of its policies, provide for its financing, and employ the teacher, it is a social system which operates on the neighborhood level. In 1918, there were 196,000 one-teacher schools. By 1958, the number had been reduced to 25,200, in keeping with the reduction in the number of school districts through those years from 127,530 to 44,170, of which 21,703 were rural.[9]

The children who attend a one-room country school come from the immediate vicinity. Because they are generally from families with comparable environments, occupations, and culture, contact with other pupils in the school does not ordinarily present any challenge to the values and behavior patterns which exist in the homes.

In the South, separate systems have been maintained for Negroes and whites. The U.S. Supreme Court has ordered an end to this system of "separate but equal" schools. In some localities this decree has led to an intensification of interracial tension and conflict; in others integration has taken place.

Sims considered the quality of instruction in one-room rural schools to be poor. He was convinced that most of the teachers were immature girls who were poorly trained, inexperienced, and interested in teaching primarily as a premarriage occupation. He also observed that school terms were generally shorter than those of urban schools, and that in addition farm children were frequently out of school to help with farm work.[10] Many of the same objections were cited by Baldwin and associates, who advocated the establishment of consolidated schools,[11] and Cubberly also criticized the one-teacher rural school severely.[12]

Very few recent writers have found anything to praise about the rural one-room school. Landis, however, has indicated that in his opinion the picture is not wholly black. Among the possible benefits, he suggested that a pupil in such a school learns to work without much direction in the midst of noise which forces him to concentrate if he is to learn. He also considered that the long walk to and from school might have some benefits and thought that some beginning teachers might have more enthusiasm than is commonly found

[9] R. S. Fox, ed., *Teaching in the Small Community*, National Education Association, 1956; W. H. Gaumnitz, *Small Schools Are Growing Larger*, U.S. Office of Education, Circular 601, 1959.

[10] Sims, *op. cit.*, chap. XX.

[11] B. T. Baldwin, Eva A. Fillmore, and Lora Hadley, *Farm Children*, Appleton-Century, 1930.

[12] Cubberly, *op. cit.*, pp. 104-106.

among more experienced teachers. On balance, however, he concluded that the disadvantages outweighed the advantages.[13]

Considered as a social system, the central group in the one-room rural school is, of course, the teacher and her pupils. It is to be regarded as a formal rather than an informal group since it is established by law and the pupils are required to attend if able-bodied and if they have not completed the eighth grade by a certain age. Cliques may exist among the pupils.

Leadership within the school is provided by the teacher. She has the responsibility of organizing the program of instruction in accordance with the course of study established by higher authorities. She must also supervise the conduct of the pupils both in the classroom and on the playground. Usually she is also the janitor and has the responsibility for starting fires, providing drinking water, and cleaning the building.

Although the teacher is the leader of the pupils, she is not a free agent; she is herself subject to many controls. She performs her multiple roles in relation to persons outside the immediate classroom group. She is employed and supervised to some extent by the school board. She also is supervised by the county superintendent of public instruction. The continuation of her career as a teacher depends upon her ability to maintain discipline and to establish satisfactory relationships with her pupils and their families, with whom she normally has direct interpersonal relationships regardless of whether or not they are organized into a formal parent-teachers association.

In her role as a leader of young people in the school system, the teacher is ordinarily expected to instruct not only by precept but also by example. Her actual teaching function is not restricted to intellectual matters but extends into the realm of ethics; parents who do not themselves fully conform to all of the moral standards of the community may nevertheless demand that the teacher's conduct be exemplary.

The problem of maintaining interest and discipline and achieving satisfactory educational progress in a one-room school is very difficult, especially if the teacher has all eight grades and a large number of pupils. With 20 to 40 classes a day, it is obvious that

[13] Paul H. Landis, *Rural Life in Process*, 2nd ed., McGraw-Hill, 1948, p. 28.

none can be very long. There is a great temptation for pupils to listen to the recitations of others rather than make preparation for their own subsequent lessons. The task must have been formidable for the teacher who had among her pupils one or more children whose progress in school had been retarded, as was sometimes the case on the frontier. Under these conditions, preference was given to strong male teachers who were able to maintain order through a display of their physical prowess. Corporal punishment is now little used in maintaining discipline, although in some rural communities it is still sanctioned if considered by the teacher to be necessary.

Brookover, analyzing the role of the teacher, has indicated that to be successful she must be friendly but still must establish control of the situation and demand respect.[14] No unvarying rule can be laid down on the question of how much social distance the teacher must keep to achieve this balance. As Lowry Nelson has observed, some teachers maintain order by punishing offenders who violate rules and regulations. Others are able to establish discipline by arousing the pupils' interest in the subject matter, manifesting personal interest in the progress of their pupils, and otherwise motivating pupils to perform adequately.[15]

The professional role of elementary-school teacher is now well established. Most are now married women, although until quite recently the majority were single.[16] Except on a temporary basis when adequately trained persons are not available, teaching positions are open only to those who have been certified by a public body such as a state board of education. Standards for certification are usually prescribed by state departments of public instruction, and include completion of a specialized curriculum which includes training in elementary school subjects and teaching methods, some practice teaching, and sometimes a special qualifying examination.

The greatest concentration of one-teacher schools is to be found in the midwestern states of Iowa, Nebraska, Wisconsin, Minnesota, Missouri, Illinois, South Dakota, Kansas, Michigan, and North Dakota.[17]

[14] Wilbur B. Brookover, *A Sociology of Education,* American Book, 1955.
[15] Lowry Nelson, *Rural Sociology,* 2nd ed., American Book, 1955, pp. 379-380.
[16] *Ibid.,* p. 395.
[17] U.S. Office of Education, "Statistics of State School Systems, 1953-54," *Biennial Survey of Education in the U.S., 1952-54,* 1956.

CONSOLIDATED ELEMENTARY SCHOOLS

The great reduction over the last 40 years in the number of school districts is due to the consolidation of small districts into larger ones. Ordinarily the schools within consolidated districts are located in towns or villages and not in the open country.

From the standpoint of educational services, consolidated schools are better able than one-room schools to provide high-quality instruction in the same subjects for two main reasons. First, the teacher is able to be something of a specialist; she does not have to cover every subject taught in all eight grades. Second, the district has greater financial resources, which means that it is able to pay better salaries and hence attract better-qualified teachers.

The consolidated school is able to offer opportunities for children to develop themselves in art, music, dramatics, and in subjects of other types which cannot effectively be offered by one-room schools, and it may also provide more health care and instruction. Furthermore, it can provide systematic instruction in physical education and recreation and gives the pupils the chance to participate constructively in student affairs; these activities are believed to assist them in learning how to "get along" with other people. The consolidated school which transports farm children to and from home by bus the same day does not, of course, provide opportunities to participate in extracurricular activities equal to those available to village children.

In terms of social development, however, the most important aspect of the consolidated school is the exposure of the pupils to standards of behavior and values other than those which prevail in their own families and neighborhoods. It removes to a very large extent the limited social participation which traditionally has been characteristic of farm children. It provides access to more adequate library facilities, and it has undoubtedly had a tremendous impact upon the patterns of family management exercised by farm parents. As noted in the discussion of the family,[18] the trend among farm as well as nonfarm families is toward the democratic and away from the authoritarian type of management prevalent in rural America until quite recently. To a considerable extent this change may be

[18] See Chapter 14.

attributed to the influence of the school contacts of young people with each other.

If the one-room country school is a neighborhood institution, the consolidated school may be considered as a community institution, serving a town- or village-centered area including both village and farm families.[19]

Considered as a social system, a consolidated school has some of the same characteristics as a one-room, one-teacher school, but has as its core a number of teacher-pupil groups, depending upon the size of the faculty and the number of classes involved. In the consolidated school there is likely to be more formal organization of relationships between parents and teachers, usually including a parent-teachers association. In addition to informal cliques, the pupils frequently associate according to their interests in formal athletic, forensic, dramatic, and social groups.

THE ELEMENTARY SCHOOL AND ITS COMMUNITY

As a community social system, the consolidated school has many relationships to the adults of the community as well as to the children and young adults who participate in its formal educational program and extracurricular activities.

The board of school directors acts to some extent as an intermediary between the school system and the electors. In addition, most school systems of any size organize parent-teachers associations for the purpose of involving the parents more fully in the problems encountered by the school, and frequently the teachers are encouraged or required to schedule periodic conferences with the parents of their pupils to discuss progress and problems.

Some school systems have enlisted the active participation of community leaders in the study of school-community relationships. An outstanding example of this was the program conducted in a suburb of Seattle, Washington.[20] A recent action-oriented study in the state of Washington involved the cooperative effort of school

[19] Dwight Sanderson, "Criteria of Rural Community Formation," *Rural Sociology*, December, 1938, pp. 373, 384.

[20] See Grant Venn, *The Development of a Long-Range Educational Plan in Bellevue, Washington*, unpublished Ed. D. thesis, State College of Washington, 1952.

authorities and community leaders and representatives of the Rural Sociology Department of the State College of Washington in the collection, analysis, and interpretation of information dealing with the interest of teen-agers in community betterment projects.[21]

SECONDARY SCHOOLS

One-room country schools do not normally provide instruction beyond the elementary level. Prior to the advent of the consolidated school, which normally provides secondary education at public expense to all pupils in a district which includes farm as well as nonfarm families, the farmer who wished to give his son or daughter a high-school education had to make his own arrangements for transportation of the child to the high school or for housing and board in a village or town. As Galpin noted in his study of Walworth County, Wisconsin, such schools were regarded as town schools.[22] The farmer had no voice in their management, nor did he contribute materially to their support. This situation apparently intensified mutual antagonism between farmers and townspeople.

Relatively few farm youths obtained a high-school education until quite recently. If the farmer was inclined to be suspicious of education in general, he was particularly likely to be hostile toward the high school. He felt, not without justification, that the high school had a tendency to educate the child away from farm life; once the child had been exposed to high school education, he was likely to be lost to the farm forever. In most farm families today, this is no longer a matter of grave concern, for because it is clear to many parents that they will not be able to provide adequate opportunities as farmers for their children, they are more likely to be sympathetic to providing them with additional education since they naturally want them to succeed.

Like the consolidated school, the high school may be regarded as

[21] See W. L. Slocum and Carol L. Stone, *A Summary of the Responses of Teenagers to a Questionnaire on Activities and Social Relationships in Four Washington Communities,* State College of Washington, Department of Rural Sociology, August, 1957. (Mimeo)

[22] See C. J. Galpin, *The Social Anatomy of an Agricultural Community,* Wisconsin AES Research Bulletin 34, May, 1915, for a discussion of this matter as perceived by farmers in Walworth County, Wisconsin, in 1914.

a social system which includes a number of groups. The central groups are the classes for which the teachers provide leadership. More than at the elementary level, there are school-sponsored student groups. In most cases these have some adult leadership provided normally by teachers who serve as advisors. As in the case of the elementary school, there is normally a high-school parent-teachers association. This is, of course, a school-sponsored rather than a citizen-sponsored organization in most cases, and attendance and participation is frequently quite superficial.

HIGH-SCHOOL OFFERINGS FOR FARM YOUTH

High schools provide preparatory subjects for those who are planning to attend college. They also provide a general orientation to certain aspects of life, principally through social studies courses such as civics, sociology, economics, history, and geography. A certain amount of vocational training is also offered, presumably directed primarily toward those who intend to terminate their formal education upon completion of their high-school career. These courses include vocational agriculture, home economics, secretarial studies, and certain other technical and trade instruction available in large school systems.

Special attention will be devoted here to the program of vocational training in agriculture which is carried out through the high schools.

Although there was some instruction in agriculture in schools prior to its passage, the Smith-Hughes Act of 1917 marked the real beginning of a systematic program of agricultural education at the high-school level. This legislation provided funds on a matching basis for instruction in the work of the farm or the farm home of persons over 14 years of age who were preparing to be farmers or farm homemakers.[23] Additional funds for this purpose were made available by the George-Barden Act of 1946. Local school systems which offer vocational agriculture and home economics courses are expected to pay part of the cost, the remainder coming from state and federal sources. At the state level, the supervisory agencies are the state boards for vocational education which maintain staffs in agricultural education and home economics.

[23] Public Law 347, 64th Congress, February 23, 1917.

A major purpose of vocational agriculture training in high schools is to prepare students for employment in occupational roles in agriculture. Training is related directly to the major types of farming found in the area served by a particular school, for example, dairying, poultry, wheat ranching, or cattle ranching. Some training is also provided for occupations associated with agriculture— for jobs in industries which process agricultural products, farm credit, agricultural education, agricultural communications, and special agricultural services—and there is considerable interest among vocational agriculture teachers in these occupations as outlets for students of their courses.[24] Persons who want such work, however, ordinarily have to obtain additional specialized training either on the job or in schools which provide the desired type of training.[25]

The vocational agriculture program at the secondary-school level involves both classroom instruction in various agricultural subjects and planning and participating in a supervised farming program. This is usually done on the family farm with the support of the father. Such activities not only serve to increase the knowledge of the student but tend to increase the parents' knowledge of modern farm practices.

RURAL SCHOOLS SERVING MINORITY GROUPS

Separate school systems, established during the so-called Reconstruction Era following the Civil War, are maintained for rural Negroes in most southern states. These are conducted in substantially the same manner as schools for white children.[26] In answer to mounting criticism that Negro schools do not provide equal facilities, many of the southern states have substantially increased expenditures for the Negro schools. In North Carolina, Tennessee, and Virginia in 1952 the average salaries of Negro teachers were higher than the average salaries of white teachers.

Subsequent to the May 17, 1954, decision of the United States Supreme Court outlawing segregation in the public schools, racial

[24] J. McMahon Bryon, "Agri-business: What Is It?" *County Agent and Vo-ag Teacher,* June, 1957, pp. 2-3.

[25] Butterworth and Dawson, *op. cit.,* pp. 176-177.

[26] Harry S. Ashmore, *The Negro and the Schools,* University of North Carolina Press, 1954, p. 9.

integration has started in some areas. Integration has been most rapid in the border states between the North and the South. Relatively little integration has yet occurred in the states of the deep South, where at the present time feelings are running very high. In the fall of 1957, federal troops were sent to Little Rock, Arkansas, to enforce the school integration decision of a federal court. This action evoked widespread criticism throughout the South, and it now appears that the ultimate date of full racial integration in the schools is fairly remote.

The federal government maintains elementary and vocational schools for Indians on the federal Indian reservations. Teachers in these schools are civil service employees of the federal government. There are some indications at present that American Indians will eventually be integrated into the general population, but this is likely to be a long-term enterprise.

QUESTIONS FOR FURTHER STUDY AND DISCUSSION

1. Discuss the problem of school integration in a southern rural community.
2. What were the major factors in altering the traditional attitudes of farm people toward formal education?
3. Describe the roles and interaction patterns involved in a specific school system with which you have personnal experience, using the terminology of the text.
4. What are the principal advantages and disadvantages of consolidated elementary schools from the standpoint of families living on isolated farms?
5. Describe a parent-teachers association, indicating clearly how the operations of this organization influence the school system with which it is associated.

SELECTED REFERENCES

Ashmore, Harry S., *The Negro and the Schools,* University of North Carolina Press, 1954.

Baldwin, B. T., Eva A. Fillmore, and Lora Hadley, *Farm Children,* Appleton-Century, 1930.

Brookover, Wilbur B., *A Sociology of Education,* American Book, 1955.

Butterworth, Julian E., and Howard A. Dawson, *The Modern Rural School*, McGraw-Hill, 1952.

Kreitlow, Burton W., *Rural Education: Community Backgrounds*, Harper, 1954.

National Education Association, *Rural Education—A Forward Look, Yearbook 1955*, 1955.

Sims, N. L., *Elements of Rural Sociology*, 3rd ed., Crowell, 1940.

22

Other Educational Systems

Although the educational level of the adult farm population of the United States has been increasing, rural farm people are less well educated than urban residents.[1] As noted in the previous chapter, this appears to a large extent to be a result of the rather deeply held attitude dating from early times that book learning is impractical. Nelson attributes this showing to the failure of rural farm parents two generations back to encourage their children to attend school or to provide educational facilities.[2] This is unquestionably true.

There is a growing appreciation among farm people in the U.S. of the value of education. This is clearly demonstrated by information from the national census showing that with the passage of time, more and more farm adults have taken advantage of opportunities for high-school and college education.

Formal education in America is most often organized in terms of specific age levels. It would be unthinkable for a mature farm operator or homemaker to enter elementary school or even high school as a regular student. Relatively few older people are found in classes even at the college level.

The major educational systems other than the public schools in which farm people are involved are the land-grant colleges and universities, rural libraries, and veterans' farm training programs associated with public high schools.

LAND-GRANT INSTITUTIONS

Land-grant colleges and universities, a unique American development, have played a central role in the transformation of American

[1] See Chapter 21.
[2] Lowry Nelson, *Rural Sociology*, 2nd ed., New York, American Book, 1955, p. 411.

agriculture from a magic-oriented, animal-powered art to the present science-oriented, highly developed technology found on leading farms. They have influenced agricultural technology and rural life, as noted previously, through innovations made by agricultural research workers. These have been communicated to farmers and their families through resident teaching at the college level, through the teaching of vocational agriculture at the high-school level, and through the work of agricultural extension services, an integral part of the land-grant colleges.

Land-grant institutions, of great importance in the historical development of farm technology, exert a continuing influence in the direction of further applications of science in agriculture; the magnitude of their educational operations is indicated by the fact that 1,428,000 students were enrolled in 1958 in 68 land-grant institutions, 16 of which were predominantly Negro.[3] Therefore, it seems worth while to examine in some detail the internal organization of these social systems as well as the relationships which American farmers and their families have with "democracy's colleges."[4]

THE HISTORY OF THE LAND-GRANT COLLEGE IDEA[5]

Although there had been earlier attempts to establish agricultural colleges, the development of land-grant institutions as they exist today really dates from the passage of the Morrill Act of 1862. This act, which was approved by President Lincoln, donated "public lands to the several states and territories which may provide colleges for the benefit of agriculture and the mechanic arts." Their development and eventual acceptance by farm people was gradual and fraught with many difficulties. Some of the problems involved can be better understood if we recall that in 1862 institutions of higher learning devoted themselves almost exclusively to classical subjects. They viewed their mission to be that of imparting classical educational culture to sons of upper-class families. In addition, they provided specific training for those going into the high-status

[3] U.S. Bureau of the Census, *Statistical Abstract of the United States: 1960,* 1960, p. 128.

[4] See Earle D. Ross, *Democracy's College—The Land-Grant Movement in the Formative Stage,* Iowa State College Press, 1942.

[5] See Edward Danforth Eddy, Jr., *Colleges for Our Land and Time: The Land-Grant Idea in American Education,* Harper, 1957.

professions of law, medicine, and the ministry. Coeducation was unknown. There was no well-established public system of secondary education to provide a substantial flow of students qualified for college entrance. The free elementary school system, although in existence by that time, offered little more than rudimentary subjects taught largely by rote.

At the time the Morrill Act was passed, agricultural research as it exists today as well as the experiment station, was virtually non-existent. There was therefore no tested body of knowledge relative to agricultural practices, and the suspicion frequently voiced by farmers about "book learning" was perhaps justified.

The research and teaching activities of most land-grant colleges are not restricted to agriculture, home economics, and engineering, as the "mechanic arts" are now construed, although some do devote their major activities to these areas. Many other fields are also covered, among them natural and biological science, social science, the humanities, and the professions of law, medicine, and social work.[6] Because of the traditional separation of church and state in America, however, the land-grant colleges do not provide theological training. With this single exception, viewed collectively they offer instruction in all branches of higher learning.

The contributions of the land-grant colleges are well recognized by contemporary leaders in the field of agriculture, a large proportion of whom are graduates of such institutions. However, at the present time the colleges do not view their function as primarily that of training individuals to go directly into farming. Still, the Agricultural Extension Service does maintain what is universally recognized as the largest adult education program in the world which takes the information from agricultural and home economics research to farm families in their own homes and communities.

The research conducted by agricultural experiment stations and made available to farmers through the extension services has played a major part in increasing the productivity of American agriculture, although this revolution in farm technology has not resulted in higher farm incomes. On the national level, the basic problem is that production of agricultural products has outrun effective demand, and as a

[6] In recent years many of the state legislatures have changed their designation of land-grant institutions from state college to state university.

result, farm earnings have not kept pace with nonfarm incomes. Productivity has risen dramatically during a period when federal farm programs have ostensibly attempted to control production, for improvements in farm machinery, farm practices, crop varieties, and animals have enabled commercial farmers to produce more on fewer acres and with less labor.

If we consider the world as a whole, it is evident that no real surpluses of food or fiber exist. However, under current conditions the improverished people of Asia and other underdeveloped areas do not have sufficient buying power to constitute a good market.

There is general agreement that the control measures to limit production which have accompanied price support programs have been unsuccessful. There is apparently a widespread feeling in the nonfarm sector that farm programs are ineffective and constitute an unwarranted charge which has to be met from taxes. (See, for example, the statement by Kenneth Galbraith in *U.S. News and World Report,* November 21, 1960.) An uncomplimentary image of farmers as tax eaters has been fostered and encouraged by some urban magazines.

Because the majority of the people in the United States now live in urban areas, with less than 9 percent directly engaged in primary agricultural pursuits in 1960, there is grave danger that state and national legislators may in the future take unfavorable action on proposals aimed at alleviating farm problems unless these are perceived as in the *general* interest. It should be noted that neither of the candidates for the presidency paid very much attention to the farm problem in the 1960 campaign.

Recently some of the land-grant colleges have undertaken systematic studies of some of the economic and social problems associated with the current situation in agriculture. Iowa State University has taken the lead by establishing what is called the Center for Agricultural and Economic Adjustment. A recent publication of the Center has set forth the problem in the following words:

The problems of agriculture and rural people are changing. A major one is the failure of the adjustments in agriculture to keep pace with the current rates of economic change in the industry. These lags are creating acute local, state and national problems. These adjustment problems have reached the stage where rural people are saying that they must be given attention by the educational institutions the same as they give to the problems of technology.

The Colleges of Agriculture, the Agricultural Experiment Stations and the Extension Services were created when the problems of rural people were largely technological. For this reason, most of the work of the agricultural institutions was largely technically oriented. Technical progress was so slow that it was assumed that the adjustments that must accompany progress would automatically take care of themselves. But they have not. To meet the problems of rural people today, therefore, involves broadening the scope of the activities of the Land-Grant Colleges. The situation calls for reorientation of their programs, the development of new subject matter and the use of new educational approaches to meet these new types of problems.[7]

It is too early to say what the outcome of this attempt at reorientation will be, but it certainly seems reasonable to look to the land-grant colleges and universities for sound information for use in making new agricultural policies.

Determined efforts have been made since the cessation of hostilities after World War II, particularly under the Point 4 Program and its successors, to make the agricultural technology developed by the land-grant colleges and associated agricultural industries available to underdeveloped countries. Many land-grant institutions have played a leading role in this, sending staff members to various areas of the world under the stimulus of the federally sponsored program of technical cooperation. Some have helped with similar programs sponsored by the United Nations and financed in large part by the United States. Marked success of these efforts could materially reduce world markets for American farm products, but this possibility has not acted as a deterrent up to the present time.

INTERNAL ORGANIZATION OF A LAND-GRANT UNIVERSITY

Although there are many variations in administrative structure, the work of the typical land-grant university, which is oriented toward agriculture, may be considered in terms of the three-fold mission of the land-grant institution: research, resident teaching,

---

[7] Iowa Sate University of Science and Technology, Center for Agricultural and Economic Adjustment, *Agricultural Adjustment: A Challenge and Opportunity for Land-Grant Colleges*, AAC-66, May, 1960, p. 2.

and extension. Because these activities are to some extent separate, even though in a larger sense they are interdependent, they and their relationships to farm people will be discussed separately.

Agricultural Research

The agricultural research activities of the land-grant college and university system are carried out within the agricultural experiment stations. These were established pursuant to the Federal Experiment Station Act of 1887, commonly known as the Hatch Act because of its sponsorship by Representative Hatch of Missouri. This and subsequent federal statutes, such as the Purnell Act of 1925 and the Bankhead-Jones Act of 1935, provided authorization for continuing federal appropriations to the states for agricultural research.

The federal grants, though important, are substantially less in total than the sum of state appropriations.[8] In addition to these funds, research may be financed by sources like the Ford Foundation, by agricultural cooperatives, by business organizations, and by branches of the federal government other than the Department of Agriculture. In recent years, funds from the Atomic Energy Commission and the Defense Department have been of considerable importance.

Ross has noted that the idea of agricultural experimentation and research was stimulated by the experiment stations established by Germany, France, and England which had made some efforts to test agricultural innovations.[9]

Although substantial federal appropriations are made annually for research at the state experiment stations, research workers at these stations are employees of the land-grant colleges and subject to administrative supervision and other personnel policies of the several institutions. Funds are allocated to the stations in accordance with established formulas based upon agricultural production and farm population or other provisions of the federal statutes.

There is some federal supervision over the work involved in the expenditure of federal funds. Before these funds can be used for any specific investigation, a project outline covering the work must be submitted to the Cooperative State Experiment Stations Service of the Department of Agriculture for prior approval. In addition, the

[8] U.S. Office of Education, *Statistics of Land-Grant Colleges and Universities,* Circular No. 541, 1957, p. 43.

[9] Ross, *op. cit.,* p. 137.

Service sends representatives to each of the state experiment stations annually to inspect vouchers and other documents reflecting expenditures, to obtain information regarding the progress of the work on every federally approved project, and to discuss progress and plans with research workers and local administrators. This supervision has been exercised in such a way as to minimize the extent of federal direction, placing the emphasis upon the needs of the various states and allowing the individual investigator wide latitude in following his own initiative and independent judgment.

The research conducted by the experiment stations in the field of agriculture has dealt principally with problems in the production of food and fiber. Experiments in nutrition, genetics, and pest control have been enormously successful, and the diffusion of the results to American farmers has helped them achieve tremendous increases in productivity. There has even been some criticism of agricultural research, principally from people not directly associated with farming, for enabling farmers to produce so much, and a few have gone so far as to call for the cessation of research until such time as burdensome surpluses of agricultural products have been disposed of.

The continuing surpluses, reduced only in the wartime period, have led to emphasis on marketing and utilization research designed to find new markets for agricultural products. It has also led to interest in off-farm employment as a means of increasing the income of farm people.

Some research has been conducted in social science fields, a large part of it also oriented toward production increases, notably diffusion research by rural sociologists and farm management studies by agricultural economists. Other problems of rural people have also been investigated in research conducted by home economists, rural sociologists, and agricultural economists. The Hatch Act, as amended, provides the following authorization:

It shall be the object and duty of the State agricultural experiment stations through the expenditure of the appropriations hereinafter authorized to conduct original and other researches, investigations, and experiments bearing directly on and contributing to the establishment and maintenance of a permanent and effective agricultural industry of the United States, including researches basic to the problems of agriculture in its broadest aspects, and such investigations as have for their purpose the development and improvement of the rural home and rural life and the maximum contribution by agriculture to the welfare of the consumer.[10]

The majority of experiment station professional workers have dual roles—their appointments involve both research and resident instruction. A few have joint appointments in the agricultural experiment station and the agricultural extension service, and some are named for all three posts. To some extent, these dual or triple occupational roles involve conflicting expectations and loyalties, but they are most often complementary in their demands. This is especially true of research and resident teaching roles.

The role set with which an experiment station worker is concerned in the performance of his role involves other professional workers and administrative officers of his department, the division of agriculture, and the university. Normally he does not have any direct contacts with the board of trustees or regents. Outside the university he maintains contacts with other members of his academic discipline, and does his research with an eye to obtaining the approval of eminent professionals in his field. Most of his research is directed toward the application of scientific principles to problems which are of economic concern to farm people, and consequently he will normally also be in touch with farm leaders and other lay people who are prominent in affairs pertaining to his specialty. A poultry scientist, for example, may expect to have contact with poultrymen and poultry organizations in his own state and perhaps also regionally and nationally. One who works on problems associated with particular commodities may be under considerable pressure from commodity organizations to channel his activities toward questions which are of immediate economic concern to the organizations and the associated industry. These pressures tend to maximize applied research and minimize fundamental research concerned with the discovery of principles which have no immediate application.

Resident Teaching

Resident teaching in a land-grant college or university, as noted above, may cover any or all branches of learning except theology.

[10] U.S. Department of Agriculture, *Federal Legislation, Rulings, and Regulations Affecting the State Agricultural Experiment Stations*, rev., Miscellaneous Publication 515, January, 1959, p 1.

Within the division of agriculture, emphasis is upon the applied sciences as they pertain to various branches of agriculture. The student of agriculture is ordinarily required to take courses in English, mathematics, the humanities, and the social sciences offered by other divisions of the institution. Home economics instruction is administratively placed within the division of agriculture in some Land-grant schools, while in others it is an independent division which reports directly to the dean of the faculty or the president. There is, of course, little similarity between the professional curriculum in home economics and that in the several branches of agriculture.

The number of technical courses in agriculture have increased with the continual growth of knowledge accumulated through the research conducted by the agricultural experiment stations. Consequently, the course load tends to be very heavy, with relatively little latitude for electives or for required subjects in fields other than agriculture. The proliferation of courses has been such that consideration is being given to reorganizing the curriculum and eliminating certain introductory courses which duplicate work available at the secondary level or in other departments.[11] The alternative seems to be the addition of a fifth year, which already exists in some agricultural fields, particulary agricultural education.

Undergraduate courses are designed to prepare students for farming, for work in industries associated with agriculture, for teaching positions in vocational agriculture at the high-school level, and for agricultural extension work. Graduate courses may be regarded as professional in character; they are designed to prepare students for eventual participation in teaching, research, and extension as fullfledged professionals in a particular specialty. In this respect, the graduate training does not differ from that provided by colleges and universities in other fields. It involves the same degree of commitment in terms of the standards and ethics of the profession, the same general sort of preparation, and the same types of tests or "rites of passage." The preparation for the doctoral degree requires course work, satisfactory performance on a preliminary examination before admission to full candidacy, and the acceptance of a thesis reporting

[11] Such a change has been made at Michigan State University and is receiving consideration at Washington State University.

research conducted under the direction of a committee of the graduate faculty.

Land-grant colleges and universities also provide systematic instruction for the benefit of farmers and specialists of various kinds who are employed in the field of agriculture. These short courses usually do not carry credit for a degree, although some kind of certificate or diploma may be awarded after satisfactory completion of a prescribed term of study. Attendance at the short courses may be large or small depending upon cost, reputation, and accessibility of the institution.

The role of the resident instructor, as we have said, is frequently combined with that of research worker, but is seldom combined with that of agricultural extension teaching. The role set of significant others with whom the resident instructor interacts within the institution include other members of the department, other members of the institutional staff, administrators, and, of course, students. Contact is maintained with professional organizations. Normally there is little or no contact with parents of students or with outside groups, organizations, or agencies while one is performing the role of resident instructor.

The sociological function of this work is to transmit pertinent aspects of the established culture, in this case the principles arrived at by experimentation and research in the particular scientific disciplines involved. At the undergraduate level it does not put any substantial emphasis upon innovation or the development of the student's creative ability, which are given some attention at the graduate level.

The Agricultural Extension Service

The most important adult education agency for farmers and farm homemakers is the cooperative agricultural and home economics extension service. It has a total staff of more than 12,000 professional workers, and is, as noted, the largest educational organization dealing with farm adults. Its mission is not exclusively adult, however, since it does carry on a youth program popuarly known as 4-H work.

ORGANIZATIONAL STRUCTURE. The agricultural extension service in each state is an agency that operates under the authority of and by means of appropriations from the federal government, from the

states, and from the counties in which agricultural and home agents
are located. Within each of the several states, extension workers
are associated with the land-grant college or university; at the county
level, the county agent reports to the county commissioners or board
of supervisors.

EDUCATIONAL SERVICES. The educational services provided are
both specific and general in character. Specifically, one of its major
responsibilities is the dissemination to farmers and farm homemakers
of the results of experiment station research which can be used to
improve the farm, the home, the community, and the nation. Its
general mission is described by Mathews as "not so much to make
two blades of grass grow where one grew before, but to develop
self-confident, effective and understanding men, women, and youth
who will be capable of meeting leadership responsibilities."[12]

There are both male and female county agents, called respectively
county agents and home demonstration agents in some states and in
others both called county agents. Those who deal primarily with the
youth program are often called 4-H agents. In some states, the youth
program is the responsibility of all extension workers.

With respect to the content of the extension teaching program,
Mathews reports that historically agricultural production has received the greatest attention from agricultural agents.[13] This consists
of information and assistance in planning for various farm enterprises. In some counties there will be specialists in horticulture,
weeds, agronomy, poultry, and other enterprises or commodity
programs. The agricultural phase deals with problems of livestock
and crop production of all kinds, including soil and water conservation, soil improvement, wildlife management, and farm management.
Some attention is also given to marketing and distribution programs.

The home demonstration agent, on the other hand, finds her work
primarily in the areas of foods, clothing, home furnishings, and other
phases of home life including, to an increasing extent, questions dealing with family relationships and child development.

The youth program is organized around social groups with adult

---

[12] J. L. Mathews, "The Cooperative Extension Service of the United States,"
in C. P. Loomis et al., Rural Social Systems and Adult Education, Michigan
State College Press, 1953, p. 55.
[13] Ibid., p. 63.

leadership. The child who is a member of a 4-H Club undertakes a project under the supervision of the leader and with the assistance in many cases of the parent. Representative projects for boys include such enterprises as raising calves, pigs, or rabbits, and for the girls, having a garden, sewing, and canning.

Other aspects of rural life in which the agricultural extension service has an interest include community development, health, recreation, and discussions of social and economic problems and agricultural policy.

Of particular interest to rural sociology is the extension community development program. The extension service in many states has helped community leaders to establish communitywide development programs, to improve town-country relationships, and to train other community leaders. Mathews has reported that in 1950 extension agents assisted 34,100 communities with their recreational facilities, 57,600 community groups with organization problems, nearly 7,000 communities in obtaining library facilities, and 2,266 communities in building community houses. In 1951, 25 states had full-time community organization specialists.[14]

TEACHING METHODS. The teaching methods used by the agricultural extension service are generally informal in character; relatively few programs employ formal classroom methods. The traditional approach used in the early days of the service was the result demonstration. This method is still employed, but it has been supplemented with tours, work through local leaders, and work with groups. A study by Wilson and Gallup indicates that the result demonstration is less effective and more expensive than some other methods.[15]

Recently the extension services have adopted a method of working intensively with individual families or groups of families to teach the principles of effective decision-making in plans for their homes and farms, a process variously known as farm and home development, the farm and home unit approach, and farm and home planning, depending upon the state. This method involves detailed and repeated contact with the family by a county agent and a county

[14] *Ibid.*, p. 69.
[15] M. C. Wilson and Gladys Gallup, *Extension Teaching Methods*, USDA, Extension Service Circular 495, August, 1955, p. 21.

home demonstration agent. As conceived in the state of Washington, it involves interaction between husband and wife in planning for the future of farm operations in terms of the attainment of family goals. This is not a simple matter of disseminating information about specific techniques. It is a complex process which involves intimate interpersonal relationships over a period of time between the extension staff and the cooperating family. The method was introduced at federal suggestion and has been financed to a major extent by funds obtained from federal appropriations.[16]

EXTENSION WORK IN FOREIGN COUNTRIES. Especially since the termination of World War II and the provision of various types of aid to underdeveloped countries by the United States and the United Nations, there has been a great deal of interest abroad in the methods employed by the Agricultural Extension Services. Many county agents and other extension employees have spent some time in various foreign countries helping to establish similar organizations and programs, modifying them, of course, to meet the local culture.

RURAL LIBRARIES

Libraries may be regarded as agencies which have educational as well as entertainment functions. Ordinarily a public library is maintained by some unit of local government. Kolb and Brunner feel that the number of rural libraries is inadequate, and Nelson agrees.[17] Unlike the agricultural extension service, a library is essentially a local social system. As such, its growth is not stimulated by some larger agency which has a vested interest in it and which offers encouragement, financial and otherwise, for the promotion of library services. This probably explains the great variation from state to state and from county to county in the provision of library services. The President's Advisory Commission on Education proposed that the federal government make grants-in-aid to states in order to expand library services.[18] The proposal was incorporated

[16] See Chap. 13 for a summary of a Washington study of the effectiveness of the method.
[17] John H. Kolb and Edmund deS. Brunner, *A Study of Rural Society*, 4th ed., Houghton Mifflin, 1952, p. 348; Nelson, *op. cit.*, p. 423.
[18] Nelson, *op. cit.*, p. 427.

in a general plan of federal support for public education, and no such program has been enacted.

In Oregon, Illinois, and Louisiana there are state libraries which extend their reading programs to any individuals interested.[19]

After a comprehensive survey of public libraries in the United States, Ruth Warneke concluded that the potential of adult education through libraries in rural areas is largely undeveloped. She pointed out that two-thirds of American rural areas had no library services in 1951 and those which existed generally lacked the financial support necessary to provide adequate library facilities and programs.[20]

Considered as a social system, a local rural library usually has a small staff headed by a chief librarian, and a board of directors which sets policy, helps to gain public support for the library from the community, and acts as an intermediary between the library and the source of public funds. Relationships between the library and individual citizens are usually on an individual basis, although services may be provided to groups in some cases.

In addition to stocking books and periodicals, libraries also sometimes carry films on topics of current interest. Libraries in some states maintain traveling "bookmobiles."

ADULT EDUCATIONAL PROGRAMS CARRIED ON BY PUBLIC SCHOOLS

Public schools in a number of states provide vocational and general programs of adult education. These programs are available both in rural and in urban areas. In 1950-1951 more than 300,000 adult males were taking evening classes in vocational agriculture. The heaviest enrollment was in Texas, followed by Georgia and South Carolina.[21] The majority of those who were seriously enrolled in vocational agriculture in 1950-1951 were undoubtedly farm veterans of World War II. Table 17 shows the average number of

[19] Ruth Warneke, "Public Libraries," in Loomis et al., p. 188.

[20] Ibid., p. 198.

[21] John F. Thaden, "Adult Education in the Public Schools and the Community," in Loomis et al., op. cit., pp. 24-51; U.S. Office of Education, Digest of Annual Reports of State Boards for Vocational Education, Fiscal Year Ending June 30, 1951, pp. 88-89.

TABLE 17.   Average Number of Veterans Enrolled Annually in Institutional On-Farm Training Under Laws Administered by the Veterans Administration, United States, 1945-1955[a]
(In Thousands of Veterans)

Fiscal Year	Total	Public Law 346	Public Law 16	Public Law 894	Public Law 550
1945	0.2	0.1	0.1	—	—
1946	12.0	11.5	.6	—	—
1947	99.8	91.7	8.2	—	—
1948	232.4	208.4	24.0	—	—
1949	309.2	272.6	36.7	—	—
1950	348.7	305.6	43.1	—	—
1951	320.8	285.0	35.8	—	—
1952	252.3	229.8	22.5	—[b]	—
1953	135.1	122.1	11.7	.2	1.1
1954	70.6	53.2	5.5	.5	11.4
1955	47.5	16.6	2.6	1.1	27.2

[a] Public Law 346, 78th Congress (Servicemen's Readjustment Act of 1944), is popularly known as the GI Bill for World War II veterans. Public Law 550, 82nd Congress (Veterans' Readjustment Assistance Act of 1952), authorized education and training benefits to veterans of the Korean emergency period. Public Law 16, 78th Congress, authorized training benefits for disabled World War II veterans found to be in need of vocational rehabilitation. Public Law 894, 81st Congress, authorized an extension of Public Law 16 benefits for disabled veterans of the Korean emergency period.
[b] Less than 50 veterans.
SOURCE: United States Veterans Administration, cited by J. V. McElveen, "Family Farms in a Changing Economy," USDA, Agricultural Information Bulletin 171, March, 1957, p. 29.

veterans in training each year from 1945 to 1955 under federal programs administered by the Veterans Administration.

In the period following World War II, adult programs in vocational agriculture were established in many parts of the United States under the provisions of the G.I. Bill and the Vocational Rehabilitation Act. These were generally operated by the high schools, although they had little connection with the usual programs of vocational agriculture. Ordinarily, additional personnel were employed to teach the classes and supervise the on-farm activities of veterans.

Because it combined classroom instruction with supervised farm experience, the program was known officially as the institutional on-farm training program. The on-farm phase was available on a farm controlled by the veteran or operated by another farmer who had proved to be qualified and equipped to give this type of training.

A large number of veterans participated in these programs, doubtless motivated in part by the fact that the Veterans Administration paid tuition and subsistance allowance to participants. More than 9 out of 10 of the institutional on-farm trainees took their training on a farm under their own control through either rental or ownership.[22]

Training was provided for veterans who wished to become established as farm operators, managers, or specialists in certain types of farming. The training course included instruction in various phases of production, processing and marketing farm products, record keeping, soil conservation, and basic principles of farm management.

While in training the veterans were required to attend regularly scheduled classes and also to devote full time to farming activities under the supervision of qualified instructors. Classes were customarily held in the evening, usually in the high-school agricultural room or building.

Training at government expense could not exceed four years for a farm operator or two years for a person who took his training under another farmer. Participation in the program was restricted by law to those who were able to demonstrate that they needed training. The G.I. Bill contained a requirement that a veteran who trained on a farm under his own control was required to operate a farm "which . . . if the veteran intends to continue such farm at the close of his course, will assure him a satisfactory income under normal conditions."

A study of the operation of the veterans' training program in the state of Washington led the writer to conclude that perhaps half of the men included in the sample would not have been per-

[22] U.S. Veterans Administration, *Report on Education and Training Under the Servicemen's Readjustment Act as Amended from the Administrator of Veterans Affairs,* printed for use of the U.S. Committee on Labor and Public Welfare, 1950, p. 37.

mitted to enter the training program on the farms they were operating if the rules had been applied strictly. Many of the farm units were marginal or submarginal in the economic sense:

> Not all of the veterans will be able to make a success of farming. Some will fail because of inadequate financing, poor farming methods, poor land and equipment, poor motivation, or a combination of these things. . . .
>
> There will remain, after the failures have dropped out of the running, a solid and substantial group who will be successful farmers and who will also, in most cases, be well adjusted to community life. There are indications that many of these veterans will be leaders in agriculture and community affairs. . . . the educational program does not appear to be sufficient by itself to provide all of the assistance needed by a veteran who wishes to become a farm operator. The veteran in most cases needs help in locating a good farm. He also needs financial backing and favorable credit terms.[23]

The World War II program has, of course, largely disappeared. This review of its accomplishments and problems is chiefly of value as an indication of what might be accomplished through systematic courses for adult farmers. In this connection it is interesting to note that most of the Washington veterans studied were found to be serious-minded and persistent in their studies. Their instructors reported that 57 percent had adjusted themselves very well in their communities. Most of the veterans who gave an evaluation of the training program were quite well satisfied with it.[24]

QUESTIONS FOR FURTHER STUDY AND DISCUSSION

1. Prepare a report on the social organization of a land-grant college or university in your state, following the outline of this chapter.
2. Discuss the function of short courses for farmers, indicating whether you consider this to be a proper use of university funds.
3. What is your opinion on the desirability of continuing research by agricultural experiment stations which is designed primarily to increase agricultural production?

[23] W. L. Slocum, *Adjustment of Veteran Trainees to Farming and Rural Life,* Washington AES Bulletin 541, April, 1953, p. 20.

[24] W. L. Slocum, *Agricultural Training for Veterans: A Report on Reactions of Participants,* Washington AES Circular 206, October, 1952.

4. In many states part-time farming and rural residence have increased to the point where the majority of people in rural counties are now not engaged in full-time agriculture. This situation has made it very difficult for the state agricultural extension service to plant programs within its proper scope of operations. Discuss this matter with a representative of your extension service and give his opinions plus your own concerning the proper clientele for the service. Should it give its attention to full-time commercial farmers only or should it also include others who have problems involving various agricultural techniques, community development, or family matters?

5. Two-thirds of rural America had no library services in 1951, and most of those which existed were classified by Warneke as inadequate. How would you improve this situation?

6. What is your opinion about the feasibility and desirability of providing systematic classroom instruction in agriculture for farm adults? What about general education?

SELECTED REFERENCES

Loomis, C. P., *et al.*, *Rural Social Systems and Adult Education*, Michigan State College Press, 1953.

Ross, Earle D., *Democracy's College—The Land-Grant Movement in the Formative State*, Iowa State College Press, 1942.

Wilson, M. C., and Gladys Gallup, *Extension Teaching Methods*, USDA, Extension Circular 495, August, 1955.

23

Rural Religious Systems

Religious social systems include both the concrete local networks of interrelationships known as congregations or churches and the abstract groupings represented by the major world religions. Our interest will be focused principally upon the former, with special reference to the rural United States. We should be aware, however, that the forms of religious organization and the associated systems of belief and practice found in this country differ in major respects from those of people in Asia, Africa, and other parts of the world who profess other faiths than Christianity.

Considering the entire population of the world, it has been estimated that approximately 820,000,000 people in 1960 were Christians, of whom about 207,000,000 were Protestants. There were about 416,000,000 Moslems, 300,000,000 Confucians, 300,000,000 Hindus, 150,000,000 Buddhists, and 50,000,000 Taoists to mention only those believed to have as many as 50,000,000 adherents.[1]

The rural population of the U.S. is predominantly Protestant.[2] At the time of the 1936 census of religious bodies, the most recent comprehensive nationwide church census, some Protestant denominations such as the Norwegian Lutheran Church (now the Evangelical Lutheran Synod), the American Baptist Association, the Southern Baptist Convention, and the Church of the Brethren were

---

[1] Dan Golenpaul, ed., *Information Please Almanac Atlas and Yearbook, 1961,* McGraw-Hill, 1961, p. 365.

[2] Lowry Nelson, *Rural Sociology,* 2nd ed., American Book, 1955, p. 350; A. L. Bertrand, ed., *Rural Sociology,* McGraw-Hill, 1958, p. 240; Glen W. Trimble, *Two Worlds of Church Life in the United States,* National Council of the Churches of Christ in the U.S.A., March 28, 1959.

predominantly rural in membership.[3]

These data mean, of course, that great care must be exercised in applying information from empirical studies of rural American religious systems to rural people elsewhere. Furthermore, it should be borne in mind that there are very substantial differences in this country among local religious bodies affiliated with different Christian denominations.

RELIGIOUS CULTURE

Every major religious system possesses a more or less distinctive set of beliefs and practices which may be regarded as religious culture and whose influence on the attitudes of the believers may be very profound.

Religion as a set of ideas or values within a culture system appears to be at once a dynamic force and a stabilizing influence. It is dynamic in the sense that it influences human behavior; it is stabilizing because it usually makes its appeal in terms of moral and spiritual values handed down from the past. Loomis and Beegle have concluded that the influence of the rural church is more likely to be conservative than to facilitate change.[4] This appears to be a correct judgment.

The Christian religion is considered by most Americans to be one of the great character-building forces in their society. It is generally regarded as the basic source of prevailing concepts of morality and of ethical standards for interpersonal relationships. As Kimball Young has pointed out, its influence is both direct and indirect.[5] The influence of the golden rule and other Christian precepts extends beyond the doors of the church to the entire culture of America, affecting the behavior of many who are neither members of nor participants in any particular church. It is taken for granted that a devout church member would be influenced to a greater extent by the values and standards of behavior which are stressed by the church than those who may profess belief but who are not

[3] U.S. Bureau of the Census, *Summary and Detailed Tables*, vol. I of *Census of Religious Bodies, 1936,* 1941; National Council of the Churches of Christ in the U.S.A., *1960 Yearbook of American Churches,* 1960.

[4] C. P. Loomis and J. A. Beegle, *Rural Sociology, Prentice-Hall,* 1957, p. 205.

[5] Kimball Young, *Sociology,* American Book, 1940, pp. 484-490.

churchgoers. However, a recent statewide study of high-school and college youth in Washington did undertake to analyze the relationship between extended participation and social adjustment. The investigator concluded that "young people who participate regularly in church activities will have fewer problems of adjustment in their homes, in their relationships with their peers (their own age group), and in school situations than those who take little or no part in church activities."[6] Nye found evidence in his study of data from three medium-sized Washington towns that church attendance by both parents and adolescents tended to be associated with lower rates of delinquent behavior.[7]

The power of religious culture to influence behavior has varied from one society to another and from one period to another within a particular stream of culture. In the U.S. at the present time religious ideology takes the form of promoting tolerance, honesty, brotherly love, and the other virtues epitomized by the Ten Commandments and the golden rule. This has not always been the case: within western civilization, history has recorded such extreme religious-associated behavior as the wars of the Crusades against the Moslems, the Spanish Inquisition which sought to exterminate heretics through torture and burning the unrepentant at the stake, and persecution of the Jews and other minorities. Many of the early colonists came to North America to escape religious persecution at home, but a good number were little if any more tolerant of those whom they themselves considered heretics to their particular dogma.

The degree of religious tolerance which now exists in America is a product of interaction among the representatives of various denominations. Sociologically it can be classified as a form of accommodation.

An interesting example of the change in religious teaching from one period to another is reflected in the current acceptance by most Christian leaders of the basic tenets of the natural and physical sciences, once considered by many devout believers as heretical. The turning point in the U.S. was probably the Scopes trial, which featured Clarence Darrow, the famous Chicago attorney, and

[6] Carol L. Stone, *Church Participation and Social Adjustment of High School and College Youth,* Washington AES Bulletin 550, May, 1954, p. 28.

[7] F. Ivan Nye, *Family Relationships and Delinquent Behavior,* Wiley, 1958, p. 35.

William Jennings Bryan, the orator and political leader, as the principal actors. The trial was conducted in a rural Tennessee town, where a high-school science teacher, John T. Scopes, who had taught the theory of evolution, was found guilty of violating the laws of Tennessee. However, the publicity given to the opposing points of view effectively broke the hold of reactionary religious leaders, and the teaching of science in the public schools encountered few if any major obstacles of this sort from that time onward.

The imagery of the Bible is rural because the Christian religion arose from the faith of the Hebrews, who were pastoral and rural people. But there is no reason to presume that there is or should be a rural religion as distinguished from an urban religion within the general framework of Christianity. In spite of this, some rural sociologists have indicated a belief that rural religion is distinctive in character.[8] It is true that the major religions differ in respect to the influence of rural traditions and the use of agricultural imagery.[9] Furthermore, there is evidence that farm people in the past have been more conservative in clinging to traditional beliefs and practices than urbanites.[10]

Particular churches located in rural communities may emphasize somewhat different rules of conduct for members than other churches of the same denomination located in urban centers, but it would be difficult to demonstrate that this is a universal condition or that the theology is, in fact, different. It seems reasonable to believe that the dogma of a particular denomination is fairly uniform in all its congregations and that differences between rural and urban churches in this respect are differences of degree only.

As we noted in Chapter 5, large numbers of non-English Europeans settled on farms in the northern United States. They brought with them their religious ideas, beliefs, practices, and forms of social organization along with other aspects of their culture. It appears from studies of the assimilation of immigrant stocks that religious ideas and practices persisted longer than certain other aspects of their culture. John P. Johansen found that the displacement of the

[8] See Paul H. Landis, *Rural Life in Process*, 2nd ed., *McGraw-Hill*, 1948; P. A. Sorokin, C. C. Zimmerman, and C. J. Galpin, *A Systematic Source Book in Rural Sociology*, University of Minnesota Press, 1931, II, 372.

[9] Sorokin, Zimmerman, and Galpin, *op. cit.*, chap. 14.

[10] *Ibid.*, pp. 375-380.

foreign language by English in South Dakota church services took place over a relatively long period of time, and was accompanied by other significant changes:

In the history of most foreign congregations one may observe three fairly distinct stages of language uses: foreign language wholly; both the foreign language and English [American]; and the native language. This change of the church language is accompanied by profound spiritual changes in the nature of the service liturgies and hymns [which] are essentially untranslatable. . . . When the language of the old country is dropped, the worship of the immigrant churches rapidly changes so as to conform in general with the democratic spirit, the urban-industrial life, and the patriotism of America.[11]

Commenting on the development of American variations of the religious culture brought by immigrant settlers, Hepple has said that the separation of church and state accomplished by the Constitution of the United States has been of profound importance because it meant that all churches were required to function as voluntary organizations. This, of course, was a marked change for some of the religious bodies which were state-supported. In his words:

For example, the Methodists became independent of Wesley and the Methodist Church of England, and the Church of England became the Protestant Episcopal Church. The Roman Catholic Church, while never to be thought of as an independent church in any country, began seeking more recognition for the church in America directly from Rome rather than by way of lesser authorities in Europe. Religious bodies·such as the Baptists, which had been organized in terms of local sovereignty, had few ties to break with Europe.[12]

The conditions on the frontier provided a challenge for the church, since churches as well as other local social systems had to be established. Hepple has suggested that the Baptists and the Methodists tended to be more successful on the frontier than the Congregationalists and the Presbyterians because their clergy took the initiative while the latter required that a congregation be organ-

[11] John P. Johansen, *Immigrant Settlements and Social Organization in South Dakota,* South Dakota AES Bulletin 313, June, 1937, p. 54.

[12] Lawrence M. Hepple, *The Church in Rural Missouri: Part I, Introduction,* Missouri AES Research Bulletin 633A, September, 1957, p. 8.

ized before a minister could be called. During frontier times there was a period of revivalism featuring "hell-fire and damnation" sermons at camp meetings. According to Hepple, "these meetings provided a temporary escape from the hardships of the frontier, an opportunity for social participation with other people, and a significant religious experience."[13]

After the passing of the frontier, some religious bodies changed their religious practices to eliminate the revival meeting. This led to the development of new denominations, including the Pentecostal, Holiness, and Assembly of God, which carried on the revival tradition.[14]

These changes in religious culture accompanied and were correlated with changes in the economic and social conditions of the members of local churches. As we will see later, certain types of religious practices apparently appeal to persons of different social rank.

SOCIAL FUNCTIONS OF RURAL CHURCHES

The major functions of rural churches appear to be the following.

1. Churches play an important part in the socialization of individual members by instructing them in the religious values of the denomination or sect through the church school and through the Sunday worship service, which usually features a sermon, prayers, and related religious rituals.

2. Churches sometimes solicit contributions from constituents for the relief of the needy, both in the local community and elsewhere. The Mormon Church, for example, carried on a major program during the 1930s for the relief of destitute members and their families. Since the major burden of meeting welfare needs in the U.S. has been assumed by local, state, and federal government agencies, church activity in the welfare field has greatly diminished. It should be noted, however, that American churches have given invaluable service in the resettlement of individual refugees and refugee families since World War II. Many local congregations have sponsored one or more refugees.

[13] *Ibid.*, p. 9.
[14] *Ibid.*, p. 9.

3. A church may provide recreational activities for members, particularly those who are affiliated with subsidiary groups such as Sunday school classes, women's societies, men's brotherhoods, or youth groups. However, the purely recreational aspects of church activities are to be regarded as supplementary rather than primary and probably are to be found to a lesser extent in rural than in urban congregations.

4. A church may provide counsel and guidance to members on troublesome personal and social relationships such as marital problems. Pastors have probably always done a certain amount of this, but it appears to be increasing, particularly in the Protestant churches.[15]

5. A church functions as an agency of social control. Every church is concerned with the conduct of its congregation and also with that of other members of the local community of which the church is a part. In Christian churches the attention of unpaid as well as paid leaders is directed to promotion of proper conduct as defined by the Christian religion. Motivation for conformity is found to a considerable extent in the dogma that individuals who live a Christian life will be rewarded after death while those who are sinful will be punished, though, as Kimball Young has alleged, fear of judgment after death is unquestionably less important than it once was.[16]

6. Churches provide solace to individuals in times of bereavement and crisis. In fact, it is common even in societies with advanced technology for people to appeal to supernatural powers for assistance in meeting difficulties of many kinds, whether they be natural catastrophies, war, or personal trials. Recognizing this, Loomis and Beegle have identified one of the major functions of religion as "adjustment to the unexpected." There are many such crises in agriculture due to the fact that weather and certain other processes of nature cannot be controlled; according to Loomis and Beegle, "In most rural areas, religious beliefs and practices serve to provide security in those realms that have not been brought completely under human control."[17]

[15] See Samuel Blizzard, "The Minister's Dilemma," *Christian Century*, April 25, 1956.
[16] Young, *op. cit.*, p. 499.
[17] Loomis and Beegle, *op. cit.*, pp. 204, 205.

RURAL CHURCHES AS SOCIAL SYSTEMS

In connection with its study of the church in rural Missouri, the Department of Rural Sociology of the University of Missouri has classified local religious systems into two categories: church-type and sect-type. Church-type groups are described as those which have adjusted to and accepted secular society, whereas the tendency to revolt against or withdraw from secular society is said to be predominant among the sect-type groups.[18] In the Missouri sample of 505 religious groups, 73.5 percent were classified as church-type and 26.5 as sect-type. Church-type groups averaged 121 members compared with 51 members for the sect-type. On the other hand, the sect-type groups were more active; 62.7 percent as compared with only 39.1 percent of the church-type bodies were full-time churches with worship services every Sunday.[19]

MEMBERSHIP

Membership in a specific church is a voluntary matter; consequently, members or constituents are relatively free to leave one church and join another. Since churches like other formal social systems are interested in growth rather than decline, this feature of membership places a premium on adapting the program of activities of the church and its suborganizations to the desires of the congregation. Active proselyting is generally frowned upon by church-type groups, but the sect type usually have no such inhibitions. Both types feel free to recruit any person who shows some interest by coming to worship services or to meetings of suborganizations.

Like other social systems, religious systems must attract new members if they are to continue active over a period of time. Coughenour and Hepple point out that in addition to meeting the specific interests and needs of participants, the suborganizations of local religious groups may also serve to some extent as recruiting agencies. The Sunday school, for example, plays a large part in

[18] Hepple, *op. cit.*, p. 33.
[19] Milton Coughenour and Lawrence M. Hepple, *The Church in Rural Missouri: Part II, Rural Religious Groups*, Missouri AES Research Bulletin 633B, September, 1957.

preparing children and youth for eventual church membership.[20]

The membership requirements of local religious systems are ordinarily determined by the denomination or sect with which they are affiliated. These differ greatly. Some, like the Amish, are closed and accept no new members except by birth. Catholics are members at birth if born into a Catholic family, and others may join by conversion after systematic instruction in the religious beliefs and practices and a public confession of faith. Most Protestant denominations require an affirmative and voluntary confession of faith by older children and adults. Some local religious systems are easy to join, others difficult.

In most Christian religions, membership in a local church is generally terminated through death, transfer, or long failure to attend. It is rarely revoked except for violation of the religious mores. The Catholic Church uses the sanction of excommunication to maintain social control. Excommunication involves withdrawal of membership privileges including confession and the last rites administered to the dead. The Amish use such means as forbidding worldly pleasures and contacts with outsiders under pain of social shunning or ostracism.

Some churches attempt to discourage withdrawal by social pressure. Those who leave may be called backsliders or other uncomplimentary names. Loomis and Beegle have described the methods used by the old-order Amish in some detail; among the devices used for restricting interaction with members of other social systems are distinctive clothing, hair style, and headdress.[21]

Some Protestant denominations maintain special departments in their national headquarters devoted to rural churches. The Catholic Church operates a special rural organization known as the Catholic Rural Life Conference. Some seminaries have special courses for rural clergymen.

ORGANIZATIONAL STRUCTURE

Small Protestant congregations usually have relatively simple organizational structures consisting of the congregation as a whole with a board of trustees and few other officers or subgroups. With

[20] *Ibid.*, p. 90.
[21] C. P. Loomis and J. A. Beegle, *Rural Social Systems*, Prentice-Hall, 1950, pp. 229-230.

growth, however, the number of activities tends to increase as does the number of subsidiary organizations devoted to the development of such activities. In addition, with increasing size subsidiary organizations may become more complex and formal. For example, a small rural church may have one women's group and a small number of educational classes or suborganizations. Contrasted with this, a large congregation which includes both farm and nonfarm members may have several women's groups, one or more men's groups, a number of specialized youth groups, and several educational groups. There may also be special groups comprised of people of comparable ages and interests. For example, the Mormons have a comprehensive program of social recreation for members, including supervised social dancing for young people.

The Missouri study collected information about the frequency of occurrence of seven major types of subgroups, which included 91.2 percent of all the suborganizations reported by the 505 local religious systems studied.

	Percent of Churches Reporting
1. Sunday school	94.7
2. Women's organization	60.6
3. Youth organization	44.6
4. Choir	34.1
5. Men's club	14.5
6. Young adult organization	6.2
7. Older adult organization	2.2

SOURCE: Milton Coughenour and Lawrence M. Hepple, *The Church in Rural Missouri: Part II, Rural Religious Groups,* Missouri AES Research Bulletin 633B, September, 1957, p. 97.

Some churches had more than one of a given type of suborganization; 5.3 percent of the total number of churches reported none whatever and 34.1 percent had Sunday schools only. All the rest had two or more. However, some groups existed only on paper as a part of the formal structure of a few of the rural churches studied. Many of the suborganizations which were actually operating were found to be multipurposed, having numerous supplemental functions and aims in addition to the central one.[22]

[22] Coughenour and Hepple, *op. cit.,* p. 101.

WORSHIP SERVICES

The most important collective activity of a religious system is the worship service. With the exception of such groups as the Mormons and the Quakers which emphasize lay leadership in worship, the service is generally under the direction of a priest or pastor. The principal services are ordinarily held on Sunday.

Because of the differences between denominations in the way religious services are conducted, it is not possible to present a pattern which would be characteristic of all rural Christian religious social systems. Ordinarily there will be a sermon by the priest or pastor or by some lay member of the congregation who has been assigned this responsibility. In addition, there will frequently be reading of portions of the Scriptures, responsive readings, prayer, and participation in singing hymns. Coughenour and Hepple have observed that the worship service promotes sociability and the solidarity of the group because it is at this time that the largest number of group members meet together.

In addition to Sunday worship services, some local church groups conduct services during the week and some conduct revival meetings. In 1952, 78.6 percent of the rural churches in the Missouri study reported revivals as a part of their church program. One of the purposes of the revival is, of course, the recruitment of new members. In the Missouri sample, 4.2 percent of the religious groups reported a program of "visitation evangelism," a plan that provides for pairs of lay members of the church to visit prospective new members.[23]

ACTIVITIES OF SUBORGANIZATIONS

The activities of church suborganizations for which information was collected in the Missouri study included religious education, fund raising, recreation, social reform, sponsorship of youth organizations such as boy scouts and 4-H Clubs, welfare, and other activities; as noted above, some of the subgroups carried on a number of different activities.

The Missouri study found that with the exception of the Sunday

[23] *Ibid.*, p. 85.

school, which was approximately the same for the church-type and the sect-type groups, religious education activities were provided by a much higher percentage of the former than the latter. Nearly 8 out of 10 of the suborganizations reported some recreational activities, which were found more frequently in church-type than in sect-type groups. These recreational activities included church suppers or picnics; recreation for children, youth, adults, and older adults; and the provision of a nursery during worship services.

A high proportion of the suborganizations in the Missouri study conducted various social services, including sending flowers to the sick and to funerals, visitation of the sick and the aged, sending Christmas and Thanksgiving baskets, and providing medical service. All but 14.5 percent of the organizations carried on these activities, and the differences between the church-type and sect-type groups were not substantial.[24]

RURAL CHURCH LEADERSHIP

Most American religious systems employ professional leaders. Notable exceptions to the general rule are the Latter-Day Saints (the Mormons) and the Society of Friends (the Quakers), both of which depend upon lay leadership. Paid leaders may be called priests, preachers, ministers, pastors, or clergymen. In this discussion we will use the last term.

It should not be thought, however, that churches which employ paid leaders make no use of laymen whatever; there is a considerable amount of lay leadership in the subsidiary organizations. Men are more likely to occupy leadership positions than women. Kaufman found that men in open-country churches comprised 42 percent of the membership but held 59 percent of the offices.[25]

In most denominations, the clergyman carries the major responsibility for not only worship services but also most other activities of the church. He may not hold the major leadership roles in subgroups, but he is likely to be consulted frequently on the program of activities and perhaps on the nomination or appointment of the

[24] *Ibid.*, pp. 105, 107, 116.
[25] Harold F. Kaufman, *Religious Organization in Kentucky*, Kentucky AES Bulletin 524, August, 1948, p. 33.

leaders of suborganizations as well. Because of his importance, it seems desirable to consider selected aspects of the clergyman's motivations, characteristics, economic remuneration, and roles.

The Decision to Enter the Ministry

The first questions which arise relate to occupational choice. What are the primary factors in the decision to enter the ministry? It may be assumed that the *processes* of occupational choice are the same as those for other occupations.[26]

When asked to give the reasons why they had chosen their vocation, rural Missouri clergymen offered three principal reasons: the call to preach, home influence, and the desire to serve people. Frequently more than one reason was involved. More of the sect-type (84.7 percent) than of the church-type (61.9 percent) listed the call to preach as one of the major reasons for entering the ministry. Hepple comments:

"It is frequently mentioned that the sect-type religious groups and clergymen tend to place greater emphasis on the religious experience of conversion than the church-type, since the latter [have] come to place considerable emphasis upon religious education. According to this hypothesis the typical sect-type position is that joining the church must be accompanied by the genuine religious experience of conversion which in most instances is highly emotional. It also follows that the *call to preach* should be a genuine religious experience."[27]

Rural ministers are predominantly from rural families. Of the rural clergymen included in the Missouri Church Study, 84 percent had lived in rural areas prior to entering the ministry. More than half (54.2 percent) of their fathers were farmers, while only 7.5 percent of their fathers were clergymen. Many had been active in church activities—Sunday school, choir, youth organizations—before entering the ministry. Hepple has expressed the opinion, undoubtedly correct, that clergymen probably participated in more church activities prior to entry into the ministry than their peers. Only about one out of five had entered the ministry without first having held some other occupation. The majority of both church-

[26] See Chapter 13.
[27] Hepple, *op. cit.*, p. 183.

type (52.3 percent) and of the sect-type (76.5 percent) ministers were part-time leaders who occupied dual occupational roles at the time of the study.[28]

CHARACTERISTICS OF RURAL MINISTERS

The Christian ministry in the United States is predominantly an occupation for men. In 1950, according to the U.S. Census Bureau, only 4 percent were women. In addition there is a tendency for ministers to be men of mature age. In 1950, 48 percent were 45 years of age or over. Nationwide information on the characteristics of rural ministers does not seem to be readily available.

Confirming the national statistics, relatively few of the ministers in the Missouri rural sample (only 2.6 percent) were women. With respect to age, there was some concentration in the upper age categories, but nearly 3 out of 10 (29.4 percent) were under 35.[29] The study revealed that sect-type clergymen had much less formal education than the church-type; 82 percent of the former as compared with 29 percent of the latter had less than a college education, and only 1.2 percent as compared to 33.1 percent of church-type clergymen reported seminary training.

Kolb and Brunner indicate that there has been some improvement in professional training of rural ministers, but that this has occurred to a greater extent in villages and towns than in open-country churches.[30]

Many of the Missouri rural clergymen devoted only part of their time to the ministry; only 41.7 percent were full-time. Sect-type ministers were much more likely to be part-time ministers—only 23.5 percent were full-time in comparison to 47.7 percent of the church-type.[31]

ECONOMIC SITUATION OF RURAL CLERGYMEN

Many rural sociologists have called attention to the relatively low salaries of rural ministers. Kolb and Brunner have said that

[28] *Ibid.,* pp. 169, 176.
[29] *Ibid.,* p. 176.
[30] John H. Kolb and Edmund deS. Brunner, *A Study of Rural Society,* 4th ed., Houghton Mifflin, 1952, p. 371.
[31] Hepple, *op. cit.*

while there had been some improvement since the depression of
the 1930s, salary increases up to 1952 had not kept pace with either
the increased cost of living or the higher incomes of farmers.[32]
Lowry Nelson has commented that reliable information on this
subject is not readily available, but he concluded that information
from census sources indicated a marked improvement between 1940
and 1950.

After careful analysis of the economic circumstances of Missouri
rural clergymen, Hepple suggests that it would be a mistake to
regard a rural minister's salary as an adequate indicator of his
total economic situation.[33] As noted above, the majority of the
Missouri rural clergymen occupied dual occupational roles and
hence received income from other sources than the ministry. In
addition, 47 percent were provided with a parsonage and 17.7 percent received a travel allowance.[34]

Many rural ministers receive gifts of food and clothing in addition
to their cash salary, fees, and other perquisites. Considering all
sources, however, there is little doubt that the rural minister's
compensation is generally very modest.

Robert L. Skrabanek has observed that the limited financial resources of rural churches and low salary scales have led to the
practice, apparently of long standing, of one minister's serving more
than one congregation. In 1926, 62.5 percent of rural ministers
served two congregations or more.[35] Carr, a young southern pastor,
has alleged that low salaries make it difficult to keep ministers in
rural churches.[36] Skrabanek has called attention to the use of open-
country churches as training opportunities for those who will later
become urban ministers, and has noted that the rural ministry in
the U.S. has been characterized by rapid turnover.[37] In the rural
Missouri study, 60 percent of the ministers had served the same

[32] Kolb and Brunner, op. cit., p. 372.
[33] Hepple, op. cit., Chapter 14.
[34] Ibid., p. 202.
[35] Cited by Nelson, op. cit., p. 362, from C. Luther Fry, The U.S. Looks at Its
Churches, Harper, 1930.
[36] J. M. Carr, Bright Future: A New Day for the Town and Country Church,
John Knox Press, 1956, pp. 34-35.
[37] Robert L. Skrabanek, "The Rural Church: Characteristics and Problems,"
in Bertrand, ed., op. cit., pp. 247-248.

church for only two years or less; only one in five had remained at the same church five years or longer.[38]

ROLES OF CLERGYMEN

Clergymen as professional religious leaders perform a number of different roles in and with reference to local religious systems. Two sociological studies have investigated certain of these roles. Blizzard identified and studied the following six roles performed by Protestant clergymen in the United States: administrator, organizer, pastor, preacher, priest, and teacher.[39] However, he found no evidence of rural-urban differences in the self-images that a national sample of Protestant ministers held with respect to the performance of their roles.[40]

Hepple identified eight roles of rural Missouri clergymen, and also collected information about the performance of selected activities related to some of them. Hepple's description is of interest here because it provides a basis for understanding the functions performed for local churches by rural clergymen.

Role 1. Symbol of Religious Ideals. The personal life of a clergyman is expected to conform closely to religious ideals. Thus, he is regarded as a living example of the teachings of his church.

Role 2. Prophet. As a prophet, a clergyman is expected to interpret God's will through his sermons. The responses of rural Missouri clergymen indicated that most of them tended "to state their messages in broad and general religious terms. . . ." They apparently did not ordinarily point out the application of religious principles to the problems of daily life.

Role 3. Priest. The role of priest includes performance of religious rituals at "worship services, communion or mass, baptisms, weddings, and funerals." Nearly all of the rural Missouri clergymen interviewed conducted at least one worship service every Sunday and many conducted two or more. Almost two-thirds reported one or more weddings and nearly 8 out of 10 reported one or more funerals during the survey year.

[38] Hepple, *op. cit.*, p. 167.
[39] Blizzard, *op. cit.*
[40] Samuel Blizzard, "The Parish Minister's Self-Image and Variability in Community Culture," *Pastoral Psychology*, October, 1959.

Role 4. Student. As a student, the clergyman devotes time "to study, Bible reading and meditation, and general reading of books and periodicals." Many rural Missouri clergymen apparently gave relatively little time to reading. Fourteen percent had not read a single book other than the Bible during the survey year while 52 percent of the sect-type and 19 percent of the church-type ministers read less than six books. The typical minister read four periodicals regularly. Hepple has suggested that the limited reading is probably related to performance in other roles. In this connection, it may be noted that the majority of the rural Missouri clergymen were busy men who had other jobs and performed their ministerial functions on a part-time basis.

Role 5. Pastor. This role "includes serving as counselor, advisor, and spiritual guide in the conferences, confessionals, and visitations which take place between the clergyman and his people." In rural Missouri churches, local church problems, family relationships, and religion were the three topics most frequently discussed in conferences involving the role of pastor.

Role 6. Administrator. This role includes property management, formulation of church policies, integration of the functions of sub-organizations, and promotion of church-related activities.

Role 7. Supervisor. As a supervisor, a clergyman has the responsibility of advising and training lay leaders.

Role 8. Representative of the Church. The clergyman is expected to be the symbol of and spokesman for his local church as he participates in meetings and activities in the community. Hepple found that most rural Missouri clergymen were not active either in community affairs or in organizations outside the church. The majority (62 percent) had not attended a single community meeting during the survey year. Only 31 percent had attended a meeting of a luncheon group or a fraternal order. The study also showed that few ministers did much public speaking outside the pulpit. Evaluating the responses, Hepple said that "one is forced to conclude that these clergymen tended either not to serve as the church's representative in society or to do so only on a minimum basis."[41]

[41] Hepple, *op. cit.,* pp. 210-218.

PARTICIPATION IN CHURCH ACTIVITIES

Participation is not the same thing as membership. According to surveys made by H. P. Douglass only about half of the members attend church services.[42] On the other hand, Rockwell Smith found in Wisconsin that rural churches had more constituents than members.[43] More farm people are *members* of churches and *participate* in church affairs than of any other voluntary social organization.[44] Some studies have indicated that church participation tends to be higher among urban than among rural people,[45] but a nationwide study made for the *Catholic Digest* indicates that on the national level attendance at Sunday church services of city and country dwellers did not differ greatly (Table 18). There were, however, very substantial differences between Protestants and Catholics.

Not all farm people participate in church activities to the same extent. Some attend services regularly, some do so infrequently or not at all, and others seldom attend formal church services but may participate in one or more of the auxiliary church groups.

Much information on participation in the rural church has been gathered in various parts of the country. In 1952, Hostetler and Mather abstracted relevant information from 73 such studies. The major conclusions from their review may be summarized as follows.

1. Farm people who participate in church activities also tend to be more active in other organizations.
2. Women tend to be more faithful in church attendance than men, though men are more likely to be selected as church officers.
3. Participation tends to be more common among older rural people.

[42] H. P. Douglass, "Some Protestant Churches in Rural America," *Town and Country Church*, January, 1950.

[43] Rockwell C. Smith, *The Church in Our Town*, Abingdon Press, 1955.

[44] John A. Hostetler and W. G. Mather, *Participation in the Rural Church*, Pennsylvania State College, Department of Agricultural Economy and Rural Sociology, Journal Paper 1762, October, 1952. See also C. P. Loomis *et al.*, *Rural Social Systems and Adult Education*, Michigan State College Press, 1953, pp. 322-323; Nelson, *op. cit.*, p. 324.

[45] See H. M. Bell, *Youth Tell Their Story*, American Council on Education, 1938; M. J. Taves, *Factors Influencing Personal Religion of Adults*, Washington AES Bulletin 544, November, 1953; Stone, *op. cit.*

TABLE 18. Frequency of Church Attendance of American Adults

Frequency of Church Attendance	Total Population	Rural Residents	Farmers	Roman Catholics	Protestants
Every Sunday or Sabbath	32	32	30	62	25
About three times a month	13	16	15	8	16
About twice a month	12	14	14	6	13
Once a month or less	11	10	11	6	14
Don't attend	32	28	30	18	32
Total	100	100	100	100	100

SOURCE: "Do Americans Go to Church?" *Catholic Digest*, December, 1952, p. 5.

4. The size of rural churches is directly related to density of settlement—the denser the settlement, the larger the congregation.
5. Newcomers in a community generally participate in church activities less than old-timers. This is related to land tenure; farm owners are more likely than tenants to be church members, and owners, of course, have greater residential stability than tenants. Furthermore, owners tend to be more active in church affairs.
6. Church members and participants tend to have higher incomes than others. As might be expected, there is a direct relationship between income and the amount contributed to the church.
7. Negroes and whites nearly always belong to different local religious systems.
8. Most people are brought into religious social systems as members of families. In the words of W. A. Anderson, ". . . If husbands participate, wives usually participate, and if wives and husbands participate children usually do, so that participation is chiefly a family trait."[46]
9. Church membership is positively related to formal education. In

[46] W. A. Anderson, "The Family and Social Participation," *American Sociological Review*, 1943, p. 420, cited in Hostetler and Mather, *op. cit.*, p. 23.

addition, church officers tend to have more formal schooling than those who are not officers.[47]

Actual participation in religious groups and activities may decline to some extent with advanced age. The majority of those interviewed in a sample of older people in Thurston County, Washington, reported that they were less active in church functions than they had been when they were younger. This study also indicates that participation through personal attendance is not necessarily an adequate criteria of the religious interest or activities of older people: "Even though a substantial proportion of the respondents neither belonged to a church nor attended church services, 89 percent of the women and 78 percent of the men reported that they listened every week to some religious program on the radio or on television."[48]

In response to the question, "Judging by your experience, do you think your church is taking sufficient interest in its older people?" 50 percent answered in the affirmative and 11 percent in the negative. Six percent believed that the church was showing sufficient interest in some ways but not in others. The remaining 33 percent were undecided or unwilling to offer an opinion. The responses indicated that some churches had special programs for older people. Those who had a church connection and also made suggestions for the improvement of services to older people most frequently emphasized a desire for visits from church members and for transportation to and from church.[49]

THE CHURCH AND ITS COMMUNITY

Local religious systems have relationships as social groups with other social organizations. Furthermore, church members share certain common interests both as church members and in their roles as members of other social systems in the community. The survival of rural churches as community-oriented institutions depends in large measure on the services performed for their constituents. These, in turn, are seriously affected by the resources of the con-

[47] Hostetler and Mather, *op. cit.*, p. 30.
[48] Carol L. Stone and W. L. Slocum, *A Look at Thurston County's Older People*, Washington AES Bulletin 573, May, 1957, p. 41.
[49] *Ibid.*, pp. 41-42.

gregation in terms of active membership and financial support. Obviously, small churches are unable to provide the same set of services as larger churches; neither are they able to attract or retain professional leadership of the same quality.

There has long been a trend toward concentration of the membership of rural churches in villages rather than in the open country. Some open-country churches have moved to the trade centers because of the obvious advantage of central location, though many have had the strength to remain. In the Far West, there are relatively few, since rural churches were generally established initially in the village trade centers. In other parts of the country, improved transportation facilities have made it easy for farm families to reach villages or cities on the Sabbath, which has tended to increase participation in larger churches with more facilities. Kolb and Brunner have offered the opinion that the villageward trend will continue.[50]

Shifting the community base of the church from an open-country neighborhood to a town-country community obviously broadens the range of interaction of farm residents by bringing them into fellowship with nonfarm people.

Douglass has called attention to the tendency for small villages with a population of less than 500 to have from two and a half to three times as many churches per 100 persons as larger villages and towns.[51] This may result in poorer rather than better religious service and undesirable social consequences within the community; excessive competition between churches disrupts community solidarity and tends to aggravate divisions between factional groups. Kolb and Brunner have correctly noted that competition between churches is not entirely a matter of differences in religious doctrine; the basic factors in many cases are social or economic, including such matters as race, ethnic background, tenure status, social class, and occupational affiliation.[52]

To meet the problem of providing adequate religious services to people in small rural communities, various types of cooperation among Protestant churches have been proposed. One suggestion is federated churches, which are local mergers of the congregations

[50] Kolb and Brunner, *op. cit.,* pp. 364, 365.

[51] H. Paul Douglass and Edmund deS. Brunner, *The Protestant Church as a Social Institution,* New York, Harper, 1935.

[52] Kolb and Brunner, *op. cit.,* p. 374.

of two or more denominations into a single religious system for purposes of worship. In a federated church, however, individual members still retain their affiliation with the original denomination. Another type is the denominational community church; under this system, group of cooperating denominations may assign a community to one of the cooperators. Usually this is done on the condition that the surviving denomination broaden its terms of membership and adopt a "definite community outlook."[53] Still another variation is called the larger parish, which involves the integration of two or more churches of the same denomination into a single organization having a unified staff that provides religious services to all the constituent groups. This permits staff members to specialize. In this plan the previously existing open-country church buildings may be retained for neighborhood meetings, recreation, and religious education, but the Sunday services are concentrated in the trade center.[54]

Mark Rich has set forth the potential contribution of the rural church in community development enterprises,[55] which no doubt can be a very large one. However, information from the Missouri survey cited above indicates that the professional leadership in many rural churches has little or no community orientation or consciousness of social problems existing in the community.

QUESTIONS FOR FURTHER STUDY AND DISCUSSION

1. Describe the social organization of a rural church with which you are familiar.
2. Many rural sociologists have discussed the problems of so-called over-churched communities in rural areas. What is the solution to these problems?
3. What is the larger parish idea? What merit has it for solving problems of weak open-country churches?
4. What connection, if any, is there between religious beliefs and agricultural rituals and practices?

[53] Douglass and Brunner, *op. cit.*
[54] Kolb and Brunner, *op. cit.*, p. 376.
[55] Mark Rich, "How the Church Can Contribute to Community Programs," in Irwin T. Sanders, *Making Good Communities Better*, University of Kentucky Press, 1950.

5. Describe the differences between membership and constituency. Discuss the impact of this difference on local churches.

6. In your opinion, what are the reasons for low salaries of rural clergymen? What solution would you propose?

SELECTED REFERENCES

Coughenour, Milton, and Lawrence M. Hepple, *The Church in Rural Missouri: Part II, Rural Religious Groups*, Missouri AES Research Bulletin 633B, September, 1957.

Hepple, Lawrence M., *The Church in Rural Missouri: Part I, Introduction*, Missouri AES Research Bulletin 633A, September, 1957.

Hepple, Lawrence M., *The Church in Rural Missouri: Part III, Clergymen in Rural Missouri*, Missouri AES Research Bulletin 633C, December, 1958.

Kolb John H., and Edmund deS. Brunner, *A Study of Rural Society*, 4th ed., Houghton Mifflin, 1952.

Loomis, C. P., and J. A. Beegle, *Rural Sociology*, Prentice-Hall, 1957.

Nelson, Lowry, *Rural Sociology*, 2nd ed., American Book, 1955.

Rich, Mark, "How the Church Can Contribute to Community Programs," Irwin T. Sanders, *Making Good Communities Better*, University of Kentucky Press, 1950.

Sorokin, P. A., C. C. Zimmerman, and C. J. Galpin, *A Systematic Source Book in Rural Sociology*, The University of Minnesota Press, 1931, vol. II.

24

Governmental Systems: Local, State, and Federal

The actions of farm people in all parts of the world are influenced by laws and regulations established by governmental systems. The degree of influence depends upon the prevailing political philosophy and other aspects of the relevant culture. There are, of course, great differences between nations. In a totalitarian country like the USSR, farmers have little if anything to say about running the government at any level, although their daily lives may be largely controlled by its decisions. In a democratic country like the United States, the political ideology in most sections of the country, except the rural South where Negroes are rarely encouraged to vote, seeks to encourage participation of all citizens who have attained adult status. In countries like India and Pakistan, which are still rather more feudal than either totalitarian or democratic, decisions of the central governments have only minor direct effect on the lives of agricultural villagers, although the indirect influence may be very considerable indeed. Participation in local governmental systems in various parts of the world ranges from a high degree of democracy to extreme authoritarianism.

Like other citizens, American farmers are affected by and participate in local, state, and federal systems of government. The influence of all levels of government appears to be much more pervasive than it was a generation ago. Laws and governmental regulations continue to proliferate as citizens make demands upon government to provide expensive services and benefits.

All persons who enter the territorial boundaries of a state, municipality, county, or other local governmental system are influenced to some extent by the regulations established by such systems. Those who are residents naturally have a greater stake in the decisions of these governments than do nonresidents. Membership in governmental systems is ordinarily referred to as citizenship, and is involuntary for persons born in the U.S. to parents who are citizens. Membership in lower levels of government is largely voluntary because of the relative ease with which migration now takes place within the boundaries of the United States.

Residence determines whether one is regarded as a citizen of a particular state or local governmental system. However, members of the armed forces, employees of the federal government, and members of Congress do not lose their voting rights in their state of origin even though they may be stationed elsewhere for many years.

In the U.S., active participation in elections is restricted to adults who meet specified requirements. There are always residence and age requirements, and some states levy poll taxes. Sometimes, as in parts of the South, there is also a literacy requirement which on occasion is administered so as to prevent Negroes from voting. Aliens who seek American naturalization and who have entered the U.S. under quotas established by federal law may be admitted to citizenship after passing an examination on American history, language, and law and taking the oath of allegiance.

Federal and state governments may be considered from one point of view as abstract collectivities. In both, however, there are concrete inner subsystems of officials and clerks who occupy specific status roles and perform specific functions for their constituents. The interaction between members of these inner systems, or bureaucracies as they are called, may be quite intense; however, their inner workings are not of primary concern in the present context except to the extent that such operations affect the lives of farm people. Pertinent relationships will be discussed later.

The most important functions of governmental systems in the U.S. are (1) to furnish a framework for the operation of systematic processes of decision-making on matters of common concern to citizens of the particular level of government; (2) to provide for the defense of the United States against external enemies (this function is exclusively federal); (3) to maintain social control by providing for the enforcement of laws established by legislative bodies; (4) to grant benefits authorized for various categories of citizens; and (5) to collect taxes.

LOCAL GOVERNMENTAL SYSTEMS

Local systems of government in the U.S. include counties, incorporated and unincorporated towns and townships, villages, school districts, and other special districts. These systems represent for the most part a gradual evolution of forms imported from the old world, especially from England.[1]

As noted previously, the New England colonists established agricultural villages. Decisions of importance for local government were reached in the famous New England town meeting, a public gathering of all eligible electors who settled outstanding issues by majority vote after oral discussion. The town meeting is part of American folklore and is frequently referred to as the standard for the attainment of decisions by communities. With the westward surge of settlement, as we have already seen, agricultural villages gave way to a pattern of isolated farmsteads surrounding a trade center. However, emphasis on local participation persisted and township governments were established in most of the midwestern states, though they are not found in the South or the Far West. In the southern colonies, the local government was in the hands of high-ranking owners of large plantations, and the county became the important local governmental system in the South.[2] Townships are found in 22 states, all of which are in the North and all of which, except for Washington, are east of the Rocky Mountains.[3]

Record keeping, tax collection, administration of poor relief, and some aspects of law enforcement were the major initial functions of local governments. Other functions have been added with the passage of time to meet new situations. However, local governmental systems are not very responsive to new developments; they are normally involved in a great deal of routine and are not very

[1] T. Lynn Smith, *The Sociology of Rural Life*, 3rd ed., Harper, 1953, p. 484.
[2] *Ibid.*
[3] Lowry Nelson, *Rural Sociology*, 2nd ed., American Book, 1955, pp. 442-443.

aggressive. Those which are established for the accomplishment of specific purposes, like some of the special districts to be discussed later, are exceptions to this rule.

COUNTIES

The county (called the parish in Louisiana) is the universal unit of local government found in all the continental states; in 1952, they numbered 3,049.[4] Except in New England where the town predominates, the county is the most important local governmental system for American farm people.

Counties are not uniform in size; they range from 25 to more than 20,000 square miles in size.[5] Furthermore, there is a tremendous variation in population, both absolutely and per square mile. Some counties consist only of farmers and the residents of small trade centers who serve them, whereas others contain substantial rural nonfarm and urban populations as well; we are not concerned here with the characteristics of purely urban counties. The nature and degree of farm people's participation in county government is obviously influenced by the physical size of the county as well as by the size and composition of its population. In sparsely settled areas, relationships between citizens and county officials tend to be on a face-to-face, first-name basis, whereas in urbanized counties they become more impersonal.

Like other units of local government, counties are legally subdivisions of the state. State constitutions and statutes prescribe their functions, and generally establish the rates of pay and duties of county officials.

The essential features which distinguish county government from the state are the following: (1) officials are elected by local citizens rather than appointed by the state; (2) there is a closer and more intimate tie between local citizens and county officials; (3) there is ordinarily no county executive, although a few have county managers; and (4) there is relatively little legislation.

The functions of counties at the present time include tax collec-

[4] U.S. Bureau of the Census, *Governments in the United States in 1952*, State and Local Government Special Studies No. 2, 1953.

[5] William Anderson, *The Units of Government in the United States*, Chicago, Public Administration Service, 1949.

tion, administration of specified benefits, keeping public records, and participating in law enforcement.

The officials who perform these functions usually include the following.

1. *The County Superintendent of Schools.* This official, who is frequently a woman, has some responsibility for the supervision of the public elementary and secondary schools. In some states the county superintendent is regarded as part of the administrative and supervisory organization of the state superintendent of public instruction. Generally, the county official has little or no influence on the employment of teachers, which is a function of local school boards, but he does have some responsibility for the curriculum and for educational standards. He is generally expected to visit each school once or twice a year. Superintendents sometimes conduct institutes for the purpose of familiarizing teachers and school directors with mandatory curricula and other matters.

2. *The Sheriff.* The sheriff is the principal law-enforcement officer at the county level. In larger counties he may be assisted by a substantial number of deputies. The sheriff is almost invariably a man.

3. *The Prosecuting Attorney.* This official, sometimes called the state's attorney or district attorney, has the responsibility of prosecuting offenders in court. In many rural counties it is a part-time job, and the prosecuting attorney is allowed to maintain his private practice while holding office. Frequently the compensation is fixed at such a low level that additional income is essential if he is to maintain his family at a level of living commensurate with local standards. In such cases the post is frequently filled by a succession of beginners.

4. *The Auditor.* The auditor is the principal fiscal officer of the county. In this capacity he audits the transactions of every county department. In some states he also serves as secretary to the board of county commissioners and keeps a record of their transactions. He may also have the duty of recording legal instruments; otherwise, this is an independent function assigned to an official called the registrar of deeds. In all counties, the maintenance of court records, records of marriages, births, deaths, and real estate transactions, and other legal records is an important part of the routine work.

5. *The County Treasurer.* The treasurer collects taxes and money due the county from other sources, such as fines, state grants, etc.

6. *The Assessor.* This official has the duty of assessing real estate and personal property for taxation purposes. In some states he is a township official, and in others a county or state official.

7. *The Board of County Commissioners or Supervisors.* This board has the responsibility for making such policy decisions as are required for the conduct of county government, including approval of budgets, authorization of expenditures, and related matters.

8. *Other Officials.* In some states there are other county officials such as a county engineer who may be responsible for the construction of roads, a coroner who conducts inquests, and a clerk of the county court. In addition to these elective officials, there are now a number of other functionaries at the county level who are appointive. They perform various services in connection with public benefits for eligible citizens. The county agricultural agent is a cooperative employee of the county, the state agricultural college, and the federal agricultural extension service. The county welfare director is an appointive employee of the state welfare department, and the county public health officer is usually also an appointive employee. Some county offices are extensions of the federal government and will be discussed in greater detail later.

Relationships between county officials and local citizens is generally on a coordinate rather than a subordinate-superordinate basis throughout most of the country. Except for the rural South, individuals with high social rank very seldom hold any public offices at the county level in rural America;[6] in fact, the elected county officials are generally considered servants of the people. Incumbents usually conduct themselves in a responsive rather than an authoritarian manner, calling local people by their nicknames or first names and stressing personal service more than emphasizing efficiency and impersonality. There is evidently some tendency for county officeholders to move from one office to another as they complete their statutory terms and thus to constitute a "courthouse gang," as it is sometimes known, consisting of a clique or friendship group of incumbents who share many social activities together. There is some

---

[6] C. P. Loomis and J. A. Beegle, *Rural Sociology*, Prentice-Hall, 1957, p. 279.

danger of corruption and collusion in this sort of situation,[7] but it is of course not inevitable. In many counties the officials apparently tend to be physically disabled or to have some positive reason for wanting to work as local officials; the pay is usually comparable with that of clerical positions in small businesses and obviously is not a point of attraction.

Because most local officials are elected and the professional qualifications, except in the case of the superintendent of public schools, are not very exacting, primary emphasis is upon personal qualities and interpersonal skills. That is, the successful candidate is usually personally popular with the electorate. It does not follow, however, that elected officials are always the most important political leaders in a locality. In many cases they are under obligation to the real leaders who prefer to stay in the background and rely on informal means and pressures to obtain what they want from county boards or officials.[8]

TOWNSHIPS

From New York westward to the Dakotas, the township is recognized as a subdivision of the county. In the Dakotas and adjacent states townships exercise few local government functions; but in New England they are the most important units of local government, and perform functions which elsewhere belong with counties. In these states the principal activity of counties is in providing state services to local people.[9] Townships in New York, Michigan, and Wisconsin are organized local governmental systems with a town board of supervisors consisting of three or more members, a clerk, a treasurer, a highway overseer, and sometimes law-enforcement officers. In some states the township assesses property for taxation purposes.

In New York, New Jersey, Michigan, Illinois, and Wisconsin, the county boards of supervisors are comprised of township supervisors, whereas in Pennsylvania, Ohio, Indiana, Minnesota, Iowa, Missouri,

[7] C. P. Loomis and J. A. Beegle, *Rural Social Systems,* Prentice-Hall, 1950, p 591.

[8] Loomis and Beegle, *Rural Sociology, op. cit.,* p. 279.

[9] Smith, *op. cit.,* p. 491.

North and South Dakota, Kansas, and Oklahoma there is no formal connection between the township and the county. In the latter states the county commissioners or supervisors are usually elected without reference to townships, which in these states are served by boards of supervisors elected independently who thus owe no allegiance to the county board.[10]

INCORPORATED VILLAGES

People who live in a farm trade center that has incorporated under the laws of their state have a system of local government which is confined to the corporate limits and excludes farmers and others who live outside. Incorporated villages, towns, or cities have the authority to levy and collect certain kinds of taxes; to obtain funds through bond issues for school building, street maintenance, construction, and certain other purposes; and to enforce the law within the corporate limits. Municipalities also have the authority to enact ordinances covering parking, building, and certain other activities. Commenting on the powers of the incorporated village Nelson has said, "It is about the most significant type of local government in rural America, from the standpoint of the services which it can perform for its citizens and the degree of local autonomy which it enjoys."[11]

It should be noted in passing that unincorporated centers such as hamlets and small villages do not have governmental powers commensurate with those of incorporated places.

The legal division between residents of incorporated villages and the farmers who live on isolated farms in the surrounding territory, as noted earlier, has sometimes led to strained feelings between farmers and villagers.[12] The village, being located as it is in the center of the town-country community, is an inner social system within a social system which excludes from decision-making farm people who sometimes feel they have a rightful claim to membership. In areas where consolidated school systems have been established embracing both village and surrounding open-country areas, town-

[10] K. H. Porter, *County and Township Government in the United States,* Macmillan, 1922.
[11] Nelson, *op. cit.,* p. 445.
[12] See Chapter 12.

country relationships have been greatly improved. School districts as a type of local government were discussed earlier.[13]

SPECIAL DISTRICTS

The inflexibility of established systems of local government has led to the creation of many local special-purpose systems. These include irrigation and drainage districts, rural fire protection districts, soil conservation districts, and similar units.

The powers of special districts are specified by state legislation and may include taxation, the right to issue bonds, and the power to enforce restrictions against certain types of land use.[14]

SOME PROBLEMS OF LOCAL GOVERNMENT SYSTEMS IN THE UNITED STATES

Students of the subject have concluded that many of the existing systems of local government in the rural U.S. are inefficient and poorly organized to cope with modern problems.[15] It has been said that some small counties have a set of officials sufficient in number to service large populations, and it is widely believed that local governmental positions attract only people of very modest ability because of generally low salary scales and the disregard of educational or professional prerequisites. Perhaps even more important, the work conditions provide few if any incentives to improve ability to perform the functions of local elective offices. To a great extent, the county in rural America is administered by a government which is really without any executive direction. The county board of supervisors has very limited jurisdiction over the elected incumbents of the statutory positions. Many of the functions provided constituents by old-line officials of local governments are routine in character and present relatively little challenge. Furthermore, these routine functions attract little interest on the part of citizens in general.

In some areas of the country, as noted above, local government systems have apparently fallen into the hands of cliques, the mem-

---

[13] See Chapter 21.

[14] Nelson, *op. cit.,* pp. 446-447.

[15] *Ibid.,* pp. 448-451; John H. Kolb and Edmund deS. Brunner, *A Study of Rural Society,* 4th ed., Houghton Mifflin, 1952, chap. XXIV; Smith, *op. cit.,* pp. 490-491.

bers of which may manipulate the offices for their own personal ends. However, this does not seem to be a general complaint.

Various proposals have been made for the improvement of local government, among them that county boundaries be relocated in the interest of efficiency and economy. However, where this has been attempted, very little support has been found for county consolidation; this was the case in western South Dakota where an election was held to determine whether the residents of two adjoining counties would agree to consolidate. One exception to the generalization that it is virtually impossible to change the form of local governments is the great progress made in many states in school consolidation,[16] which indicates that changes in local government structure and functions can be achieved; however, they do require consistent effort and application of sound principles of community organization, as well as an understanding by the local citizenry of the benefits to be derived from the proposed changes.

STATE GOVERNMENTS

State governments are far enough removed from the local scene that most farmers seldom come into direct contact with state officials. Ordinarily their participation in state government affairs is restricted to elections to the legislature and to the principal state offices. In most states, the departments of state governments established prior to the 1930s are represented on the local level by elected county officials, who are not generally subject to detailed supervision or to removal by state officers except in the case of corruption or other malfeasance.

The newer departments of state government, which have been established since 1933 pursuant to federal legislation, generally have appointive local officials. The most important of these departments is the department of welfare or public assistance. Public assistance benefits do not generally come from local taxation but are derived from state and federal sources. Welfare employees are appointed and subject to direct supervision by state officials. Members of the public welfare bureaucracy have some security of tenure; they are supposed to be appointed on a merit basis and promotions are presumably given for meritorious service. Furthermore, capricious or

[16] See Chapter 21.

arbitrary removal without cause is forbidden by the regulations. Local citizens, whether receiving benefits or not, have little or no voice in the policies or procedures of the welfare department.

The agency of the state government most likely to come into contact with farmers is the state department of agriculture. This department, which is found in most states, does not generally operate through county departments of agriculture but rather has its own field staff. Various regulatory functions required by state law have been assigned to the state department of agriculture, for example, insuring compliance with regulations concerning pure seed, adulteration of food, compliance with sanitation regulations, and vaccination of animals against various diseases. In California plant inspection stations at the ports of entry guard against the introduction of plant diseases and insect pests.

Recently a number of states have undertaken promotional programs designed to increase agricultural income. No less than 30 states have enacted legislation giving state backing to compaigns to increase consumption of 40 agricultural commodities. In Washington, for example, the Washington State Apple Commission, composed of elected representatives of eligible growers, is empowered by statute to levy a tax on production for the purpose of advertising the product of the apple growers. In addition, volume control programs have been put into effect on selected agricultural commodities by California, Colorado, and New York.[17]

FEDERAL GOVERNMENT AGENCIES

Nations are political social systems in which all citizens participate to some extent. Governmental systems differ considerably from one country to another, but all have specific requirements for citizenship and rules that govern participation in policy-making.

Because of the great territory and large population of the United States, the average farmer's contacts with the federal government, except for specialized agencies of the Department of Agriculture which will be discussed below, are impersonal and infrequent. Nevertheless, farm people, like their nonfarm fellow citizens, do have a voice in the formulation of national policies, principally through

[17] *Wall Street Journal,* January 12, 1961.

the lobbying activities of farm organizations and through direct participation in elections for national offices.

The federal government of the U.S. is a large and complex social system composed of many specialized subsystems or agencies. The three major branches established by the Constitution are the legislative, the judiciary, and the executive, which are of course related, although they perform different functions.

AGENCIES AND PROGRAMS OF THE U.S. DEPARTMENT OF AGRICULTURE

The United States Department of Agriculture has a number of agencies charged with the responsibility of conducting specialized programs authorized by Congress. Some of these agencies have established offices in rural counties and local districts which are staffed by federal officials subject to civil service rules and regulations. These functionaries are not supervised by local or state elected officials but rather by the federal departments concerned. There is relatively little effective coordination of federal programs for agriculture in spite of the fact that nearly all are administered by the secretary of agriculture. Some attempts have been made to bring about coordination at the local level by housing all of the local branches of the U.S. Department of Agriculture in a single building.

Direct intervention of the federal government in agricultural production and distribution came only after a severe economic crisis when it became clear that individuals, farm groups, and states were powerless.

The problem of agricultural surpluses began in the 1920s. The application of science and technology to American agriculture after about 1910 greatly increased the productivity of American farms. At the same time, industrialization and the consequent growth of large urban populations of consumers encouraged farmers to produce for the expanding market. Favorable prices during and immediately after World War I provided economic incentives for increased production.

The economics of commercial agriculture, at least on family-sized farms, are such that price reductions tend to be accompanied by efforts to increase output in order to maintain farm income. Thus the loss of many foreign markets after 1918 and the consequent drop in farm prices led to further increases in production and the continued adoption of more efficient methods of agriculture. The agricultural depression actually started not in 1929 but in 1921 when farm prices dropped sharply due largely to the loss of foreign markets.[18] Farm production was further increased during the 1920s by the release of millions of acres previously used for horse pasture and feed production as farmers adopted tractors for power. Demand did not keep pace, and the situation became immeasurably worse with the onset of the depression of the 1930s. Farm organizations demanded federal legislation for farm relief and obtained commitments from candidates for federal offices for a positive federal program for the relief of agriculture. With the consent of President Roosevelt, representatives of farm organizations had a major part in writing the Agricultural Adjustment Act of 1933 which sought to reduce agricultural surpluses through acreage controls.[19]

During World War II and the immediate postwar period, there was sufficient demand for the products of American agriculture to provide a ready market at good prices. From 1943 to 1949, acreage allotments were not used except for certain kinds of tobacco. After the termination of the Korean war, however, further increases in productivity here and abroad coupled with some shifts in urban consumption habits resulted in still greater surpluses. On June 30, 1959, the value of agricultural commodities owned by the Department of Agriculture exceeded $6,200,000,000.

The laws established by the federal government for the economic relief of farmers and the subsequent control of production are of great importance to nearly all American farmers. The economic welfare of producers of commodities like wheat, cotton, and tobacco is directly affected by the level of price supports and the acreage limitations on their crops, as are local markets by federal government measures to dispose of agricultural surpluses abroad. Enforcement of federal regulations respecting the amount of certain chemicals on food products may spell disaster for some growers, as in the case of the 1959 cranberry episode.[20]

[18] Kolb and Brunner, *op. cit.*, p. 127.
[19] Nelson, *op. cit.*, pp. 457-458.
[20] Just before Thanksgiving, 1959, the Secretary of the U.S. Department of Health, Education, and Welfare announced that some cranberries in Oregon had been found to have residues of a chemical that could produce cancer in

During the 1950s the executive branch attempted to persuade Congress to reduce the level of price supports. Mounting agricultural surpluses required tremendous government outlays for agricultural subsidy. Some urban organizations and private citizens have conducted vigorous campaigns for the reduction or abolition of agricultural subsidies, and a number of farmers and farm groups have taken the view that the federal government's control over agriculture should be greatly reduced.

Withdrawal of federal supports in the face of great agricultural production would doubtless mean that the prices of farm products would fall, and many farmers, including some of the large operators, might be forced out of agriculture. Until the present, at least, this action has not been considered as in the national interest since, as we have seen earlier, the long-time agricultural policy of the United States on the federal level has been support of the family farm.[21]

Farmers give less attention to and have less influence over these broad considerations of agricultural policy, despite their great importance, than the manifestations of these programs which touch him on the local level.[22]

There is a great deal of discontent with the specific programs developed for agricultural relief, and further, there is little likelihood that the problems of American farmers will cease to have nationwide implications in the foreseeable future. This means, of course, that federal government actions which affect agriculture and people dependent on agriculture will continue to be of concern to students of rural life. At the same time, the tradition of local government is quite strong in many sections of rural America; direct and equal participation in governmental decisions of the type exemplified by the town meeting of colonial New England is still generally idealized,

---

rats. He announced that berries from areas which had used this chemical should not be eaten until they had been certified as safe for human consumption. Coming as it did just before Thanksgiving, this nearly destroyed the large market for cranberries traditionally used with Thanksgiving turkey. Various public figures including the Vice-President and various presidential candidates had pictures taken of themselves consuming cranberries. Many public officials in cranberry-producing states condemned the action of the Secretary (see *Time*, November 20, 1959).

[21] See Chapter 15.

[22] However, discussions of agricultural policy by farmers and scientists are being stimulated by the land-grant colleges and universities (see Chapter 22).

and other forms of political decision-making are frequently criticized as failing to meet this standard.

Those who would like to emphasize "grass-roots" democracy frequently deplore the growing tendency for important policy decisions affecting agriculture to be expressed in general terms through federal legislation and subsequently to be elaborated through administrative decisions by federal agencies. There is evidence that the trend toward centralization in governmental decision-making is fairly widespread, not only in the United States but also in many other sections of the world. To some extent this is due to the fact that technological developments in communication and transportation have virtually destroyed the possibility of any large nation's maintaining an isolationist position.

In contrast to the relative stability of local government systems, the agency systems of the U.S. Department of Agriculture have experienced considerable reorganization from time to time. Changes in their missions and organizational structures will very probably continue to be made in the future.

At the federal level, the Department was reorganized in 1961 into six major groups:

Agricultural Economics, Director: Economic Research Service, Statistical Reporting Service

Marketing and Foreign Agriculture, Assistant Secretary: Agricultural Marketing Service, Foreign Agricultural Service, Commodity Exchange Administration

Federal-States Relations, Assistant Secretary: Agricultural Research Service, Forest Service, Soil Conservation Service, Federal Extension Service, Farmer Cooperative Service

Agricultural Stabilization, Assistant Secretary: Agricultural Conservation and Stabilization Service, Commodity Credit Corporation, Federal Crop Insurance Corporation

Departmental Administration, Administrative Assistant Secretary: Office of Administrative Management, Office of Budget and Finance, Office of Hearing Examiners, Office of Information, Library, Office of Personnel, Office of Plant and Operations[23]

Individual farmers seldom if ever come into direct contact with national officials of the Department of Agriculture. Their direct re-

[23] USDA Employee News Bulletin, August 16, 1961, pp. 2-3.

lations are restricted for the most part to the agencies named above which maintain local staffs. The Agricultural Extension Service has been discussed elsewhere.[24] It seems worth while at this point to examine selected aspects of the local operations of some of the divisions listed.

Agricultural Stabilization and Conservation Committees

A substantial portion of the Agriculture Department's regulatory functions are carried out through state and county committees which, since 1953, have been called Agricultural Stabilization and Conservation Committees.[25] At the county level, committee members are elected by farmers who produce crops which are eligible for price support and subject to production controls. In addition to 3000 county groups, there are also community committees with elected members as county or community committeemen. About 90,000 farmers serve every year.

These committees are responsible for the local administration of acreage allotments and marketing quotas, the Soil Bank, price-support loans, purchase agreements, incentive payments, the Sugar Act, and the agricultural conservation program. The price support programs are the most important action programs of the Department of Agriculture.

Each county committee employs an office manager who is in charge of day-to-day office operations and supervises the activities of other employees.

In an effort to bring production into line with demand, acreage allotments are made for five basic crops: cotton, wheat, rice, peanuts, and tobacco. Marketing quotas may also be used in connection with acreage allotments if at least two-thirds of the producers vote for them. When quotas are accepted, production in excess of the quota is subject to penalties.

Price-support operations involve wheat, corn, cotton, peanuts, rice, tobacco, butterfat, milk, wool, mohair, honey, tung oil, barley, oats, rye, sorghum, grain, flaxseed, soybeans, dry edible beans, cottonseed, and crude pine gum. Loans, purchases, purchase agreements, and incentive payments are used to support prices.

[24] See Chapter 22.
[25] This discussion is based upon CSS *Background Information Releases* issued by the Commodity Stabilization Service, November, 1959.

The Soil Bank is a program authorized by Congress in 1956 designed to withdraw agricultural land from cultivation by providing payments to farmers for the unused land. It has three major objectives: (1) to reduce agricultural surpluses, (2) to increase farm income, and (3) to promote soil and water conservation. Farm owners can take part in the program by contracting to withdraw crop land from production for periods of 3, 5, or 10 years. During this period the land must be built up by the use of approved conservation practices. To discourage speculators and other nonfarmers from taking advantage of the payments to acquire land at government expense, the Soil Bank was initially restricted to farmers who owned land prior to 1956 and their renters. In 1958 there were 27,600,000 acres, or about 7 percent of the crop land reported by the 1954 census, under Soil Bank programs.

Acreage control price-support programs seem to have operated to increase rather than decrease the production of price-supported commodities. The higher yield is the result of improved farming practices such as better crop varieties, better tillage methods, more efficient use of fertilizer, and retirement from production of poorer land.

Efforts to dispose of surplus wheat, cotton, and corn to needy countries at reduced prices have met with opposition from other surplus-producing countries like Canada and Australia. There are still many food shortage areas in the world comprising hundreds of millions of undernourished people. Some of the surplus food stocks of the U.S. are made available to such countries on a virtual gift basis, but as yet satisfactory methods have not been worked out for the free flow of these stocks to people who could use them but have little purchasing power. At the same time agriculture in underdeveloped countries is not adequate to cope with the problem of feeding the ever-increasing population, and the great cry in many parts of the world at present is that there is need for family limitation to avoid still lower levels of subsistence.

Farmers who produce commodities which qualify for price supports are of course influenced greatly by the general and specific rules of the Department of Agriculture regarding their crops. Acreage allotments to individual farmers are made in terms of the history of previous allotments and may bear little relationship to the actual

extent of productive land on a farm. County and community committeemen have the responsibility of informing farmers of their allotments and of checking them for compliance with acreage limitations
and soil conservation programs for which payments are claimed
under applicable federal legislation.

Although the sanitation aspects of operations of dairy farms are
regulated by health departments, livestock farmers, among others,
have resisted attempts to have the federal government stabilize conditions in their industry. Part-time and self-sufficing farmers generally do not come under the programs to any important degree if at
all.

Soil Conservation Service

The Soil Conservation Service (SCS) has its policymakers and
chief administrators in Washington, D.C., with lesser administrators
in seven regions and in the headquarters maintained in each state.
About three-fourths of American farm land is included in 2418 soil
conservation districts.[26] In 1959, about 40 percent of all U.S. farmers
were cooperating with the SCS (Fig. 24).

The activities of the Soil Conservation Service are designed to promote the maintenance and long-range improvement of the agricultural land resources of the country. It was established by federal
legislation in the 1930s when Congress recognized that soil and water
erosion presented problems of major concern for the national welfare.

The Service encourages farmers to utilize soil-conserving practices
which are adapted to local soil, topography, and climatic conditions.

Each soil conservation district is directed by a local board of
supervisors (directors or commissioners), usually elected by members of the district. These boards enter into formal agreements for
assistance from the SCS and other agencies of the Department of
Agriculture. The principal services available to farm owners include:

1. Making a detailed soil and land capability map of farm or range
   land (see Figs. 25a and 25b).
2. Providing local and specific information about the safe use of

    [26] T. W. Longmore, "Special Agencies Within the Department of Agriculture,"
in C. P. Loomis et al., *Rural Social Systems and Adult Education*, Michigan
State College Press, 1953, p. 152.

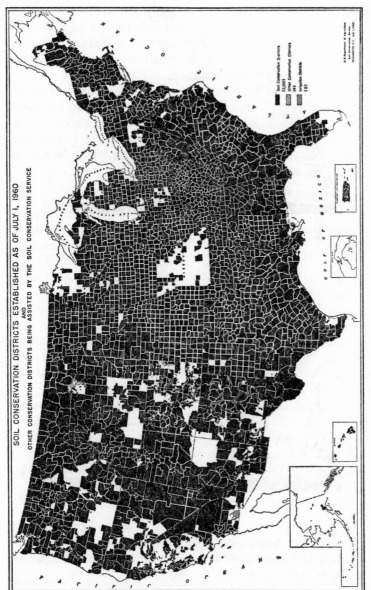

SOIL CONSERVATION DISTRICTS ESTABLISHED AS OF JULY 1, 1960
AND
OTHER CONSERVATION DISTRICTS BEING ASSISTED BY THE SOIL CONSERVATION SERVICE

Fig. 24.

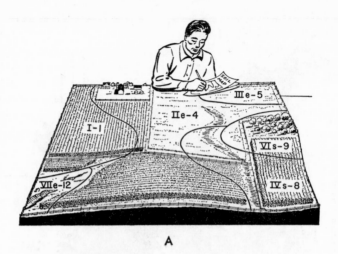

A

B

Fig. 25. The Farmer and the Soil Conservation Service.
A. Analyzing the Soil Map to Determine Land Capability.
B. Planning Acording to the Capability of the Land.

different crops and other uses of each type of soil on the farm (such as for grasses, trees, and wildlife).

3. Providing information about applicable conservation practices.
4. Making consultation with a professional soil conservationist available for drawing up a conservation plan for the farm.
5. Providing technical assistance for designing and checking construction of dams, terraces, or other soil-conserving structures.

In addition, many districts provide other services and facilities for cooperators, including specialized equipment for rental, nursery stock, and scarce seeds and fertilizers.[27]

The method of operation is to place a technical specialist in soil conservation in each soil conservation district. This expert works directly with cooperating individuals and with groups of farmers called "neighbor groups" by the SCS. Longmore has classified these sociologically as informal friendship or clique groups rather than as neighborhoods; each neighbor group consists of a small number of families who live relatively close to each other and have bonds of mutual interest and friendship. The technician attempts to locate the "natural leaders" of such groups and works rather closely with them. Based on the counsel of rural sociologists, the SCS has developed a guide for locating existing neighbor groups and identifying their leaders. Longmore has described these steps as follows:

1. Consult with several overall district, or county-wide leaders to secure the names of the most important community leaders.
2. Talk to these community leaders and gather all information possible about neighbor groups and their leaders.
3. Using the names secured in this manner, talk to enough people in each neighbor group to verify the membership of the group and determine as positively as possible who the leader or leaders are.
4. Consult with the leader and check with him as to the membership of the group. Let him decide where borderline cases fit. Likewise, find out from him whom he considers to be the real community leaders.
5. With the leader, determine the group's interest and understanding of soil conservation. Plan with him the course of action to be taken with the group to move them along in soil conservation work.

[27] U.S. Department of Agriculture, Soil Conservation Service, *Soil Conservation Districts,* C-1-9, May, 1959, pp. 2, 3.

6. Call on the community and overall leaders to encourage and assist the neighbor group leaders.[28]

A soil conservation district enters into a formal agreement with each cooperating farmer or rancher. He prepares and follows a conservation plan on his farm, and the district provides a soil and land capability map, technical assistance, and other services and materials in carrying out the plan.

Some disagreement has arisen between the land-grant colleges and the U.S. Department of Agriculture over the educational functions involved in soil conservation. The colleges have taken the position that educational activities, as distinguished from activities concerned with the distribution of monetary benefits, should be conducted through the existing agricultural extension services. The SCS has not accepted this point of view. The result is that information on agricultural practices that would be beneficial in soil conservation is disseminated both by the agricultural extension services through the county agents and by the SCS through the district conservationists.

Farmers Home Administration

The Farmers Home Administration (FHA) is basically a rehabilitation agency which has the mission of assisting economically distressed farmers who cannot get credit from other sources to become self-supporting. It has developed from the earlier farm rehabilitation programs administered by the Farm Security Administration and the Resettlement Administration, both lineal ancestors of the FHA.

The great economic depression struck with special severity the already depressed agricultural segment of the population. At the bottom of the depression in 1935 approximately 2,500,000 rural families were on relief, and it has been estimated that in the period 1931-1937 there were 3,500,000 rural families on relief at one time or another.[29] Initially relief was dispensed to farmers as well as others by the Federal Emergency Relief Administration, but in 1937 the Rural Rehabilitation Division of the FERA was abolished and its

[28] Longmore, *op. cit.*, p. 154.

[29] T. J. Woofter and Ellen Winston, *Seven Lean Years,* University of North Carolina Press, 1937; Rupert B. Vance, *Rural Relief and Recovery*, WPA, Social Problems Pamphlet 3, 1939.

functions taken over by the Farm Security Adminstration of the Department of Agriculture. At this time the program was enlarged to include assistance to tenants in purchasing farms, migratory farm labor housing, and homestead projects. However, the agency's principal activity was to provide low-income farm families with credit and sound advice concerning farm and home management.

The Resettlement Administration, one of the predecessors of the Farm Security Administration, undertook as a major activity to relocate farm families in certain areas of the country who were operating land that was considered submarginal for agriculture. A study of the short-term results of one such effort in the state of Wisconsin led the authors to the following conclusion:

> The analysis . . . causes one to question the thesis that the welfare of all families can be enhanced by resettlement alone. Resettlement, as proposed for the purchase area, was a selective process which left out of consideration a large proportion of the families living in that area. The best provisions for resettlement were made for those who already seemed to be succeeding and in many ways were living nearly on a par with the families in the area to which it was proposed to move them. Other families with the lower levels of living and with the greater needs were not eligible for assistance under the proposed projects.[30]

The impact of relocation upon established systems of relationship among the families who resided in the purchase area was, of course, very great.

During the year ending June 30, 1960, 181,000 farmers either received loans or used credit advanced by the FHA in previous years. Operating loans were made to 69,888, emergency loans to 9,203 and real estate loans to 8,830 farmers during this period. On June 30, 1960, outstanding loans totaled $1,164,969,000.[31]

For FHA clients, relationships with the agency are, of course, extremely important; but for other farmers, comprising roughly 95 percent of the total, the operations of the agency have little significance, even indirectly, at the present time.

---

[30] G. W. Hill, Walter Slocum, and Ruth O. Hill, *Man-Land Adjustment*, Wisconsin AES Research Bulletin 134, February, 1938, p. 69.

[31] Ezra Taft Benson, *Report of the Secretary of Agriculture, 1960*, USDA, 1960, p. 73.

The FHA is a centralized organization with headquarters in the Department of Agriculture and four field offices; there are state offices in 40 states and, in 1951, 1619 county offices, some of which served more than the state or county where they were located. All of these offices had a field supervisor, and there were 77 women home supervisors.

Each of the county offices is assisted by an FHA county committee consisting of three local persons, at least two of whom must be farmers. In most cases, these farmers are not FHA clients. The committee's function is to approve FHA loans at the local level, review the progress of borrowers annually, and give other advice.[32]

Perhaps the most significant feature of FHA operations from a sociological standpoint is the direct and intimate relationship between the farm family and the FHA supervisor. The borrowing family makes annual plans for managing the farm and home with the help of the supervisor, who has the responsibility of giving advice throughout the operating year. The intention of this supervision is, of course, to insure sound work practices, such as maintenance of adequate records and the use of approved techniques including soil conservation methods. Those who purchase a farm under the farm ownership loan program of the FHA receive more detailed supervision than those who take only annual operating loans.

In addition to these personalized relationships, the FHA also uses group techniques for analyzing borrower progress and educating borrowers in better farming methods.[33]

It is obvious from the nature of the relationships between supervisors and individual borrowers that the latter might be subject to exploitation in the absence of adequate safeguards. This aspect of the situation has evidently not been objectively studied but so few complaints have been made public that it is doubtful that there is or has been much abuse.

Rural Electrification Administration

The Rural Electrification Administration (REA) was established by executive order of the president, May 11, 1935, and the Rural Electrification Act of 1936 gave it permanent status. It has been an

[32] *The USDA, Organization and Function, op. cit.*, p. 15.
[33] Longmore, *op. cit.*, pp. 147-151.

agency of the Department of Agriculture since 1939. The REA makes loans for the purpose of helping farmers obtain electricity and telephone service. When it was established, only about 11 percent of American farmers had electrical service from central power stations. Due chiefly to the stimulation provided by the agency, rural electrification has proceeded rapidly since that time, although only about half of the farms served by electricity are members of REA-financed cooperatives. In 1959 all but 4 percent of the farms in the U.S. had electricity from central power stations. Electricity is being used for an ever-increasing number of purposes on American farms: consumption more than doubled between 1952 and 1957.

Loans for rural telephones were authorized October 28, 1949. Only 38 percent of farms had telephones in 1950, but the figure had increased to 65 percent in 1959 due chiefly to REA loans for this purpose.[34]

The REA cooperative is a local unit controlled by its members who obtain loans at favorable rates from the agency. Loans are made on a 35-year amortization plan at the low interest rate of 2 percent. The activities of the REA have been attacked by private power companies,[35] and in at least one rural county—Stevens County, Washington—members of the REA cooperative voted to sell out to the private concern. It should be noted in this connection, however, that prior to the time Congress authorized the REA farm service was not considered by many private power companies to be a lucrative field as evidenced by the very low rate of rural electrification noted above.

THE FARM CREDIT ADMINISTRATION

The Farm Credit Administration[36] was first established in 1933 to coordinate and supervise federal agencies dealing with agricultural credit. Until 1953, when it became independent, it was a semi-independent agency within the U.S. Department of Agriculture. It includes the Federal Land Bank, Bank for Cooperatives, Federal

[34] REA news release, January 11, 1960.
[35] H. S. Person, "The Rural Electrification Administration in Perspective," *Agricultural History*, April, 1950, pp. 70-89.
[36] See U.S. Farm Credit Administration, *The Cooperative Farm Credit System*, Circular 36a, December, 1959, on which this discussion is based.

Intermediate Credit Bank, and the Production Credit Corporation. It is a cooperative system which provides long-, intermediate-, and short-term credit. Fig. 26 shows how farmers share in the control of the system.

The federal government entered the field of farm credit in 1916 when Congress enacted legislation which created the 12 Federal Land Banks and the local associations through which land-bank loans are actually made. Prior to this time, farm mortgage credit was expensive and was generally available only for periods of 5 years or less. Federal land-bank loans are made for periods of not less than 5 nor more than 40 years. Interest rates at present range from 4½ to 5½ percent for new loans, which are paid off on an installment basis with interest charged only on the unpaid balance. In 1959, more than 370,000 farmers and ranchers were members of about 800 land-bank associations. Each association elects its own board of directors which hires a manager to carry on day-to-day operations.

The majority of farm mortgage loans are made by commercial banks, insurance companies, and private individuals. Nevertheless, the policies of the federal land banks brought about a virtual revolution in the field of long-term credit. Most private loans are now made at reasonably competitive interest rates. Furthermore, most farm mortgage loans are made for relatively long periods and are repayable in installments.

In 1959, there were 494 production credit associations (PCAs) which provided short-term, low-cost production loans to 270,000 of their 500,000 members. Fig. 27 illustrates the growth in number and dollar value of their loans.

Members of each PCA elect their own board of directors, which determines local policies and hires a manager to conduct local operations. Local PCAs are supervised and assisted by the 12 Federal Intermediate Credit Banks, which obtain funds by selling short-term bonds in the investment market. These funds are used to buy and discount farm-production loans made by PCAs, national or state banks, trust companies, agricultural credit corporations, and livestock companies.

As noted in Chapter 20, most farmers belong to one or more cooperatives. The 13 Banks for Cooperatives provide loans to cooperatives engaged in marketing agricultural products, purchasing farm

How Farmers in each of 12 Districts Share in Control of Cooperative Farm Credit System

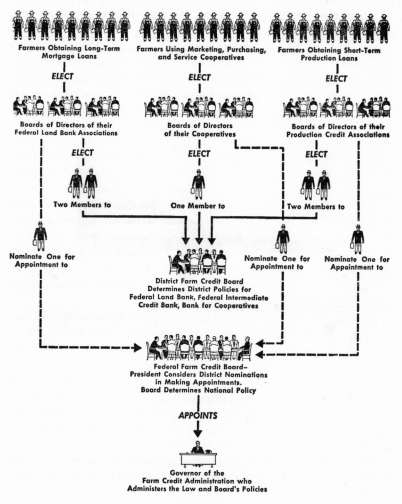

FIG. 26.

supplies, or furnishing farm business services. In 1959, about 30 percent of the capital of the Banks was owned by cooperatives.

There is no doubt that the policies of the Farm Credit Administration have had a major influence on the development of current farm credit policies. In contrast to the Farmers Home Administration, there is little direct supervision of individual borrowers. The land-bank and production credit associations are cooperatives, but they

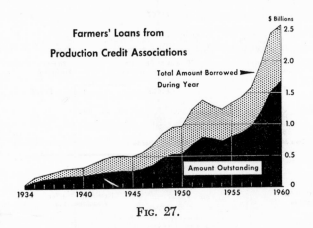

FIG. 27.

are operated on business principles. All expenses of the Farm Credit Administration are met by contributions from the banks and credit associations which it supervises.

WELFARE AGENCIES

In addition to the agencies discussed above which provide specific types of economic assistance to various categories of farm people, farmers are eligible to receive the benefits offered by general welfare and social security agencies.

As Kolb and Brunner have pointed out, prior to the programs introduced during the 1930s there had been little change in rural welfare since colonial times.[37] Those who accepted poor relief, farmers and nonfarm people alike, were required to take a pauper's oath which in some states deprived them of citizenship privileges.

[37] Kolb and Brunner, *op. cit.*, p. 452.

The widespread economic distress during the 1930s brought the federal government into the welfare field, which in turn greatly altered the administration of assistance to the needy.

The public assistance program established under the Social Security Act of 1935, as amended, is a federal-state undertaking administered by appointed officials. The benefits available include monetary assistance to those who are in need, as grouped into five general categories: (1) the aged, (2) mothers with dependent children, (3) the blind, (4) permanently and totally disabled persons, and (5) the unemployed.

Although public assistance agencies dispense benefits locally, policies and procedures including criteria for eligibility are established at state and federal levels. Local citizens have little or no voice in these functions, and consequently, from a sociological standpoint, the local offices of welfare agencies are not to be considered as local social systems. Interest centers therefore upon the relationship between these local representatives and welfare recipients. As Loomis and Beegle have observed, the profession of social worker has largely developed since the enactment of the Social Security Act of 1935, although there were some social workers in urban areas prior to that time.[38] The social worker is an additional specialist performing certain functions for particular categories of the farm as well as the nonfarm population.

SOCIAL SECURITY

Amendments to the social security law in 1950 and in 1954 made the provisions of the federal social security system applicable to farmers and farm workers. These benefits are administered by federal agencies outside the Department of Agriculture.

Studies of provisions made by farm people for old age in various states indicate that relatively few farmers have adequate savings to provide for retirement.[39] Consequently, the benefits available under the Old Age and Survivors Insurance Program (OASI) will have a number of consequences for farm participants. For one thing, farm-

[38] Loomis and Beegle, *Rural Sociology, op. cit.,* p. 394.
[39] See Walter C. McKain, Elmer D. Baldwin, and Louis J. Ducoff, *Old Age and Retirement in Rural Connecticut,* Storrs AES Bulletin 299, June 1953; Bertrand, ed., *op. cit.,* pp. 296-297.

ers may be able to retire at an earlier age, making it possible for younger people to take over the lands. As Loomis and Beegle have pointed out, the impact of the program on the postretirement activities of farmers and their wives cannot be foreseen at this time,[40] but the general effect will doubtles be beneficial. A recent Iowa study by Bauder reveals that OASI has already become a major factor in farmers' plans for retirement income.[41]

As in the case of other federally administered benefits, this program is characterized by a minimum of local participation in decision-making. The rules are established at the federal level pursuant to general provisions enunciated in federal legislation. Those who are eligible make their payments to the Social Security Administration and receive benefits directly from that agency when they reach retirement age. Consequently, while the activities of the agency may have a great impact on individual farm people, the relationship is one of agency and constituent and does not involve local social systems.

FUTURE PROSPECTS FOR FEDERAL GOVERNMENTAL SYSTEMS

The information presented in this chapter shows clearly that many vital functions affecting farm people are performed by governmental systems established under federal and state legislation. The amount of direct participation in these systems is, of course, much less than that found in purely local governmental systems. Basic policies are formulated by the Congress and state legislatures and amplified by administrative regulations issued by federal and state administrators. In most cases, the participation of the local farmer is restricted to receiving the benefits offered by the agency. His part in the decision-making is indirect. Except for referendums conducted by the Agricultural Stabilization Committees, the two principal channels open to a farmer to influence federal farm programs are (1) his farm organization and (2) his contact with his elected representative or senator.

[40] Loomis and Beegle, *Rural Sociology, op. cit.,* p. 392.
[41] Ward W. Bauder, *Iowa Farm Operators' and Farm Landlords' Knowledge of, Participation in and Acceptance of the Old Age and Survivors Insurance Program,* Iowa AES Research Bulletin 479, June, 1960.

QUESTIONS FOR FURTHER STUDY AND DISCUSSION

1. Organize the class into committees representing each of the major departments in your county. Have each committee study the most recent county budget and prepare a budget covering activities proposed for the coming fiscal year. This may be presented as a sociodrama with some members of the class playing the roles of members of the board of county commissioners.
2. Discuss the prospects for consolidation of counties.
3. To what extent do the "welfare state" activities of the Federal government operate to reduce local individualism and initiative?
4. Is there any discrimination in your county in the distribution of various benefits available from various government departments? If so, what is the nature of the discrimination?

SELECTED REFERENCES

Kolb, John H., and Edmund deS. Brunner, *A Study of Rural Society,* 4th ed., Houghton Mifflin, 1952.

Longmore, T. W., "Special Agencies Within the Department of Agriculture," in C. P. Loomis *et al., Rural Social Systems and Adult Education,* Michigan State College Press, 1953.

Loomis, C. P., and J. A. Beegle, *Rural Sociology,* Prentice-Hall, 1957.

Weidener, E. W., and Jack Preiss, "Rural Local Government and Politics and Adult Education," in C. P. Loomis *et al., Rural Social Systems and Adult Education,* Michigan State College Press, 1953.

V

COMMUNITY
DEVELOPMENT

The modern rural community does not stand alone as an isolated social system. It is greatly influenced by national and international developments. However, community development does involve the cooperative effort of local people to make their own communities better places in which to live. In an earlier day, informal mutual aid met many comparable problems. Today, however, most rural communities are so complex that formal organization is required for effective social action. Systematic research is required to identify both the crucial problems and the unutilized human and physical resources which may be mobilized to meet community needs. This, of course, brings various specialists into the picture.

The process of organizing a community for social action to solve its problems can be facilitated through the application of relevant principles based upon the findings of basic research in the social sciences.

25

Organizing Programs of Social Action in Rural Communities

In recent years there has been an upsurge of interest in community development programs in many countries. Throughout the United States, thousands of farm families have participated in community efforts to improve local conditions; state and federal agricultural extension services, the Grange, and business organizations have provided stimulation through prizes and professional assistance.

Recognition of common problems by people residing in a locality often leads to cooperative efforts designed to solve those problems. However, rarely are the majority residents involved; more often only a minority participate, generally motivated to act because of self-interest or a common bond with others through common social systems of various kinds.

Although social action in a community frequently involves one or more local government units, its processes are not essentially political in nature as the word is defined in America.

RURAL COMMUNITY DEVELOPMENT IN THE UNITED STATES

Emphasis upon local enterprise and initiative in the solution of area problems is traditional in agricultural communities in the U.S. The early settlers were unable to call upon outside agencies or organizations for help, and consequently such progress as was made in the development of community facilities came from local efforts. The New England town meeting is still regarded as a model of democracy. It was not until the 1930s that the concept of the welfare state took root in America. This has undoubtedly stimulated many farm people to look to government for help.

Few rural communities during previous generations possessed many community facilities. People were exhorted to labor long and vigorously. During the busy seasons, farm work began before dawn and continued until after dark. Under these circumstances there was little or no awareness of community needs in fields other than religion and elementary education. Furthermore, there was a tendency to consider that it was sinful to devote time and energy to economically unproductive enterprises.

The erection and support of churches and schools by rural communities was not accomplished at the urging of community development specialists; neither was any professional advice available as to the best procedures. Nevertheless, these facilities were established and served the felt needs of the people.

It does not follow from the foregoing that contemporary farm people would be satisfied with either the community facilities or the community organization methods of past generations. As rural life has become more urbanized and leisure has increased, additional community needs have appeared. The growing complexity of rural social organization requires a more sophisticated approach than that of the pioneers.

Community work in urban areas preceded and stimulated interest in rural community problems. Local community surveys in urban areas were undertaken by various investigators prior to 1900, among them Jane Addams of Chicago's Hull House and Robert Woods of Boston's East End House.[1] These studies revealed undesirable economic and social conditions and stimulated more liberal labor laws, showing that surveys of social and economic conditions could lead to social action.

In 1909, the Russell Sage Foundation financed a study under the direction of Paul Kellogg, of the effects of urbanization in Pittsburgh, the findings of which were published in six volumes in 1914. The Pittsburgh survey stimulated civic consciousness and community

[1] Pauline Young, *Scientific Social Survey and Research*, 2nd ed., Prentice-Hall, 1949, p. 22.

development in that city and elsewhere.[2] It was followed by a number of studies of social welfare problems in many American communities, and the investigations led to urban community action to solve these problems.[3]

Widespread interest in the problems of rural communities in the United States was aroused by the appointment of a Country Life Commission by President Theodore Roosevelt in 1907. The Commission conducted investigations and published a report in 1909, and their work eventually led to the development of rural sociology. Dr. C. J. Galpin was employed as a part-time rural sociologist in 1911 in Wisconsin, where he spent much time and energy working with community clubs.

The Purnell Act passed by Congress in 1925 authorized "such economic and sociological investigations as have for their purpose the development and improvement of the rural home and rural life."[4] Concomitant with the development of rural sociological research in the agricultural experiment stations, many state agricultural extension services undertook to stimulate rural community improvements and employed community organization specialists to assist in the solution of local problems. This trend has been gradual and has not assumed the proportions of a social movement. The extent and nature of such efforts varies considerably from one state to another.

During the 1930s, the federal government, under the leadership of President Franklin D. Roosevelt, urged states, municipalities, and local units of government to lay plans as a basis for action. At one time most states had planning boards that received assistance from the National Resources Planning Board and the Works Projects Administration (WPA). The boards established research staffs which conducted studies of various social and economic problems and made recommendations on how to solve them to state legislators and others. The state planning boards were not specifically agriculturally oriented but covered agriculture as one phase of social and economic

---

[2] *Ibid.*, p. 27.

[3] Murray J. Ross, *Community Organization*, Harper, 1955.

[4] See Paul H. Landis, *Rural Life in Process*, 2nd ed., McGraw-Hill, 1948, p. 511. This language also appears in the amended Hatch Act which provides authorization for federal government support of agricultural experiment station research.

activity. The planning movement ended with little to show for its
effort when the National Resources Planning Board was abolished
by the Congress shortly before the entry of the U.S. into World War
II.

A somewhat similar planning effort directly aimed at the rational
and efficient use of land was undertaken during the same period
under the leadership of the U.S. Department of Agriculture: County
Land Use Planning. In most cases one or more counties in a state
were designated as pilot or experimental. The program was dominated by salaried employees of the Department of Agriculture and
other federal and state bodies. In Hand County, South Dakota, a
total of 22 representatives of various state and federal agencies
acted as consultants and advisors to the County Land Use Planning
Committee. This effort to promote better land use through official
stimulation did not prove to be very popular or effective. Work was
discontinued by congressional action about the time that major attention was given to problems associated with the outbreak of World
War II.

More or less sporadic efforts to improve town-country relationships
and specific aspects of community facilities or relationships have
been undertaken in various parts of the country from time to
time. For the most part, these have been stimulated by local Cham-
bers of Commerce, by the community organization specialists of the
state agricultural extension services, and by the efforts of farm organizations like the Grange. In Washington, for example, the State
Grange conducts an annual community betterment contest, and the
Washington State Extension Service for a time conducted an
annual community planning workshop which was attended by leaders from rural communities in all parts of the state.

In many cases, local leaders have asked universities and other organizations concerned with community development to help in
studying their situations and developing programs of action. The
University of Washington at Seattle, the University of Southern Illinois at Carbondale, and other institutions maintain bureaus of
community development which provide assistance of this type to
small communities.[5] These studies are frequently focused on the

---

[5] See Richard W. Poston, *Democracy Is You*, Harper, 1953; W. W. Biddle,
The Cultivation of Community Leaders, Harper, 1953.

trade center and only incidentally on the problems of farmers in the trade area. Most of the assistance available to the latter has been provided by state agricultural extension services.

There is now a national program (Rural Areas Development) to stimulate American rural people to make greater efforts to solve the economic and social problems which exist in their own communities. A pilot program was initiated by the federal government during the late 1950s in most of the states which have substantial numbers of low income farms. The heaviest concentration of effort was in the southeastern states, but demonstration counties were also selected in the Lake states cut-over area and elsewhere. The agricultural extension services of the states with pilot counties were allocated federal funds with which to employ extra county agents. It was their job to stimulate local interest in social action to solve specific local problems. It was hoped that the program would spread spontaneously beyond the boundaries of the pilot counties but this did not occur.

The results were sufficiently impressive, however, to motivate the United States Department of Agriculture in 1961 to make a concerted effort to interest people in other rural counties. In low income areas (including rural counties) designated by the United States Department of Commerce as redevelopment areas under Public Law 87-27, 87th Congress, financial assistance in the form of loans and grants is available for community facilities and for industrial development designed to increase employment opportunities.

COMMUNITY DEVELOPMENT IN FOREIGN COUNTRIES

American experiences with rural and urban community development have been drawn upon heavily in connection with technical aid given by the United States to underdeveloped countries in various sections of the world.[6] American specialists in community development have played important roles in planning government-sponsored programs to stimulate community development in India, Pakistan, and other countries. Many of the people who were active in the land-use planning movement as well as in urban community development have served or are serving as community development experts overseas.

[6] A. L. Bertrand, ed., *Rural Sociology*, McGraw-Hill, 1958, pp. 98-100.

Review of the progress of community development efforts in India and Pakistan indicates that cultural differences require extensive modifications in American methods.

COMMUNITY DEVELOPMENT GOALS

The approach to community development by most American specialists understandably carries the imprint of American social and political values. We should be surprised, as sociologists, if we were to find an absence of democracy in these procedures. It should be made clear, however, that there is wide divergence of opinion concerning the best ways to serve democratic interests. One school of thought offers a blueprint for restoration of "grass roots" democracy if its program for community self-study is carefully followed in complete detail.[7] Another holds that emphasis should be placed on problems that local people consider to need solution through community action.

The goals of social action on the community level are defined in terms of societal and community values. Generally, to make a successful appeal to community members, improvement of community services or facilities must be emphasized.[8]

At an earlier point, we noted that few rural communities exist in which members have a psychological bond of interest in common problems. We also observed, however, that interest in common problems can be created.[9] It is in this sense that the concept is used here.

ASSUMPTIONS UNDERLYING COMMUNITY DEVELOPMENT

Ross has listed seven underlying assumptions in community development methods.

1. People have or can develop the capacity to solve their own problems.
2. People desire change.
3. People should take an active part in change in their communities.

[7] See Poston, op. cit.
[8] Dwight Sanderson and R. A. Polson, Rural Community Organization, Wiley, 1939, p. 77.
[9] See Chapter 19.

4. Changes developed by community members will last longer and be more meaningful than imposed changes.
5. Problems have multiple causes.
6. Democracy requires local social action.
7. Assistance from community organization specialists may be required by some communities.[10]

Many of these are value statements. Most of them would be readily accepted by members of a modern democratic society, but it cannot be taken for granted that people necessarily desire change or that they can readily be stimulated to cooperative social action to solve their own problems.[11] The nature of the culture must be taken into account. Furthermore, in some underdeveloped countries and in Communist states the decision-making ability of citizens is not likely to be encouraged to any substantial extent; the hazards to vested interests would be too great.

THE PROCESS OF COMMUNITY SOCIAL ACTION

Social action may be defined as effort involving two or more members of a social system. In this discussion interest centers on cooperative rather than antagonistic social action. In its simplest case, social action is generally informal and impulsive. For example, one member of a family suggests, "Let's go to the movie tonight. I've heard it's a good show." Some or all of the others agree to the suggestion, and two or more members cooperate to solve a transportation problem and actually go to the movie together.

Not all social action is simple; much of it is complex and formal, and while impulsive participation is undoubtedly very common, there may be rational bases for participation. Furthermore, it is sometimes possible to guide social action into relatively rational channels.

The progress of social action in a community from its initiation to its culmination may be divided into a series of stages. As Beal and Capener have pointed out, certain ones may be omitted or may occur out of their logical sequence.[12] The stages set forth below apply

[10] Ross, *op. cit.*, pp. 85-91.
[11] See Howard W. Beers, "Social Components of Community Development," *Rural Sociology*, March, 1958, pp. 13-24.
[12] George Beal and Harold Capener, *A Social Action Model*, unpublished paper presented at the Rural Sociological Society Meeting, August, 1958.

to social action in a social system which is sufficiently complex to place a premium on the introduction of rationality in reaching and implementing group decisions, for instance, a voluntary formal organization, a community, or an agency. In less elaborate form, these stages might also be found in social action by a farm family.

STAGES IN COMMUNITY SOCIAL ACTION

The following stages may be identified for the purpose of analyzing the factors and processes involved in democratic social action by a community to solve a local problem.

1. Initiation of a proposal
2. Diffusion of concern
3. Organization for analysis of relevant information
4. Group decision-making
5. Planning the campaign
6. Action
7. Evaluation[13]

It should be emphasized that this set of stages represents a set of postulates rather than a set of tested hypotheses. Fruitful analyses can doubtless be made in terms of other models.

There are not many systematic research studies of the relative importance of specific types of action during various stages of the social action process. Those which do exist primarily concern specific concrete social situations involving social action within the cultural framework in a particular locality, and consequently the findings cannot be generalized. Nevertheless, there is a good deal of information about community action, consisting for the most part of rules of thumb developed by community organization specialists and presented in manuals on the subject. These guides undoubtedly contain a great deal of .wisdom, but our earlier study of the importance of cultural relativity even within a general culture area such as the United States suggests that some caution must be used in applying these rules.

In addition to the rules of procedure which have grown out of

[13] See *Ibid.;* Irwin T. Sanders, *Making Good Communities Better,* University of Kentucky Press, 1950.

practical experience, there is a considerable body of partially tested theory based upon sociological and social-psychological research.[14] Insofar as these disciplines are themselves well founded, these findings may be taken as a more appropriate basis for action than folklore or even the wisdom of practitioners where it runs counter to theoretical principles or research findings. Most of the practitioners who have written on the subject of community action have drawn heavily upon the literature of these fields, and many of them, in fact, are sociologists, social workers, or social psychologists.

All social action takes place either within or with reference to one or more social systems. Consequently, the course and fate of a proposal for action will be determined primarily by the nature of the social structure, culture, and current situation in the affected systems. For the purposes of this discussion, reference will be to democratic social action by a rural community designed to improve some aspect of community life.

Let us now consider the stages in greater detail with emphasis on factors and procedures which may lead to either success or failure.

Initiation of a Proposal

An idea for social action in a local community may originate with any individual member of the community, or it may be proposed directly or indirectly by the representative of some organization or agency with headquarters located outside the community area. In either case, the idea will not take root in the community unless other persons can be induced to accept it. To be acceptable, regardless of its source, the idea must not conflict with important values held by members of the community. For example, a proposal to establish a birth-control clinic would not get very far in a Catholic-dominated community. The chances of acceptance are greatly improved if the idea is one which gives expression to felt but unfulfilled needs of a substantial number of influential people in the community.

A realistic review of the situation indicates that external stimulation by some responsible private or governmental agency or organization is essential for social action on any substantial scale at

[14] See Ross, *op. cit.*

the community level. This is not to say that enlightened local leaders may not take the initiative in organizing their communities for action on specific local problems, but even where the educational level is high, encouragement and support from outside sources is likely to be required.

Still, ideas do not necessarily stand or fall on their own merit. It has long been recognized that an idea which might be scorned if advanced by a low-ranking member of a social system is likely to be accepted enthusiastically if advanced by a high-ranking person, meaning that the initial success of a proposal may be greatly influenced by the social standing of the initiator. If he does not belong to the upper echelons, he will be well advised to obtain the approval of high-ranking persons at an early stage. The latter, who are not necessarily leaders in the positive sense, are to be found in all social systems. Because they are looked to by others as persons of sound and mature judgment, they have been called *legitimizers*.[15] Proposals they endorse are thought to have a legitimate claim on the attention of others.

Because of the importance of this matter, experienced community organization specialists sometimes take great pains to identify the persons who occupy positions of power and influence and solicit their active support and participation or at least their tacit approval.

At the initiation stage, a small group of people who have an interest in the idea explore its possibilities on the basis of their knowledge of the local situation, and usually evolve at least a preliminary plan of action for presentation to others. Although the formal role structure of the relevant social systems in the community may not be analyzed in detail, this group is likely to take into account such matters as power relationships, the identification of legitimizers, communication channels, and group loyalties and prejudices of leaders. The group should also consider the impact of the new idea on established values held by influential members of the social system and evaluate the chances of success in terms of the previous relevant history of the social system, including conflicts and co-operative efforts. The initiators should also make a more or less thorough analysis of the current situation, estimating how people

[15] Beal and Capener, *op. cit.*, p. 9.

will feel about the idea and their readiness to act.[16] If these considerations are systematically and thoroughly explored, the chances of success are likely to be improved. Early detection of possible barriers to action may lead to successful measures to overcome the barriers or abandonment of the idea prior to heavy involvement.

Diffusion of Concern

At this stage, the initiators talk to others, perhaps issue publicity, and in various ways seek to enlist the interest of a larger segment of the social system.

Particularly in the U.S., with its democratic ideology, widespread recognition of the existence of a problem which can be solved by social action would seem to be essential in preparing the way for the decision to act and subsequent support for the program planned. Depending on the nature of the social subsystems involved and the associated systems of culture, this decision may be taken by a small group or by substantial numbers of the citizenry.

Primary interest centers upon channels and methods of diffusing concern. In a small community, oral communication may be relied on to a major extent, but in most of rural America local newspapers, radio stations, and perhaps television will also be used. Essentially the same principles apply to the diffusion of concern as applied to initiation of the proposal. As the social rank of the originating group is often of prime importance, so the chances that the idea will be accepted are improved if those charged with diffusing the idea are able to point out that persons of prestige—the legitimizers—have given it their sanction. Appeals may also be made to community loyalty and to the benefits the action will bring.

Research has indicated that some ideas spread through local opinion leaders,[17] and these should not be overlooked as a channel of communication. Persons who have the time, skill in communication

[16] Beal and Capener have pointed out that in many localities there is a history of past experience with some kind of social action, and that the patterns of communication, leadership, role expectations, and attitudes thus established have an important bearing on the potential success or failure of new social action.

[17] See Paul F. Lazarsfeld, Bernard Berelson, and Hazel Gaudet, *People's Choice: How the Voter Makes Up His Mind in a Presidential Campaign,* Duell, Sloan, and Pearce, 1944.

and organization, and access to people are essential.

Organization for Analysis of Relevant Information

Conscious organization for systematic analysis of attitudes, factual materials from surveys, and discussion of the issues involved may be regarded as a prelude to group decision-making. This stage may be omitted, or it may be included as a phase of the process of group decision-making. It is important, however, because it is the point at which rational principles may be applied to the social action process with greatest effect. This stage will nearly always be found in programs of social action which receive guidance from community organization specialists, and conversely, it is often absent in cases where social action is spontaneous or the product of illiterate persons. Fundamentally, it rests upon the assumption that the solution to community problems can be developed better if relevant information is gathered systematically and carefully analyzed and interpreted within the context of the social situation.

At this stage, if it has not already occurred, there will frequently be a formal division of labor to insure coverage of various aspects of the social action process.[18] The steering group must decide what they want and need to know as a basis for policy decision, what groups or subcommittees will gather specific facts, and whether expert advice and/or assistance will be required in obtaining and interpreting the needed information. Some sort of procedure must be set up for processing the data received, interpreting it, and reporting to the decision-making body.

In social action involving various aspects of community life, some of the essential information can be obtained from official records maintained by school systems, various branches of local and county government, the census, and similar sources. However, much of it will be either out of date or not specifically relevant to the problem. Consequently, it will frequently be necessary to organize a survey to obtain firsthand reports from people in the community on their

[18] The question of the proper type of organization is sometimes troublesome. The alternatives seem to be (1) an entirely new organization, (2) a community council composed of representatives of existing organizations, and (3) leadership by one existing organization. All of these alternatives have advantages and disadvantages so that it is not possible to render a judgment in the abstract. The decision has to be made by specific communities on the basis of local circumstances.

circumstances and attitudes. In some cases, members of the local community who possess the required background and skills may make a community self-survey;[19] or the problem may be of such complexity that it requires the assistance of specialists in the subject. For example, a community committee in a tri-city area of the state of Washington became interested in a program to combat juvenile delinquency. As a stage in the social action process, the committee enlisted the assistance of a sociologist from Washington State University who conducted a survey of factors associated with delinquent-type behavior, and subsequently provided information on this subject to the community committee.[20] The committee used the report as a basis for considering programs of corrective action.

There is a division of opinion among community organization specialists concerning the degree to which experts should participate in the collection and evaluation of information on a community problem.[21] A general observation might be that action to solve a simple problem can be based on information collected by members of the community with little guidance. However, unless the community contains people with very specialized professional training, it ordinarily could not conduct a useful self-survey on a complicated issue. In such cases reliance on specialist assistance, even if it entails substantial expense, should lead to much sounder results.

Group Decision-Making

At this stage, people in the community who are concerned about the problem must arrive at a decision with respect to social action, possibly during the course of a communitywide meeting. In an American rural community there would ordinarily be a considerable amount of discussion and perhaps some opposition to the proposals advanced by the steering committee. Obviously, a large meeting attended by scores or even hundreds of community members is not to be considered as a planning body. Some smaller group has probably already made tentative decisions and plans, in which case it will present these to the larger group for ratification. Group decision

[19] See Poston, *op. cit.*, for a community self-survey guide covering nearly all aspects of community life.

[20] See F. Ivan Nye, *Family Relationships and Delinquent Behavior*, Wiley, 1958.

[21] Biddle, *op. cit.*

may be made by formal vote, acclamation, or other means of ascertaining consensus. Sometimes a legal decision must be obtained through a public election before further action can be taken, but even so, there would ordinarily be a commitment by a small deliberative group, and the action of the larger group could be regarded as confirmation of the decision.

Because a proposed action may have adverse implications for the economic, political, or social interests of some individuals or special interest groups in the community, there may be efforts to discredit the proposal. Sometimes the motives of the proponents will be questioned or impugned. In such cases both sides may have recourse not only to the objective facts collected during the course of the preceding stage but also to the goals of the program as these are related to the fundamental values of the members of the community.

Planning for Social Action

After a decision has been made by a communitywide group to support a proposal, it is still necessary to plan the program of action carefully if it is to be fully successful. This is a task that can best be accomplished by a relatively small group of people, who may or may not be those who initiated the idea in the first place. At this stage, information must be obtained about alternative solutions. Frequently experts are called upon to provide cost estimates, building plans, or other advice. The solution to the problem should be one which can be achieved with the economic and human resources available in the community.

Action

In putting the program across—the climax of the social action process—members of the community should be kept informed of the objectives, the problem, and progress toward the approved solutions. Since all social action involves individuals, it is necessary to get individuals to assume responsibility for carrying out definite phases of the action program. Success requires leadership and persistent effort. The specific plan of action chosen depends substantially on the type of support required from the community. For example, if no contributions are to be obtained from members of a community and the work is actually to be accomplished by a contractor or by outside experts, acquiescence may be all that is needed. If, however, community members are to participate directly, a more vigorous publicity campaign and a detailed plan of organization will be required.

Evaluation

The evaluation stage may not seem to be a matter of primary concern to members of a specific local community, particularly if the program is designed to solve a specific problem. However, if the action undertaken is regarded as one of a possible series or if it is sponsored by some outside group that has made financial and other contributions to the program, evaluation may be a matter of considerable importance.

In any case, periodic reports on the progress of the program will certainly help gain the support of members of a local social system, and an evaluation at various stages by persons of prestige will help maintain the ego involvement of the participants. Systematic and scientifically organized programs of evaluation will bring to light a useful set of principles for community leaders and organization specialists to use not only in weighing results but also in analyzing the interaction processes involved at various stages.

CITIZEN VERSUS SPECIALIST

As would be expected because of the growth of specialization in American life, the use of specialists in community organization as well as in recreation, health, and other fields appears to be increasing rather than decreasing. Dependence upon the specialist does not necessarily mean that the citizen is left to play a less essential role, however. His interest and his support, financial and otherwise, are essential if we are to continue to make progress toward the democratic solution of problems at the local community level. Experts can perform a useful function in giving direction to specialized aspects of a community program. They cannot and should not attempt to do the job alone.

QUESTIONS FOR FURTHER STUDY AND DISCUSSION

1. What are the principal cultural barriers to community development in underdeveloped countries?

2. Is the community development process restricted to democratic societies? Explain your answer.
3. What is your opinion concerning the proper roles of citizens and specialists in community development?
4. Do you believe that community development programs offer a means of preserving "grass roots" democracy?
5. Propose a research design for a study of the social action process in a community.

SELECTED REFERENCES

Biddle, W. W., *The Cultivation of Community Leaders*, Harper, 1953.

Nelson, Lowry, C. E. Ramsey, and Coolie Verner, *Community Structure and Change*, Macmillan, 1960, chap. 20.

Poston, Richard W., *Democracy Is You*, Harper, 1953.

Ross, Murray J., *Community Organization*, Harper, 1955.

Sanders, Irwin T., *Making Good Communities Better*, University of Kentucky Press, 1950.

Index of Names

Index of Subjects